Neighbors, You're Beautiful!

Mini-Biographies of Fascinating Personalities Living in and
Beyond Squirrel Hill—enlivened with a Touch of Humor.

(1962–1974)
By SARA ROSENBLUM

WOLFSON PUBLISHING CO., INC. • PITTSBURGH, PA.

PREFACE

Compiling my articles published in the Squirrel Hill News during the past twelve years is done for several reasons:

Newspaper clippings disintegrate with age, fall apart and disappear. The talents and accomplishments of the distinguished personalities herein deserve permanence. To be remembered by their loved ones, friends and our community—with admiration and pride—now and in the years ahead.

A life-time active member of the Pittsburgh Chapter of Hadassah (Hadar) I am familiar with the urgent needs in Israel. And how important it is to our own country to support that little nation—the only Democracy in the Middle East. Thus, with financial aid from my sister (Naomi R. Blum, Great Neck, N. Y.) entire cost of publishing this book is our responsibility. All proceeds will go to the Pittsburgh Chapter of Hadassah. Contributing to a great cause is more meaningful while yet living than you-know-when.

My sincere thanks to Don Brockett and Margery Weiner for their delightful Forewords. Also to my friends Ella Eisman and Ethel Peresman who were helpful in some necessary tasks prior to publication. And Lorraine Briskman, public relations.

I would like to add that our community has countless more personalities whose beautiful talents and deeds merit recording. But one must stop somewhere. So it's 250 as of July 1, 1974.

Sara Rosenblum

Through the generosity of the author—a lifetime active member of the Pittsburgh Chapter of Hadassah (Hadar Group)— entire funds derived from the sale of this book will go to the Pittsburgh Chapter of Hadassah. These funds will help further Hadassah's work in the United States and Israel.

Marty Wolfson, Publisher
WOLFSON PUBLISHING CO., INC.

FOREWORD

A chronicler is supposedly a recorder of events. In this delightful book one finds Sara Rosenblum chronicling people. The following pages—a record of outstanding personalities interviewed by the author—are replete with warmth, enthusiasm, candor and humaness.

The interviews are with nationally and internationally known people as well as the prosaic man-in-the-street who also has a fascinating story. She sprinkles humor throughout her articles, maintaining a light touch but never missing the essence nor the spark of the personality.

Miss Rosenblum has touched many lives through her interviews contained in these pages, and many lives have touched her. And that touch is reflected in the honest discussions with people in so many interesting fields. Although she has chronicled community characters, this book should have universal appeal, for there may be a little of us in each of the vignettes.

A distinctive woman who has enjoyed a distinctive career has thus compiled a distinctive book that gives distinctive pleasure. And what's more, all proceeds go to a distinctive cause.

Margery Weiner, President
Pittsburgh Chapter of Hadassah (1972—75)

FOREWORD

In my travels around the country, whenever people ask me what part of Pittsburgh I am from and I say "Squirrel Hill" it invariably invokes a lyrical grin and a response such as "Are you one of the squirrels there?" It's not that they know anything about Squirrel Hill, it's just that they think the name is funny. Maybe it is. All I can say is that I am proud to be one of the "squirrels" in Sara Rosenblum's warm and wonderful book about 250 neighbors who have contributed to the vibrancy of our city.

For the past twelve years she has been writing these mini-biographical sketches published in the Squirrel Hill News. Now, under hard cover, you can read about artists, civic leaders, entertainers, philosophers, scientists, teachers and a host of other interesting personalities that appeared in the pages of our neighborhood News. The articles are filled with love and humor, thanks to the nature of the author who looks at her subjects through rose-in-bloom colored glasses.

All 250 of these provocative life histories have been collected into this edition. Bravo! In my business, a standing ovation would be in order. For anyone who grew up or spent any amount of time in or around our community, this is must reading. Here we have a valuable record of a place and a time. It is history, biography, sociology and besides, it is great fun.

So sit back and start reading, and before long you may be able to understand what Sara means when she says our so-called "squirrels" are *Beautiful People.*

DON BROCKETT

TABLE OF CONTENTS

Neighbors, You're Beautiful!

Mrs. Marcus (Barbara) Aaron II
Enterprising, Charming Neighbor

This is being written on an unbelievably sunny day in February. And although the Ides of March still face us, one gets the feeling that spring is just around the corner. Also around the corner is a charming and enterprising neighbor. She's Mrs. Marcus Aaron II of Wightman St. Everyone affectionately calls her Barbara. And again around the corner is spring housecleaning. Which reminds us of those no-room for unwanted books that are gathering dust in your home.

But before we find out what's all this about books, let's learn a little about our remarkable neighbor — the former Barbara Goldman from far-off San Francisco. Barbara is the lovely missus of Marcus Aaron II, a well-known Downtown attorney. And who do you think his mom is? The indomitable president of our School Board — Mrs. Maxine Aaron, a Vassar graduate.

When Marcus Aaron II was a youthful bachelor he took a trip to San Francisco to visit his sister. And on a blind date met beautiful Barbara Goldman, a Bryn Mawr graduate with an A.B. degree. Unlike the fella who left his heart in San Francisco, he brought her home as his bride. This was in February, 1955. By now they are the proud parents of three lively girls: Susie, Judy and Barbie — aged 10, 8 and 6 respectively. All attend Ellis School.

And now for the piece-de-resistance. The Bryn Mawr-Vassar annual BOOK SALE — the largest and greatest sale of second-hand books for miles around. It takes place April 17, 18 and 19. At the Greek Orthodox Cathedral in Oakland. Similar sales are being held in important cities throughout the country. Our neighbor inaugurated them here five years ago. The experience and know-how she gained during her San Francisco days make her a natural as leader of this fabulous project.

As a graduate of Bryn Mawr, Barbara long ago joined other alumnae from her famous college, together with those from equally-famous Vassar, to work on the Book Sales. Proceeds from them go toward full scholarships to Bryn Mawr and Vassar for qualified young women from Western Penna. — deserving women financially unable to make it on their own. Last year's Sale netted over $9,000 for two scholarship funds (one for each of the two colleges), thus helping a dozen area girls attend either Bryn Mawr near Phila. or Vassar in Poughkeepsie, N.Y. The first-mentioned college has eighty-some alumnae in Western Penna. The other, 300 in this area. These sweet girl-graduates sort the books, clean them, price them and box them for the coming Sale. They have established book depots throughout Allegheny County — and even as far away as Greensburg. To receive the thousands of books (yours too, of course) which change hands as you clean house, settle estates, etc., etc., etc. . . .

So take a look. A GOOD look. In your attic, basement, behind the piano or under the bed even. And call Mrs. Robert Tate (phone 521-8039) and she'll arrange for someone to collect them.

When the slam-bang Book Sale is completed and everything accounted for, our neighbor resumes full time with home and family. The Aarons enjoy Tennis. On fall week-ends they go sight-seeing in the Pennsylvania Dutch country, Washington and Williamsburg. They have fun hiking along the Forbes Trail. And go ice-skating in North Park.

You know the old saying: The family that has fun together, stays together. Nice, isn't it — having such wonderful neighbors?

Gloria Abdou
Foodland Is My Land

As this is being written, higher food prices are again forecast. Oy vey! Like adding insult to injury. So it might ease the hurt to learn about a fantastic gal highly skilled in food buying. You hear her on TV and radio, telling how to buy the mostest for the leastest. During baseball season she follows Bob Prince on the air. He describes the games. She speaks about foods. So meet lovely Gloria Abdou, a nearby neighbor from Shadyside. She's Director of Customer Services for Foodland Markets (105 of them).

Born in Squirrel Hill, her first job at 16 during Sacred Heart High was at Newman's Youth Center, Forbes near Murray. Her mom (Anna Abdou) was the store's manager then, and still works there part-time. She's known and admired by the moms and grandmas of our community, having waited on their offsprings through the years.

And now more about daughter, Gloria. After High School she entered the Pittsburgh Playhouse of the Theatre and the Microphone Playhouse, studying voice and acting technique for ten years. Talented and dynamic, she played leads in various Playhouse productions including "Pygmalion", "Strange Bedfellows", "Detective Story" and a host of others. Her last stage appearance was in 1955, followed by three years at Kaufmann's where she displayed merchandise throughout the store. She then became WTAE's radio Director of Women's Activities for 17 years. Her daily programs included news and commentaries on home, fashions, entertainment, civic and cultural affairs. She interviewed local and world-famous celebrities, like beautiful Marie Torre does on KDKA. For a year Gloria was Director of Publicity and Sales Promotion. In 1964 she joined Foodland. Remember? She ends her broadcast commercials with "Foodland is My Land."

Incidently, her grandmother owned and operated a small neighborhood grocery store in Chicago's Polish district for over 40 years.

In addition to TV and radio, this gifted personality presented talks on supermarketing at women's clubs, civic and fraternal organizations, high school teachers and students. For free. Non-commercial. She's unfortunately not in position to lower food prices but she tells you how to stretch the dollar.

She lives with her mom, sister, Aphia (a medical illustrator in the Oakland Vet Hospital), and brother, Elias (Ass't. Professor of English at the Community College of Allegheny County, North Side campus.) All do the household chores in their Roslyn Place spic-and-span three-story home. No outside help. Gloria even does the windows!

For diversion our today's personality attends the Symphonies, Operas and Stage Productions, the Pittsburgh Playhouse in particular.

Eva Gabor, as it says in the newspapers, just took on husband No. 5. So Gloria — nu? How come not even one? With a charming smile she says she enjoys her independent life-style and finds it plenty stimulating. So go do her something!

Mrs. Martin D. (Ann) Adler
Donor Chairman With Much Charm

Dear Hadassah-ites—all 4800 of you—and hopefully countless more: If you think the last two Donor Spectaculars were the talk of the town, you ain't seen nothin' yet. For this year's will be at the Magnificent Heinz Hall for the Performing Arts.

With a program only Hadassah women—bless 'em—know how to arrange. Inspired by the motto "The Dream and the Deed" the committee has been working like mad since May to give you the bestest and the mostest. Since it's the Chairman who carries the greatest responsibility, let's learn a little about the gal with much charm, imagination and heart.

She's the former Anna Frances Stark, affectionately called Ann. And the lovely wife of Dr. Martin D. Adler, Associate Professor of Pitt's Graduate School of Social Work. Ann herself is a major graduate of its School of Physical Ed. Dr. Adler hails from New Jersey. In 1949, a handsome bachelor, he came here for a national convention. Ann was there too.

So was Cupid who hovered around til one enchanted evening June 1951 Martin said so-long to bachelorhood and became Ann's devoted husband. They went housekeeping in Braddock and 11 years ago moved to our neighborhood in Hobart St. Unlike Tevye the Adlers have only 3 daughters: Randi, Sherri and Lori—16, 14 and 12. The latter goes to Colfax. The others to Allderdice.

Last summer Randi spent 7 weeks in Israel. Her parents were there in 1966 when dad was asked by Israel's Ministry of Health to do research there. And mom looked into the education projects. They made a second trip 2 years later. Next February another trip is in the offing. And still another next May. For her own Hadassah Group Sinai Mrs. Adler was Recording Sec'y; Donor Chairman, and President for 2 years. Also Chapter Youth Commission Chairman 3 years.

The phones at the Adler home are constantly ringing. And of course when mom's in the shower. Because of the countless Donor meetings—here, there, everywhere—dad sometimes must wait for his supper. But being equally dedicated, he's proud of his busy missus. In fact, as it says in the commercials, he thinks he'll keep her.

Surrounded by enemies, under constant threat of war, needing 80 per cent of her income for defense, yet Israel's accomplishments are outstanding. The advances in open-heart surgery, cancer detection by Dr. Chloe Tal and hopefully its prevention will benefit the world. All at the Hadassah-Hebrew University Medical Center. Its Community College, the vocational schools, social services, community health programs, participation in Youth Aliyah and JNF—all Hadassah projects in Israel—are second to none. Its efforts on behalf of the Jews in the Soviet Union, the oppressed Jews in Arab countries and elsewhere means Hadassah truly cares. We could go on and on but space is limited. One thing is certain, However. The State of Israel cannot exist without the support of American Jewry. Nor is there much hope for American Jewry without Israel.

The Donor Spectacular will be held Saturday, February 19, 8 p.m. Even if you must look under your mattress for some dough, be on hand. Get a hair-do or wear your pretty wig. Step into your nicest dress or pantsuit. Or short pants, hot pants—or whatever. And come join the Beautiful People at Heinz Hall and have yourself a ball. You'll be the happier for it.

P.S. And bring your husband and male friends.

Mrs. Elliot (Freda) Alber
'Jill' of All Trades

Today you'll meet a veritable Jill of all trades — a neighbor whose talents are many splendored things. So pull up your chairs, kick off your shoes, relax. And learn about popular Freda Alber of Albemarle Ave. Her well-known husband Elliot is a partner of Alber & Leff Foods Co. on College Ave.

Freda, a professional actress has accepted — in addition to her many personal commitments — the chairmanship of the fabulous Hadassah Luncheon being held Feb.

11th at the Hilton. She's had an additional phone installed. And boy, are the bells ringing! And often — wouldn't you know it — when she's in the shower.

Hadassah, as you doubtless know is the largest women's organization in the U.S., with a national membership of 318,000. Locally there are 4400 members. Through fund-raising and education it supports a program of healing, teaching and research in Israel. It includes the Hadassah Medical Center in Jerusalem. Also the former Hadassah hospital on Mt. Scopus, in disuse since the 1948 War of Independence. Now it is being rebuilt and restored to its original use as a rehabilitation and geriatric center as well as a youth hostel. Their services are available to all peoples — Christians, Arabs, Jews. No discrimination whatsoever.

Freda and Elliott were in Israel several months ago. In Jerusalem they prayed, with countless others, at the Western Wall. And now a bit of ancient biblical history. The first Jewish Temple, built by King Nehemiah was again destroyed by the Romans 1900 years ago. All that remains of that Temple is a beautiful and lonely Wall. Access to it was closed to the Jewish people by the Arabs for many years. The Israelis won it back last June. Praying at The Wall is an emotional experience.

And now about our neighbor's personal background. The former Freda Cazen whose dad owned a kosher food store on lower 5th Ave. is a graduate of Carnegie-Mellon Drama School. Their son Stephen, almost 23, graduated W & J. He's now a creative copy writer for Batten, Barton, Durstine & Osborn — an international advertising firm.

Freda can't remember when she wasn't in plays. In "Tevya and His Daughters" (5 of them) at our Playhouse years ago she made Sholom Aleichem's charming play popular long before it become Broadway's smash - hit, "Fiddler on the Roof". She played — you guessed it — Tevye's wife Goldde. In addition, her variety of roles at the Playhouse include the Queen in "Hamlet", Beatrice in "A View from the Bridge", Signore Fioria in "The Time of the Cuckoo", Peppina in "The Rose Tattoo" — to name a few. She also starred in "A Majority of One" in the Saint Fidelis College Cultural Series. In a recent Alcoa production "The 39th Witness' on WQED she played the wife — the only wife — who pleaded with her TV husband to phone the police when a shrieking woman was being murdered on the street below. You remember? None wanted to be "involved". But Freda convinced the husband and he phoned. Even though, by then it was too late.

Our neighbor also acted with the Guignol Theatre, Lexington, Ky. And the U.S. Signal Corps. She directed and produced festival plays for the children of Rodef Shalom Temple for 9 years.

The Alder home contains 9 rooms and 3 baths. Freda has outside help 3 days a week. Her mom, Mrs. Anna Cazen, has charge of the cooking. Her famous recipe "Mrs. Cazen's Sponge Cake" was recently published in our morning PG. You don't have to be Jewish to make the best sponge cake, but it helps.

Who will be guest speaker at the Hadassah luncheon? None other than the Consul General of Israel with the status of Ambassador to the U.S. — the Honorable Michael Arnon. See you at the Hilton.

Bessie Frank Anathan

Gracious Philanthropist

Remember the famous movie "Miracle on 34th St.?" Well, a miracle happened in our community too. At Murray Ave., to be exact.

On a sunny, warm, beautiful day Sept. 8, 1963 the sparkling new Simon J. and Bessie Frank Anathan House for Older People opened wide its doors. How to describe this miraculous place? There are no words. But the hundreds of senior citizens of all faiths whose lives are enriched by it say it's a "World of Enchantment." And the throngs of visitors all agree.

The gracious, generous lady — Bessie Frank Anathan — who made the Anathan House possible through her fabulous gift of $125,000 wants credit given to others. Like, for instance, her close friends Mrs. Abe Bluementhal and Mrs. Isidore Goldsmith. Their artistic talent and know-how in furnishings resulted in comfort to the body and refreshment to the eyes. And Mrs. Irving Sommerman, the director whose varied activity programs enliven the mind and lighten the heart. And of course there are others.

Mrs. Anathan, who cares for the happiness of others, is the daughter of the late Isaac W. and Tinnie Frank. Dad Frank was Chairman of the Board of United Engineering and Foundry Co., which he founded. And a board member of National Steel. Her grandparents on both sides all came to Pittsburgh in 1840. One of her ancestors was knighted in 1739. She has the family coat of arms.

In 1913, after a romantic meeting in Atlantic City, Bessie Frank married the late Simon J. Anathan, department store owner of Steubenville, Ohio. As a young boy he helped support his family. His brothers later became partners in his store. He was a prominent leader of the Steubenville community. It was his wish that a home for older people be made possible. The former Council Lounge for Senior Citizens, through Anathan philanthropy, came into being 13 years ago. Now the Anathan House stands in his loving memory.

The Anathans were our good neighbors for 30 years, in a beautiful home on Beacon St. Daughter Frances is Mrs. Joel Spear Jr. Jane is married to Alan Lehman. There are five grandchildren.

Recently Mrs. Anathan moved to an apartment. It is flooded with light and sunshine and filled with lovely objects of art from far and near. Especially prized are five glass bottles made during the Civil War in her grandfather's glass factory. Soft blue in color, they're encrusted with a cannon; American flag, 13 stars, an olive branch and clasped hands. With her is Mary, her devoted maid for 20 years.

During the Civil War Bessie's grandmother was president of the then Ladies Sanitary Society. Now it's the world-famous Red Cross. Later these ladies founded the Pittsburgh Improvement of the Poor, with grandma Frank on the Board until her death at age 96.

When Bessie Frank was nine, she and other youngsters made and sold lemonade. The proceeds helped toward a kindergarten built by the then Columbian Council of Jewish Women in Allegheny. Now it's the National Council of Jewish Women.

Is it any wonder, then that Mrs. Anathan has been so interested in Council activities — and given so much? And wait. She's on the Board of 10 other organizations. Too many, she says.

The hundreds whose hearts she has gladdened—in fact our entire community—are proud of Bessie Frank Anathan. We wish her long life, good health and great happiness. Who deserves it more than she?

Paula Atlas

Art Festival Secretary

Our neighborhood personality of the week is Mrs. Ralph R. (Paula) Atlas. And what do you know — she says she's not important enough to be written up! That, in our book, makes her extra special because humility is an admirable virtue. Especially in a woman. So pull up your chairs and let's learn a little about our likeable neighbor who lives at 1151 Wightman St.

Paula Atlas is Executive Secretary of the Three-Rivers Art Festival. This 7-day carnival of culture gladdened the hearts of thousands who thronged Gateway Center last spring. If you were among them you'd understand the skill, experience and know-how a position like hers requires. She worked hand-in-hand with the Director — planning, arranging, putting over. And this in between being a wife, mother and running a private metal fabricating business. She runs this business from her home — a big old house tastefully furnished. Paula likes to "do things" with bricks. So what happened? She built a patio, with the skill of an honest-to-gosh bricklayer.

Paula graduated and received her B.A. degree from Penn State University. Before her marriage she was a buyer of gifts for a stationery supply house in Philadelphia. For two years she was on the Board of IKS and associate chairman of Advance Gifts of the UJF.

And now about Paula's interesting family. Husband Ralph is a consulting engineer, having received his B.S. in Engineering at Carnegie Tech. He lived most of his life in Israel; and before it became a state held an important post with the Israeli Army which then was known as the Haganah. Ralph speaks Hebrew, Arabic and Russian fluently.

Daughter Rosanne Skirble, 15½ was cheer-leader and captain of junior school at Allderdice. For the past two years she wrote a weekly column for the Squirrel Hill News titled "Junior Corner."

Joel Skirble is 18 and an honor graduate of Allderdice. He attended Duquesne University six months and this fall will start at Penn State. His mother says he's a "fabulous salesman." So you guessed it — he'll take up Business Administration.

Paula and Ralph lived and worked in Mexico City for six weeks. And recently returned from a visit to Stratford, Canada, where they attended the Shakespeare Festival there. Both are interested in the Pittsburgh Council for International visitors. Their home is a rendezvous for people from Kenya, Africa, Yugoslavia and from other far corners of the world. They come for dinner, over night and sometimes for several weeks' stay. They bring their own interpreters, but in the Atlas family, so versatile in languages, who needs them.

In among the comings and goings of the Atlas household is a lively little mutt, "Blackie" by name. He's non-descript and unpedigreed, but who cares? Everybody loves him — even his neighbors.

Paula Atlas is average in height and the youngest-looking mother of grownups you ever saw. Her hair is plain and uncluttered — with the hair-do's you see all around. However, psst! listen but don't tell anybody: Paula has a wig! And when the proper occasion arises she looks as glamorous as the best of 'em.

Mrs. George (Marie) Aurentz

Talent for Politics

They say poets are born, not made. It's like that with politicians, too, sometimes. And that's how it's been with Mrs. George Aurentz, affectionately known as Marie by all Democrats — and by many who aren't.

Marie, residing in the General Forbes Apartments, was born in Pittsburgh and has lived in our city ever since. She graduated from St. Mary's High School in Lawrenceville and later attended Ursaline Academy. At the ripe young age of 17 she met George Aurentz, a coal and coke executive. A year later they married.

A professional career, least of all politics, was far from her mind then. Marie became a busy and happy housewife and developed into a devoted mother. But when son George Jr. married and daughter Betty became Mrs. Andre I. Brown, things started to look a little different.

The clock began tolling arrival of middle age. Spare time seemed important, precious and pressing. However, not until after her husband's death in 1932 did she become serious about "working at something." It was then her latent talent for politics came to the fore. With her abundant energy, and swept by enthusiasm, it wasn't long before she became a well-known and popular political figure. On the Democratic side. And she has been at it — successfully — ever since.

Marie was employed in the Allegheny County Court House for 25 years and retired just four years ago. But she still holds a voluntary, non-paying position as Democratic County Vice Chairman. She was appointed to that position 11 years ago by Allegheny County voters and is considered an elected official. On this voluntary job she works full time during all campaigns. And even pays her own expenses. That office is in the Democratic headquarters, 14 Wood St., downtown, where the women of the party meet and discuss campaign plans.

Last year she served as Pittsburgh chairman of the Cancer Crusade. She worked on it for three months, organizing the women workers.

A former resident of Homestead she was interested in all civic projects. She served as general chairman of the March of Dimes, Crippled Children; Old Newsboys Fund; Rosalia Foundling Home, Ladies of the G. A. R. of Swissvale, and she is past president of the V. F. W. Post 373. Marie is a past officer of the State Federation of Democratic Women. She truly can be called a dedicated "Servant of the Democratic Party."

While Mrs. Aurentz is modest about it, you should know that the Democratic women honored her with a dinner-dance last August at Rockwell Hall, Duquesne University, for her many years of service to the party. Over 1,000 attended — all elected officials. And who was the belle of the ball? You guessed it!

Her hobbies? She likes nothing better than a good political campaign — with the Democrats winning, of course. She loves traveling around the county to all political meetings.

In between campaigns she enjoys visiting Fairless Hills, Pa. There live her son George, a machinist at the USS Fairless plant; and daughter Betty Brown. And her four lively grandchildren: Tommy and Georgeanne Aurentz; and Tommy and Jimie Brown. The one grand-daughter, Georgeanne Aurentz recently became Mrs. Fred Kludis. Marie has a hilarious time with all of them.

We have enjoyed telling you about Marie Aurentz not only because she's a well and favorably known Sq. Hiller, but also because she's our cross-the-hall neighbor. And a good neighbor.

The only person we know who doesn't like Marie is the one who said, with typical American candor: "How can I like her? She's a Democrat — ain't she!!"

Howard Balsam

Sabbath Holiday Special Event

Ever since those "Six-Days-in-June" the word miracle has become a household word. So today you'll learn about other miracles. Tiny ones — in comparison — but miracles just the same. And since a learned and dedicated fellow in our neighborhood has an important part in them, let's get better acquainted with him. Meet dark-eyed easy-to-look-at Howard Balsam, our neighbor at Beacon St. He has just been elected president of Yeshiva Achei Tmimim, a Hebrew day school. Yeshiva in Hebrew means "to sit." To sit and study. There a child gets intensive religious learning and at the same time complete secular schooling approved by the Board of Education. Years ago a Yeshiva was unheard of outside of New York City. Elsewhere Jewish youngsters were given religious training in the synagogue, after regular school. But Balsam, when a little tike, had it made as the saying goes. His beloved grand-dad did the teaching. A grocer by trade, grandpa had a religious scholar's know-how — a natural as teacher. When the Yeshiva was first founded 25 years ago by Rabbi Sholom Posner, it was considered a novel idea. There were only 10 youngsters enrolled, Howard included. Grand-dad was one of the teachers of religious subjects and the well-known Fannie Sachs taught them the three R's. The project caught on and accelerated. Currently there are 100 pupils. And now Fannie is principal of the secular department.

Remember the old Soho Bath House in the 2400-block Fifth Avenue? Where people congregated to get washed, steamed, rubbed, scrubbed? That's where the Yeshiva is now located. And the Bath House is no more. In its place stands a new lovely modern building complete with up-to-date educational facilities. And a swimming pool even. Arranged for by people who care. The youngsters study, learn — and like it. And there are no drop-outs. A miracle?

And now about president Balsam. In private life he's in the insurance and real estate business. Though an ordained rabbi, he says he "practices but doesn't preach." What does it take to be president of a Yeshiva? A thorough knowledge and love of one's religious faith; giving of one's self to help others without personal advantage and an awareness of moral and social obligations. Balsam has all these — and more. Read on.

After Bar Mitzvah Howard went to the Mesivta Torah Vodaath, N.Y., for higher study of Torah — comprising Bible Prophets, Ethics, Mishna and Talmud (code of Jewish Law). Graduating, he went on to Ner Israel Ribbinical College, Baltimore. There he was ordained a rabbi by the world-famous Talmudic scholar, Rabbi Jacob Ruderman. Then followed a year of Talmudic research in the Kollel (the College's Post Graduate School). His undergraduate work he did at Johns Hopkins University and got his M.A. degree in Education and Psychology at Loyola College.

Somewhere along the line Cupid stepped in. The rabbi attended a Chassidic wedding and there met beautiful Elsie Najjar, an American-born Yeminite. A teacher in New York's public school system, she's now assistant principal of the Yeshiva here. Howard and Elsie have been blessed with three bright lively children: Shoshana 10; Naomi 8, and Avrom 6. And where do they go to school? You guessed it. At Yeshiva.

Our neighbor is one of the founders of the new Yeshiva Gedola-Talmudic College here. Having just started, it takes much leg-work by interested orthodox lay people. His evenings are chock-full of civic activities. But all through the Sabbath dad Balsam is home with his family. After attending synagogue services together, the family goes home for the nicest special meal of the week. With the best linen and silver. All wear their newest clothes.

If ever parents and children have an opportunity for direct communication it's during the Balsam kind of Sabbath. No business is conducted. No one dials or answers the phone. No radio nor TV. And no movies. Just family warmth, intimacy, togetherness. They discuss what happened to one another during the week. Read together, sing special songs together. And you'll never believe it — the youngsters can't wait until Sabbath arrives. Neither can the parents. What do you think neighbors — another miracle.

Mrs. A. L. Barbrow

Known Around the World

Did you know that a charming widow in our neighborhood gets letters from fellas from the far corners of the world? Letters of love, affection, appreciation. Curious? And a little jealous mebbe? Well — gather 'round and find out who, why and how come.

However, since first things come first, let's start at the very beginning.

Our neighbor in question is none other than Mrs. Freda Barbrow of Wightman St., widow of a well-known physician, the late Dr. A. L. Barbrow. She has lovely natural white hair and a school-girl complexion.

The former Freda Seiger graduated Schenley High and married at 19. She then started at Pitt. But you know how it is with young marrieds. She became pregnant. And in due time baby Eleanor arrived.

Time marches on. Eleanor herself is now married — to Dr. Leonard Cohen, a Whitehall physician. Another daughter, Jane, is the wife of Allen Broff, owner of Broff's Jewelry. Son Stanley owns the Photocopy Supply Co. in Downtown. There are nine lively grandchildren.

Like countless other neighborhood women, when her youngsters started being on their own, Mom Barbrow became active in all local organizations. She was treasurer-auditor for the Ladies Hospital Aid Society's fund-raising campaigns. She thought up a clever seating-system for the Hadassah donor luncheons and other huge affairs.

And has been on the board of the Jewish Home for the Aged.

Now her greatest interest is the Council of Jewish Women projects, helping in practically every one of them.

Well, if other women do these things, what's so remarkable about Mrs. Barbrow? Here's what: three years ago like Humpty Dumpty, she had a great fall. And after numerous stays in the hospital is still an invalid

Most of her time is spent in bed, using a walker to get around. And she must have round-the-clock nursing aid. Other women in similar circumstances would doubtless "let go" talking about their operations. And even showing off the stitches. But not Freda Barbrow, she conducts all her activities just as if nothing happened. They bring her the records. She does the rest. From her bed.

At home our neighbor is chairman of Serve-a-Camp sponsored by the Conference of Jewish Women's organizations. She sends packages to Jewish servicemen overseas — in Korea, Turkey, Greece, Okinawa, Vietnam — all over. Last Passover she sent 100 "Solo Seder" boxes of kosher food — each a complete meal — to boys on radar posts in the middle of the high seas and other isolated places. Also prayer books for the High Holy Days.

Right now, upon request from a chaplain-of-camps Freda is busy mailing necklace mezuzahs — the Ten Commandments in miniature Hebrew, attached to a slender chain to be worn around the neck. For our boys in Berlin. Also Jewish records. All packaged from her bed, mind you.

Those love letters? They're pouring in from everywhere. In the words of Jimmy Durante, "there are millions of 'em." Well, hundreds, anyhow.

Like for instance from a soldier in far-off Ankara: "When we saw those Passover bundles from you we literally jumped for joy." And from Korea. "I was fortunate to receive a JWB Passover package with your name inside. God bless you."

Another from Clear, Alaska: "We were delighted with your CARE packages. The gefillte fish will qualify for the Farthest North seder in the history of Manishevitz."

Our neighbor was recently honored with a 2,000-hour service pin. And was named First Lady of the Day by WRYT for "out-standing service and contribution to the cultural, social and civic progress of the Greater Pittsburgh area."

Housed in, handicapped and often in pain, Freda Barbrow puts TLC (tender loving care) in every package. She thinks it's a challenging world and doesn't want it to STOP — nor to GET OFF.

Dr. Shepard Bartnoff
Scientist Values His Bible

Simply fantastic, isn't it, the interesting personalities we have in our neighborhood? As for instance Dr. Shepard Bartnoff, our neighbor at Marlborough Rd. He's been with Westinghouse for 11 years, in various research development projects involving nuclear reactors.

Recently he was appointed manager of CVTR (Carolina-Virginia Tube Reactor) at its Atomic Power Division in our city. In this position he will administer the company's contribution to the post-construction research and development program of CVTR.

Westinghouse, a leader in the area of nuclear power, must be very choosy about its top men. So how come Dr. Bartnoff? For one thing, our neighbor's experience and background reads like a Who's Who.

Prior to Westinghouse he was associate professor and executive officer of the physics department of Tufts University. He also taught in the same department at Massachusetts Institute of Technology; and also Syracuse University.

His B.A. degree in mathematics and his M.A. in physics he earned from Syracuse. And his Ph.D. in physics from M.I.T. He's a member of the American Nuclear and the American Physical Societies. Yet, with all his degrees our neighbor doesn't care if you address him as Dr. or just plain Mr.

Unassuming, to say the least. A rare attribute these days.

Forty-four years ago, when Shepard Burtnoff had reached the ripe age of one year the family left their little town in Poland for the Land of Liberty. They didn't travel on the Queen Mary or the S. S. Shalom. Nor by jet. By the time they settled in Syracuse little Shepard was five weeks older. Time marched on.

July, 1945, our new American had graduated Syracuse University. And also received a thorough Jewish education. His dad, steeped in tradition, spoke only Yiddish to his family, so they would not forget the language. He wrote a weekly column on Syracuse news events for New York's National Yiddish newspaper. Shepard and his sisters attended an all-Jewish Institute after regular school.

They made and kept up many friendships, until each married and scattered.

When student Bartnoff was a Syracuse University freshman he took a jaunt to Brooklyn to look up relatives and his dad's "landsleit." On that enchanted evening, across the crowded room, was lovely Irene Tennenbaum. Before you could say Jack Robinson, catching trains and subways Syracuse to Brooklyn became a gentle habit.

Then you know what? He didn't want Irene to sit under that Brooklyn tree with anyone else but him. So he did what came naturally. Married her.

Now there are three lively, lovely daughters. Judy, 17, is a senior at Allderdice. She's on the school's debating team specializing in extemporaneous speaking. They have tournaments in all Pittsburgh and surrounding schools. Also she plays violin in the Pittsburgh Youth Symphony. She just left with a Young Judea group for the summer in Israel.

Dad and Mom Bartnoff recently returned from a trip there. Come next April Judy will graduate Allderdice. At the same time her Mom, who has been attending Pitt, will receive a B.S. degree in education.

Then there's Debbie, 14, also in Allderdice. She's in its Scholar's Program and plays in the All-City Orchestra. Young Donna is nine and goes to Wightman School. All three attend Hebrew Institute after school and are active (especially Debbie) in the Young Peoples Synagogue. Dad Bartnoff was its president for two years. He's a member of the board of directors and the educational committee of Hebrew Institute.

Shepard and Irene, with two other married couples meet every Friday evening at one another's home. To play Poker? No, not even Canasta. But to read from the Hebrew Bible. Over a cup — or maybe a glass — of tea they discuss what they read. They look up and study the commentaries. They are now finishing the second Book of Kings.

In his all-girl family, would our neighbor physicist want boys? With four adoring women constantly spoiling him, who needs boys!

Donald G. Beaman

His Is Theater's Magic

Hi, everybody — and particularly those of you who love the theater.

When the curtain rises on the first act — that magic moment before any actor appears — you are at once transformed into the mood of the play, filled with anticipation for what is about to follow.

Want to know what puts you into that spell so easily, quickly? The scenery, of course.

And the artistic fellow who creates and puts life into scenes here, there and everywhere is our closeby neighbor, Donald G. Beaman.

At 30 he is a young man with talent, ambition and a terrific enthusiasm for the theater.

He and wife Myrna (also talented) live in a five-room third-floor apartment which they both decorated at Beacon St.

Their star boarder, roomer and master of all he surveys — and reaches for — is baby Alexander Benjamin, just turned 18 months.

Now set-designing isn't like Uncle Tom's Topsy who "just growed."

It takes planning, imagination, skill.

Mr. Beaman reads a play and gets the feel of its content. He starts the ground-work like an architect. Then he confers with the director of the play, and both decide what, which, how.

His scene-shop has a technical director and carpenter who do the drafting of the flats (canvas walls). Don himself does the painting.

Designer Beaman did the scenery for most of the Pittsburgh Playhouse and White Barn strawhat theater productions.

Last year he did 15 plays, 22 the year before, and 15 the current season. Comedy, tragedy, operetta, classic and contemporary drama each has its own inner rhythm of time and place.

Take for instance a few of his many plays: "The Beggar's Opera;" "Dark at the Top of the Stairs;" "Bye, Bye Birdie;" "South Pacific;" "Come Blow Your Horn;" "Little Mary Sunshine;" "Thurber's Carnival."

Each of the three Playhouse theaters presents special problems. And the children's Theater brings still another audience that must be enchanted as well as amused.

His genius for changing the mood and style to fit the occasion — that's art in the purest form.

Don and Myrna met while attending Carnegie Tech, and married shortly after graduation in 1960.

She's from the place where a tree grows — Brooklyn. Myrna is a playright and composed a scenario of an opera on a Greek Drama — and another play about White Russian Jews escaping from that country (her grandparents came from Odessa).

She and Don just finished a children's story, each writing half. Don did the illustrations. They are now looking for a publisher.

Myrna taught acting at the Playhouse on Saturdays. Who baby-sat those Saturdays? Dad, of course.

Don Beaman is working on his PhD in Art History for scene designing. He is going back to Tech for his masters degree. During that time he will be teaching second-year scene designing. He also wants to study in Europe.

What about baby Alexander Benjamin? His mom and pop hope he'll steer clear of the theater.

In the meantime, at the sound of music, he immediately begins to swing and sway. A dancer mebbe? Well, Fred Astaire and Gene Kelly didn't do so badly.

Dr. Wallace Beardsley
The Dust-Cloud Watcher!!

When Ranger 7 landed on the moon recently, someone important was conspicuous by his absence — that MAN in the moon.

Moon scientists — unconcerned with romance — couldn't care less. But for poets and young lovers it was quite a let-down. So to soften the blow let's turn to the stars instead.

For Squirrel Hill that's easy because in our neighborhood there's an honest-to-goodness star-gazer. No, not the kind who looks at the stars and tells you whom you'll marry.

But for a fellow with scientific know-how and a carload of experience, meet Prof. Wallace R. Beardsley, research astronomer par excellence — our neighbor at Shady Ave.

Answering a call from our Allegheny Observatory to study the stars, Wallace Beardsley came here 10 years ago from Seattle, Wash. The observatory high on a hill in North Side's Riverview Park, is affiliated with our university.

In addition to star-gazing, Astronomer Beardsley will teach at Pitt two days a week beginning this month. He is a research assistant professor. And now listen to this. If you want to "see stars" tune in on KDKA-TV 2 beginning Sept. 14. Our neighbor will host a week-day program titled "Astronomy: In the Space Age." Between 6:30 and 7 a.m. If the kids don't wake you, set the alarm.

Beardsley graduated from the University of Washington in Seattle with two degrees — a B.S. in mathematics and another in physics. At the University of Chicago's Yierke's Observatory he had additional training, which won him an M. S. degree in astrophysics.

Astronomy is the oldest of sciences which probes the heavens for secrets. And to learn more about the age and life expectancy of the stars and their distance from the earth.

Asking his students why they study astronomy, the usual answers he gets are "useful in navigation" or knowledge for the sake of knowledge." Quite true.

But the compelling reason, he says, is that astronomy provides information on the properties of matter and energy not attainable in the laboratory. They are the building blocks of the universe. In astronomy you can take the studies of matter and energy to the very universe itself.

On lovely nights when the stars blanket the Pittsburgh skies, our neighbor starts gazing. At the observatory he uses a 31-inch reflector telescope. Often he becomes so engrossed that the sun begins rising before he knows it. When this happens on an early Sunday morning, he hurriedly drives home for a few hours sleep.

Then he goes with wife Natasha to our neighborhood Church of the Redeemer where she teaches Sunday nursery school. And he sometimes ushers. They first met eight years ago at the All Saints Episcopal Church on the North Side where they both sang in the choir. She's a lovely soprano; he a masculine bass.

The Beardsleys have an absorbing hobby — collecting antiques. They own a chipped plate dated Apr. 8, 1850; a Pittsburgh post-card album with cards dated from 1900 to 1910. They find it fascinating to study the stamps. And our professor also loves boats and steamships. His family had a summer home on Puget Sound when he was a youngster and he went on many boat trips. Their rooms are filled with pictures and data of early boats and steamers.

And now back to Ranger 7. When it was on its way up there, our astronomer at the observatory was glued to his telescope watching for dust clouds at the landing. Maybe THAT MAN is underneath.

Mrs. Marian Beck
A Busy Helping Hand

You'll never believe it but this week's neighborhood personality, who does so much for others, doesn't think she's important enough to be written up.

Fact is, she had to be literally coaxed into it. That, in our book, makes her extra special because humility is a charming attribute — particularly in a woman. So let's learn a little about our likeable neighbor.

She's none other than the well-known Marian Beck, living at Bartlett St. — volunteer worker second to none.

Pittsburgh born, the former Marian Schwartz is the wife of merchant Steven Beck. The Becks have two children — Stanley, 12½, and Arlene, 9. Both attend Hillel Academy.

While Mrs. Beck does much for many other important projects, Hillel is her special love. Just where and what is Hillel Academy?

Located at 5685 Beacon St., it's a new-looking two-story buff brick building — so unpretentious that in passing you'd hardly give it a second glance. But if you stepped inside you'd pause in wonderment.

It's alive with teaching, learning and accomplishment in an atmosphere of dignity, devotion and joy. You see, it was named for Hillel, one of the greatest sages of the Talmud, living in the first century. Rabbi Max B. Posnansky is principal and Rabbi Isadore Marine executive director. Both are learned Talmudic scholars.

Hillel Academy is a private Hebrew day school sanctioned by the State Board of Instruction. Serving 300 or more students from ages 3½ through high school, it includes general studies plus an intensive Hebrew education.

Many graduates have received scholarships to Ivy League schools like M.I.T.; and some go on to institutions of higher Jewish learning.

Marian Beck was treasurer of the Hillel Women's Club and served in many other capacities. Now she's Brownie leader, is active in their Gift Shop, clears the scholarship boxes, helps plan the President's Day and Donor programs and does the decorations.

As a photographer she's firstclass and takes pictures at the drop of a hat, when needed in a hurry. Two years ago Marian was official co-chairman of the National PTA convention.

As for the Jewish Home for the Aged, the Poale Zedeck Sisterhood, Hadassah Group 2 Israel Bonds — actually she has "a finger in every project." And comes by it naturally. You see, her beloved dad — the late Morris Schwartz — was high in the Hillel tradition.

And Mom Helen Schwartz, living in the Wendover Apartments, is equally engrossed in many welfare causes.

At home, wife Marian, is the best cook ever. Her chocolate cakes, cookies and fudge brownies melt in your mouth, not in your hands. And the numerous sweaters she constantly knits have delighted and warmed many youngsters.

Like her husband, Marian loves sports. She goes in for swimming and ice-skating. During an extended trip to Europe and Israel several years ago she and Steve flew to Rome for the Olympics.

Hillel's President Adolph Schoenbrun, well-known civic leader, says of Marian Beck: "For sincerity, interest, honesty and loyalty she has no equal."

All this — and humble too.

Jacob Becker
Diogenes Gets His Man

Remember Diogenes, that ancient Greek philosopher who went searching in daylight with a lantern for an honest man? And was hard put to find one?

Well, if the time were now and he made it to our neighborhood he'd have the surprise of his life. For among us is a fellow so truly honest that the most hardened cynic would have a change of heart. Honest Jacob Becker is our personality of the week. A former butcher he worked for a meat firm 33 years.

Ill health forced him into early retirement at 62. With minimum social security and a modest government pension he recently took a small apartment in the new highrise Garfield Heights development — a federal government project for senior citizens regardless of race, creed or color. Naturally the rent is minimum. Until then he was our neighbor for 16 years on Douglas Street.

Having no family he prepares his own meals and keeps his place spick and span. Four days a week he divides his time working as a volunteer at the Veteran's and Montefiore hospitals. Full six hours a day, for absolutely free. In their Hobby Shop he teaches the patients to create and make all sorts of interesting novelties which, upon convalescence, they take home. Becker himself is an outstanding penman and addresses letters and cards for discriminating people who like the best.

And now for the piece de resistance. Last May Jake was invited by his cousin to come to Miami Beach. Renting a room in a small hotel he remained nine weeks. The living was easy and the bathing healthful. One day — well, let's quote in part from the Miami Beach Sun, later reprinted by our ever-alert neighborhood NEWS.

"The chain of circumstances, set off by a sudden downpour ended in a sunny note for Polish born Frank Lozorowitz, a 39-year-old Fort Myers merchant. His wife and little girl were bathing at the 4th St. beach when the rains came. Lozorowitz dashed into the public rest-room to dress and then drove off with his family. Minutes later Jacob Becker entered the rest-room. He too had been driven from the beach by the storm. There on the floor lay a well-worn billfold. Opening it he found $251 in bills, a gold watch, a diamond wedding band. And pictures of a laughing baby. No identification.

If a Rockerfeller or a Rothschild made such a find and returned it — money shmoney, who needs more. And no credit due them. But to one of meager circumstances, keeping it would mean some extra comforts in the years ahead. A great temptation. But it was furthest from Becker's mind.

Finding a piece of brown paper from a discarded paper bag, he wrote on it: "Anybody who lost money please contact J. Becker, 510 Ocean Drive, Bentley Hotel." He not only wrote it in English but Yiddish too. And pinned it on the wall. Then hurried to his hotel for a shower. Soon he was interrupted by a knock on the door. There stood Lozorowitz with the note in his trembling hands.

Our former neighbor handed him the wallet and contents. Offered $20 reward, Becker would not think of it. But he did accept an invitation for dinner at their home "To meet all the family." He had the time of his life being smothered with attention and affection. Several of Becker's friends called him a fool for not keeping the find. But Jake slept awfully good that night.

And here's a bit of irony. Lozorowitz in his youth lived in Poland — when that country was seething with Anti-Semitism. Children were brought up to hate all people of Becker's faith.

Born in the Ukraine young Jacob migrated to the Land of Liberty at 18. In night school he learned English. He also speaks Russian, Polish, Hebrew, German, Italian. And of course Yiddish. During World War 2 he soldiered in Uncle Sam's Personnel Dept. of the secret DEML. He's a member of the Jewish War Veterans Post 49.

So what else is news? Nothing. Except, as they say — honesty is the best policy.

Mr. & Mrs. Yehuda Berdugo
Husband And Wife Gladden The Heart

Today it's a double feature. About a husband and wife team that will gladden your heart. Meet Verdina and Yehuda Berdugo, our Beechwood Blvd. neighbors. Both teach at Hillel Academy, a private day school, Named for Hillel, one of the greatest sages of the Talmud living in the first century, it's sanctioned by the State Board of Instruction and serves about 350 students, 3½ through high school age. It includes general studies plus an intensive Hebrew education. Located on Beacon St. the Academy is a 2-story buff brick bldg. Inside it's alive with teaching, learning and accomplishments. In an atmosphere of dignity, devotion and joy.

Our neighbors met 15 years ago at Teachers Seminary near Kibbutz Yavneh, Israel. There they studied together and learned to love each other. After two years they were married under a "huppa" in Haifa by a military rabbi. The groom was still soldiering at the time. He is a grandson of the then Chief Rabbi of Morroco. After marriage he taught in the Yavneh school, Haifa. Also in the Carmel school on Mount Carmel. And is a graduate of Haifa University in Jewish and General History.

Mrs. Berdugo, a native of Rumania graduated from the Teachers Seminary and attended courses at Bar-Ilan University. She also taught at Carmel School there. Before coming to our city, both had been sent to Belo Horizonte, Brazil by the Torah Dept. of the Jewish Agency as the first teachers of the Hebrew Religious School there. During their 3-year stay they built the foundation of true Yiddish-keit. And were asked to remain another 3 years. Which they did. Then back to Israel.

At Hillel both teach Hebrew Language, Prophets and History. Between them Verdina and Yehuda speak 23 languages. Son Yigal, 5 is Brazilian-born. Nehama, 10 is a sabra. The children communicate in Hebrew but "scrap" in English. Our language they quickly picked up from their school friends and watching "Sesame Street" and "Misterogers Neighborhood". Mom cooks various exotic dishes. Like for instance, Brazilian Feijoada (rice, black beans and meat); Israeli Fallasel; Morrocan Dafina (cholent), and Rumanian egg plant. Mostly for Sabbath meals. During T.V. she manages to crochet sweaters and dresses for the children.

Why did the Berdugos come to America? Love of travel, to know people and places. They went all through Europe before arriving here. And the joy of teaching the Hebrew Bible to bring the spirit of Israel to the children. They like Squirrel Hill and its friendly neighbors.

The Berdugos all go to Hillel (their second home) together. Mom works from 9 to 3:30, brings the children home, prepares lessons for the next school day. Then dinner. Dad, after school goes to Pitt to study History toward a higher degree. Next term he plans attending Duquesne for counseling.

If ever parents and children have real communication, it's during the Berdugo kind of Sabbath. No one dials nor answers the phone. No radio nor T.V. and no movies. Just family warmth, intimacy — a blessing for the spirit and the body. They read together, sing special songs, and you'll never believe it, the kids can't wait till Sabbath arrives. Neither can the parents.

Did you watch the "Youth Salute to Israel Parade" recently? The expression of unified solidarity by the youth in the Tri-State area toward the bastion of democracy in the Middle East? The Berdugos all were in it too. After marching from Frick Park, the parade ended at — you guessed it — Hillel Academy. To dance, sing, socialize. And rest.

Sidney M. Bergman
His Golden Years Truly Golden

We all know retirees, fumbling around to keep dat ole debbil boredom away from their door. Their lifetime work was their one and only interest. And at its end they find themselves completely lost. How refreshing, then, is a fellow like Sidney M. Bergman whose golden years are truly golden.

Currently living in Morewood Ave. he was our Beacon St. neighbor for 17 years. Prior to retirement in 1962 Mr. Bergman was Executive Director of Montefiore Hospital for 29 years. During 12 of those years he taught Hospital Administration and History of Hospitals in Pitt's School of Public Health.

It was a natural for him. His venerable father was a founder and first president of the first Jewish Hospital in New England. Mr. Bergman's vast experience with medical and lay personnel, with patients and people in general would fill a book. But this is primarily about his retirement years, so let's just learn a bit about his educational and personal background. Then take it from there.

Boston born, Sidney graduated Boston Latin School founded by the Puritans in 1630 and patterned after Rugby. Six years later, to continue the boys' education, Harvard was established. Young Bergman entered that School. Then came WW II and he enlisted for Uncle Sam. Upon honorable discharge the ex-soldier was admitted to Harvard Medical School. Later he had charge of building and improving 3 hospitals:

Beth Israel in Boston (connected with Harvard); Sinai Hospital in Baltimore (associated with Johns Hopkins), and in 1943 our Montefiore which he came to develop as a teaching and research hospital. Many administrators he trained are now heading hospitals around the world, including 2 in Israel.

In 1924, guess what? Sidney fell in love. With beautiful Esther Cabe from Virginia, a librarian in Baltimore. Esther came to visit her aunt in Boston. You know — where "The Cabots speak only to the Lowells and the Lowells speak only to God". The man in love not only spoke to Esther but after just one week he proposed! Good thing she said yes because their marriage turned out like it was made in Heaven. Besides encouraging her husband in his hospital work, she became fascinated by his life-time avocation: Anthropology and Archeology. Every year they traveled in far-off places to add to their store of information. When Mr. Bergman retired, they took a year-long trip around the world visiting archaelogical sites.

And now for the piece de resistance — his retirement occupation. Mr. Bergman was made honorary associate Curator in the Section of Man at Carnegie Museum. Now he's a member of the International Assoc. of Glass Historians whose headquarters are in Leige, Belgium. Let's quote Mr. Bergman: "When one contemplates the 4,000 years of glass history, especially in the Near East, one becomes aware of the incalcuble debt civilization owes to early glass-makers and their descendents who, in the face of unending war, pestilences, conquests, invasions and migration, persevered — despite long periods when the world was dark — in bequeathing to us the useful and often beautiful commodity — glass".

He says that when peace is restored, Israel will be one of the most glorious archeological sites in the world. Mr. Bergman accumulated for the Carnegie Museum the first library of books on ancient glass in Western Pennsylvania.

Our remarkable retiree spends at least part of each day, 5 days a week, at the Museum. On the voluntary basis. Next time you're at the Carnegie Museum take a look at his magnificent glass collection. It's refreshment for the eyes and a lift to the spirit.

Any children? Yes, a son, Charles, living in NYC. A graduate of Harvard he's Executive V.P. of the Academy of Religion and Mental Health. And pssst! Listen! The handsome fellow's a bachelor. But don't let it get around.

Dr. Aksel A. Bothner-by

A Personality With Intriguing Name

With a preponderance of Cohens and Kellys in our neighborhood, the name Bothner-by stands out as interestingly intriguing. So it is. And the fellow who owns it is not only that but much, much more. So it's a privilege to tell you a little about him. Meet Dr. Aksel A. Bothner-by of Darlington Rd. A specialist in nuclear magnetic resonance and organic chemistry, he was named Dean of the College of Science at C-MU. April 1st of last year, to be exact. Since 1958 he had been a Staff Fellow, Director of Research and Member of the Advisory Committee of Mellon Institute.

Four years prior to that Dr. Bothner-by was Adjunct Professor in Pitt's Chemistry Dept. When Carnegie Tech merged with Mellon Institute in 1967 our neighbor served as Chairman of its Dept. of Chemistry for 3 years. In 1971, as mentioned above, he was named Dean. You think you climb up that far in the ladder one-two-three? Just like that? You'll find out differently if you read on.

Born in Minneapolis to Norwegian parents, Aksel spent his youth with his folks part in the U.S. and part in China. After some study at Univ. of Nanking he continued at Minnesota U., earning a B. of Chem. degree in 1943. Then came WW 2 and the youthful student served Uncle Sam with the coast artillery, military intelligence, and infantry. After an honorable discharge he continued studies for advanced degrees, obtaining his M.S. from N.Y.U. While at that school, guess what? The tall handsome student did what comes naturally. Fell in love.

With charming Christine Treuner also studying chemistry there. They married in 1949 after he had completed his Ph.D. at Harvard. And went housekeeping in Long Island. Then to Brookhaven National Laboratory. Later, from there he got a leave of absence for a year in Zurich, Switzerland as a Fellow of the American Cancer Society. Upon return to the States the Professor joined the faculty of Harvard's Chemistry Dept. And his lovely missus worked at Boston's Retina Foundation—until son Peter was born.

Dad's research at Harvard was concerned with the synthesis of the steriod hormone estrone to find out what things are made of—drugs, blood, fuel, glass, paper, you name it. You understand? Neither does anyone else except those highly educated smart fellas. A year later found them in Munich, Germany where Prof. Bothner-by was a Fullbright Lecturer at Ludwig-Maxmilian U.

While there a German stork brought baby Anne. Our neighbors live in a big old 15-room house built in 1912. Inside it reflects Christine's excellent taste and house-keeping ability with just twice-weekly outside help. In a year they'll own the place. Peter, now 14 goes to Penn Hall, Monroeville.

He likes radio and electronics. Off-hours he works at the Radio Shack next door to the Murray Ave. Guild Theatre. Anne, 9 attends Colfax. Their pet kitten "Ink" goes to no school. Dad Aksel likes to play Chess, but Spassky needn't worry. Nor Bobby either. He enjoys fencing at the C-MU gymnasium. Mom Christine is a good figure-skater, improving her skill at the Monroeville Mall Ice Palace.

So what's in a name? With such neighbors in Squirrel Hill you could truly say "There's gold in them thar hills."

Howard Braun
Loves Pittsburgh's People

High food prices got you down? Are you bored with TV commercials? And are you heart-broken that the moon heroes by-passed our fair city? Well, as the saying goes, count your blessings. That you live in the nicest neighborhood with the most interesting personalities. Like for instance Howard Braun, our neighbor at Bellerock St. Mr. Braun is Manager of Business Development in the PWR Systems Division of Westinghouse. His job's objective is the development of new businesses and products in the Atomic Power field.

.Mr. Braun is tall, easy to look at, unassuming — with a personality that wins you over in a minute. Right off you want to call him by his first name. Should you be invited to his home for Sabbath Eve dinner (as was the writer) you'd soon sense the friendly warmth of a happy family, devoted to one another and to one's religious faith. And toward the community as well. The so-called generation gap between parents and children is conspicuous by its absence.

Neighbor Braun was born in Hungary and reared in New York since age six. After finishing Boys High School there is 1941 he went on to Des Moines, Iowa, to enter and graduate Drake and Iowa State Universities — earning his degree in Engineering. Then came WW II. So the Graduate (apologies to Dustin) joined Uncle Sam's Navy in the Pacific serving three years. After an honorable discharge the ex-sailor worked in Schenectady. Single and fancy-free he would spend weekends in the

Adirondaks, the Berkshires and occasionally in New York with his folks. One enchanted weekend at home his father hinted that efsher maybe bachelor Howard might perhaps make a date with "that nice Jewish girl" from across the street — Dorothy Friedman. Those days a fella listened to his dad. And a good thing too because he found that Dorothy not only had become beautiful but interesting as well. And as an extra bonus was working as a bookkeeper to pay for a fur coat (now the coat is a short jacket, fashionable and good as new). To make a long story short, July 3, 1948, Howard and Dorothy became Mr. and Mrs. and started housekeeping in Schenectady. In due time son Steven was born, and several years later the Stork delivered Michele. But baby Janet wouldn't be caught arriving in a city that's so hard to spell. So she bided her time until much later when mom and dad moved to Pittsburgh. And that's where she was born.

But we're getting ahead of ourselves. In 1955 the Brauns moved to San Jose, Calif., where dad worked as an engineer and contractor. They loved it there so much, he tells you, that if he were to lose his job he'd be a fruitpicker there if need be, rather than leave. But eventually leave he did, when Westinghouse called him. Now, after six years in our city it's like this. Not that he loves San Jose less but he likes Pittsburgh more. Pittsburgh and its people.

Our neighbor is president of the Pittsburgh Chapter of the American Jewish Congress, developing programs along the lines of Jewish progress activism. And he's involved in a housing project for Pittsburgh Urban Improvements. Also on the board of the Hebrew Institute and the Y-IKC.

His lovely missus concentrates on being a devoted wife and mother. With no outside help in their five-bedroom home, the children make their beds, take turns at other chores. Dad sometimes goes into the kitchen to cook up something or other—mostly soup. But it comes out differently each time. And no one as yet knows what name to give it.

Son Steven is now almost 17 and will be a senior at Allderdice come September. He was on the school's track team and now is on the football team and captain of the volleyball team. Michele, 14, attends Allderdice. And goes in for folk dancing. Janet goes to Wightman. Smokey, their pet cat, goes to no school. At age 9 who needs it. He looks on in silent tolerance at the goings-on around him. Or curls up and takes a snooze. But most often just sits and purrs.

Gives you a nice feeling, doesn't it, having a family like the Brauns in our neighborhood.

Joseph Breslove Jr.
Keeps Busy As Firm's President

There's an awfully nice gentleman living in our neighborhood. He's the kind of guy who started small in the business world and worked his way up to someone quite important. His name is Joseph Breslove, Jr. With his charming wife, Peggy, and two young sons he occupies a duplex at Dalzell Place. They live downstairs. Upstairs lives someone who adores his family-the boys' doting grandma. Joseph III, age 11 and William H., 8 attend St. Bede School.

Mr. Breslove attended Wightman elementary school, Allderdice Junior High and graduated from Schenley High. He received his ME degree from Cornell University. During World War II his outstanding performance with the U.S. Navy Air Service won for him the Navy Cross, two Distinguished Flying Crosses and six Air Medals. Presently he is Commander, U.S. Naval Reserve (retired).

Our neighbor is president of the Breslove Separator Co.; and as a consulting engineer is also vice president of Safeway Steel Scaffold Co.

With a schoolboy's enthusiasm for his work, he not long ago invented an important machine. It's called a Regenerative Fly Ash Collector. Those of us who know nothing about such things will ask "What sort of a whoosit is it?" With patience and simplicity its inventor describes it as a machine that removes fly ash, soot and cinders from stack gases. And if this still doesn't have meaning to us, it sure does make sense to owners of industrial plants. His Collector has been installed here, there and everywhere. "Everywhere" includes some of the Caribbean countries. Mr. Breslove recently returned from a business trip to Puerto Rico. Martinique and Guadelupe. The sugar mills there have found his invention indispensable. However he was saddened by seeing so much poverty in those beautiful countries, even though it's not as bad as it used to be.

But nature has been kind there, he says. The weather is warm and soft and wonderful.

During his early school years Mr. Breslove was an expert at chess. Now his hobby is taking pictures through a microscope. And he loves to travel. No, he doesn't walk to his travel destinations. His trips are usually far beyond the currently popular 50-mile stroll. Mostly he jets.

Wife Peggy has no hobbies. At least not yet. She enjoys her role as a wife and mother. The boys have one mystery which as yet they have not solved. Their dad's age. It has become a tradition and source of much fun, to keep them guessing. No matter how the kids conspire to trip him with unexpected questions, he still has kept his age a deep dark secret.

How about telling your neighbors, Mr. Breslove? Delighted to. Just turned 47. But for goodness sake, don't tell the kids.

Don Brockett

Don Brockett Opens Newest Revue

Oh, for laffin' out loud! That's how it is at Beck's Patio Theatre these lovely Wednesday through Saturday evenings.

Their after-dinner revue, "Who's in Charge of This Ratrace?" spoofs everybody, everything — here, there, everywhere. There's no scenery, no bunnies and — you should pardon the expression — no strippers.

But it's a howl and the paying customers love it.

So Who's in Charge of this laugh — combine? A clever fella named Don Brockett — that's who. With special material by Joanne Pasquinelli and himself, he's aided and abetted by talented Bob McCully and Joe Negri. While Judy Knaiz and Judy O'Dea add song and sparkle. And, incidentally, keep it clean.

They've been at Beck's two full summer seasons. The winter months Don and his stooges keep you in stitches at Bill Kramer's Back Room.

And now, because he's our neighbor, let's get the low-down on Don Brockett's private life.

Want to know how he met the former Leslie Mulvihill, his charming missus of five years? She was working for TV Guide." So was Don. But it was strictly professional between them because they seemed to have nothing in common. In fact, as Don says, they simply hated each other. For four years it went like that.

Then, at the Melody Tent summer theater "Li'l Abner" was playing. Don had no date so in desperation asked Leslie to join him. She had no date either so, also in desperation, said yes.

To the surprise of both, it turned into an enchanted evening. And to the surprise of no one, they married. And are living happily ever after. When Don was playing in Palm Springs and Phoenix, Leslie was Phyllis Diller's production assistant. Now she manages their interesting household and stage-manages most of his plays.

The Brockett eight-room neighborhood home, which they own, is something to see. English Colonial, painted spanking white, it's surrounded by lovely trees and colorful flowers. Inside it's even lovelier. Their artistic taste is evidenced at every turn. Upstairs is Don's music room with a small bar piano. There many wonderful tunes are born. Next is his study where he creates his lyrics and comedy. A gardener cuts the grass and trims the hedges. A barber comes once a month to snip Don's bangs.

Always there are actors, dancers, singers — coming in, going out, waiting, talking. Like Grand Central Station. But it's lots of fun and they enjoy it.

Even though he's up late for his night shows, Don gets up early every morning to work on the many things constantly facing him. So how can he burn the candle at both ends, as the saying goes? Well, he's smarter than most guys. He leaves the night show immediately it's over, not stopping for drinks nor nuthin'. Straight home he goes. And listen to this: Every afternoon, regular as clock-work, rain or shine, he takes a nap. In polite society they call it a substantial snooze.

Our talented neighbor has just completed his first musical-comedy — "Love Song." It made its debut Tuesday at the Rabbit Run Theatre. Madison, O. In addition, he and Janice Friedman wrote and staged "The Fiddler" for the local chapter of Brandeis University. An instant smash hit. Now it's being offered to charitable groups for fund-raising affairs. Like your church, synagogue, Hadassah, B'nai B'rith and the like.

But that's not all. Don's also writing a revue for ORT for their convention at the Hilton in October.

Nice, isn't it — having such a fantastic fella as our neighbor?

Dr. Elliott (Steve) Brodie
Dentist During Day, Hypnotist at Night

During the day Dr. Elliott Brodie is engrossed seriously and conscientiously at his chosen profession, dentistry, sharing his office suite with his chiropodist brother Dr. David Brodie. At night, however, he happily turns to his lifetime hobby as hypnotist and magician.

How does one come by such an unusual hobby? About 20 years ago Dr. Brodie (now affectionately known as "Doc" or "Steve") watched the then famous hypnotist-magician Howard Klein perform. That was it! Steve's compulsion to master that art immediately took form and soon he became Dr. Klein's avid pupil. Klein was gracious and Steve learned fast. Before long he became a performer on his own merits.

Steve's first performance was at the Squirrel Hill Boys Club (now the Irene Kaufmann Settlement). He helped raise $4,000 for charity, and put 15 boys to sleep. And he has been putting people to sleep ever since. He even used his skill on some Pittsburgh Pirates some years ago. The things he had them do under his hypnotic spell would make a wooden Indian rock with laughter. And quite recently, at the Edgewood Country Club, Steve performed his amazing feat of snatching a man's shirt off his back without removing the subject's coat.

Doc Brodie is a member of the Enoch Rauh Club; Alpha Omega Dental Fraternity; the Oakland Lodge Masonic Temple; the Odontological Pennsylvania Dental Society; the American Dental Society, and the International Brotherhood of Magicians. Also a member of the Captain & Managers' Club of the University of Pittsburgh. All this and a world champion swimmer, too. At Pitt in 1962 he was captain of the swimming team and was the quarter mile national record holder.

Through the years Steve has entertained millions of persons and raised countless funds for all kinds of charities — Catholic, Protestant and Jewish alike. A number of years ago the late Father Regis of the Toner Institute wrote him:

"You have done much to brighten the lives of boys who have been deprived (through no fault of their own) of the better things the world has to offer. God bless you!"

Perhaps the Father's blessing came true, because Steve got an interesting break. While on a Florida vacation he met up with several executives of the big liners that go to the Caribbean countries. It didn't take long for him to connect up on several of their cruises as lecturer and entertainer. He had several 14-day cruises with stops in Haiti, Puerto Rico, Jamaica, Dominican Republic and the Virgin Islands. And on to Trinidad, Aruba, Caracas and the Panama Canal. He put on shows "with never a dull moment." Steve also lectured on hypnotism on two Italian Liners leaving Port Lauderdale. He enjoyed the cruises and the passengers loved his entertainment.

Doc lives on Darlington Road with a sister Mrs. Ethel Simon. Why with a sister? Well, you see, Steve is a bachelor. Why a bachelor, you may ask? Our guess — and it's only a guess — is that it's not easy to hypnotize a hypnotist. But your guess is as good as ours.

Mrs. Charles (Rose) Bronk

Charity Extends Beyond Call of Duty

Our personality of the week is the dynamic and well-known Mrs. Charles (Rose) Bronk of nearby Maxon Towers. Learning about her should put a zing into your day.

Rose Bronk has been a dedicated organization worker all her adult life. But so have countless other wonderful women in our neighborhood. However, what's unique about Rose is that she carried her charity work over and above the call of duty and even during her stay in Miami Beach the past two winters. Most people who leave the snowing and blowing of winter for sunny Florida go there to escape the deep freeze and responsibilities. They mostly laze around, go nightclubbing and have fun. Rose did these things too, but much, much more. She got many wealthy women interested in her current pet charity project, and raised a raft of money.

But first let's learn a little about our neighbor's background and how she became such an example of the human spirit.

The former Rose Gusky met handsome Charles Bronk where the boys are. In public school. They went through the grades together and both graduated South High School. Charles went on to Penn State College to become a mechanical engineer. And Rose worked in Kaufmann's. When they were 20 and 21, respectively, Rabbi Reuben Grafman (of blessed memory) made them Mr. and Mrs. Fifty years ago.

The young husband worked in the engineering department of Koppers Co. a year and another for the B. & O. Railroad. Then opened a store for Ladies on the North Side. His bride worked right along with him. In 1924 the Bronks opened a Ladies Store in nearby Irwin. By the time Charles semi-retired and left the business in the hands of a manager, it had grown to two stores. And became a landmark, selling everything for ladies except bikinis with no tops on top.

Somewhere along the line the Bronks became parents of three sons. They're all grown by now. Bernard is a financier in N.Y.: Robert, a local builder. Burt received his Ph.D. at Princeton and is a nuclear physicist. He's doing research at Brookhaven Laboratories. The sons presented mom and pop with 11 grand-children — seven girls and four boys. And that's not all. Rose has seven devoted brothers. Six are "The Gusky's of S.S." The seventh is Bill Gusky, a well-known Squirrel Hiller.

During her busy years as housewife, business partner and raising her boys, one day Rose decided she wanted to do something for others. In no time her charitable activities progressed like a house on fire. Now she wears a charm bracelet, a symbol of her accomplishments. One charm is for 42 years in Haddasah, enrolling 14 life members. Another is for life membership in B'nai B'rith. Two for Eastern Star. Several more for Hadassah. And a pearl-encrusted one for Phi Epsilon Pi — her husband's and sons' fraternity, which she organized. Then there were her services for Red Cross, teaching First Aid and transporting blood to the Blood Bank. And enlisting volunteers during WW 2. She helped arrange a Library for the dear hearts and gentle people of the Jewish Hospital and Home for the Aged. And a host of other projects too numerous to list.

December before last husband Charles underwent major surgery. And the doctors prescribed Florida sunshine. They left for Miami Beach, renting an apartment in the beautiful Sea Coast Towers which boasts 1,000 tenants in a complex of three buildings. No sooner had they settled and Charles started recuperating, than Rosy got busy. She maneuvered to meet many of the Towers' wealthy women. And before you could say Jack Robinson they organized the Suncoast Chapter of the Women's American ORT. They held teas, luncheons. And next January the group is taking a Caribbean cruise. They've planned a masquerade ball, cocktail parties. And money will be raised for ORT, you may be sure.

Just what's ORT? It's an Organization for Rehabilitation through Training. For deprived and dispossessed persons. ORT has training schools in all countries of Europe, Asia, North and South America and Africa. And of course, Israel. It's the largest voluntary vocational training system on earth — a global force in the struggle against defeat and despair.

The Bronks are home now — tanned and fit. And come Aug. 12 they'll celebrate their 50th wedding anniversary. Couldn't happen to nicer people.

Dr. Henry W. Brosin

Psychiatrist Finds Meaning in Movement

Remember the popular song of yesteryear — "Every Little Movement has a Meaning All It's Own?" It seemed to hint at saucy romance. But today's psychiatrists find deeper meaning in Movement. So much so that they can probe into mental illness, understand the patient better and help guide him toward normality.

A prominent Psychiatrist who heads this fascinating study is Dr. Henry W. Brosin, our neighbor on Northumberland St. Dr. Brosin is Professor and Chairman of the Department of Psychiatry in Pitt's School of Medicine. And is also Director of the Western Psychiatric Institute and Clinic in Oakland. He's been there since 1951.

Before attempting to tell you about this important research, it might be nice to learn a little about our interesting neighbor's background. So pull up your chairs. Born in Blackwood, Va., in 1904 young Brosin grew up and went to school in various other cities. In 1923 he enrolled at the University of Wisconsin, earning his A.B. and M.D. degrees there.

Then followed a year's internship at the Cincinnati General Hospital, three years of training at the University of Colorado, and three additional years at the Institute for Psychoanalysis, later becoming a staff member of the Psychiatry Department at the University of Chicago. He started serving Uncle Sam 10 months before Pearl Harbor, heading a 200-bed Psychiatry Unit in an Army Hospital in New Orleans for 2½ years.

Then became Consultant to the Third Service Command in Baltimore. In 1945 he was made a full Colonel and the following year received the Legion of Merit. At war's end he traveled for the Army in Germany, France, Austria and Korea. While in France Col. Brosin was accompanied by his lovely wife — the former Ruth Hatfield of Nebraska. A wife?? Where did it happen? In Chicago. How did they meet? In the darndest way. They were introduced! And by mutual friends yet. Their interesting son Lloyd is now a graduate at the University of Wisconsin. He's a specialist in Library Science and History. And girls — sorry to disappoint you. Lloyd too is married. And is the dad of a lively little girl named Rachel, all of three.

As to our neighbor's membership in Professional Societies — local and national — limited space won't permit listing. But honestly, their number is so great they would fill a book. Maybe a library even. Suffice it to say our Junior Chamber of Commerce gave him "The Man of the Year" Award last January. And the United Mental Health Services of Allegheny County presented him with a Special Award last May.

So what about those Movements — remember? Dr. Brosin's researchers have been probing movements, for the past six years, in a remarkable study of human behavior. Amazingly they have found these slight message-bearing movements going on almost continuously while you talk. Even more surprising: the movements you make are synchronized perfectly with the actions of the person you're talking to. In effect, you and he engage in a fantastic dance together even though neither of you is aware of it.

If you like each other, the researchers have found, you dance in harmony more than if you don't. However if you have a severe mental illness, you may not "dance" with other people at all. Dr. Brosin's group made a study of 1,000 eye-blinks and a slow-motion scrutiny of films taken of the heroine in "The Three Faces of Eve." The movie is about a mental patient who, at different times, showed three entirely separate personalities. The scientists took a count of the number of abnormal eye movements of each of the three.

The eyes of Eve Black — who was the sexy, wild, irresponsible personality — strayed apart fully 16 times as much as those of the depressed quiet Eve White. Jane's strayed about a third as much as Eve Black's. When the patient was fully cured, her eyes stopped straying entirely.

All of this may be very interesting. But what good is it? The answer lies in the study of the movements of mentally ill people. And may be helpful in transforming their infantile anxieties into mature ones. Are you confused, mebbe? Well, our brilliant professor isn't. And our community is proud of him.

Dr. & Mrs. Shlomo Brovender
Headlines, Smedlines - News Isn't All Bad

No matter what the headlines say, the news isn't all bad. Especially in our neighborhood composed of so many interesting personalities - natives as well as those here far-off countries for special study and work. Today let's say welcome to Dr. and Mrs Shlomo Brovender of Shady Ave.

They came here from Israel - that dangerously-surrounded little country whose people's ancient and present history defines courage, sacrifice, vision and a deep love for learning. How did the Brovenders meet? Shlomo didn't need to stand on a corner in Jerusalem watching all the girls go by. He was invited to a party at a friend's home. Shulamit Zitman, affectionately called Shula, was there too. That was it. After four months of dating they married in that lovely city. In 1962, to be exact. Two years later they came here.

Let's see now. Since Women's Lib hasn't as yet been completely finalized, you'll learn first about husband Brovender. Then of his beautiful Shula.

Dr. Brovender, after earning his M.A. and Ph.D. degrees from Pitt, is now Assistant Research Professor at its Graduate School of Public Health. His current work is closely related to what he plans to do when they return to Israel.

Mrs. Brovender was sent here by the Jewish Agency and teaches Hebrew at our neighborhood Beth Shalom synagogue, Beacon and Shady. For just several hours late afternoons, when the Jewish children come there after regular school. Thus mom has time to take care of their 5½ room apartment and their own three youngsters — all boys. All were born here. In other words, they're all dyed-in-the-wool Yankees. Their ages are 4½, 2½ and 8 months. Because later the family plans to return to Israel, the children were given Israeli names, as follows: The eldest is Shahar, meaning Dawn. Next is Shai (Gift) and the baby is Shamir (Strong Rock). The first one speaks Hebrew and English. The middle boy Hebrew and a little bit of our language. Baby Shamir makes known his wants in a language all his own but which the family readily understands. While mum is away teaching, a baby-sitter keeps a watchful eye on the kids. The sitter's job is a cinch because the youngsters are deeply engrossed in TV's "Sesame Street" and "Misterogers Neighborhood" Fascinated and learning.

Our neighbors love music and regularly attend our Symphony concerts. Husband Shlomo also likes photography. And deep-sea fishing. The only thing, there's no ocean here — not even at Forbes and Murray. The parents learned English in Israel and speak it with only a slight accent. But to master it completely, they feel, one must use it in the country of the language. Meantime their accent is charming. Maybe they should leave it as is.

Are "hot-pants" the range in Israel as they are in USA? Actually, shorts have been worn by the Israeli young women in the army for years. Shorts because of the heat and boots for marching. But compared to here, they're not so short and not so tight and not so "hot".

Don't you wish our neighbors would live here permanently? But since it will be otherwise, our community wishes them the best of everything now. And in the years ahead.

Jack Brown

Couple Eagerly Awaits Premiere Performance

Come October 24th we'll be "climbing to the stars to see the stars." Atop Mt. Washington on Shiloh Street. That evening the Open Stage Theatre, seating approximately 430 persons will have its premiere performance. Formerly a moviehouse the newly arranged Theatre will make its performances intimate, bring them closer to the audience.

The talented fellow with a beard in whose eyes the stars gleam is well-known and popular Jack Brown. He lives in our neighborhood of course, at Darlington Rd. Jack was recently named Managing Director of Open Stage. Also President of the Pittsburgh Performing Artists Foundation — a non-profit, tax-exempt cultural, educational institution. Backing Director Brown is a non-salaried Board of Trustees and Advisory Council made up of civic, commercial and theatrically oriented individuals. Like for instance Jules Fisher, Earle Gister, Gabriel Rubin, Omar K. Lerman, William H. Putch, and Reuben Katz. And working with him even more closely is Jack's beautiful blue-eyed Brazilian-born missus, Ana.

And now let's learn what's with our important neighbor. After graduating Taylor Allderdice Jack studied Acting at Carnegie Tech (soon to be known as Carnegie-Mellon University). Several weeks before his senior year he was rehearsing in their play "Waiting for Godot." After rehearsal someone said "Come meet some of the new students." So Jack sauntered in. Looking down his senior nose he said hello — nothing else. An unpleasant fellow, thought Ana Edler, the first Brazilian actress to win a Rockefeller Scholarship. And started talking with another student about her country and experiences there as an actress. Brazil—An actress—those lovely blue eyes! Jack was electrified. And invited Ana for coffee at Tech's Skibo Hall. That summer he took her to a play at the White Barn strawhat theatre. And one enchanted evening— who can explain it—who can tell you why—wise men never try—Jack told her: "I'm going to marry you." Hm! Married she can always get.

But Jack too had his share of charm. Besides they had so much in common. Soon they were winging to Brazil for her parental blessings. And said their I-Do's in a Jewish synagogue there. The young bride appeared in every major theatrical company and TV station in Rio de Janiero. And Jack managed and directed a number of successful theatre productions in that city. Both inaugurated the first Repertory Theatre in Brazil and also a nationally-acclaimed Drama School.

Baby Deborah, now five, was born in Rio. She attends Colfax Kindergarten. Arthur, a real live Yankee, was brought by the stork in the Magee Hospital. He's all of two years now and goes to the Mother Goose Nursery in Penn Hills. The bus picks him up early mornings and off he rides, with other toddlers, clutching a small bag. Cigarettes mebbe? No—not even cigars. Just a few clean diapers. In a toddler's day changes are often made. He's completely housebroken by now, has started walking and had his first fight already, ending with a swollen eye. Another tike wanted to sit on his little wagon. The nerve! As to the Open Stage Theatre—little Arthur couldn't care less.

What does it take to start a new theatre in our city? Takes talent, inventiveness imagination. Jack and Ana have much of all these. And it takes money too. The fund-raising goal of the Pittsburgh Performing Artists is $200,000. It's being supported by the Commercial and Industrial sponsors, founding members, charter members other contributing members and foundations and charitable trusts. Wanna call the Browns for more facts? Dial 421-8875.

Jack and Ana have great expectations. Let's wish them a whopping success.

Dr. Peter M. Bungay

Award Winner Pleasant Neighbor

As this is being written it's a sad day in our fair city. The mighty Pirates have struck out, after many, many wins. But don't despair. The season is young, the soft beauty of spring is here, buds are bursting out all over and hope is in the air. So let's turn our attention and be even more happy about a most interesting neighborhood personality.

Meet Dr. Peter M. Bungay of Northumberland St. — tall, youthful-looking, stream lined and plenty brilliant. A biomedical Engineer at Carnegie-Mellon, he recently won a post-doctoral fellowship from the North Atlantic Treaty Organization (NATO). Dr

Bungay, one of 45 Americans to receive the NATO award will conduct biomedical research at McGill University, Montreal. For one whole year beginning next September. He was selected from among 432 applicants appointed by the Research Council for the National Science Foundation (NSF), administrators of the NATO program in the U.S.

Born in the city where a Tree Grows, young Peter graduated Brooklyn Technical Hi. In 1963 he earned his Bachelor of Chemical Engineering degree from Cooper Union. Then went on to Houston's Rice University for graduate work in his chosen field. Part of his duties was doing research in the artificial heart program (long before heart-transplants were headlines in the world's newspapers). After two years in Houston his unusual ability and experience began showing and Carnegie-Mellon called him here. September 1965. To work with one of the Profs whom he had met several times before and through whom he became interested in biomedical engineering.

Now that our neighbor will soon be leaving for Montreal, let's peek into his personal life before he goes. His lovely wife, the former Janet Duval (a History major) originally from Baltimore but whose folks now live in Fairfax, Va., Came to C-MU a year later. To work as Administrative Ass't. in the Chemical Engineering Dept. Before very long they met. You know, where boy often meets girl—on the campus. August 1967 they became Mr. and Mrs. They had intended marrying at a Methodist Church in Connecticut by a minister Janet knew. But decided to wed at her parents' home in Fairfax. And who do you think lived right across the street? A Presbyterian minister no less. Since one must love one's neighbor they simply had to ask him to tie the knot. He gladly did, with the added bonus of kissing the bride.

Our neighbors haven't (as yet) added to the population explosion. They live in a private house made into 3 separate furnished apts. Theirs is on the 3rd floor, walk-up. At their age, who minds running steps! The owners (on the first floor) are none other than prize-winning sculptor Henry Bursztynowicz and his artist-wife Louise. No wonder the apartments are so artistically furnished.

Husband Pete bought a bird-feeder for outside their window. And guess who came to dinner? First guests were cardinals and chickadees. Then the species increased and became so varied that identification is confusing. All are hungry. All know when dinner is ready. All enjoy the assorted seeds menu. But none are bold enough to venture inside. However they seem to linger outside, perhaps enjoying the classical music of the Bungay stereo set.

Before starting work at McGill in Montreal, Pete and Janet plan to travel throughout Europe for 3 months this summer. While at Carnegie-Mellon they had become close friends of faculty members and students from Germany, Czechoslovakia, Austria, Holland, et cetra. How better to learn and enjoy a foreign country than through the eyes of its nationals. They won't need to pursue happiness. It will be waiting for them.

Our neighbors enjoy ice-hockey and are entranced by concerts, particularly organ music.

Henry Bursztynowicz
Hard To Pronounce Name, But Famous

Sometimes, when a fella has an unpronounceable name, he changes it, shortens it, makes it easier for all concerned. But not Henry Bursztynowicz, our neighbor at Northumberland St.

He feels that if it was good enough for his beloved Polish pop, by gum it's good enough for him. And believe it or not, many agree — and admire him for it. Especially the former Louise Evans Scott.

Just a few months ago she up and accepted that name as his Mrs., for better or for worse. You'll be sure it's for better when you learn how much of many things Henry and Louise have in common.

Sometimes a husband wants to talk shop with his wife but the little woman knows from nuthin' what he's saying—which is frustrating. But our newlywed neighbors both speak the same language, as the saying goes.

They both graduated from Carnegie Tech; both are artists and sculptors, and both have had prize-winning careers. Louise studied sculpture with the world-famous Henry Moore in England. Husband Henry went to Cranbrook Academy of Art in Florence.

He's on the Board of the Arts and Crafts Center and has had many one-man shows. At Westmoreland Museum of Art in Greensburg he displayed 80 pieces of Sculpture. These were of wood, marble, copper, slate, limestone and brazed metal, requiring a variety of skills and imaginative artistry.

At the Arts and Crafts Center he teaches stone carving, ceramics, sculpture and rug-hooking. Wife Louise paints at home and does sculpting in his East End studio work shop. And it's likely he doesn't charge her rent.

Our neighbors' honeymoon—several months belated—was spent in Mexico, lasting five weeks. They made the trip in a huge red Chevrolet "Greenbriar." They returned with the most fascinating objects of art only Mexico can produce.

These are now arranged in the Bursztynowicz home. From the outside, their house is unimpressive, but inside it's a viewer's paradise, created with artistic skill by hands that care.

You see no wall-to-wall carpeting. Instead the gleaming hardwood floors are partially covered with goat-skin rugs—white with black spots. The bed covers are of shaggy white sheep skins, while Mexican serapes are artistically draped on chairs and sofas.

As to pictures, a layman has no adequate words to describe them. Same is true with the various carvings of all shapes and sizes—gracefully standing here, there and everywhere. Even on the patio.

Their back yard is aglow with Western Pennsylvania wild flowers and trees. It takes on exotic atmosphere, touched as if with magic.

Should you happen in on our neighbors some Friday during dinner, it's likely you'll be served delicious home-made clam chowder in a most interesting wooden or clay bowl. All their dishes, linens and dinner-ware come from far off places.

Henry and Louise Bursztynowicz think it's a mad, mad, mad, mad world. But they don't want it to stop and they don't want to get off.

Fact is, they like it. And our community likes them as neighbors.

Fred Calfo

From Kid to Cop And He Loves It!

Many years ago a little boy was asked what he wanted to be when he grew up. Immediately he said A Policeman. Kids still have such lofty dreams but their mommas and poppas often side-track them into other professions. Humdrum ones, like for instance a doctor, a lawyer, or a businessman even.

But our youngster in question really made it. In 1931 he became a Police Officer with the Department of Public Safety. He's Fred Calfo of Coyne Terrace in nearby Greenfield. And you'll be delighted to learn that Patrolman Calfo watches over the safety of all who live in and around the Forbes-Murray section — our very own neighborhood. Let's learn a little about this dependable, loyal fellow with a no-nonsense attitude.

Young Fred attended Greenfield and St. Rosalia schools. In grade eight he became a dropout. Not to join gangs or speed a motorcycle. And "flower children" were unheard of then. He quit school simply to work and earn. In no time he learned the carpenter trade, including painting and cement work. And became expert in these jobs. Takes more than a Policeman's salary to bring up and educate children. Like many dads who hadn't the opportunity to go through school, he wanted his kids to have the best education possible. Aided by his capable and devoted wife, the former Elizabeth Krauss — and the children themselves — they're all on their own now with an exceptional background.

Officer Calfo has been married 35 years. To the same wife, he proudly boasts. And small wonder. His Elizabeth to this day is not too proud to do housework several days a week for personal friends, to help meet the bills.

They have been blessed with four wonderful children. Fred, Jr. works with NASA in its Missile Department in Cleveland. He's married and the father of two boys and a girl. Daughter Dolores is Mrs. Louis Angel. Her husband is an electrician for Jones & McLaughlin.

They also have two boys and a girl. Frank is a CPA. He was awarded a scholarship from Duquesne University. And worked for Rust Engineering Co. in Cleveland during the day. At night he was assistant professer at Case-Western Reserve University there. He graduated as recently as June 12 and is moving to our city to work for Rust here. His baby-boy is all of nine months and has just started to walk.

Daughter Louise is Mrs. Robert Curry and lives in Grafton, W. Va. The Currys have a boy and a girl. Even without a computer you can count nine grandchildren. And that's not all. There's one great-grandchild. At home is Raymond, 23. He operates and repairs IBM machines for Consolidated Coal Co. And listen girls, Ray is a bachelor. So you take it from there.

The Calfos own their six-room brick house. Mom is the best cook ever and Pop often does the dishes.

Our Patrolman starts his beat at 3 P.M. and continues till 11. From Forbes & Murray he walks to Beechwood Boulevard, up Beacon as far as Hobart. Then down Hobart to Murray, ending at Forbes. He checks the doors (front and back) of all business places. Sensing trouble he calls from a patrol phone for a police car.

Suspicious characters are questioned and searched for weapons. (Since the Kennedy tragedy the Supreme Court made the new ruling on weapon-searching). Recently Calfo noticed four swarthy-looking fellows speaking a foreign language. He followed them from across the street. They sauntered up Forbes into the popular Chicken Palace. After eating, they went away. Must have been just hungry for good chicken. No trouble. But Calfo takes no chances.

Neighbors, if you're up to no good and contemplating mischief, think twice. Our Policeman is the most likeable fellow with a stick you ever met. And he's fair and square. But strict as — you-know-what. So behave yourselves — you hear?

Josie Carey

Kids Have a Pal in Josie Carey

As to this week's neighborhood personality, everything is coming up talent. Because, you see, she's none other than the popular and gifted Josie Carey, our Beechwood Boulevard neighbor.

However, she's been written up so much so often with rave reviews that adding more of same now would be like gilding the lily. So you'll get just a few important highlights of her successful career. Then we'll snoop a little into her personal life — which for Squirrel Hillers is much more fun to read.

Josie's maiden name was Josephine Marie Vicari. Eleven years ago she married Henry J. Massucci, a home improvement contractor. Professionally, as you already know, she uses the charming name of Josie Carey. Since graduating Butler High in 1948 Josie has become a writer, song-writer, singer and a noted KDKA-TV and radio star.

She joined WQED in 1953 featuring "The Children's Corner." For this entertaining program she won the 1955 Sylvania Award. Besides hosting her own programs ("Funville" with Sterling Yates; "Storyland" and "Josie's World") she appeared on Dave Garroway's "Today" Show, also "Captain Kangaroo." If you don't recall these entertaining programs, ask the kids. They remember.

Our Junior Chamber of Commerce named our neighbor The Top Woman in the Entertainment Field. In 1960 she received both the Speaker of the Year Award as well as the National TV-Radio Mirror Award for the best children's programs.

Josie is also the author of several children's books. She's featured in Who's Who in American Women. And have you read "This is Pittsburgh and Southwestern Pennsylvania," sub-titled "We Live Here — We LIKE it!? Josie wrote its scintillating—and often poignant—verses while collaborator Marty Wolfson furnished the vivid, exciting illustrations. They won raves here, there, everywhere.

Our neighbor is a buoyant brunette, not much over 5 feet in her spike heels. She has a dazzling smile, lovely speaking voice and has won the adoration of every small fry within a 50-mile radius. Now she's writing lyrics and comedy for "The Vagabonds" and does specialities for Lee Tully.

And if you've been wowed recently by Dory Sinclair at the Ankara, Josie is responsible for writing the act.

And now pull up your chairs. Where and how was it first-love for Josie and Henry? In a convertible? Guess again, A Volkswagon? Nope! It was at an old-fashioned Hayride given by the ISDA Lodge 15 years ago.

Teenagers, get your moms to tell you about hay-rides. They'll sigh—maybe swoon—as they recall the scent of new-mown hay, the leisurely trot of friendly horses down unpaved country roads. They'll remember the hum of bees, the soft evening breezes, the moonlight and the star-studded skies. Need more be said?

Josie and Henry now live in a lovely 12-room house which they own. Josie's mother, Angeline Vicari, lives with them. In their adjoining conservatory Angeline raises geraniums, orange trees, orchids—you name it. Josie herself tends African violets. She has 200 plants in their sun-porch.

She also is expert in needlepoint for which she won an award. And she has gone in for the new crewel work which is gaining in popularity. They have a maid twice a week but mom does the cooking.

Naturally she concentrates on Italian dishes. Her specialty is lasagne. You don't have to be Italian to make it come out delicious—but it helps.

And listen to this. Josie teaches Sunday School at the Bellefield Presbyterian Church.

Now that you've learned a little about our talented neighbor you'll enjoy her show all the more. She will delight you and your youngsters with Misterogers on Channel 4.

Fantastic, isn't it—what interesting neighbors we have.Our community wishes Josie Carey, husband Henry and mom Angeline the best of everything. Now and always.

Lawrence Carra
Gifted Stage Director At Arena

It's simply fantastic what interesting personalities we have in our neighborhood. Take for instance Lawrence Carra. He's our across the street neighbor, Stage Director of the summer Civic Light Operas at the Arena. Has been, to be exact, for five years - even when they were held under the big top - remember?

As to the operas, you're familiar with all or most of them. You know they're top-flight entertainment, often leaving you with a smile on your face and a song in your heart. But don't forget - the Director is back of everything. While you're out front watching the show - say, for instance "The Merry Widow". - another one is going on in the basement of the Arena, rehearsing and preparing for the week following. Director Carra and staff are constantly dealing with two casts, two plays, two plots at the same time. One you see. One you don't.

But this is just during summertime when for some of us the livin' is easy. The rest of the year he has an even more important profession. He teaches Stage Directing at Carnegie Tech.

Lawrence Carra received his B. A. Degree at Harvard in - believe it or not - Pre-Med! Then went on to the University of Rome Medical School. At both universities he always somehow got involved in their theatrical productions. And loved it. So the inevitable happened. He decided to make a career of theatre work and entered Yale University Drama School.

In no time something else important happened. He fell in love with a charming and talented student of dancing, Marguerite by name. Then you know what happened? They did what came naturally - they got married.

After graduation and receiving his masters degree at Yale, Mr. Carra taught drama at Chicago's Northwestern University. Then at the University of Texas. At Palo Alto he was Guest Director of Drama at Stanford University. With this remarkable background, experience and know-how, Carnegie Tech claimed him. In 1946 to be exact. Except for five years when he went to New York to lend his talents to the American Broadcasting Company for TV work, repertory commitments and off-Broadway plays, the Carras have graced our neighborhood ever since.

Their large three-floor apartment, shaded by a cluster of Forbes Avenue trees, is furnished in excellent taste. Uncluttered, airy, cheerful, comfortable. A real home. Wife Marguerite, having been a professional dancer, held classes until recently in modern dance technique. And she has translated several Italian plays into English. They are in the publication stage.

And, oh, their gorgeous sons! Three of 'em. The eldest is Lawrence, Jr., 24. He is working on his masters degree at Kent State University, Kent, Ohio, in physical education. Vincent, 20, is a Graphic Arts major at Carnegie Tech. Both graduated from Allderdice. Richard, 13, is in the 8th grade at Allderdice. And listen to this. He's star pitcher for the Allderdice Little League Baseball team which won last year's pennant. You ask him what about the Pirates? No answer. Just a broad engaging smile.

The Carras think it's an interesting world and they don't want it to stop - nor to get off.

Maria Caruso
Pianist, Dancer, Flutist at 9

A girl of 9 in our community is not only sugar and spice but much, much more. She's chockfull of talent — in music, in dancing.

And right off she has the lovely name of Maria. Maria Caruso. Also she is blest with parents who, by virtue of their Italian heritage, love the arts and are giving her every opportunity to develop her talent.

And as if that weren't enough, she has an extra bonus of a goodlooking brother (Ralph, Jr., 12) and a lovely little siste, Carole 7.

Maria is their inspiration and a challenge. So what happens? They are taking piano lessons too. And never have their parents needed to prod them with "Go practice!"

The parents — Ralph and Joy Caruso — have been married 15 years. Ralph is a chemist. Joy owns and runs a well-established Beauty Shop in the basement of their recently built home, Frank St.

Sometimes children of working mothers run wild. But not Joy's. In between shampoos, fingerwaves and manicures she manages to know where the children are, what they are doing and what they need to do.

Many a time, while her women are under the dryers reading Harper's Bazaar — or better yet, True Confessions — she has hurried upstairs to prepare lunch for the children and enjoy it with them.

Ralph is a devoted husband and father. Many of his evenings are spent at home with all of them — some reading, others studying or practicing, and a reasonable amount of TV-ing. The parents have discovered that their children practice better when someone listens. So they listen — and encourage. And often, when the young musicians know the women downstairs are listening, they really produce a concert!

The children attend the John Minadeo public school at Lilac and Saline Sts., and get good marks. But of course, Maria, to whom everything seems to come easy, has been a Grade A student since her first day; and recently she was chosen to help write the school newspaper.

Summers they attend the Chatham College Music Camp. There they get not only music instructions but enjoy all the healthful summer activities as well. They are well-behaved, self-reliant and happily busy.

Maria has been studying the piano for only three years. She is now being tutored by Victoria Modarelli. In a recent recital at Joseph Horne's auditorium, sponsored by the Pittsburgh Piano Teachers' Ass'n, Maria was a star performer. She played "Allegretto" by Haydn and performed with the skill and poise of a seasoned artist — and with youthful charm.

In addition, every Saturday for three years Maria has been attending the Chatham Laboratory School of Ballet. The well-known director, Mrs. Karl Kritz, says Maria has truly captured the magic of a ballerina. She performed in a group ballet for the Young Children's Symphony Concerts at Syria Mosque last year. And "just as a hobby" she has been taking lessons on the flute, the recorder and the bells, under the direction of Patty Grossman — also of Chatham. This has enabled her to play in the school's orchestra.

All this and only nine years young! In the words of Maurice Chevalier, "Thank Heaven for Little Girls."

Mrs. Edward F. Casassa
What's The Menu For Your Family?

Maybe this should be read before sitting down to dinner. That way, what a remarkable neighbor did recently, to help in an experiment, would be better understood and appreciated. Meet Mrs. Ethel Casassa of Burchfield Ave. She was one of 36 mothers of middle - class families, who volunteered to budget, plan and prepare meels for an entire week on the weekly welfare allowance which is $44.55 for a family of 5. And it has to provide also for clothing, household items, repairs, etcetera, etcetera.

Before learning the why and wherefore of our neighbor's informative experiment, let's first learn a little about her personally. The former Ethel Zaiser was reared in Philly, and attended Temple University there. And later received her Ph. D at Columbia University. Then went to M.I.T. to do research work on hemaglobin. Being also a good pianist, she joined two others for a Chamber Music Trio. Another girl was violinist. And who do you think played the cello? A handsome M.I.T. student — none other than Edward F. Casassa. Soon the pianist and cellist began going steady. And in 1954 became Mr. & Mrs. They started housekeeping in Madison, Wis. where the young husband had a job at the University there. The bride kept house, and did part-time work. Two years later, when son, David, was all of 4 months old, dad was called to our Mellon Institute now a part of Carnegie-Mellon University. David is now 14, and a student at Allderdice. Brother Michael, 13 goes there also, and has an extra job before schooltime delivering the morning P-G to the neighbors. Without prodding from mom, he hops out of bed 5:30 A.M. His earned "fortune" will pay for a summer at a Boy Scout Camp in New Mexico. Sister Anne is 11 and goes to the John Minadeo School. Their pet cats Fritzie and Missy go to no school.

The plan to have middle-class families live on welfare for a week was proposed here by the Women in the Urban Crisis, Welfare Rights organizations and the Citizens Association to Interpret Rights. Our neighbor learned of the program through their church, and like other volunteers, was paired with a family actually on welfare. The first thing Mrs. Casassa did was put away the food already in the house, with instructions that those cupboards were not to be touched. Everyone cooperated. The kids didn't even ask for between-meal snacks. She then shopped for the cheapest foods — cabbage, onions, turnips, potatoes. Slicing down a picnic ham — the cheapest cut — they each were permitted one slice. What was left went into pea soup for the week-end. They had alternately baked hamburger patties, fried beef liver and several meatless menus such as frozen fish fillets, macaroni and tuna casserole. That way they could manage chicken for Sunday dinner. A complete report on how the other families made out has not been received yet. But one of the mothers told Ethel that on the 6th day they were down to oatmeal! She wouldn't be surprised to learn that some dropped out altogether.

The children learned and gained appreciation for their bounties, feeling that their "cup runneth over." On welfare they'd have no music lessons, no boy and girl scouts, no weekly allowance, no newspaper, no riding lessons. No car. And no $2 for cat food. Fritzie and Missy could, in good conscience, just walk out on them! They are also more eager to help mom keep their 10-room house clean — a house built some 60 or 70 years ago. Mrs. Casassa recently returned from a conference on "Hunger" held in the nation's Capitol.

As everyone knows — human nature being what it is — there are always fraudulent welfare claims. But by and large, living on it is no picnic. And those who must, endure great hardships and deserve sympathetic understanding and concern.

And now, at your house — what's for dinner?

Dr. Wing-Tsit Chan

Sees Eventual Resolve

This is being written as snow is gently falling — a pleasant day to tell you about a most interesting closeby neighbor. Especially since he's from China, the country that daily headlines our newspapers.

Meet Dr. Wing-Tsit Chan, professor of Oriental Philosophy at Chatham College. He also teaches that subject once a week at Columbia University. He flies to New York in the morning and returns the same evening. His Chatham class consists of 80 young women. At Columbia they are mostly older men. Will the twain ever meet? Who knows. Dr. Chan is not a "Shadchan".

Our professor was born 65 years ago in China. At age 4 he started school, and by 11 could recite all the 13 Confucius classics. At 16 he went to Canton's American-sponsored Protestant missionary school. There he picked up modern education. And it being a co-ed school — you know, where boy meets girl — he met beautiful Wai-Hing. It was love at first sight.

However, not yet ready for marriage, they both came to the U.S. on the same boat — she to study piano at the New England Conservatory and he to continue Philosophy at Harvard. At the time there were no scholarships for foreign students, so young Chan worked his way through Harvard as a waiter. After 4 years they became Mr. & Mrs. at a Harvard professor's home. And started housekeeping in Boston for a year, until he got his Ph.D. Then they went back to China.

Prof. Chan became Dean of his Alma Mater and Wai-Hing taught piano in Canton's National University. Their three children were born in China. Daughter Jean, now 34, is married to an American, a professor at the University of California. Son Low-Wi is an architect in New York and also teaches at Columbia there. Gordon, 23 studied Sociology in Italy and September entered Pitt's Graduate School. In spite of the beautiful Italian women and the lovely Pitt co-eds, he's still a bachelor. Well — married he can always get. There are 5 beautiful grandchildren.

In 1937, when Japan invaded China, Wing - Tsit took his family to Hawaii, teaching at the University there. His house at the top of a hill looked down on Pearl Harbor. When tragedy struck he saw everything, but thought it was military practice — until several hours later. The people feared Japan would occupy Hawaii so the University was closed down. He volunteered as a censor of Chinese letters for whatever information they would contain. Later he left for Dartmouth where he taught for 24 years. In 1966 he was called to Chatham.

Recently our professor was guest on the morning Ron Jaye Show. When questioned, he predicted that Communist China and the U.S. will solve their differences without resort to a major war. The Chinese people, he said, are more interested in building up a strong and prosperous country. He gets letters from a niece in Canton. She writes nothing political — only personal news.

The past summer the Chans were in Aspen, Colorado where dad was a scholar -in-residence. The entire expense was furnished by U.S. Steel.

Dr. Chan received the Guggenheim fellowship in 1948. At Dartmouth he was appointed chairman of the Division of Humanities — the first Chinese to receive either of these honors. He has spoken at many synagogues. He lectured in New York's Hebrew Seminary at the invitation of Rabbi Louis Finkelstein. And in the Cincinnati Hebrew Institute. He's among 30 top intellectuals from all over the world, including Israel where he hopes soon to visit. He was in Jerusalem in 1928, long before Israel became a State. He says the Chinese and Jews have the same tradition — love of family and love of learning.

Our professor does his shopping in Sq. Hill, especially newstands which he says carry the best papers. Also the bake shops. But he doesn't know the difference between bulkies and bagels.

In Yiddish Dr. Wing-Tsit Chan would be called a real "Mensch" — meaning a gentleman in the true sense of the word.

Mr. and Mrs. David F. Chen
Chinese Family With Quite A Background

At this writing, the headlines feature Nixon's flight to Moscow. Thus his visit to Communist China last February seems almost "old hat". Nevertheless, today you'll learn about a fantastic personality from that far-off country who has graced our community for six meaningful years, and his beautiful wife and lovely daughter.

Since the Chinese philosophy says nothing about Women's Lib, we'll dwell mostly on the man of the family. Say "nin ho — hello — shalom" to David F. Chen, our Eldridge Street neighbor. Because of his unique talent, experience and know-how, he was called here in 1966 by WQED. His first assignment, among others, was "Misteroger's Neighborhood" - you know, those lovable half-hour educational programs that keep the small fry (and oldsters too) glued to Channel 13. Weekdays 8 a.m. noon, 6 p.m. to enjoy and learn.

And now about our neighbor's background and earlier days ... Born and named Fu Ying 40 years ago in Hanchow during the Sinom-Japanese war, most of his childhood was trying to survive war's ravages. In 1948, sadly leaving his loving parents and three brothers, he migrated to the Democracy of Taiwan. Overcoming countless hardships and loneliness with serious study, he earned a BA degree from Taiwan Normal University. He completed his undergraduate work as a music education major in Formosa.

His first successful job was advertising assistant for a magazine. Then he produced a classical radio program of his own — "Music Appreciation". Somewhere along the line Fu Ying (David) fell in love, and married a beautiful young high school teacher, Mei. In due time, a Taiwanese Stork brought baby Kailin (Catherine). Now a family man, he was ambitious for greater adventure broadcasting, possible only in America.

Tearfully embracing his loved ones good-bye (till he'd be financially able to have them follow), he left for the U.S., settling in Seattle. For gratis to gain experience, David volunteered as a crew member in a TV studio, where he learned the technical tricks of production. He attended the University of Southern California, then to Syracuse University, completing his master's degree in 1965. A year later, upon starting his WQED work he sent for Mei and Catherine. The first thing he did was take Mei to dinner at a Chinese restaurant. But you know what? She had never heard of chop suey! In their immaculately-clean duplex, she cooks REAL Chinese food which dad loves.

But Catherine prefers American menus; so they compromise. They've become as integrated into our community as ham and eggs, kosher delicatessen, bagels and lox.

Mrs. Chen works full-time for Fred Roger's "Family Communications, Inc.". Catherine, 14 attended Colfax and now goes to Allderdice in its 8th Grade Scholar Program.

Having studied piano for nine years, she has received a number of awards. Pop relaxes playing the organ at home, and golfing week-ends.

Having studied English in high school, Chen later went to a speech clinic in Detroit to help eliminate his Oriental accent. You'll never believe it, but his English is just about perfect.

Remember the Heinz Hall gala Opening Night? Our neighbor directed a six-color camera live-coverage of the entire fascinating event. And now listen to this: For the first time in our city's history "The Great TV Auction" will be televised on WQED, June 5 to 11 inclusive. And who do you think is producing it? You guessed it. He suggests you "Watch, Bid, Buy and Have Fun".

Our community wishes this Americanized charming little Chinese family the best of everything now and in the years ahead.

Mrs. Harold (Florence) Chernoff
Mother-Artist Combines Talent With Know How

A funny thing happened to a would-be critic on his way to the art gallery. It was old Khrusch in Moscow. He took one look at an abstract painting and hit the ceiling. For the benefit of those who don't read newspapers, we quote: "What kind of smear is this?" he bellowed. "Looks like it was daubed by a donkey's tail."

You should pardon the expression but many modern art viewers hereabouts have made similarly humorous comments. So perhaps it's a good idea to talk things over with a real artist — and maybe learn a little. Let's meet our artist-neighbor, Mrs. Harold Chernoff of 5860 Solway St. Mrs. Chernoff is the former Florence Brasley. Husband, Harold, is a manufacturers' representative. Their two sons attend Shadyside Academy. Michael, 18, graduates this June. John, 16, is a Junior.

Florence Chernoff didn't have a formal art education. She simply went to Tech night school for many years, studying sculpture. Then she married Harold, and art lessons stopped. When her boys started school she began classes again, this time with Jean Thoburn, on water colors. She still attends these classes.

Ten years ago she became a member of the Pittsburgh Water Color Society, later becoming its president. Five years ago Florence started classes with Pittsburgh's famous Samuel Rosenberg, and still attends. She has been a member of the Arts & Crafts Center's Board for three years, having been its first Vice President. Now she is its President. The more time Florence spends at the Center the more she feels that it fills the needs in our community — for the pupil, the practicing artist and for the public who comes to see and to work. Florence also belongs to the Associated Artists of Pittsburgh as well as the Craftsmen's Guild.

Five years ago Mrs. Chernoff drove to Mexico City and attended the world famous Friday Market. On market day the Mexican natives bring their produce and other wares either aboard a burro or, as often as not, on their own heads. The scene is colorful, noisy, smelly and fascinating. With her paints, brushes and other paraphernalia, Florence sat down on the curb to paint. Soon she was surrounded by on-lookers; and moments later, by policemen who politely told her she was obstructing traffic. She had to pay a fine.

The Chernoffs spend summers at Beach Haven, Long Beach Island, N.J. At its Art Foundation staffed by well-known artists Florence became interested in mosaics. She bought kilns and now makes her own tiles in her home studio. She rolls the clay, glazes and fires it. Recently Mrs. Chernoff had a one-man show at the Squirrel Hill

Theatre. The throng of viewers "oohed and awhed" — and bought! Her paintings are lovely to look at, done by hands that care. So what about abstract moderns, you ask? Well, pull up your chairs, everybody.

Florence says people still want realistic or recognizable pictures on their walls. But she feels that non-objective modern art is full of meaning. You get something from it every time you look at it. It will stimulate you, she says. It will, that is, if you have an open mind.

Rev. Hugh S. Clark
Beatles Don't Bug the Rev.

It's mid-summer now and the foliage is abloom. A pleasant time to learn about an equally pleasant and interesting neighborhood personality — the Rev. Canon Hugh S. Clark, for 28 years paster of the nearby Church of the Redeemer. The Rev. Dr. Clark lives in the rectory at Darlington Rd. next to the church.

Also next door is St. Edmond's Academy. It's an Episcopal parochial school of which Dr. Clark is chaplain and teacher of the Bible. His church serves as the school's chapel for the 180 children and their teachers. Should you happen to be passing the school's Forbes Avenue side at recess play-time, you'll see a riot of color in motion.

Youngsters in red, green, and blue sweaters and shorts — running, sliding, swinging, laughing. And right alongside, in a separate play-yard are the small fry of our neighborhood Y-IKC, likewise having fun.

Each group is friendly with the other. A nice environment for the "Love thy Neighbor" policy that Dr. Clark so earnestly believes in and teaches.

And now let's learn a little about our likeable neighbor's personal life. First off, Dr. Clark is a bachelor. And you'll never believe it but he brews and serves the most delicious coffee you ever tasted — should you be lucky enough to have occasion to visit him.

The rectory in which he lives has five rooms. The walls of his library are lined with the best books. You'll even find one written by our famous neighbor Gladys Schmidt— "Rembrandt" in its colorful wrapper.

Dr. Clark is originally from Lancaster, Mass. After graduating from Harvard with a BS degree he went to Berkely Divinity School. There he earned his master's and doctor's degrees. For a year, he studied in Oxford, England, and taught at Groton School, Mass. He was minister in Birmingham, England, and later at our city's Calvary Church.

Our neighbor has someone come in twice a week to keep his place clean. As to meals, he is constantly invited to parishioners' homes. It's like one big family. But when he needs to, he prepares his own dinner. And the delicious coffee — remember?

Neighbor Clark's hobby is gardening and horticulture. His lawn, the freshly-clipped hedges lovely flowers and young trees indicate TLC (tender loving care). He also enjoys camping and mountain-climbing.

Recently he took off on a three-week trip to Iceland in the North Atlantic just south of the Arctic Circle. Contrary to its name, there's no ice there except some magnificent glaciers.

Iceland is rich in bird-life and interesting Arctic flora. From the capital city of Reykjavik he took a nine-day sight seeing tour with an international group — French, Dutch, English, German, Danish. He was the only American. The guide was multi-lingual and could explain the sights in any language.

Otherwise they managed with hand motions and shrugs. During his absence a Pitt student occupied his home here. Upon return he was surprised — and delighted — to find everything ship-shape. The student deserves an A-plus.

In July and August Dr. Clark conducts what he calls "a quiet service" — without a sermon. They go into the parish house for an informal discussion and coffee. This time the women make the coffee. On Christmas Eve, the minister always holds "Open House" before the midnight service.

Last Christmas he had a few sleepless nights beforehand. As is customary, the church sends out a leaflet to members only, announcing the Christmas program. This time our "Squirrel Hill News," a bit too ambitious, reprinted the leaflet verbatim, including the notation "All are Welcome." What if the whole neighborhood turned out and jammed the rectory? Well, Squirrel Hillers are intelligent and can read between the lines. Only a scattered few outsiders showed up. And a Merry Christmas was had by all.

And now what about the earthshaking words of wisdom uttered by Beatle John Lennon? Our neighbor was in far-off Iceland when the hullabaloo started. And he says Iceland was not "shaking".

So let's forget the Beatles, the cost of living. And ponder, instead over a design for living — as exemplified by the Rev. Canon Hugh S. Clark. And wish him the best of everything now and in the years ahead.

Dr. Anna F. Cohen
Her Friends Ask: How Does She Do It!

As this is being written our Pirates who early in the season were languishing in the cellar, have swept out the Mets and are now in first place. A happy day to tell you about a fantastic neighbor, even though her skills are far removed from baseball.

Meet Dr. Anna F. Cohen of Albemarle Street. Last year, she was appointed professor and chairman of the Department of Mathematics and Physics at Point Park College. And what's more, her brilliant husband, Dr. Bernard L. Cohen is professor of Physics at Pitt and director of the Scaife Nuclear Laboratory. But him you already met through your NEWS several years ago; today we're concentrating on his charmingly dynamic missus.

Pittsburgh-born, the former Anna Foner attended Schenley Hi, then graduated Allderdice. Through its special program, she became interested in Chemistry. Later, at Pitt, fascinated with Physics, she decided to take that course and in addition, Engineering — earning a BS degree in both. While still an undergraduate, Anne took a summer job at Gulf Research and later at Westinghouse.

Studying and learning, she saw she could continue graduate school in Physics at Tech (C-MU). So she up and earned an MS in that subject, continuing and earning a doctor of science degree. Somewhere along the line, guess what? She met a fellow-student. Brilliant, modest Bernard L. Cohen. And fell head-over-heels. A few months later (March, 1950) they said "I do" to a rabbi, and May they graduated together. The newlyweds went on to Oak Ridge National Laboratory, Tennessee, to do research and set up housekeeping.

During the eight years there, a "y'all" southern Stork brought them three beautiful children. Don, now 20, will be mathematics senior at C-MU come September. And Judy, 18, a pre-med and Psychology junior at Pitt. Freddie, 15 will continue at Sewickley Academy; Ernie, 11 and born in our city, will resume at Falk School.

Summer of '42 —pardon, '68—the Cohen family traveled through Europe, Russia, Greece, Bulgaria, and of course Israel. In a Volkswagon camper, they were able to see ten times as much as routine tourists. Wish there were space to describe their experiences, especially in Russia. A camera buff, mom Cohen's travel pictures are a treat for the eyes and spirit. Anne also plays the violin and harp, and is a talented artist, having studied with well-known Samuel Rosenberg. A member of Associated Artists, she recently held a one-woman Painting and Sculpture Show — 67 pieces. Proceeds from sales went to the Emergency Fund to help harassed Jews in Russia migrate to Israel. Want to do likewise? Just pick up the phone (683-0326). Anne will gladly guide and help you. And says: "Try it — you'll like it".

A born learner, Anne will probably be learning the rest of her life. How does she do it — with a full-time professional job; in the process of writing a book "Ideas in the Physical and Human Sciences"; a 10 room house; all four children at home; a ready companion to them and her equally busy husband; with only twice-weekly outside help? Easy. Only nine when her mother died, Anne learned early how to cook. She still does it all. Husband, Bernard, enjoys bringing home the groceries, often taking the kids along to teach them the art of shopping. They take turns at making beds, setting the table, clearing it, putting dishes away. The kids have fixed it so that pop takes his turn, too. As yet he hasn't found a diplomatic way to maneuver himself out of it.

Where can you find such a beautiful family other than in our neighborhood?

Dr. Bernard L. Cohen
Common Name, But Accomplishments Add To Its Luster

What's in a name, Shakespeare asks. The name Cohen, for instance is anything but unusual, filling page after page of our phone book. But many outstanding personalities have added luster to the name through their remarkable accomplishments. An interesting example lives in our very neighborhood. Dr. Bernard L. Cohen of Albermarle Ave.

Dr. Cohen is professor of Physics at Pitt and a director of the Scaife Nuclear Laboratory. For an unschooled layman to attempt describing what our neighbor's intricate work involves would be like they say — "Fools rush in where angels fear to tread." So let's settle for just a few highlights. And later take a look into his personal life. Which, for Squirrel Hillers might be more fun to read.

The Scaife laboratories include a new three-stage Tandem Van de Graff accelerator and a 47-inch cyclotron. What are they, for goodness sake? Don't ask the writer! As the director, Dr. Cohen's research has been in experimental nuclear physics, using the said whatever-they-are. And now, you know what? Let's skip the whole thing and learn about his background and life in general.

Our neighbor was born and bred in Pittsburgh. So was his brilliant and lovely missus, the former Anne Foner. And guess what. She too is a physics expert and teaches in that department at Tech. His dad and mom, the Samuel Cohens live in the East End. And the favorably-known neighborhood physician, Dr. Norman Cohen is his brother. His sister, Mrs. Natalie Appel, also a Squirrel Hiller teaches English and Social Studies at Westinghouse High.

Neighbor Cohen is so unassuming that after 10 minutes you want to call him by his first name. Strongly-built, sun-tanned by occasional golfing, he has the most pleasant smile you ever saw. The Cohens have four lively children. Donald is 14 and will be in the 10th grade at Allderdice High School. Judy, 12, is in the 8th grade at Falk School. Freddie, almost 10, is in Falk's 5th grade. Little Ernie has reached the ripe age of 5 and is about to start at Falk. He has much schooling under his belt, being an alumnus of the Poale Zedeck and Hillel nursery schools. About his pop's nuclear work he couldn't care less. He likes Pop-eye more. And Captain Kangaroo. But the commercials fascinate him even more. He knows all the products by heart. He'd make the most discriminating shopper. The only thing, he has no credit card. Not even a checking account.

Bernard and Anne met while students at Tech. Both got their doctor of science degrees there. And became Mr. and Mrs. shortly before graduation — in 1950. He did undergraduate work at Case Institute of Technology (Cleveland) where he received his BS degree. His master's he received from Pitt and his doctorate at Tech. He was at Oak Ridge, Tennesse, the Atomic City for eight years. Then he joined the Pitt faculty. Professor Cohen is the favorite adviser to graduate students. They appreciate him, his adoring wife tells you — and are inspired to study harder because of his influence.

Neighbor Cohen has written 80 scientific articles for journals and text books. His latest, "Heart of the Atom" is being published by Doubleday & Co. It's one of the well-known science study series. He has lectured on his research in 14 European countries, including five behind the Iron Curtain. Also in Israel. And at about 70 universities and major laboratories in the U.S. and Canada.

Wife Anne is not only a physicist but an artist as well. And is a member of the Associated Artists of Pittsburgh. If you take a look into their nine-room home which they own, you'd know immediately that interesting and artistic people live there.

Soon everybody in our neighborhood will be wishing their Jewish friends a Happy New Year. Let's be the first to wish the Bernard Cohens and all their dear ones the best New Year they ever had.

Mrs. E. R. (Dorene) Cohen
Dynamism Her Main Forte'

Women — bless 'em — are the salt of the earth. Especially if they're youthful, pretty, imaginative, dynamic and use their innate generosity toward things worthwhile. There are numberless such in our neighborhood. You'll meet an outstanding one today. Say hi to Mrs. Eugene R. (Dorene) Cohen of nearby Beacon St. Dorene is Special Projects Chairman for the Pittsburgh region of ORT. The women of ORT's 17 chapters are preparing Jewish foods for the annual March of Dimes Food Fair at the Civic Arena come September 17 and 18. Instead of taking it easy during the hazy, lazy days of summer, they're up to there in planning and preparing. This is the first year ORT has joined hands with the March of Dimes.

As you doubtless know, the March of Dimes raises funds for the fight against polio and the ever-widening scourge of birth defects. ORT stands for Organization through Training. It's the largest voluntary vocational training system on earth — for the deprived and dispossessed. The U.N. has called on ORT to set up its entire education program. And the late President Kennedy asked ORT for suggestions when setting up the Job Corps and Poverty Program.

Now let's learn a little about our dynamic neighbor. The former Dorene Binstock was born in the East End. At age 7 she became a Squirrel Hill-er. (so did her parents). Her dad owned the Binstock Jewelry Store at Forbes near Murray for years, until his recent retirement and settling in Israel. Dorene helped in the store soon as she was tall enough to be seen behind the counter. She went through Colfax and graduated Allderdice, and on to what is now known as Point Park Junior College. In no time she got a job as medical secretary at the Children's Hospital in the Cardiac Clinic. At 19 Dorene did what comes naturally. Got married. To handsome bachelor Eugene R. Cohen, now owner of the C & M Furniture Co., Braddock. And something else came naturally to her — the well known Binstock tradition civic responsibility. She's been active in ORT for 13 years and was chairman of arrangements for the Beaux ORT Ball. And regional Health Chairman. She's active in Hillel Academy and was V.P. for its annual concert. She and husband together were chairmen for the Hillel Spring Carnival. And both are active in various other charitable organizations.

Our neighbors have been blessed with three lively interesting children. Jeffrey is now 14 and goes to Allderdice. He enjoys playing the guitar and is helping raise money for the children of Biafra. Cathy, 11 attends Colfax and takes tap and ballet at the Y-IKC. Brian is 7 and goes to Hillel Academy.

And now the Food Fair again. Doors will open 10 a.m. and close 10 p.m. Admission free. Two hours before closing —both evenings — foods will be auctioned off. After spirited bidding there will be bargains galore. Famous delicacies from many varied nationalities will be available. But since the Jewish food booths (8 of them) will be first timers, let's get an idea what's for dinner. Gefillte fish, borscht, lockshon kugel, potato pancakes, blintzes with sour cream, sweet and sour meat balls, homemade pickles, etcetra, etcetra. So September 17 and 18 head for the hills leading to the Civic Arena. And "break a bagel" with your friends.

The Fair's over - all chairman for the past 14 years is the popular Mrs. I. H. Kantrowitz, wife of a well-known downtown CPA. Also Squirrel Hill-ers.

As to neighbor Dorene Cohen ORT's food chairman, her motto is: Raise funds, do good and have fun.

Eugene S. Cohen

Neighbor Cohen Anything But Ordinary

Dear neighbors: Today you'll learn about a fellow with the plainest sort of last name who is anything but ordinary himself. Fact is, he's extra special and a credit to our community. He's none other than well-known Eugene S. Cohen, our neighbor at 1301 Beechwood Blvd.

Comparatively young, easy to look at, with friendly charm, he wins you over in a minute. And right away you call him Gene.

Born in Wampum, Pa., our neighbor graduated Allderdice and went on to Pitt for his BS degree. After completing an executive training course at Gimbel's he became a salesman for RCA. Then came World War 2. And Eugene Cohen began soldiering in the Tank Corps, for five years. At war's end he was assigned by the Supreme Allied Command to 2½ months investigating concentration camps in Germany and Austria. Here is no place to dwell on what he learned of the unspeakable Nazi atrocities. He came home a sobered and mature man. With the determination to do everything possible to help preserve and fortify Jewish life and culture.

Meantime our ex-soldier started his business career. In 1945 he helped found the B & G Mfg. Co., later to become the Pittsburgh Aluminum Alloys, Inc., with plant and offices in Murrysville, Pa. Soon he became the firm's vice president. Then somewhere along the line, what do you think happened? Our VIP fell in love, with beautiful Marion Weis. But wait — before that he had been dating her sister Norma.

The Cohens now have three lovely, lively daughters. All attend Ellis School. Peggy, is 16, summer counselor at Emma Kaufmann Camp at Harmony, Pa. Ann is 15 and counseling at the Y-IKC "Happy Land" day camp. Sue is 11 and a camper at Wohelo in Waynesboro, Pa.

Dad Cohen is vice-president of the Y-IKC in charge of developing the new Emma Kaufmann camp and building in East Liberty, soon to be opened. And plans are afoot for a day camp and family recreation area in Monroeville. He's now president of the United Cerebral Palsy Assn. of Allegheny County. And a member of the Health & Welfare Assn., Citizen's Committee. He works actively in the neighborhood Youth Corps— a part of the Poverty Program. He's a board member of Rodef Shalom Congregation and also of the Jewish Chronicle.

Gene was recently honored by the International Executive Service Corps (IESC), America's executive-level "peace corps" — an arm of the State Department. And sent to Thailand to assist in the aluminum industry. With him was his wife.

They spent six weeks abroad, in Japan, Hong Kong, India and Lebanon. In Bangkok, capital of Thailand, there are just 13 Jewish families, Gene says. They hold Sabbath services the first Friday evening of every month. Also on the High Holy Days, at the Israeli Embassy. And the lovely art things they brought back. Their nine-room house looks comparatively unimpressive among the many magnificent Beechwood Boulevard homes. From the outside, that is.

Inside it's a viewer's paradise. You know in a minute that interesting artistic people live there.

The Cohen home is kept spic and span by their capable and loyal housekeeper, Louise Matras. They actually consider her a member of the family. The children call her their second mother.

Gene's wife Marion, is a substitute teacher in our public school kindergarten, and a volunteer in the Poverty Program.

Our neighbor's mother, Lena Cohen, is the most fastidiously dressed Golden Ager in the Morrowfield Apts. And who do you think is his big brother? That fabulous "At Random" fellow at the Drama Desk of the Post Gazette — Harold V. Cohen. As they say — what's in a name?

Sidney J. Cohen
They Went, They Played, They Conquered!

Our neighborhood personality of the week is dark-eyed, easy-to-look-at Sidney J. Cohen of Solway Street. He is personnel manager of our famous Pittsburgh Symphony. He also plays a priceless viola made in Italy in 1683.

Mr. Cohen had an important hand in preparing and completing our symphony's recent fabulous 12-week concert tour throughout Europe and the Middle East - a trek of some 25,000 miles.

The ups and downs of an orchestra's foreign tour are many. In their 10 tons of cargo they had 10 double basses and 12 cellos which had to travel in separate trunks. Their only loss was one trombone. In Rome, of all places. Good thing they didn't have 76!!

After traveling further and longer than any trombone in history, it finally caught up with them.

The greatest thrill was when the orchestra played our national anthem at the various countries. To see the expression on the faces of our own embassy's staff members put a lump in one's throat. The 121 personnel in the group spent 17 days behind the Iron Curtain. They were briefed beforehand on political angles and situations there. They were also told what to eat - and what not to eat.

Neighbor Cohen is married to the former Fannie Mattes. Remember Eddie Spector of Broadway's "Any Wednesday" fame, who used to be the symphony's business manager here? She was his secretary. And Sidney was a frequent visitor in the office. One day he up and invited Fannie as his guest to a Friday night concert. As the saying goes, music hath charms. So guess what? Two years later Rabbi Hailperin pronounced them

Mr. & Mrs. Their son Carl, now 12, goes to Allderdice. He has a talent for singing. Until his voice starts changing and going this-away and that-away, it's a high soprano. He's also a star pitcher on the Little League Baseball team. Last summer he pitched it into championship.

Summers the Cohens rent a cottage in Chautauqua, N.Y. Sidney and 12 other Pittsburgh musicians are members of the symphony there. He also is manager of "Gateway to Music," an organization composed of principal players of the symphony, broken down to string quartets and woodwind and brass quintets. They are giving 300 concerts in this area, and approximately 170,000 children will be thrilled hearing them.

Mr. Cohen also manages the Pittsburgh Symphony Symphonetta, playing at colleges in this area which can't afford full symphony concerts and have no halls large enough.

Violinist Cohen received his musical know-how and experience in New York City where his folks still live. But he thoroughly disliked that city. Says people there are calloused, hard, rushed and pushed. Pittsburgh? He loves it here. He says there's a warmth generated by almost everyone he meets. Even strangers.

Of our colorful Symphony Director Dr. William Steinberg, Mr. Cohen says: "He's unique among conductors, combining all worthwhile traits. As a director he's first-rate — a humane gentleman with a wonderful executive-type mind which is always clear and reasonable in conducting orchestra business." Mr. Cohen adds that if Dr. Steinberg left our symphony, many members would also consider leaving.

Our neighbor likes baseball, fishing, reading fiction and playing gin-rummy. When world famous violinist Isaac Stern comes here annually, they have a gin-rummy game. Stern often wins enough to pay his Pittsburgh expenses. But you know how it is in cards — he as often loses to Sidney.

Next time you watch Conductor Steinberg gracefully lift his baton for a soul-stirring concert, sit back, relax and enjoy, enjoy. And later think about the things you have learned from and about our interesting neighbor, Sidney J. Cohen. You'll appreciate our symphony all the more.

Yaacov Cohen
Musical Talents Equal To Stature

Like Charlie Brown, our personality of the week is a good man: good husband, a good father, and has a good voice. He also plays the mandolin good. And comes from Israel. So let's say "shalom" to Yaacov Cohen, our new neighbor at Wendover Street. And learn a little about him.

Yaacov, his lovely wife Ahuva and their four lively, interesting children came here a little over a year ago from Jerusalem. The youngsters are: Michal, Miriam, Ruhana and Merav — 10, 8, 5 and 3, in that order. They all go to nearby Hillel Academy on Beacon St. Their dad teaches Hebrew there. Also Oriental music and Israeli songs which he accompanies on his Italian mandolin.

After graduating Beth Hakerem High School in Jerusalem, Yaacov did what all the youths in Israel do — joined the Army, serving 2½ years. Later he attended the University Teacher's College in Israel. He organized 40 school choirs and was master of ceremonies at their concerts, often performing on radio. As a boy scout leader he composed music and lyrics for their shows. And wrote poems in Hebrew.

Somewhere along that time he met his lovely Ahuva. She was a religious girl scout and later was one of the teachers chosen to plan a new method of learning the geography of Jerusalem. They often attended the same meetings. Their friendship turned to love and now these two sabras are sharing their lives together.

In age and looks our neighbor is neither a post-teen hippie nor an ancient mariner. He wears no chin foliage. Nor hair down to his shoulders. Neither does he wear a long scarf slung around his neck. And he doesn't walk barefoot in the park. On the contrary, our Yaacov is mature, clean-shaven, lithe, slim, with a friendly charm that wins you over in a minute. Several years ago when world-famous violinist Yehudi Menuhin (child prodigy now grown to manhood) was in Israel and heard Yaacov perform, he offered him a scholarship in Oriental music at the Hebrew University. But Yaacov had by then committed himself to Hillel here. His four brothers and one sister all are singers in Jerusalem.

When Hillel held its annual anniversary concert last year at Carnegie Music Hall, Yaacov conducted the high school choir — a highlight of the evening. He has entertained on a volunteer basis, numberless charitable organizations with his sing-along program. Like for instance the Anathan House and the dear hearts and gentle people of the Jewish Home & Hospital for the Aged. In May he will sing on the Israeli Independence Day program.

In their 3-bedroom apartment lovely Ahuva holds sway. With no outside help she keeps everything spic and span. The children help some and Yaacov tries to. In addition to Israeli dishes such as flaffel (an Oriental mixture popular there) she has learned to make the best gefillte fish in Squirrel Hill.

Because there was as yet no TV in Israel before our neighbors left, the kids revel in it here. From "Misterogers" and "Sesame Street" they learn many new English words and phrases. Both Hebrew and English are spoken in their home. However, Friday evenings TV is completely out. At the Shabbas meal, instead of the traditional Kiddush wine mom serves grape-juice. And because there's always company that evening, the children entertain with plays, games and singing they learned during the week. That's part of their educational program — learning to relax and express themselves through activities. Their harmony songs are in both languages.

On their trip here, Yaacov and his family flew over. When they return to Israel at the end of the year they plan to go by boat. Imagine the exciting things the kids will have to tell their friends in Israel, about America and especially Squirrel Hill. Our community wishes them the best of everything.

Morton Coleman
Years Belie Triumphs

Today our neighborhood personality of the week could be easily termed as a Young Man with a Purpose.

And because that purpose has been developed and is bringing much good to countless persons in our city, you naturally want to know him — and learn what he's up to.

Meet Morton (Moe) Coleman, our neighbor at Pocussett St. Mr. Coleman holds down not one but two important jobs. He's special assistant to Mayor Barr's Manpower Training Program. Using federal funds, so far 2,000 men and women have been retrained and work found for them. Of these 80 per cent had been previously unemployed.

He also was co-ordinator for developing the Pittsburgh Poverty Program. Sargent Shriver calls the Pittsburgh program "a model for the rest of the nation." By now, these are running smoothly and require only a part-time look-see. So he's able to work full-time as faculty member of Pitt's Graduate School of Social Work. At Pitt he earned his BA and MSW degrees.

Coleman is a member of the Health and Welfare Committee for development of the program for school dropouts. And he belongs to many governmental and civic organizations in our city.

Neighbor Coleman is tall, dark, easy-to-look-at, energetic. And young. Scarcely past 30. And he likes what he does. An ideal combination for a man with a purpose. Oh, yes. He's something else. Married! To the former Greta Gold, a dyed-in-the-wool Squirrel Hiller.

She's a third-grade teacher at the Baxter School in Homewood. There are two lively sons. Howard (Howy to his buddies) is 12 and attends Colfax. James (Jimmie) is all of five and proudly marches off to Davis School.

Moe Coleman used to be with the Y-IKC since he was 14, on a part-time basis. He worked for two settlement houses, the Anna B. Heldman and the Kingsley House. There he had charge of delinquent gangs and his experiences with them were at times hair-raising, pathetic and also magnificent. One of the gang is now a successful commercial artist for Alcoa. Another is attending medical school.

As teenagers, Moe Coleman and Greta Gold were counselors at the Emma Farm Camp. Summer after summer. One fine summer, whether it was the perfume of honeysuckles, the moonlight or the soft glow of the camp fire — he up and proposed. And to the surprise of no one, she said yes. Several summers later, something new was added: Son Howy, all of six months. And you know how it is with young marrieds — they took him along to camp for the summer.

What baby became the pet of the entire camp and adored by all? You guessed it. Never was a child made so much fuss over and had his diapers changed by so many counselors so many times as little Howy. He took it all in stride, grew healthy and happy. And maybe some day he will do likewise for some, other baby. His very own.

Robert L. Cook
Kindly Master, English Bull Inseparable Duo

Remember seeing a sedate, elderly gentleman daily walking his huge dog — an English bull— along the various streets surrounding Forbes & Murray? The well-fed pet is Radar, 12 years old.

His kindly master is Robert L. Cook, 85 years young, our neighbor at Murray Ave. His home, built long before Murray Avenue was paved, sits sturdily between the Sixth Presbyterian Church and the Anathan House. The surrounding grounds are his too.

There are 15 rooms, three baths and a spacious porch. And contains the most interesting antiques you ever saw. A large grandfather's clock is built right into a beautiful mantelpiece. A huge china-closet with glass doors display on its shelves 200 English bull-dogs of all sizes, made of china, 18 of them Royal Dalton. The six colonial-type beds, instead of springs, have rope slats. And here's a bit of old-time history. In those days when a young man called on his girl he hitched old Dobbin to a nearby post.

At going-home time, should it be raining, snowing, blowing, he was asked to stay over night. That is, if he and the girl were engaged. The horse was given lodging in the barn. The fella slept in the same bed with his girl. But wait — listen — don't go away! A wooden partition was put in between the slats, manueuvered so carefully the couple was completely separated. And any hanky-panky was impossible. Next morning the fiance and his horse were each given a king-sized breakfast — with a different menu, or course. Beats the modern way — sleeping in a rumble seat. The partition process was called "bundling" and books were written on it. They were "best sellers" and sold on the turnpike.

Bulldog Radar rules the house. Has the best chair, snoozes on the nicest bed and phooey on bundling! Four years ago he started losing weight and pep. The Veterinary made him a special diet menu (not sold in stores). Now Radar is again fat and sassy. And woe to a prowler who might lurk in the shadows. He likes their houseman who comes three days a week to keep things spic and span. And tolerates the meter-readers. The mailman he hasn't taken a nip at but is thinking about it. He romps joyously when gardener Polito comes to beautify the trees, hedges and rock-garden.

And now about Mr. Cook himself. He attended the old Miller Street School. At 10 he moved to Webster and Duff, considered a substantial neighborhood.

Young Bob began work at 16 in the Howe-Brown Mill, working 12 hours a day seven days a week. No diversions. Just work, eat, sleep. Then he got a job at the Pressed steel Car Co. Same ungodly hours. Later he was apprenticed in the Engineering Dept. of the Pressed Steel Car Co., from which he graduated. In 1910 — guess what? The love bug bit him. He met lovely Luella Martin on a blind date at the Rittenhouse, then a popular dance hall. They did the Newport, Schottische, Bunny-hug and of course the waltz. Saturdays he took Luella to the matinee at the Davis Vaudeville Theatre and for an ice cream soda at Reymours.

Neighbor Cook was a Republican County Committeeman and 14th-Ward Chairman for 24 years. During that time they brought in 12,000 majority Republicans and you could find only three Democrats in the whole Ward. Those were the days that were!

Years ago couples from Ohio and West Virginia came here to be married. Because Mr. Cook lived next to the Church they took him for a minister. And rang his bell. He never turned them away. Always phoned a minister of their choice and acted as Best Man. His fee was a kiss from the bride.

What does our neighbor think of the mini skirts that are getting mini-er and mini-er? He likes 'em. And prays he will live three more years when he hopes the limit will be reached.

Mr. Cook, childless and now a widower has a charming younger sister in Dormont. And an aunt in Beechview who is spry at 102. He shares his spacious home with his wife's cousin, former Congressman Howard Campbell. And listen, everybody — Mr. Campbell is a bachelor! But don't let it get around.

Rege Cordic

Chuckles For Breakfast

Farmers, as we all know, get up in the wee hours of the morning. With the chickens, as the saying goes. But a likeable fella in our neighborhood hops out of bed at 5 a.m. No chickens or nuthin'. Just gets up — period.

And exactly an hour later he's at his demanding job at Gateway One. Of course, it's Rege Cordic — who else? — of KDKA's famous Cordic & Company 6-to-10 a.m. broadcasting show.

While the small fry are dreaming of snow men and space ships and oldsters are cozily snoozing, Rege starts his daily program of enjoyable nonsense.

By the time his thousands of listeners are up, they've heard the news, what's with the weather, listened to music and commercials — and they've also had many good chuckles.

Let's see — what does it take to amuse drowsy people first thing in the morning? Takes imagination, skill, inventiveness — that's what. And neighbor Cordic has all these aplenty.

Much has already been said in all the newspapers of his wondrous talent and goings on. So let's just snoop a little into his private life and learn how he got that way.

First off, Rege Cordic is tall, dark and easy to look at — with or without the beard. And his personality wins you over in a minute. He's only two years younger than Jack Benny. Thirty-seven, to be exact.

Rege landed his first radio job as a junior announcer on Davy Tyson's Kiddies broadcast from the old Enright Theatre.

In 1943 he advanced to fulltime announcing at WWSW where he remained — with time out for two years with the navy in the Philippines. Then he did what comes naturally. He got married. To WWSW's lovely Diane Dundon.

Although he had been reared in Squirrel Hill, they settled in Sewickley. But it was too far a drive to his city office. So they moved back to our neighborhood — at Northumberland St. And we're glad they did.

In 1954 Rege joined KDKA. Six years ago "Cordic, Incorporated" came into being His contract with KDKA calls for 24 hours weekly on the air.

This takes much preparation. And he writes two days a week for his programs.

And now listen to this. A funny thing happened to Rege Cordic on his way to the Shadyside Theatre recently. He showed his shorts and the packed house rocked with laughter. No, not the kind you wear. Movie shorts — two of them.

From that performance he raised $2,500 for the Old Newsboys' Club for Children's Hospital.

One short shows you what happens when, instead of walking you slide around in electric shoes. The movie is full of droll slapstick that had them rolling in the aisles.

Another shows how to check your bowler without having to tip the hat-check doll.

And now he's talking of inventing a musical snow shovel — with shimmy dancing lessons on the side.

His shorts will travel throughout the U.S. and later, with foreign narrations, continue through Europe and beyond. After all, Europeans like to laugh too.

Rege attended Tech's night school for two years for voice and speech. Then Pitt for two years in liberal arts.

He spent a summer at New York University in broadcasting. His family spent last summer at Fire Island, N.Y. Rege had planned to fly there weekends but never found enough time. During his three-week vacation, however, he joined them full time.

His children? Jennifer, 9 and Nanette, 7 attend Winchester School.

As to their dad's shenanigans, they don't understand as yet what they're all about — and couldn't care less. And one-year-old Claudia ain't talkin'.

As for little Johnny, age 2, it's like this. It's not that he loves his pop less but he likes Popeye more.

Ken Costigan

Like Show Business Motto

As they say, there's no people like show people. And with the theatrical season begun, you'll want to meet at least one of them. Say hi to Ken Costigan, Artistic Director of our popular Pittsburgh Playhouse. He was recently promoted to Associate Producer.

When Executive Director S. Joseph Nassif must be elsewhere for meetings and fulfilling commitments in other cities throughout the country, he knows someone capable is on hand here and that everything will come up roses.

And so it already has, with the first play of the current (37th) season — "Your Own Thing". It got the best reviews ever. Anderson of our PG ended his enthusiastic comments with "a fresh start for a fresh season". And more to come. Let's name them: "Everything in the Garden"; "Room Service"; the musical "No Strings"; romantic mystery "Catch Me If You Can"; an old-fashioned melodrama "Under the Gaslight" (you will want to boo the villain); Neil Simon's "Plaza Suite", and the musical "Guys and Dolls".

Ken Costigan, son of a successful practicing M.D., was born in NYC 36 years ago. And had the advantage of the best possible education. He has a BS degree in Communication Arts from Fordham, an MFA in Drama from Yale, and attended the New York College of Music. Ken was stage manager and actor in Rhode Island's Theater-by-the-Sea which starred Walter Matthau. Then in New York's off-Broadway "The Hostage" by the late Brendon Behan.

Later, on Broadway, in "Gideon" starring Frederic March. Soon he begin directing Package Plays, starring successively Molly Picon, Margaret O'Brian, Joan Bennett, you name them. He was also connected with plays in Minneapolis, Baltimore and Princeton University. Ken toured cross-country with Rod Steiger in "A Short Happy Life" and ditto with Sylvia Sidney in the "Matchmaker". You know — the play "Hello, Dolly" comes from. In December, Costigan will play the leading role in "Room Service" at the Playhouse, with Nassif directing. It had a long run on Broadway.

Of Irish descent, Costigan and his brother-in-law spent last July in — you guessed it — Dublin. Not far from Belfast where the civil-religious fighting was going on at the time. But the shooting didn't quite reach them. And now listen to this. One evening, at a Pub, minding his own business and blissfully relaxing over a mug of Ireland's national favorite drink (stout), another fellow was doing likewise. The next minute they were hugging and back-slapping each other with surprised delight. The guy had played with Ken in New York in "The Hostage". A small world!

Our man Costigan is not actually a full Squirrel Hiller but lives so close to us that we consider him a nearby neighbor. An easy-to-look-at and charming bachelor, he lives right smack across from the Playhouse — almost a stone's-throw from here. In his kitchenette apartment he fixes his own breakfast. And many of his girl-friends invite him for dinner. However, should one of them forget sometimes, Ken doesn't go hungry. The Stage Door Club Restaurant downstairs of the Playhouse serves most delicious meals.

You'll never believe it but our nearby neighbor never smoked, doesn't now and has no intention of starting. So he doesn't need to go through the agony of trying to quit. And another thing, he doesn't boast about it to those who do. It's a free country.

With the excellent plays on tap for this season and the good food you'll doubtless want to take advantage of, it looks like there'll be lots of fun and warmth on Craft Avenue in the cold months ahead.

Doris Crozier
Debunks Old Hat

Usually an assistant to the president of a famous college is a highly educated man Women, they say, aren't smart enough to reach that pinnacle. Well, we have news for the say-ers. The president of our neighboring Chatham College (Dr. Edward Eddy has as his capable assistant a brilliant women and a lovely one at that. She's Doris Crozier of Murrayhill Ave. — a farmer's daughter who made good in various cities Ours included. Let's learn a little about our interesting neighbor.

Doris Crozier grew up on a farm in Vermont and earned her B. A. degree at Trinity College in Burlington. Her first teaching job was in a 1-room school. There she had to fire-up the round coal stove in the center of the room. The children would put their lunches near the stove and go fetch water from the next farmhouse. After a year the youthful teacher made it as principal of a 3 room school, staying three years. Then advanced to high school to teach Math and as basketball coach. From there she went to Hartford to teach her subject in high school for a year. And on to Danbury High to teach Math, Triginometry and Geometry. For 8 meaningful years.

During the U.S. occupation of Germany the experienced teacher became principal of the American School in Bremen — a civilian employe of the Army. After two years Doris was back in Connecticut for her masters degree in Anthropology. Then started teaching that subject and also Math at Western Connecticut College. In 1958 our current neighbor traveled to Cambodia as adviser to the government in setting up its first Teachers College. During her three years there she had a chance to travel all around Burma, India, Bali, Singapore, to name a few. And was decorated by the Cambodian government with the Order of Chevalier for helping establish the country's first Teachers College. Then back to Western Connecticut College to teach Anthropology. While there Miss Crozier was elected on a Commission to consolidate the town and city of Danbury.

And all the while she commuted to New York University evenings and week-ends for her PH.D. The major professor of that University recommended her to the Phillips Foundation. That did it. From the Foundation she received an academic internship to our Chatham College. And after a year's interning Doris Crozier became Assistant to Cath128's President. That was in 1964, to be exact. At Chatham our lovely neighbor has found her work interesting and stimulating.

She's met all kinds of famous personalities who come to the College to lecture, exchange ideas and hold conferences — each on a 3-day visit. Like for instance Helen Hayes, Agnes Moorhead, Otto Koerner and many more. Her 3-room apartment near Chatham is furnished with furniture she brought back from Hong Kong. And is a rendezvous for the neighborhood children who stop in daily. Not exactly to admire the furnishings but to dip into a huge jar of candy their hospitable host has ready for them. It's not that they love teacher Doris less but they like her candy more.

Miss Crozier is on the board of N.E.E.D. and also a board member of the International Forum, as well as the Chamber Music Society. She has two sisters: one an Anesthesist in North Carolina and another a Vermont housewife. Does Doris smoke? Sh-h-h-h-! She doesn't. Not even cigars. Any interesting men in her life? No answer. Just an engaging smile.

And now, guess what. Our charming neighbor will be leaving Chatham the end of the 1968-69 academic year. She's been elected the first Dean of the Coordinate College for Women Kenyon College, Gambier, Ohio.

Pretty remarkable for a farmer's daughter, doing it alone. Meantime our community wishes her the best of everything now and even more when she trots off to Gambier. Chatham's loss will be Kenyon's gain.

Jennifer Darling
She's In Plays While Husband's Away

A funny thing happened to our neighbor Jennifer Darling on her way to the YWCA. Instead of a room there she wandered — bag and baggage — into a man's apartment.

He's a cad, of course, And what's more, two other fellas inhabit the place. Only these two don't go for girls. They go for each other.

So what happens to Jennifer shouldn't happen to your daughter. But before you rush out to save her from a fate worse than death, just relax. It's not for real.

Jennifer Darling is starring in "The Knack," a comedy currently wowing them at the Playhouse. So gather up the wife but not the kids and see for yourself. You'll have much to laugh about, think about and talk about.

And because Jennifer is young very talented, cute as Christmas and lives in our neighborhood, you naturally want to know about her. Pull up your chairs.

Doubtless you best know her as Joan. Jennifer is her professional name. In private life she's Mrs. Paul Itkin. Paul, too is an actor. Both attended Tech Drama School and graduated together last June. They've been Mr. and Mrs. for 1½ years.

Jennifer's parents are Nathan and Mary Darling. Dad is owner of the various Darling drug stores. Brother Macy has an interior design shop in Georgetown, D.C. And sis Esther is married to Marvin Resnick, an executive of Hertz-Rent-a-Car.

You theatre lovers have doubtless seen Jennifer with William Ball's ACT at the Playhouse last summer in "Servant of Two Masters," "Rose Tattoo," "Six Characters in Search of an Author "And" a "Midsummer Night's Dream." In her undergraduate days Jennifer acted with several theatres. At the White Barn in Irwin she played Baby June in "Gypsy," Mammie Yokum in "Lil Abner" and Zipporah in "Milk and Honey." For the Three Rivers Festival she played "Romeo and Juliet."

At Wooser (Ohio) Arena Theatre she played Winnifred in "Once Upon a Mattress." When only 14 she won the Ted Mack Original Amateur Contest.

Our neighbor has other talents too. For 12 years she studied dancing at the Gene Kelly studio. And singing for three years with teacher Belle Bernfield.

Husband Paul, too — you learned — is an actor. So what's with him? Well, it's like this.

His career was nipped in the bud by Uncle Sam. Several weeks ago he left for Fort Jackson, S.C. You'd hardly call it a stone's throw from his lovely bride. They dismantled their little artistic apartment and she moved in with mom and dad at 401 Shady Ave. She plans to go to New York for a look-see into the theatre world. Already she has several "maybe's."

Separated from her ever-lovin', she plans to keep busy. And is proud that Paul can be of service to our country. For a petite blonde with a BB hairdo, skirts an inch or two above the knees, it surprises you to hear her say serious things like that.

As the saying goes, it's what's inside that counts. And our neighbor has plenty there.

Let's give Jennifer Darling a big hand. And send our kindest and bestest to husband Paul soldiering in the Deep South. And don't forget "The Knack" at the Playhouse. It was shown in movie-form at our neighborhood Guild Theatre. Remember?

Marylin Davis

A Real 'Go-Go' Girl

Do you happen to be a secretary? And are you stuck with a ho-hum job where you sit for hours typing names and addresses from the phone book?

Or your boss stutters his dictation and you can't read your notes? And you keep watching the clock wishing it were five already?

Then you'll admire — and maybe envy a little — a neighborhood "Girl Friday" whose boss is tops and her job fascinating. She's Marylin Davis of Hempstead Road.

Marylin is secretary to well-known Richard Hoover, general manager of the Pittsburgh Playhouse.

Marylin is a tall, graceful redhead. She smiles easily and seems to love life. As a teenager she attended the Playhouse School. And later graduated from the University of Toledo with a bachelors degree in psychology. Her mom is Mrs. Evelyn Davis, same address. She, too, is a secretary — for the United Jewish Appeal. And honestly, she's so young-looking that you have to squint to determine which is mother and which is daughter!

Brother Robert is 23 and has been assistant manager of A. S. Beck Shoe Store at South Hills Village since 19, Bob too is good-looking.

Everything that happens at the Playhouse originates in Boss Hoover's office. So Marylin's duties are many, varied and often fascinating. Working hand-in-hand with "Playhouse Plus" — a group of prominent women who plan diversions for the actors — she's constantly in the swing of things.

As you often hear, there's no people like Show people. On the stage they're someone else. Socially they're warm, friendly, delightful. And not all the fellas are married, either.

Though Marylin's job is primarily 9 to 5 Monday through Friday, she often gives up evenings to them because it's such fun. On opening nights she takes an active part as official hostess. During the "Mad Show" Marylin was dressed as a bunny (in tights, mind you) handing out balloons and smiles to the delighted audience.

As a publicity stunt, when the Madmobile was stationed at Mellon Square and Gateway Center during the noon-hour, our neighborhood bunny was on hand. With her curvacious figure, an otherwise sedate executive remarked: "I don't want a balloon. I'll take the bunny." Just then mom Davis came strolling along during her own lunch-hour. So what happened? Nothing. Darn it!

Last summer Marylin up and purchased a 25-foot cabin cruiser. And named it "Redhead." It's been a lively spot all summer long as it bobs against its moorings at Oakmont. And you guessed it. The Playhouse people are welcome guests.

Recently the whole cast of "The Knack" was invited aboard for a cruise down river to the Point and back. Took three hours. And ditto for the delightful "Mad Show" five.

Between the eats that Marylin prepared in the cabin kitchen and what the guests came with, no one left hungry. Nor thirsty. And nobody rocked the boat. And no one fell overboard.

Our neighbor has just returned from a vacation in New York City. What did she do there? Saw the top-notch Broadway shows. She was even taken to Sybil Burton Christopher's Arthur".

Now let's cut out all the nonsense and get down to cases. With all those men she meets — some being bachelors — does Marylin "go steady" or just play the field? No answer. Just an engaging smile.

So your guess is as good as ours.

Mrs. J. M. (Sarah) Davis

Radiant Personality at 82

Our community is proud of its many active older adults. But there's one in our midst who's so extra special that you want to know her better. Say "hello, doll" to Mrs. Jack M. (Sarah) Davis, neighbor down Murray Ave. At age 82 (repeat —82) she's vibrant, radiating enthusiasm and warmth, giving her time and effort for others. Blest with good health she considers it a privilege and joy to help when needed.

Hadassah in particular, being a charter member for 55 years. Many mornings of each week for the past 4 years Mrs. Davis punches the clock at its office in nearby Maxon Towers. For free, of course. A vital organization of some 4,800 dedicated members has plenty jobs. When there are special thank-you letters and other important mail not socially proper to type, Sarah writes them by hand in her neat, feminine back-hand penmanship. When the multigraph machine breaks down she addresses envelopes — volumes of them — by hand. And helps out on other clerical jobs that constantly need doing.

And now let's go back 82 years. The former Sarah Treelisky was born in Oakland in a house under the Schenley Bridge. She attended Bellefield grade school but no further. Mom thought Jewish girls don't need high school. Even Rabbi Sivitz (of blessed memory) said all they need is to keep house, marry and have children. (Women's Lib, take note). Dad Hyman owned a Dairy. Everyone affectionately called him "Chaim the Milkman". The late Tom Schubb — that fabulous surgeon — and a few of his pre-med student friends used to walk a mile to the Dairy, not for a Camel but for a glass of fresh, foamy milk right from the natural donor.

In her early teens Sarah raised $600 for the first "ad" booklet of the YMHA's beginning. The opening meeting was held at brother Jesse Treelisky's home on Erin St. He was its first Treasurer with 14 members present. She volunteered 8 years service for the Hebrew Ladies Sick and Relief Society. And was the first Superintendent of the B'nai Israel Sunday School when they met in a small building on Collins Ave. 52 years ago. Later Sarah was on a committee of 13 men and women to supervise Saturday night dances at the Zionist Institute, Center Ave. Admission 15 cents plus 5 cents for the hat-check boy (no girl bunnies). Handsome bachelor Jack Davis couldn't go to those dances. His men's store was open Saturday nights. But he did attend the monthly dances of the Kadima Zionist Institute. A bit classier — admission 25 cents. Later, at a YMHA Sunday night program Sarah came with a girl-friend. Who walked in, big as life but Jack Davis.

And escorted her home. Cupid must have followed because that very night Jack proposed. Her family was flabbergasted. Four months later (Feb. 29, 1920) they became Mr. and Mrs. and went to NYC for their honeymoon. They started housekeeping in an apartment near their store. After 15 months the Stork brought baby Herbert Jesse. Three years later Saul Charles arrived. Then tragedy struck. At age 47 their mom was widowed. She took over her husband's scrap iron business but after 2 years decided it was not a woman's work. And opened a small grocery store in Homewood. Then moved back to Sq. Hill, becoming credit interviewer for Frank and Seder's and Gimbels, to support her boys.

When they left home mom was called to our nation's Capital for 6 months to do secretarial work. She stayed 16½ years, working 7 days a week till she reached 71 — the mandatory retirement age. She then returned here to the same apartment where she and her boys had lived previously.

At age 77 our widow was elected recording sec'y for Hadassah Group 1 (now Henrietta Szold) for 3 years. She also did clerical work for the Jewish National Fund. And as a member of Beth Shalom Sisterhood, addressed 1,000 envelopes by hand. Sarah was also president of the Beth Aaron Sisterhood. At age 80 the Sisterhood honored her by planting a tree in Israel. And on her 82nd birthday Judge Ellenbogen did likewise. She also received 6 citations from the USO.

Son, Herbert, now manufactures uniforms. And goes to Pitt 4 nights a week to further his education. He presented his mom with 3 grandchildren and 2 great-grandchildren. Saul was an actor for 13 years. Now he's Service Mgr. for the Norman M. Morris Corp. A bachelor, he refuses to call her "mother". Says she's too young. So he calls her "Sadie". When our neighbor's "mispacha" come here for a re-union, 14 people sit down to dinner she herself cooks in her 3-room apt. As they say in French — no, in Yiddish — "umbaschrien".

And don't tell Jack Benny, but Sarah Davis looks younger at 82 than he at 39. Lord bless and keep her!

Sharon & Marilyn Davison
Sisters Gain Widespread Success

As this is being written it's snowing and blowing like mad outside. But it might as well be spring for it's like a whiff of fresh air telling you about two youthful sisters in our neighborhood. They're Sharon and Marilyn Davison of Ludwick St. Though a mere 19 and 22, respectively, they already are climbing fast up the ladder of success as "The Musical Sisters of Song." Not only because of their talent but their dynamic enthusiasm and love of what they're doing.

Both wear mod clothes most of which they themselves design, decorate and sew. But nothing bizarre. Sharon, with brown hair to her shoulders, eyes aglow with expression, accompanies their songs with a guitar — either 6-string, 12 string or electric. Marilyn shakes the tambourine, morrocos, and her hips too when the song requires it. Her dimpled smile adds charm to their act.

The Davison repertoire is a melange of diverse ethnic songs. The girls are equally at home with folk, pop, bossa nova, calypso, jazz, country-western, show tunes and Beatle types. They sing "Spanish Eyes", "My Wild Irish Rose", Russia's "Kretchma", French "Alouette", Mexican "Cucuracha", Greek "Never on Sunday", Italian "Quando Quando", and African "Kumbaya".

Also West Indian "Girl from Ipenema." Their ethnic specialties are Hebrew and Yiddish songs (the latter learned from mom). In great demand are "Tum Balalaika", "Have Nagilah", "Chiribim Chiribom", "Trinkt Le Chaim" (the Jewish Wedding Song), "Hevanu Shalom Aleichem" (Peace to all), Sabbath prayer from "Fiddler on the Roof", "By Mir Bistu Shein", "Tzenna Tzenna" — the list is endless.

They've performed on stage, TV, radio, at Ben Gross's Restaurant, The Edge, Hilton, Westmoreland and Baldoc Country Clubs, the Catskills — you name it. Also at Carnegie Music Hall, many Hadassah groups as well as numberless other worthy organizations. Tiny Tim, while at the Holiday House recently, invited them on stage. The applause was thunderous.

Their deservedly proud parents are Ted and Sylvia Davison. Dad is an auto supply jobber. One or both come along when the girls perform — especially at night. The kids must have had solid up-bringing because they have a keen sense of values. They know the difference between quality and triviality. They belong to Hillel, the student branch of B'nai B'rith. Smoke? They don't. And what's nice too, don't brag about it. Sex education in school? They learn more at home from their parents— especially from mother. Both date but not steady. Sometimes they must cancel out because of unexpected last-minute performance requests. The fellas understand and phone again— AND AGAIN.

Both girls graduated Allderdice. Marilyn attends Pitt for Music Education courses. Sharon ditto at CMU. They composed three songs which have been copyrighted in Washington. At a social affair honoring Roberto Clemente where they performed, he taught them the Spanish words of his favorite song "La Bomba", which they played and sang. This thrilled him as much as slugging a home-run for the Pirates. In addition, Marilyn does ceramic and acrylic work. Also paints oil and water colors. Her paintings of brilliantly multi-colored roses against a white background are being shown and sold here, there, all around. The following Show Biz personalities have her rose paintings in their homes: Tiny Tim, Marty Allen, Theodore Bikel, Elmer Willett, Tom Morgan and Hal Friedman (both of Chatham Communications, Inc.). And lovely Marie Torre.

Guitarist-singer Sharon was a tomboy-athlete in her early school years. As captain of soccer, volley-ball, baseball teams from the 7th to 12th grades her teams never were beaten. In basketball she was called "Wilt the Stilt." Since then she has come a long way, baby. And is all-woman now. In between their "Sisters of Song" concerts she teaches guitar to the lolly-pop bunch, up to and including young adults.

Honestly, ours is the luckiest neighborhood.

Diana Dean
Neighbor Key in TV Series

Dear neighbors: Especially moms who are home fixing dinner. Take a look with the small fry at a charming educational program: "Misterogers' Neighborhood".

Fred Rogers, a Presbyterian minister no less, talks to the kids as a friendly neighbor, not down to them. Week-days 5 to 5:30 Channel 13. And again 6:30 to 7 for the older ones, including pop maybe. You'll learn more in 30 minutes about numberless things than it took you months—maybe years— to grasp and remember.

And with fun instead of the boredom of long, long ago. Delightful to watch, the program speaks for itself. But what goes on behind the scenes in creativity, imagination, experience and planning is a different story. And as always in things worthwhile our neighbors are a part of them, today you'll meet one of many.

Say Hi to Diana Dean Braverman of Phillips Ave. Diana is Associate Producer for Fred Rogers' "Small World Enterprises, Inc." Rogers (a neighbor on Beechwood Blvd.); fabulous Don Brockett (also living close by), and famous guitarist Joe Negri create the ideas for the series. Diana, with a talented staff of five produce them. Way in advance— Weeks, sometimes 5 months. She started with Fred three years ago when his program went on the National Educational TV (NET) in Alaska, Hawaii, Pago Pago in the Samoa Island, and all over continental USA.

The former Diana Dean Root was born in Danville, Ill. After High she earned her BA degree in Home Economics and Theater at De Paw University. Then on to Graduate School in Bowling Green State University. She was speech director and taught dramatics in Baldwin-Wallace College near Cleveland for two years. Then got a job at the University of Illinois as typist for the Illinois Natural History Survey. And was acting in plays at the University. Bachelor Max H. Braverman was in the same university working on his Ph.D.

During one of her plays he was in the audience. That did it! Steady dating followed and they married in 1957. They did extensive traveling in Europe, the young bride accompanying her husband to Naples where he was doing research. However, the marriage ended ten years later. Since then Diana has been on her own and making progress by leaps and bounds. Limited space prohibits listing the numberless outstanding things our neighbor has accomplished.

For "Misterogers" she has produced, directed, supervised, edited and transferred to video tape 80 films. Let's name a few at random: Misterogers Visits a Windmill; How Ice-cream is Made (movies taken at the Tri-Point Dairy); How Pianos are made (at the Steinway factory), which ends with none other than the great Van Cliburn playing a sonata, followed by the puppets asking him questions—how, when, where he started lessons. (The puppets' voices are by Fred and at times by another young minister); Misterogers at the Dentist's Office; Dishwashing in a Cafeteria (at CMU Skibo hall); Chef Brockett Makes a Fast Cake; Males and Females in the Animal World. Etcetra, etcetra— on and on. The kids are fascinated, absorb and learn. And remember.

Not having added to the population explosion, our neighbor adopted two handsome Siamese cats in her 4 room apt. But the landlord said "No cats!" So Susu and Gus are now living out their nine lives at a friend's home which is minus a landlord. And in the style they had always been accustomed to.

Diana has other interests, like for instance gardening, cooking, reading, skiing and photography.

Like Fred Rogers sings at the end of his daily program, let's wish him, Diana Dean and the entire team "A Happy Tomorrow Today". And oh, yes—those cute puppets too.

Mrs. Dennis (Pat) Dewey
Loves Cats, Breeds Ribbon Winners

"Have cats. Won't sell." That's how it is with our today's neighborhood personality. She's youthful, slim, blond-silken-haired Mrs. Dennis (Pat) Dewey of Hobart St. And small wonder. One of her 3 pet cats, with the Hebraic name Ebenezer has won more blue ribbons and trophies in his 4 years of life than you can shake a stick at. More about him later. First let's meet the gal who likes cats and is the power behind his throne.

The former Pat Entress was born in suburban Morningside. And grew up in a home with plenty space inside and out, ideal for various pets whom the family enjoyed having around and caring for. After graduating St. Raphael Hi, Pat came to our city and enrolled at Pitt. In no time she met handsome, educationally ambitious Dennis Dewey, a Senior and Chairman of the schools' evening Student Council. He had graduated Central Catholic Hi in nearby Oakland.

They started dating and to the surprise of no one pronounced their marriage vows to a priest in St. Raphael's church. May 11, 1968 to be exact. And started housekeeping in a Wightman St. basement apt. Currently they occupy a 4-room 3rd floor walkup overlooking clusters of trees now in colorful autumn glory. Squirrels often hop to their window-sill for peanuts. And get them. After graduating Pitt the young bride worked as an insurance adjuster. Now she's an elementary counselor at 3 different Braddock schools. And because she loves learning, is keeping up her evening studies at Pitt toward a Ph. D.

Husband Dennis is an installer for Western Electric Co., and also goes to Pitt evenings. He will get his BS degree next April. Shortly after marriage Pat started hankering after her pet cat in Morningside. But it was already in its 8th year of life - "a senior citizen" - and too attached to its comfortable surroundings to adjust elsewhere. So guess what? Her understanding husband, as a birthday surprise came home with a furry kitten from the Northside Humane Society where it miraculously survived after having been found abandoned in dead of winter.

They named him Ebenezer. And now that you've met him you'll be interested in learning of the pride and joy he bestowed upon his adoptees during his 4 years of life with them. Orange-color, silky fur, sparkling eyes and a loveable disposition, the Dewey's entered him, at age 2 in the Tri-State Cat Club Show last October. It was held in Castle Shannon for the benefit of the Western Penna. Humane Society.

Edward P. Tremel, Human Society animal officer and Mrs. Mildred K. Schad, education sec'y were invited to distribute Humane Society literature. And Jim Horne, then with KDKA-TV and some Don Brockett Shows, was a judge. Hundreds of spectators cheered the winner. So who was the winner? You guessed it. Ebenezer was chosen Champion Household Pet and awarded 4 blue ribbons and trophies. But success didn't spoil Ebenezer. He just looked on in puzzlement at all the excitement; and after getting home curled up and took a snooze.

Being away from home so much, to keep Ebenezer from being lonely they added 2 kittens to the "family". When they hear the Dewey car drive up they all run to the door, purringly greeting them. Mrs. Dewey is only 25 and Dennis not much older. They want to have a baby of their own after they are more established and can be the best parents ever. Pat's mom used to belong to the non-sectarian Y-IKC and her best girl-friend was Jewish. That way the mother learned many Yiddish and Hebrew words and phrases. They brushed off on Pat. And maybe, in turn on Ebenezer. So let's say "Shalom" to the Dewey's. And to Ebenezer: "L'Chaim!"

Mr. & Mrs. Thomas Digman

Happily Married 50 Yrs., They'll Celebrate

How refreshing it is, these days of multiple marriages and quick divorces, to meet a couple like Thomas and Alfreda Digman.

These two have been happily married for 50 years.

However, happiness didn't just fall on their laps. They made it that way themselves.

Somehow they knew how to be humbly grateful for their blessings and to endure together, with courage and faith, the sorrows that inevitably creep into people's lives.

The Digmans were born in England 73 years ago. At the outbreak of World War 1 young Tom Digman enlisted and served in England's Royal Army Medical Corps. In the holocaust that followed he was gassed and wounded; and some time later honorably discharged.

Because his country's damp and foggy climate was injurious to his health, Tom and his young bride Alfreda emigrated to the States settling in Pittsburgh. They lost no time in becoming loyal American citizens.

When his health improved, Mr. Digman connected up with U. S. Steel Corp. and later became Supervisor of Maintenance in its Duquesne plant. He held that position for 30 years. Now, of course, he is retired.

Tom and Alfred were blest with two children: Thomas J. and Alfreda (now Mrs. Walter Kern). These children both attended Taylor-Allderdice and were graduated from there. There are two grandchildren and one great-grandchild — all boys.

During World War 2, son Thomas served in the U. S. Air Force as a bombadier. In April 1944 — six weeks before V-Day, he lost his life flying over Germany. His age? Just 24 years! On the same day 68 bombers were shot down and lost.

Many parents, confronted with that kind of a tragedy, would have spent the rest of their lives mourning. But Mr. Digman hid his sorrow in his work while his courageous wife became active in worthy causes serving others. All through the war she worked in the Salvation Army Canteen at the Penna. and P.& L. E. stations, serving sandwiches and refreshments to the soldiers as they arrived from far-off places. She continued that work for 15 years, packing boxes of food for the boys at Aspinwall, Deshon and the Veterans Hospital.

For 12 years Mrs. Digman was chaplain of the Eastern Star, Joppa Chapter 57. And is past Matron of the Hazel Court, Order of Amarenth. Her husband being a Shriner, she belongs to the Syria Ladies Social Club. The women of that club do work in behalf of the Shriners' crippled children throughout the U.S.

At a recent Bazaar they raised $2,300 for the children. Also she is a Gold Star Mother of the Fort Black American Legion. Both she and her husband belong, attend and are active in the Church of the Good Shepherd.

The Digmans live on the second floor of a nice-looking duplex, Kennebec St. The owner lives on the first floor. And never was there such good will between landlord and tenants, because the landlord is their daughter, Mrs. Walter Kern!

Thomas and Alfreda Digman are celebrating their 50th Golden Wedding Anniversary Dec. 15. They are having "Open House." The hours are from 2 to 5 and 7 to 10 p.m. They are looking forward to the pleasure of greeting all their neighbors, friends and relatives.

Our community wishes this lovely couple and their dear ones, good luck, good health and much happiness — which they richly deserve.

Jon Dorish

Many talented man also good neighbor

You, of course, know of a former actor turned Governor. Today you'll learn of ex-football player turned actor. And in between, an artist. Terrific in all three talents. So you may as well get acquainted with him, especially since he lives in our very neighborhood. Say hello-dere to Jon Dorish of Aylesboro Ave.

The youthful actor has shoulder-length blond hair, looms over 6 ft., is strongly streamlined, with a personality-plus. Dorish is the newest addition to the Don Brockett talented gang whose shows keep you in stitches in various night spots and particularly at the Ben Gross after-dinner Cabaret. Late this month will end the long-running 'Hello, Goodbye! I Love You!" at Gross'. Then Brockett will premiere his newest laugh-provoking musical "Sweet Feet". Sweet Feet?? What kind of a whoozzit is it? The nickname of one of the girls, a show-stopping soda-jerker — that's what it is. And that's where our neighbor gets mixed up in. He takes the part of a lecherous producer; and in another act as a French maid, based on Hollywood's big movies era of the 30's and 40's.

And now a little about our neighbor's background. Born in nearby Heidelberg he graduated from Chartiers Valley Hi and went on to Clarion State College for four years, earning his BA degree in Humanities. During those years he went in for football. He had a try-out with our Pittsburgh Steelers whose manager Art Rooney suggested he play for Pottstown — a semi-pro team. And he did just that. At the same time, encouraged by his close artist friend Lavern Grant of Clarion, he started dabbling in Art. No lessons. Just came naturally — out of his own head, as the saying goes. And made such remarkable progress that currently he's doing art work to sell for galleries through the Arts and Crafts Center, Fifth and Shady; at the Sandpiper, Monroeville Mall — water colors and traditional scenes, mostly of our city. He's had several one-man Shows last February. And his art adorns the walls of the Pittsburgh National Bank, Fifth and Craig. Also paintings at the Charles Pitcher Gallery. Dorish is a member of Associated Artists of Pittsburgh and the Pittsburgh Society of Artists.

While at Clarion College, in addition to football and art, he was involved in over 15 stage productions, And last year played in "Room Service" at our Pittsburgh Playhouse. After an audition with Brockett, Don quickly recognized Jon's acting talent and lost no time in nabbing him.

Neighbor Dorish has a 3-room walk-up third-floor apartment. His bedroom serves for sleeping and as his art studio. He prepares his own meals — mostly salami and hot dogs from the various neighborhood delicatessens, the kosher ones, believe it or not.

And hydrated soups. Also all kinds of fresh salads. Barbara Russell, Brockett's delightful side-kick bakes delicious bread. And keeps Jonny freshly and fully supplied. But don't tell our neighborhood bakershops. They might go out of business!

Being at the romantic and vulnerable age of 24 and easy to look at, how about girls? He says his acting work is constantly surrounded by beautiful girls. Any special girl? No answer. Just a mischievous smile. So it could be yes. Or it could be no. So go figure it out.

Mrs. Jonathan (Roberta) Duker

Donor Chairman Devotes Energies To Annual Feta

Sunday, March 3rd, it's that time again. The Hadassah Annual Donor. Proceeds to help Israel in its "Blackest Hours". The countless committee women — bless 'em — have been knee deep planning, arranging to make this year's Donor the most enjoyable ever. More about it follows. But first let's learn a little about its top gal — the Donor Chairman. She's none other than Mrs. Jonathan Duker, affectionately called Bobby.

The former Roberta Katz was born in Mineola, N. Y. After High she went to Connectcut College, New London, graduating with a B.A. degree. Somewhere along the line she met — and fell for — handsome Jonathan Duker working in New London. Among his many fine qualities he was a dedicated Zionist. It quickly rubbed off on Bobby continuing throughout their married life on to their three interesting children. Jonina 17 is a senior at Baldwin High and a merit semi-finalist. Jay is 15 and goes to Wallace Intermediate High. Judith, 13 attends Painter Middle School. When age 10 her mom made her a Hadassah life-member, explaining she couldn't be active until 17. Judy began taking messages, copying names, keeping files, then coyly asked: "So I can' be active before 17 — huh?" Dad works in the Purchasing Dept. of Westinghouse Bettis Laboratory. They live in suburban Whitehall but Bobby spends so much time at the Forbes Ave. Hadassah office, Maxon Towers, she insists she's a Squirrel Hiller.

Our today's personality was V.P. of Membership at the Chapter level for 3 years And currently is Treasurer of her Tova Group. Any hobbies? Who has time? However— but don't tell Waldorf— she bakes the best bread and cinnamon rolls in town.

And now let's digress a bit. After a visit to Israel before the Yom Kippur War, Henr Ford III said: "In all history it's doubtful if any people have ever accomplished so much so quickly and with such odds against them". Odds? Count them: With the sea on one side and a ring of hostile, ruthless neighbors on all other sides Israel has no place to run to. With 2,412 men killed in battle, over 1,800 hospitalized, cost of war billion: more than her entire economy for a year, if she loses the peace there never will be another opportunity.

Where will the current Donor be held? Gay and charmingly arranged — at our neighborhood Manor Theatre. There'll be room for all since the complete program wil be performed twice: at 2 and 8 p.m. Have your choice. And guess what? a caterer wine and cheese buffet will be served in the lobby following both performances. You' revel in the film "I Love You, Rosa". It's Israel's entry in the 1973 Academy Award competition for Best Foreign Film. Taking place among Oriental Jews in the Old Cit of Jerusalem, it's an English-speaking version, rich in authentic characterization an colorful detail. It is a beautiful, affirmative picture, reminding us of truths almost for gotten in our cynical, unbelieving age. It is rated "H" for Hadassah.

Hadassah mobilizes to S.O.S. (Safeguard our Services) for Israel. Don't anyone dare skip this year's Donor. Sunday, March 3rd, 2 or 8 p.m.
See you there.

Dr. Abraham Edelman

A Boy, A Girl and Sugar on Sauerkraut . . .

It's simply fantastic the important personalities who add luster to our neighborhood. Take for instance Dr. Abraham Edelman of Beechwood Blvd. He's a doctor of course. But if you have a "code-in-your-dose" with sniffles, don't call him. His work is far more important — and not to be sneezed at.

You see, our neighbor is director of the Division of Radiation in the Radiology Department of Allegheny General Hospital. He heads a group of doctors who do research on the effects of radiation, what it does and how to counteract it. Radiation therapy for cancer, that is.

He and his staff are trying to find ways and means to administer more radiation without harming the patient.

What does it take in education, experience and know-how to do research on this dread disease? Plenty. Let's see now. Dr. Edelman came here in 1955 from Brookhaven National Laboratory, Long Island. His AB degree he got at John Hopkins University. Then earned his MS in its medical school.

From here he went on to Ohio State University for his Ph.D. Then, wouldn't you know it, he got a brand new interest. A girl. And a pretty one at that. Rita Duker, also an Ohio State student. Often she'd walk past his dormitory with a tall boyfriend, discussing world events. So she was smart, too, he decided. He'd see her daily in the campus cafeteria. And even noticed what she chose to eat.

Once he watched her pour sugar on some sauerkraut. Must be good, he thought. And did likewise. And liked it. Eventually they met. But you'll never guess how. They were introduced! Steady dating followed. Two years later they were both saying "I do" to a rabbi in New York.

Nine years and two children later, a new company started in our city — to exploit peaceful use of atomic energy. The Nuclear Science & Engineering Corp. Dr. Edelman was called here to become head of its Biology and Medicine Department. Then was made vice president. After eight years with that firm he came to Allegheny General where he has now served two full years.

Rita Edelman concentrates on being a mother, wife and homemaker. But finds time to be active in the Technion Society. Daughter Beth is now 19 and goes to Radcliffe, majoring in Slavic languages and literature. Son Samuel, 16 is a junior at Allderdice. He is interested in science.

In 1950 our brilliant neighbor founded the Radiation Research Society and was its secretary for seven years. It's an international group of 1,200 members, many of whom are from India, France, Germany, Israel, Sweden, Norway and England. The society meets once a year in the U. S. and every three years in foreign countries. The last European meeting was in England. The next one will be in Italy. Then in San Diego, U.S.A. Also Puerto Rico. The society includes chemists, physicists, biologists and MD's. They come together to talk about their findings, exchange ideas and learn more.

Our neighbor scientist has a lighter side too. Get a load of this. While at Brookhaven he organized an orchestra in which he played the piano. Then a symphonic band. And, once a band has no need for a pianist, he was made its director, no less. They gave concerts for the Red Cross and Cancer drives. And performed at the Old Folks Home.

The golden-agers preferred band music because it's good and loud and all could hear it. Alexander's Ragtime Band? Who needs it, when they could listen to Edelman's?

It's likely our neighbor's favorite movie is "The Music Man." Because he'd like to organize a band here. But all he knows as of now is a lone flute player. Wanna join his band — anyone?

Bernard Elinoff
Theatre Manager Like Mailman

When is a theatre not a theatre? When it's converted into a House of Worship.

As happened recently at two movie houses in our neighborhood — the Squirrel Hill and Manor. During the several days of Rosh Hashona and Yom Kippur — the Jewish New Year and Day of Atonement. The marquee read: "Beth Shalom Services."

Since the idea for holding them at a theatre came from the imaginative and well-liked manager of the Manor, and he being a dyed-in-the-wool Squirrel Hiller, let's concentrate on him and find out the why, the wherefor, how come and what else is news. He's Bernard Elinoff, our neighbor at Bartlett St. Everyone affectionately calls him Bernie.

If you've passed the Beth Shalom Synagogue at Beacon and Shady you know that it's in the process of enlarging its sanctuary and constructing a new school. The digging, pounding and clutter make holding services there impossible — let alone those for the High Holy Days. What to do! So Beth Shalom's executive director Bob Fisher and Bernie Elinoff put their heads together and came up with an idea. Hold the services in the neighborhood theatres. So it came to pass.

Instead of a screen there was a silken curtain falling in graceful folds. There was light, not darkness. The Ark holding the Torah was on center stage. (Torah, as some may not know, contains the Laws of Life — the ways of justice and righteousness) Huge white chrysantemums and beautiful foliage surrounded it. The bright red seats were filled with serious worshippers. They entered with a humble heart and contrite spirit, to ask forgiveness of their sins. And prayed to be inscribed in the Book of Life for a good and meaningful New Year. The golden voice of the Cantor and the Rabbi's sermon enhanced the prayers.

Neighbor Elinoff came to the Manor last February, succeeding the late Max Silverman. Prior to that he was manager of the Squirrel Hill theatre for 9½ years. In 1937 after graduating Schenley High his first job was usher at that theater. After six months he was made assistant manager of another Stanley - Warner Movie house. And in 1940 was transferred to their main office in the Clark Building as advertising and publicity man. Then came WW II. And Bernie went off to serve Uncle Sam for three years, in the medical department of No. 127 General Hospital. The Hospital was set up to operate in England, France and Belgium.

At war's end our ex-soldier returned to Stanley-Warner's in the same department but in a different job. Then guess what? The handsome bachelor became interested in love, not war. After dating lovely Esther Snyderman for two years, they became Mr. and Mrs. in 1957. Their son Edward is now 10 and goes to Colfax. He likes baseball and is a whiz in history, knowing all about every President. Even the which-will-it-be ones. He also attends Beth Shalom religious school. And get a load of this. He not only gets to see the movies for free but can invite a buddy. As to those "For Adults Only" movies, not a chance.

Eddie's pop has many interesting plans afoot for the Manor. The much-heralded film "Star" with Julie Andrews will begin Dec. 18 on a reserved-seat basis. And the small fry are delighted with the Saturday Kiddie Shows. Parents, be at ease. Manager Elinoff likes kids and watches them carefully. Recently a youngster left the movie, crying. So what was wrong? He needed to go to the Little Boys' room. Too young to read, he wasn't sure which door to open. Heaven help a little fella if he got mixed up with girls under such personal circumstances. Shown the way and mission accomplished, the youngster returned happily to the movie.

Then there's excitement in store for the Golden Agers. Tuesdays, at special prices will show favorites of long ago. "The Student Prince," "Show Boat," "The Merry Widow," to name a few.

What does Bernie Elinoff do on his day off? He goes to a movie.

Max Elling
Neighborhood Cop Big Favorite With Kids

Ask a little girl what she wants to be when she grows up and she'll settle for nothing less than being Carey Grant's leading lady. But little boys — for reasons known only to themselves — want to be a policeman. So guess whom you'll learn about today? A policeman, that's whom. And if you're up to no good and contemplating some kind of hanky-panky, gather up the kids, pull up your chairs and listen. And listen good. Before it's too late and you'll wish you had.

But honestly now, beat patrolman Max Elling is the most likeable fellow with a stick you ever met. Strict? Bet your boots, yes. But fair and square. Many consider him the Young People's Champion.

Born in Brooklyn, young Max came here at age 10. His dad ran a fish market in the Hill district. In that neighborhood, where fists often were the price of survival, he remembers how easy it is to fall into trouble. So now, as he saunters along the streets on his neighborhood 3-to-11 p.m. beat, he keeps a practiced eye beamed on potential gangs, dangerous drifters, and any other threat to the young people he knows and likes to befriend.

Now let's go back a little. Our policeman attended Allegheny Vocational Trade School, selling newspapers during spare time. In the 8th grade he quit and got a job as an electrician's helper. His 8-hour shift included 3 hours daily traveling to and from the various jobs. His pay was $10 per week. Later he became an electrical contractor on his own. In 1929 — during the depression — he started boxing. As an amateur he boxed for medals and trophies. When he became a pro, he received $3 for 10 rounds of fighting. And earned the title "Kingfish" Elling. He completed 185 fights in all. And got his nose flattened in the bargain.

Later, together with 1700 others, Elling applied for the Police Force. And got the job. He has served 29 years, 17 of them in our neighborhood. Out of 5 Jewish policemen in Squirrel Hill, he is the oldest.

Starting his No. 6 Police Station beat, he helps the youngsters at Wilkins and Shady Aves. cross the street. And if there's a little old lady who wants across, he gallantly lends his strong arm. Down Shady toward Beechwood Blvd. and all the side streets, patrolman Elling doesn't miss a trick. Bohemian teenagers with black shoe-polish around their eyes, tight pants, long hair don't phase him. And make no mistake about it — he can tell the boys from the girls.

Until age 50 our policeman had been a confirmed bachelor. Then he up and fell in love. With lovely Betty Hecht, a bookkeeper at Bauman Chevrolet. Each had come, separately, to a dance at the Bellefield Ave. YM&WHA. After the last waltz he was a gonner. The Ellings have been Mr. & Mrs. for 5 years now. And are living happily in their own home at Winterburn St., Greenfield. After several years of being a house-wife, Better went back to "keep books" at Bauman's. They both share the household chores. Max can make their windows shine, the floors gleam, and dust instantly dis-appears at his touch. With no ash-trays to clean (both are non-smokers) it's a cinch, he tells you. He can even whip up a good dinner when necessary. Wives with husbands who don't know from nuthin' about such chores — are you jealous mebbe?

Our neighbors are members of the Tree of Life Synagogue — Max in the Men's Club, Betty the Sisterhood. He's an ardent Zionist and his missus belongs to Hadassah Group 8 and B'nai B'rith Women's Keystone Chapter. When the kids see him at the synagogue services they ask. "Aren't you a policeman any more?" After all, whoever heard of a policeman in a synagogue! Well, now you've heard. Our patrolmen's hobby is cross-word puzzles. He can't pass a newsstand without buying a paper. And he's a natural psychologist. When trouble faces him he likes to analyze the whys and the wherefores.

During World War 2 our neighbor served Uncle Sam for 18 months. In the Military Police he went after the AWOLS. So neighbors, better behave yourselves — you hear?

Mrs. H. D. Engelberg
Tree Chairman Shows Enthusiasm

A poet once said: "Only God can make a Tree". However, people plant them. So to-day you'll meet a dedicated neighbor heading the Jewish National Fund Drive. To plant trees in Israel for a Freedom Forest for Soviet Jewry. You'll understand its importance later in this article. Meantime let's learn about its capable Chairman, Mrs. Herman D. (Evelyn) Engelberg of Beechwood Blvd. Husband Herman, equally dedi-cated is an attorney and partner in Prudential Realty Co.

The former Evelyn Rosenberg, born in NYC came here when 11. She attended South Hills High on top of Mt. Washington, climbing 120 steps each day to get there. Her dad had a wholesale shoe business on Fifth Ave. She helped mind the store as bookkeeper and salesgirl. Then to Pitt. Herman Engelberg's sister, Ruth was in one of her classes. And got her to join Hapoel Hamizrachi, a religious Zionist Youth group, in which Her-man was active while attending Pitt Law School. Of course, it had to happen. They met, dated 3 years, became engaged at graduation. The marriage knot was tied by 5 rabbis, no less. At the then most popular Club, the Chatterbox. Later it burned down. But don't blame them!

And now about the Engelberg family. Daughter, Mimi (Mrs. Peter Hein) has 2 little boys, Jonathan and recent infant, Kevin. Rozy just received her master's in Jewish and Social Studies from Harvard. A cum laude graduate of Barnard she spent her Junior year at Jerusalem's Hebrew University. On her parents' first trip to Israel they planted a tree for Herman's beloved father. Sheri is in her second year at Cornell, a fine arts major in Drawing and Painting. Marcy is a Soph at Allderdice. The youngest son, Moshe goes to Hillel Academy. His hair style is mod, the bangs falling over his mis-chievous brown eyes. Dad is current president of Hillel and mom formerly was its PTA and Women's Auxiliary president. The children all are Hillel graduates. Evelyn, sister Harriet Mallin and mother, Elsie Rosenberg just planted a Garden in Israel in memory of their beloved father, Maurice A. Rosenberg. On the livelier side, Evelyn dabbles in poetry, Herman's boat ("Herm's Navy") sails the Allegheny. And mom Rosenberg is one of the best penny-ante players in Maxon Towers.

Their 9-room home, lovely to look at from without and within is kept shipshape by their capable housekeeper of 15 years. Though her name is Kelly, she cooks strictly kosher. Their huge collie arrived on the Jewish holiday of Sukkot. So they named him Sokie. He loves everyone — even the mailman. But woe be to a prowler lurking in the shadows!

Already planted in Israel are Forests in memory of John F. Kennedy, Harry Truman, Eleanor Roosevelt, Winston Churchill to name a few. And the Martyrs' Forest memorializing the 6 million Jewish victims of the Nazis. The trees, among other things have transformed malaria-ridden swamps, healed the ravaged land and brought back the birds to Israel.

The Freedom Forest for Soviet Jewry? As all know, the USSR is Atheistic and frowns on religion. However, all ethnic groups in Russia are allowed to develop their spiritual culture. All, that is, except the Jewish people. If discovered studying Hebrew by the secret police they often are fined, lose their jobs, and at times cast into prison. Some have even been executed. And what's equally tragic, they're not permitted to leave the country to join relatives in Israel. Every possible stumbling block is put in their way to hinder getting visas. Oh, a trickle has managed somehow to get out, but only a trickle. Those remaining are helplessly trapped.

Jews and many non-Jews throughout the world are watching, hoping. If and when more Russian Jewish people do manage to get to Israel, the Freedom Forest for Soviet Jewry will prove that they have not been forgotten — that people care.

The Drive's motto is: "Say it with Trees". Simply call the JNF office (521-6866). A word to the wise . . . And the kind at heart.

Rev. Dr. Carl E. Ericson

Presbyterians Show Pride in Edifice

When you pass Forbes & Murray are you sad at the lonely vacant space since the Old Asbury Methodist Church was dismantled and is no more? And unhappy with the clutter left there by thoughtless loungers on the premises? Well — just look across at the other corner and rest your eyes. There stands the stately Sixth Presbyterian Church. Its lawn, shrubbery and surroundings are fresh, clean and loverly to look at. You immediately know that someone there is very much alive and truly cares. So you'll doubtless be pleased to meet the Church's new minister, the Rev. Dr. Carl E. Ericson. He started his meaningful work there as recently as last February.

Actually, though, Rev. Ericson wasn't a theologian all his life. He is a newspaperman turned minister. Before coming here he served only one other parish — the Knox Presbyterian Church in suburban Washington. For 20 years the new minister had been a journalist. Seven of these years he was editor of a daily newspaper in Jacksonville, Ill. And for 13 years picture editor with Associated Press in Chicago and Washington. Somewhere along the line, at middle age, he had a call for the ministry. He didn't really want to stop being a newspaper man, but felt he had a call from God. To prepare for the ministry he entered and graduated from Princeton Theological Seminary, Princeton, N.J. And received his BA degree from Illinois College, Jacksonville, Ill. He was ordained to their Church in 1959, serving there until called to our neighborhood Sixth Presbyterian Church.

While in Jacksonville, love came our minister's way. At a dance he had the good fortune to meet beautiful Mary Katherine Shaw, a student at nearby McMurray College. After marriage the young bride continued teaching for 17 years. Now she just keeps house and helps her husband in his interesting work.

Their daughter Karin is married to Richard Blair, an Air Force Captain in Vietnam. Son Carl Eric Jon is editor with United Press in Washington, D. C. The youngest — Helen — goes to Pitt. Grandchildren? Four. Three Blairs and one Ericson.

During his ministry in Falls Church, Va., Rev. Ericson was clergyman - director of the Fairfax County Council of Churches.

Jail Rehabilitation Program. Prisoners have many problems they want to talk about. Visits were made on a weekly basis directly in the Cell Blocks. Listening, counseling, showing that someone cares had great therapeutic value. During the summer, college girls preparing for a church vocation visited the women prisoners. The Women's Circle made candy, put it in individual cellophane bags for the pastor to carry in to the men. Fruit — the finest quality — was distributed three times a year.

Pleas were frequently received for intervention with judges, lawyers, probation officers with respect to the prisoner's legal predicament. And requests to make a phone call, money needs, reading material—often for Bibles or text books for study—were carefully considered and arranged for. The variety was wide and wonderful.

There is no jail in Squirrel Hill because of course all our neighbors behave themselves. Or do they? Rev. Ericson is a good man to have around. He is happy in his work. His realistic approach to religion is akin to a newspaperman's familiarity with the secular. He says a Christian minister doesn't look for success. Failure is sometimes necessary and constructive. His philosophy as well as his insight into reaching people through the church helps to explain the fact that within his first month in Pittsburgh he spoke to five different churches here.

If you should drop in for Dr. Ericson's Sunday morning Services, the experience will be rewarding. Whether in conversation or before a congregation there's an almost compelling factor that makes you want to listen.

And now let's get back to the clutter across the Church's street. Recently a clean-up crew of two responsible neighbors went over there and cleaned up the mess. And who do you think they were? Members of the Sixth Presbyterian Church! It's likely the minister's lovely silver-haired Girl Friday—Corinne Smith— had a hand in it. Be that as it may, let's wish the new minister the best of everything now and in the years ahead.

Mrs. Charles (Sylvia) Feldstein
and
Mrs. Charles M. (Sybil) Schwartz, Jr.
Artists Team Up for Oldsters

To put zing into spring, today you'll learn about not just one but two interesting neighborhood personalities. A double-header as they say in baseball lingo. So turn off the commercials about beer, gasoline, dandruff and how to make your hands as lovely as your daughter's and pull up your chairs.

Our two remarkable neighbors — life-long friends — are top-notch artists. They teach the Golden Agers at the popular Anathan House for older people how to paint. For free — in an age when most everybody likes being paid for what they do.

Meet Mrs. Charles Feldstein of "Malvern Ave." We're starting with her because she's a youthful-looking blonde — the type gentlemen prefer.

The former Sylvia Goldberg graduated Schenley High and studied art at Parson's Art School in New York. Her husband Charles is an optometrist in Washington, Pa.

They've been blessed with twins, now all grown up. Son Richard practices with his dad. And just recently he did what comes naturally — got himself engaged. Twin sister Judy is Mrs. Joel Smalley. The Smalleys are parents of Michael, all of 21 months.

Our second artistic neighbor is Mrs. Charles M. Schwartz Jr. of S. Dallas Ave. The former Sybil Hart is a young-looking brunette. A fella named Richard Burton — remember? — prefers brunettes. So does husband Charles, president of the Hart Furniture Co.

Their daughter Cathy is married to Samuel Pearlman now studying law in Philadelphia. Sister Susan goes to Ohio University. Mom Schwartz graduated Allderdice and went briefly to Tech for art. Then to Penn State.

If you happened to see the cover on a recent issue of "The Jewish Choronicle," it was painted by Sybil Hart Schwartz. It was titled "Passover Among Nations" depicting a famous quotation from Isaiah ending with:

". . . And they shall beat their swords into plowshares,
And their spears into pruning-hooks;
Nation shall not lift up sword against nation,
Neither shall they learn war any more."

Their art class at the Anathan House is small because senior citizens aren't all gifted — as many young people aren't. Some prefer playing cards, listening to music or a lecture — or just relaxing and visiting with one another.

But star pupil Gertrude Friedman of Darlington Road is really going places in the art world. She's so excited with her teachers and her painting, she feels as if a new world has been opened up and she holds all the keys.

Mrs. Friedman, the youngest-looking golden age grandmother you ever saw, keeps that way by swimming daily in the neighborhood Y-IKC pool, knitting stylish dresses — and learning to paint. She even has graduated into abstracts, no less. Her pictures were accepted for a showing in Bellevue — and won acclaim.

When Grandma Friedman turns into a Grandma Moses, it will be due to her natural talent, her enthusiasm — and the teaching skill of neighbors Sybil Schwartz and Sylvia Feldstein. And our community is proud of them.

Mrs. Rudolph (Anita) Fellner
New Resident Had Role With the Stars

When a dressmaker has designed and made dresses for movie star Ann Sheridan (the Oomph Girl) and clothes for New York, Washington and Chicago, she must have plenty of knowhow. And since not too long ago she moved into our very neighborhood, it's important you get to know her. So without much ado shake hands with Mrs. Rudolph (Anita) Fellner, our neighbor at 1504 Denniston Ave.

But wait. Husband Rudolph is an important personality on his own, and you should learn about him first thing. Mr. Fellner has been head of the Opera Department at Carnegie Tech for 2½ years. He teaches the voice students how to put on operas. In the spring of last year they put on "The Carmalites".

At the well-known St. Paul's Cathedral. Bishop Wright closed the Cathedral for several days so that two performances could be given. To a large and delighted audience, by the way. In the interim the worshippers were not denied the solace of prayer. Church services were held in the Cathedral's basement. The Carmalite Order in Wheeling sent all the habits (religious costumes) for the Opera's actors. Did you happen to be in the audience maybe? Then you remember how remarkably well it was done.

And now let's find out how Rudy and Anita — of such diverse professions and countries — got together 22 years ago. Anita was born in Munich, Germany. During the Hitler regime she fled to England. Rudolph, an Austrian, migrated to the U.S. and soon became an American citizen. During World War II he joined Uncle Sam's Army.

In no time he was sent overseas for duty in Cardiff, Wales — a stone's throw from England. As was a British custom, same as here, soldiers were invited to various homes for meals. Anita's cousins in London wanted to host several American soldiers for Passover dinner. To play it fair, it was customary to simply pull two names out of a hat. One of the lucky names was American soldier Rudolph Fellner. As you surmise, Anita was on hand.

The Messiah must have entered through the door with Cupid alongside him, because it was love at first sight. But after only three enchanted dates Rudy was transferred to France. However, soldiers do get leaves, you know. And our soldier-in-love took his in London. In no time Anita became a war-bride.

After an honorable discharge the newlyweds went to Chicago to start housekeeping. The young husband entered Chicago Musical College to earn his Masters Degree. His youthful missus, having studied dressmaking and designing in England, got a job in a fashionable dress salon. In due time, you know how it is with young marrieds. Baby Kim was born. And not long after they moved to New York City.

There Anita worked in an exclusive dressmaking establishment. When the twins (Jene and Jane) arrived, Mom Fellner became a house-wife. In no time she built up a successful private clientele of her own. And soon started making costumes for the entertainers of Manhattan's famous Gaslight Club (no kissin' cousin to our local Shadyside Club of that name).

She often traveled to their branch Clubs in Washington and Chicago as supervisor. During that time she created and made about 10 costumes a month — each original, each different — never a duplication.

Daughter Kim is now 18 and a sophomore at Pitt, specializing in political science. The twins, each 14, go to Allderdice. Twin Jene wants to be an actor, of all things. Their lovable grandma Stephanie, young at 80, insists on doing all the cooking — and maybe a little disciplining — as she's done for 18 years.

Our neighbor plans to start a class teaching details of sewing — how to cut, fit and whatever else goes into high-class dressmaking. She wants five women for two-hour sessions. With several sewing-machines available in their cheerful 12-room home which they own, everything should be coming up roses. For the style-conscious ladies who don't like themselves in "boughten" clothes, Anita will whip up beautiful outfits. But the price, though right, comes high. As they say, if you want class you pay for it.

Good luck to the Fellners. And may Anita's women of fashion look lovelier than spring.

Dr. Dorothy C. Finkelhor
Code In Doze? Don't Call Her!

This is being written on a sunny spring day with blossoms bursting out all over. A nice time to learn about a remarkable neighbor. She's Dr. Dorothy C. Finkelhor of Beechwood Blvd. But listen: If you have a "code-in-your-doze" don't call her. She's not an M.D. But just as important. Maybe even more so. Let's see now.

The former Dorothy Cimberg is a native New Yorker. In her teen years she was so confused about what to study for which career, she flunked high school. You know — a drop-out. She became interested in a political party which aimed to attract college students. And attended one of their dances. That enchanted evening who sauntered in but a tall, handsome student from Columbia University. None other than Herbert Finkelhor of our city whose family was well and favorably known — and still is. Cupid must have lurked in the shadows because soon as Herb met Dottie, they could have danced all night. Six weeks later (July 12, 1922) they became Mr. and Mrs., starting housekeeping in our city. After a year, they went back to New York. But before long returned here "for good".

Love, a many splendored thing, inspired the young bride to make up for those lost high school years. Starting from scratch she enrolled at Duquesne University. By the time she reached the senior year, guess what? Baby Carol arrived. Mom somehow continued until graduation with a bachelor's and master's degree. Then on to graduate Pitt with a Ph. D. in Education. Meantime, at separate intervals, two more babies arrived: Joanne and Naomi. Needing a nurse for the youngsters she advertised, offering secretarial training in exchange for registered nursing service. A hundred replies rolled in. That lead to a Business School which she and Herb founded in 1933 — a month before the nation's banks closed down. No one had any money. The initial enrollment totaled eight girls. Between teaching, Dorothy wrote three books, the last one titled "How to Make Your Emotions Work for You," published in 1952. She lectured on that subject here, there, everywhere. Last year it was translated into Italian: "Como Utilizzari Propri Sentimenti". And was equally popular in Italy.

In 1960, Dr. Finkelhor with capable Herbert and a board of trustees, founded Point Park Junior College. Six years later it became the popular Point Park College. After seven years — against the wishes of the trustees — Dorothy retired. Then she and Herb took an extended trip around the world, including Russia and Yugoslavia. And of course Israel. Upon return, Herbert continued his activities and became Educational Consultant to six schools: Duffs College with branches in Jamaica and Barbados, Britannica Academy (one in Chicago, another here), and the John Robert Powers Charm and Secretarial Schools.

Daughter Carol, now Mrs. William Ferguson, graduated from Chicago University and Carnegie-Mellon. Joanne (Mrs. Arthur Blum) is a graduate of Brandeis with a bachelor's degree, getting her master's at Harvard. Naomi, the youngest, is a Pitt graduate and is working for her master's at Villa Nova. There are two grandchildren — and one on the way. All live in our city. Winters grand-dad takes the kids ice skating in Bridgeville. Or maybe they take him!

Meantime Dottie, still bursting with vitality with little to do, outsmarted dat old debbil boredom. She up and became Sponsor and Consultant to Britannica Academy in the Clark Bldg. It's a four-year high school. The Britannica people revised the textbooks and learning material into what is known as Program Learning. That way students progress at their own best learning rate. The bright ones aren't held back by the slow learners. And the latter are not made to feel inferior. Among the 75 students many have completed four years in two. All enjoy the experience of learning.

The Finkelhors still do much traveling. Twice again they returned to Israel. The last time they had the emotional experience of attending Yom Kippur services at the renowned Wall in Jerusalem.

Until recently when they sold their 400-acre farm, our neighbors used natural vegetables only. You know, without harmful fertilizing chemicals. They don't smoke. And drink only mountain spring water. Seldom do they eat between meals. No wonder Dorothy is still beautiful and Herb youthfully streamlined.

May they live to be 125, as it says in the Good Book.

Marguerite Fischer

Lady Cop, In the French Style

Ask a little boy what he wants to be when he grows up and mostly he'll say "a police-man."

But a policewoman? Ugh! No glamour. They'd rather be Cary Grant's leading lady— or some such. And that's probably the situation everywhere.

Everywhere, that is, except at Forbes and Wightman. There the red-cheeked little cherubs on their way to and from the Wightman and St. Edmunds schools think a policewoman is plenty okay.

That's because the pretty blue-eyed blonde in uniform who guides them across the street or waves them to a stand-still is Mrs. Rudolf (Marguerite) Fischer. She's from Paris. Wrapped in a thick yellow raincoat, maybe six sweaters, high boots, three pairs of gloves and a double woolen helmet, the French chic is completely hidden.

But little girls — and sometimes boys too — sense such things. And being a police-lady looks pretty good to them.

Trained for her duties by a veteran policeman for two whole weeks, Mrs. Fischer is now a veteran herself. Little Stevie, Wayne, Nancy, Carol, Lois, Jane and the many others whom she knows by name, are safely confident under her watchful eyes.

She's there daily during the school-rush hours: 7:45 to 9; 11:30 to 1; 3:20 to 4:20. On Jewish holidays there is a substitute.

Our Forbes-Wightman policelady was born in Paris, attended and graduated from public school there; and as a teenager worked in a pastry shop.

Husband Rudolph is an Austrian. He went to school in Vienna and later worked at Leathercraft, becoming expert in his trade. The Hitler invasion cut short his career.

Of Jewish faith, he was an easy target for the German storm-troopers. He fled to Paris, joined the French Foreign Legion and served in Indo-China for seven years. At war's end he returned to Paris. Without relatives and a lonely bachelor, Rudolph Fis-cher became a daily patron at Marguerite's bakery. He liked French pastry — and Mar-guerite. In 1947 they became Mr. & Mrs. Nine years later the Fischers and their three boys migrated to the U.S., became full-fledged American citizens and settled in our neighborhood at Flemington Ave. in a home they now own.

Mr. Fischer works at the Blumcraft Co. on Melwood St. where his leathercraft know-how is in demand. The Fischers' pride and joy are their sons. Michael, 15 and 14 year old Gerard attend Southside Vocational High, learning baking. They studied Hebrew at our neighborhood Institute, Forbes near Denniston— and were Bar Mitzvah there.

The youngest son, Bernard, 12 is an excellent student and goes to Allderdice. After school he attends the Hebrew Institute, and following his brother's footsteps will be-come Bar Mitzvah there next July 4th.

And now pull up your chairs, everybody — and listen to this. After graduation all three boys will return to Paris. There they'll enroll in the most famous cooking school in all France— to become chefs. They won't have to hurdle the language barrier be-cause their parlez-vous is perfect. And their loving Parisian grandma will open her home to them.

Meantime the Fischers are a close-knit family. They go ice-skating at South Park and the Civic Arena. Summers they take week-end overnight camping trips. And they love swimming. They do things together. They even pray together.

And oh, yes. When police-mom Marguerite comes home during the noon hour, lunch is ready. Her future French chefs prepare it.

Our community is proud of this wonderful family and wish them well.

Dr. Edwin R. Fisher

Regards Transplants Issue for Scientists

Ever since Dr. Barnard's first human heart transplant in South Africa the world has been watching, hoping, pondering. Thus a recent Channel 11 discussion on "The Moral Implications of Heart Transplants" is worth noting. Newscaster Wes Sorginson guided the discussion.

The panelists were a prominent lawyer, a Catholic priest and two medical specialists. And since one of the latter is a nearby neighbor (we're partial to neighbors, of course) you'll want to learn about him. He's none other than Dr. Edwin R. Fisher of Solway St. He's a Pathology Professor at Pitt. Pathology, as you may or may not know, is the study of diseases, their nature, causes, progress, etc.—the foundation of all medical practices.

In his early forties, Dr. Fisher's education, postgraduate training, hospital and teaching appointments as well as his Awards and Societies' memberships would fill a book. To name a few, he was given the Park-Davis Award in Experimental Pathology in 1963. And several years later our Junior Chamber of Commerce named him "Man of the Year in Medicine."

When a little tyke of 3, Edwin had his curls snipped off by a neighborhood barber, S. R. Hall. Hall, now 80 still does barbering in his Forbes Avenue shop. And still trims our professor's hair. Long ago Dr. Fisher's devoted parents — Reuben and Anna — lived on Sherbrook St. when there were only two or three houses on the street. Now they live on Beechwood Blvd. Son Edwin went to Colfax, graduated Allderdice and earned his BS and MD degrees at Pitt.

After interning at Mercy Hospital he went to the Cleveland Clinic for two years of post-graduate work in Pathology and to the National Institute of Health in Bethesda, Md. for another two years. Then he returned to the Cleveland Clinic as a staff member. In 1954 he was called to Pitt as professor of Pathology. He's also Chief of Laboratory Service at our V. A. Hospital. Dr. Fisher had many opportunities to settle in other cities, but as he says "You can take the boy out of Pittsburgh but not Pittsburgh out of the boy". He loves our city and Squirrel Hill in particular.

Our neighbor's lovely missus is the former Carole Levy. And you'll never believe it. She enjoys being a full-time housewife without outside help. Their large old house which they themselves artistically redecorated has 7 rooms, 2 baths, 2 attic rooms and a basement. Mom's the best cook ever and pop is general maintenance man. He's expert in plumbing. painting, repairing. You name it, he can do it. He used to play basketball at Allderdice and baseball at Pitt. Now it's golf. and again you'll not believe it. Wife Carole is almost as good a golfer as he. They enjoy the game together. The Fishers have two lively girls. Marjorie, 12 goes to Allderdice. Like her daddy she loves golfing. Abbe Dava is 9 and attends Wightman. She's an excellent figure-skater.

Dr. Fisher's older brother Bernard — also a Sq. Hiller — is a professor of Surgery at Pitt. Both do research together. Dr. Edwin is invited to lecture all over the country — 3 or 4 times a month. He just returned from a lecture trip in San Francisco.

So what is the moral implications of heart transplants? Dr. Fisher feels the decision to do transplants rests in the hands of the scientists involved rather than any legislative body, para-medical group or well-meaning spectators. Coming from an authority—and a neighbor yet — who inspires confidence, need more be said?

Armon F. Frederickson

Interesting Family Settles in Our District

When a brilliant college professor from the Mid-West is called to the University of Pittsburgh to become chairman of its geology dept. in new Langley Hall, it's a great asset to our city.

And when he has a beautiful wife and five lovely, lively daughters, it's even better. But when this amazingly interesting family settles in our very own neighborhood, we really like to brag a little — and want you to know about them.

Dr. Armon F. Frederickson, a graduate of world-famous M.I.T. came here with his family from Tulsa, Okla. two and a half years ago. His family consists of wife Mary and their five daughters:

Mary, 18 is a Pitt Freshman and works part time in its botany dept.; Clover 17, a senior at Allderdice has worked a year in Pitt's Biology Dept.; Penny, 15, Allderdice sophomore is a professional model and has performed on "Luncheon At The Ones". Kimberly, 11, is in the 6th grade at Linden school, and baby Sigrid, 7, is in grade 2. And there's "Granny," Mrs. Frederickson's lovable mother.

They live in a 14-room house at Beechwood Blvd. It's an old-style house, to be sure; but making the inside into a charmingly liveable home was no problem for the talented Fredericksons — particularly since wife Mary's life-time hobby has been art. Even now she is taking an art course at Pitt.

Thus "Doc" Frederickson (as his students call him) is master of all he surveys — one man with 7 adoring women. And he loves it!

His daughters were members of the Tulsa Figure Skating Club and all are expert fencers. Clover's special hobby has been collecting all sorts of animals.

Until recently her collection included a pet monkey, an Iguana lizzard 3½ ft. long; an opposum, dogs, kittens, sea horses and all kinds of South American birds.

But when the menagerie became too hard to handle the whole shebang was carefully transferred to Biloxi, Miss. to be used as pets at the biological stations there. The transfer was preceded with tears, sighs and regrets, from all the Fredericksons.

Prior to their coming to Pittsburgh, the entire family had traveled to many far corners of the world — for geological research and the enriching experience which travel affords.

They lived in Spain long enough for the girls to learn Spanish fluently. They spent a year in Oslo, Norway; and took a 6-week geological excursion on the northern coast of Africa.

They recently returned from a 3-month trip by car to Mexico—their third trek there. They traveled over 100,000 miles, covering deserts, swamps, rivers, bays, open ocean; and visited dense jungle and completely barren uplands. Mary and Penny helped in the geological research and Clover was biological assistant — with all the details that go with it.

And because many nights the group slept outdoors, the girls prepared the sleeping bags before and after use. Since they could speak Spanish, traveling and shopping were made easier. None got sick, got lost or got frightened.

Dr. Frederickson left Dec. 1st for Japan, to organize an exchange of geology professors and students, between that country and Pitt.

When home, "Fred" and Mary go to all the football games. The daughters attend every Pitt game. At daughter Mary's graduation patio party last June, 100 young guests showed up. The majority were young men!

Asked if the girls go steady, they answer: "Daddy says no—it's too soon." The father is often asked if he wished he had some boys to balance up his all-girl family. He smiles and says: "When I sit down to dinner, I am one man with 7 adoring women giving me love and affection. Who needs boys?"

Well Dr. Frederickson — we don't like to disrupt your cozy situation but there will be boys. With your 5 lovely daughters, your 4 telephones and the bells ringing, you'll have boys allright.

Ann Robin Friedland
Cary Grant's Leading Lady Soon?

B-r-r-r! This is being written during one of those freezing days — and Dear Me, the Snow is falling. So, let's warm your hearts with a neighborhood personality just 11 years young.

Not only is she sugar and spice but chock-full of talent too in music — in dancing. And right off she has the charming name of Ann Robin. Ann Robin Friedland.

Her parents are Irvin and Marilyn Friedland. Dad is with the Pennex Products, a well-known drug firm in nearby Verona. There there's kid brother Paul, 8, who likes football and rock 'n roll. Both attend Colfax School.

The piano fascinated Ann Robin in as early as age one. She picked out tunes by ear. At the ripe old age of four she began piano lessons seriously. Progress came fast. Final polish was perfected by the widely-known piano teacher Aaron Gross of Hobart Street.

Our talented little neighbor studied ballet with Mrs. Karl Kritz formerly of Chatham. Now she's continuing with Mario Melodia and Bill Bailey. Voice lessons were with the late Julia Bakaleinikoff. Classical, of course; but she loves modern jazz and rock 'n roll.

She even bought a guitar and starts strumming at the drop of a hat The Beatles' pictures adorn her bedroom walls—especially Ringo's. Now that he up and got himself married, there likely will be some changes made.

Ann Robin inherited her musical talent from Mom, Marilyn. Often they entertain together as a "Mother-Daughter" duet team. Their voices blend perfectly in harmony. Listeners enthusiastically rush up to Mr. Friedland and say: "Your daughter is simply wonderful." Then — "Oh, YOU sing well, too." No professional jealousy, however.

Our young neighbor entertains singly too. She was guest performer at a Hadassah Group 2 donor tea. Last January she was the youngest "soloist" with the All-City Chorus at Stephen Foster Memorial. And she brought youthful charm to our neighborhood Anathan House and the Jewish Home for the Aged. And made those dear hearts and gentle people feel young again.

Ann Robin Friedland is now on the "Bar Mitzvah" circuit a'la the Borsht Belt. At such happy gatherings the guests look, they listen, they like.

Would Ann Robin like to be Cary Grant's leading lady? No answer. Just an engaging smile. So it could be yes.

Michael & Lois Friedlander
Double Feature For An Afternoon

Already, through your NEWS you've met 200 fabulous neighbors. Repeat: 200! Anyone who thinks there are no more such around here should be asked to leave town. To prove the point, today you'll learn about not just one but two remarkable neighbors— A Double Feature for a Thursday Afternoon, as it says on TV. Meet Michael and Lois Friedlander of Saline St., married scarcely a year ago.

The young husband, a professional photographer is Chairman of the Art Department at the South Campus of Community College, West Mifflin. And teaches Art History and Photography there. A graduate of Pitt and with an M.A. from West Virginia U., he is currently photographer for The Pittsburgh Ballet Theatre. For the best reason in the world. His lovely and talented misses, the former Lois Friedman of Harrisburg is a ballet dancer. She teaches Music Appreciation there, and Ballet at the Pittsburgh Playhouse and Point Park College. An accomplished pianist, she studied under Natalie Phillips — you know, mom of the youthful and already famous violinist Danny Phillips.

Lois originally planned being an M.D. and earned a BS degree in Bacteriology from Pitt. Then, about three years ago she met Nicholas Petrov, founder and now Artistic Director of The Pittsburgh Ballet Theatre. Working nights so she could practice the piano during the day, she started to take a few ballet lessons. Just for fun. Soon she was hooked. And joined Petrov's Company. At first it was a small group. Now there are 45 dancers. The younger girls in the Company that are high school students at Point Park College divide their time between school and ballet. December 13 and 19 they performed "The Nutcracker Suite" to audiences that packed Syria Mosque. The dancers were from all over our city, with two big stars from the New York City Ballet: Edward Villella and Violette Verdy. Also Alexander Philipov, the youthful dancer from the Moiseyev Ballet who defected from the USSR and joined the Pittsburgh Ballet Theatre. He is now permanent guest-artist-in-residence. They'll perform again at the Mosque Feb. 26 in "Swan Lake", with additional stars.

Last year Michael had an Art Exhibit of his Spanish photographs at our Pittsburgh Playhouse. This year he exhibited Ballet pictures at the Mosque. Although his photos have appeared in various local and national publications, he laughingly comments: "I really can't take all the credit for those high leaps. It takes the ballet dancer to get up there." He's never "on stage" but very much in evidence behind the scenes. Lois suggests whom to photograph. And has taught him much about ballet. Her greatest desire now is to be a superb ballet teacher. She gets a thrill teaching dance and transmitting her enthusiasm to youngsters who are experiencing their first exposure to formal lessons.

How did our two talented neighbors meet? Through Mike's two and her three pet cats—believe it or not—with ancient Athenian names too long to spell out. The day before leaving for Spain for picture-taking, he was having dinner at a friend's home. Lois walked in to return a plate she had borrowed. Michael was worried what to do about leaving his cats for a whole month. So guess what? Lois offered to "cat-sit" during his absence. Upon his return, his pets had learned to love her and she them. It didn't take our photographer much time to get the message. Soon he started dating the beautiful "sitter" and before long they married.

Pooling their piggy-banks (and the cats too), together with a loan from a big bank they made a down-payment on their 7 room house (3 bedrooms and 2 baths). And added a large poodle named Sheba to their menagerie. There's plenty room and comfort for everybody. After all, fiddler-on-the-roof matchmakes deserve the best. All our neighborhood animals should have it so good!

And now get a load of this. When Mike's beard gets too thick, too bushy and too long, who do you think trims it? His B.W. (beautiful wife). But don't tell the neighborhood barbers."

Mrs. Alter (Janice) Friedman
Creative Writing One of Her Many Talents

High food prices got you down? And are you still heart-broken over the Pirates' Dream of What Might Have Been and Almost Was? Well, as the saying goes, count your blessings. That you live in the most interesting neighborhood, with the most remarkable personalities. Like who? Like for instance Mrs. Alter (Janice) Friedman of Murdoch Rd. Mrs. Friedman, the former Janice Segal is what you call a veritable dynamo. Quadruplets together couldn't accomplish what she herself has done.

Janice met bachelor Alter Friedman in 1951, on a blind date. And right from the start, it took. A year later they became Mr. and Mrs.

Mr. Friedman is the owner of two Ladies Ready-to-Wear stores— in neighboring New Kensington and Natrona Heights. Janice herself, for 19 years has been running a business of her own — Maternity Fashions, in the Jenkins Arcade. She had learned the ropes of business at Pitt's Bureau of Retail Training during her senior year. Prior to Pitt she graduated Allderdice where she was a drum-majorette, of all things. Through the years Mrs. Friedman has had many occasions to model her Maternity dresses, being a mother of four. Daughter Amy is now 13 and goes to Allderdice. Betsey, 10 and Cathy, eight both go to Wightman school. So does little Johnny, all of 4½ — in the school's nursery.

So what else is news? Plenty. Creative writing talent can be added to our neighbor's many-stringed bow. Janice has the unique ability to write special material for all and sundry.

Asked by the Rodef Shalom Sisterhood to "write something" for a membership affair, up came a clever comedy skit titled "Any Thursday." It centered around Rabbi Freehof's lovely wife Lillian — as a surprise to her.

Directed by our fabulous Don Brockett, it was an instant hit. For the Tri-State Israel Bonds shows in the surrounding towns she wrote "The Fiddler," with Don. Presuming him to be Jewish, an enthusiastic lady in the audience, thrilled with the show, ran up to him and said: "Only we Jewish people can appreciate the play's real meaning." With a straight face Don answered: "I'm a Catholic. But isn't everybody a little bit Jewish?"

Janice also wrote a show called "No Strings" for the Ladies Hospital Aid Society's membership drive luncheon at Green Oaks Country Club. For the Council of Jewish Women's luncheon at the Holiday House she produced and directed an original skit "How to Succeed in Council with Estelle Really Trying." She also wrote a lot of undergraduate shows at Pitt.

And do you remember the fabulous Review at Temple Sinai last Spring — "The Sounds of Sinai" that had them rolling in the aisles three nights in succession? Janice created it. And for the special kind of humor which our inimitable Esther Lapiduss puts across in Kramer's "Back Room," credit Janice and Don Brockett for the laugh-producers.

Deeply sun-tanned from golfing and a month at Margate during the summer, her flashing blue eyes show off more than ever our neighbor's dynamic and enthusiastic personality.

The Friedmans have a full time housekeeper in their nine-room home, but Janice loves to slip into the kitchen and whip up a delicous meal.

Husband Alter is no longer mad at her for doing so much. And come January is planning to take her on a trip to the Orient with a stop-over in Hawaii. It's likely he's wise enough to know "if you can't lick 'em — join 'em."

Mrs. M. H. Friedman

Talent, Like Roses, Comes Up In June

It's June and everything's coming up roses. And talent too. Much talent. Our neighborhood personality of the week has been blest with — and developed — not just one skill but three. And yet, what do you know — she says she's not important enough to be written up. Humility, in our book, makes her extra special.

So let's learn about Mrs. Minna Hirschfield Friedman of Crombie St. — singer, pianist, artist. The first two are the result of excellent training and she's been teaching them in her home studio. Her art is self-taught. Out of her own head, as the saying goes. Long before the Weinstein tragic fire, 22 of her paintings graced the restaurant walls. Quite a few were sold. Her 5-room home looks like a miniature art gallery.

Everywhere are pictures by Minna Friedman. On wood, aluminum, glass, using oil and acrylic. A nearby neighbor, lovely wife of Rev. Gorodinsky of the Poale Zedeck synagogue asked to "take lessons". She was told if she got 10 pupils an art class would be started. Early next morning 10 would-be artists showed up with paint and brush. At season's end they had progressed so well and were so thrilled they gave their teacher a thank-you luncheon. She's now continuing art lessons in an outside studio with a much larger class.

Minna studied piano and voice at Carnegie Tech (C-MU). A lyric dramatic soprano she continued voice at Curtis Institute, Phila. Her teacher, a Viennese opera singer arranged an audition for her with the NYC Light Opera Co. But Fate intervened. Two weeks prior, on a street-car headed for a lesson she was dreaming of a great career.

Suddenly, a huge truck collided with the car. The shock injured the main nerve of her vocal chords. Audition cancelled, she spent a month in a hospital. But youth is wonderful. Courage even more so. She came through with flying colors to continue singing. In 1926 our singer was one out of 60 chosen to sing with hundreds of others in "The Miracle" produced by famous Max Reinhardt at the Phila. Opera House. When KDKA first opened here, Mina Hirschfield sang ballads and played piano each week for 4 months. And started teaching.

She also had a week-end class in Weirton, W.Va. There Cupid started to make with his arrows toward the dark-eyed raven-haired music teacher. Louis Friedman of Manchester, Eng. maneuvered an introduction to her. He owned a men's specialty shop on Weirton's Main St. Five months later they married. The young bride stopped teaching and concentrated on being a housewife and later the mother of two lively boys.

After 17 years of happiness life's eventuality struck. Mrs. Friedman was sadly widowed. She returned to our city with her boys to resume teaching. Here are excerpts from one of her pupils of 6 years (quote): "What a teacher! She draws out your abilities by dancing to the tune of a Nocturne, cautioning 'Not too fast now — keep it graceful'. At other times she guides you by SINGING the difficult passages. Then again she CONDUCTS, dramatically urging you to achieve expression. Like a maestro".

Minna's sons are grown now. They too are talented. Ronald is a graduate architect and writer. He wrote for the Danny Kaye and Jonathan Winters Shows. Also Bill Cosby, Dick Van-Dyke and last year Robert Goulet's Specials. Son, Alvin, won a scholarship from the NYC Neighborhood Drama Playhouse. He studied painting at the School of Visual Arts (NYC). And invented several printing machines for advertising. He's now contemplating the writing field.

Our neighbor shares her home with a younger sister, Ruth Hirschfield Klein — a pretty red-head no less. She too paints and plays the piano. Should you get an invite to their home for dinner, say yes immediately. Minna is the best cook ever. Health and calorie-wise in the bargain.

Honestly, ours is the luckiest neighborhood.

Dr. Ely M. Gelbard

Nuclear Physicist Has Many Distinctions

This is being written as the Rain in Spain is falling Mainly in Squirrel Hill. So it might be good to put a little sunshine into it by telling you about an outstanding neighbor. Meet Dr. Ely M. Gelbard of Normlee Place. First off be warned that his work is not understood by the average layman. But just for the heck of it let's give it a try, if only to get a little educated and to appreciate more than ever what remarkable neighbors we have.

Dr. Gelbard, only 44 and a physicist, is consultant in the Reactor Development and Analysis Group at the Bettis Laboratory which Westinghouse operates for the Atomic Energy Commission. April of last year our neighbor was one of five scientists to receive a Nuclear Award Medal at the Carnegie Institute of our nation's Capital. The prize carried with it $5,000 cash, a gold medal and a citation reading: "For outstanding creative contribution in the development of modern methods for the design of nuclear reactors and for his deep insight into physical processes, his mastery of computational techniques and effective application of theoretical models to important problems and experiments". Do you understand? Neither does anyone else except those smart fellows. The Award was announced by Dr. Glenn T. Seaborg, chairman of the AEC. Last June he was awarded another medal. But that's not all. His charming missus (the former Helen Galbavy) is a mathematician in the same Laboratory. She specializes in computer programming and her husband does a lot of work in that field.

Now let's go back a little. Ely graduated high school in NYC, then went to City College there. During WW II he served Uncle Sam three years as a radar technician and instructor in U. S. and Canada. At war's end he graduated from the University of Chicago. By then his outstanding ability began showing and Westinghouse called him here. Prior to then and before she knew Ely existed, Helen graduated Hunter College with a B. A. And came here to work at Bettis, and attending evening classes at Pitt's Graduate School. This was September 1954. Ely came there the preceding June. Working together so closely, soon Cupid started buzzing around. Remember that nice Hungarian restaurant upstairs at Murray and Bartlett which later burned down? That's where Ely took Helen for dinner on their first date. But they didn't cause the fire. In 1957 they married.

Often a husband wants to discuss his work with his wife but the little woman knows from nuthin' about it. And he's frustrated. No so with the Gelbards. They speak the same language, as the saying goes. And share many delightful discussions of their experiences in the work they both so well understand. Our neighbors haven't as yet added to the population explosion. Helen enjoys gardening and household duties, assisted by her devoted mom Tessie who lives with them. At times they get outside help. The master of the house is Ghengis, a large stray dog who wondered in, liked it there and remained, endearing himself to all — even their two cats Mosca and Chebbie.

Lovers of travel, our neighbors have been almost everywhere. Before the war in Cambodia they vacationed there. Then to Hong Kong, Singapore, Bali and Bangkok. Last summer they spent a month in Japan. They saw much of that beautiful country, its magnificent Buddhist temples, majestic mountains. And spent one steaming day at

Expo 70 with about 800,000 others. What about those famous public baths where men and women bathe together — you should pardon the expression? Skipped it this time. At leaving Japan which is filled with so much charm, they said "sayonara" with tugs at their heartstrings. Now that they're back, let's say "no sho'-koku". In case you don't savvy Japanese, it means WELCOME HOME.

Our community is proud of the Gelbards and wishes them the best now and in the years ahead.

Mrs. Joseph (Mary) Gertner
Their Story is of Courage and Devotion

Today's article about a remarkable neighbor will bring you no chuckles. It's likely your eyes will fill with tears. But they will be tears of wonderment, admiration and pride that such a personality is in our midst.

Our unusual neighbor is Mrs. Joseph Gertner, a seamstress living at Douglas St.

Her husband, skilled in leathercraft, works for the Blumcraft Co. He works, that is, in between trips to the hospital.

He is afflicted with a broken spine and glacoma of the eyes. Cause of his affliction will become clear in a moment. Their son Morris is 14 and a student at Allderdice.

Now let's go back to the year 1940 in a little town of Luzk, Poland.

There lived Joseph Gertner, a Jewish merchant in the malt exporting business. In the same town, in a little cottage with her widowed aunt, lived Mary Chodin, a Roman Catholic. She had just graduated from a dress-making school.

Came the Hitler hordes. The school was converted into a concentration camp. Joseph Gertner, together with 650 others "guilty" of being Jewish, were herded into the Nazi camp.

Grain in 200-lb. sacks were stored in the basement. These sacks had to be carried to the fourth floor. Joseph and his brethren had to drag them up, day in and day out. Some simply collapsed from exhaustion; others who faltered were kicked to death.

The rest, after two years, were murdered. Only Joseph and two companions are alive today.

Why and how did these escape? Through God's mercy and Mary Chodin's compassionate courage.

From her aunt's store, Mary slipped food through the barbed wire fence to the prisoners. "What could I do?" she said in a recent interview. "They were people — and they were hungry."

Joseph begged her help to escape. On a cold November evening in 1942 Mary Chodin tricked her way into the compound, using a restaurant worker's card she had "bought" for a pound of butter.

Plans were secretly made. The next evening, through a hole in the fence made with Electrician's pliers, Joseph and his two friends slipped to safety.

In the darkness they hastily made their way to Mary's cottage, hiding in an underground room dug for them. She burned their lice-infested clothes, sewed new ones, hauled water for them every day, sneaked them food.

She did this for a year and a half.

In 1944, when the Russians occupied Poland, Mary's "guests" came out of hiding. One, Jischak Halpern is now practicing law in Israel. The other, a young medical student, is behind the Iron Curtain and contact with him has been completely lost.

And Joseph Gertner? Sympathy being a kin to love, Mary Chodin became his wife. Hating anti-Semitism, she embraced the Jewish faith.

After years of moving in uncertainty, and with the kind cooperation of a Pittsburgh cousin, Louis Berez, the Gertners came to the U. S. They are American citizens now — and our good neighbors.

Son Morris was Bar Mitzvah last May at the Poale Zedeck Synagogue.

His first present was a check for $100 from lawyer Halpern of Israel — one of the men whose life Mary Gertner had saved. Morris hopes to study medicine, even though it will mean working his way through college. In their modest Douglas Street home mother Gertner has several roomers to help with the mortgage. And she takes in sewing.

Now dry your tears — and bring your dress-making to our remarkable neighbor. She can even make plunging neck-lines for the stylish-at-heart.

Dr. Robert H. Gibson
Psychologist Here Aiding the Blind

This is being written on the first cool day after those sizzlers, when our Pirates nosed into first place. And the fans developed pennant fever.

A delightful day to learn about a fabulous neighbor living around the corner at Wightman St. He's Dr. Robert H. Gibson, associate professor of psychology at Pitt and listed in "Who's Who" in American Science. And what's more, his lovely young missus, the former Janice Thorne, also is a professor at Pitt.

Some husbands, when they want to "talk shop" with their wives are greatly frustrated because the little woman knows from nuthin' about his work. With the Gibsons it's altogether different. They both speak the same language, as the saying goes. And they enjoy sharing their respective experiences.

Janice Gibson is an educational and child psychologist. Which makes her an ideal mother. The beautiful Gibson youngsters are bright, happy and well-adjusted. Robin Lynn, 8, goes to Colfax School in the Workshop Program. Mark Gregory, all of 4, attends the Y-IKC nursery school and Rodef Shalom summer camp.

Also adjusted is their pet Siamese cat, Snowflake. And her bosom friend, Fuzzy, a miniature half-schnauzer, half-terrier. But the most adjusted personality is their capable full-time housekeeper, Mrs. Hattie Daniels. In such educational environment, she and her husband are putting their own three children through college.

The Gibsons came here five years ago from New England. During the Korean War Bob served Uncle Sam and studied electronics in the Navy. Janice was a graduate at Brown University (an Ivy League school). They married in 1957 before both graduated Brown. Then went together to the University of Virginia in Charlottesville 8 at the foothills of the Skyline Drive. There they both received their Ph.D.'s.

Summers they lived in a tent on the Drive. Robin Lynn was "almost" born on top of a mountain. Bob still has the tent. Recently friends who just married, spent their honeymoon in it — near the same mountain.

As research project director at Pitt, Dr. Gibson is working on a communication system using the skin that would help the blind. He says people perceive more through their skin than they suspect. The secret of his research is a device he built that lets him send electric currents directly into the nerves that carry "touch sensations" to brain.

He is also studying the effects of temperatures on touch and pain sensitivity. He invented a computer to be used for communication purposes with astronauts and the infantry.

Our neighbor scientist has dark hair and eyes. Scarcely 34, he's lithe, quick, imaginative and diligent, with a sense of obligation. And is blest with many extra talents. In their 11 room home which they own, he built a seven-foot high-fidelity speaker — one of his hobbies.

A photography buff, he built a dark room in the basement and does his own developing. He owns a German Porsche car. And works on the engine of a racing car in which a friend races. On the side, he himself does a bit of racing — but not in the vicinity of Forbes & Murray.

On cool evenings Bob and his missus bicycle in the neighborhood. What else, Pussycat? He also plays the violin. Some say better than Jack Benny.

The Gibsons just returned from three weeks in Europe, while the kids stayed with grandma in New England. The British government invited our neighbor to give a lecture at a conference in London, as consultant. An eminent professor at Oxford traveled 60 miles to London to hear him.

And was so impressed that he invited Dr. Gibson to leave his laboratory for a year and come work with him. Because he loves Pittsburgh, the university and his work here, he did not take advantage of such an honor. At least not now. Later? Who knows.

We hope we shall be able to brag about the Pirates come World Pennant days. Mean time, we sure are proud of our neighbors; the Gibsons. And wish them the best of everything.

Mrs. Hyman Ginsberg
Never Under-Estimate Power of 'Hadassah'

As they say, never underestimate the power of women. Hadassah women. Since last April 250 of them have been knee-deep planning, working, arranging Chapter's annual Donor celebrating Hadassah's 61st year. And you may be sure it will be the greatest. With internationally-known entertainers it's to be held March 17 and, of course, at the magnificent Heinz Hall. Since most of the responsibility for its success falls on the chairman, let's first learn a little about this fabulous gal. She's none other than Mrs. Hyman (Mimi) Ginsberg.

The former Mimi Seiner, born in Magee Hospital, lived in our community since age 5 until marriage. She attended Colfax, graduated Allderdice and later Pitt's School of Social Work. Her first job was with the IKC then located on Forward Ave. One enchanted summer she went to the "Y" Emma Farm Camp. And there, guess what? She met Hy Ginsberg, a Duquesne U. pharmaceutical grad. Three months later (1949) they stood under a hupah at Beth Shalom synagogue and said "I do" to Rabbi Goodman Rose (of blessed memory). Later, when the young husband ditched pharmacy to become a scrap dealer they moved to Stanton Heights where they still live.

But Mimi's well-known parents (Jennie and Tom Seiner) continue to be our Wightman St. neighbors. Mimi and Hy have been blessed with four interesting children: Jay now 21 is a senior at C-MU. Ellen is 18 and a freshman at Chatham. She loves to sew and after the Spectacular she'll teach mom sewing. Samuel is 13 and in the 7th grade at Sunnyside. David, 7, is in his first grade at Hillel. Their mother joined Hadassah a year after marriage and by now hers is a 3-generation Hadassah life-membership family. She was president of Group 7 (now Lieba) 12 years ago; Chapter VP 3 times also VP of Program, Organization and Membership. The generation-gap in her dedicated family is conspicuous by its absence. If supper is late and the phone bells constantly ring, all understand — and are the prouder for it. Mimi herself says she has received far more than given in her Hadassah work. But she warns: Don't take a big job unless there's family cooperation. She has it from hers — 100 per cent plus.

As you know, Hadassah is dedicated to the survival of Israel. Surrounded by enemies with the constant threat of war that little country — the only democracy in the Middle East — has accomplished wonders. And has shown the world how to use science and technology to improve man's life on earth. Recently the Hadassah Medical Center developed a blood-test that detects cancer quicker than through any other method.

We could go on and on but space is limited. And you want to know who's on the Spectacular program? First it will be "Hedva & David", an Israeli song-and-dance team honoring Israel's 25th anniversary. The other highlight is the one and only Marilyn Michaels, internationally-known song-stylist. She's been on the Mike Douglas and Merv Griffin Shows. And with the Hollywood Squares.

Chapter's quota is $142,000. Don't anyone skip the Spectacular. March 17 is Purim, a time for rejoicing. Any attire is appropriate for this exciting evening. In other words, wear what you want. And have yourself a ball.

See you March 17th, 8 p.m., Heinz Hall.

Earle R. Gister
Tech Finds a New Drama Master

A funny thing happened to a talented neighbor on his way to Carnegie Tech recently. He was named head of the Department of Drama in the College of Fine Arts.

But actually it wasn't funny. Wonderful is a better word. Because so many will benefit so much from his know-how. So who is this important personality? Earle R. Gister, our neighbor at Beechwood Blvd. He had been serving as associate head for three years. And when his boss, Bob Corrigan, left for New York, Earle was immediately made head man.

Our likable neighbor is tall dark, soft-spoken — with a personality that wins you over in a minute. His hair is black and abundant, but — with apologies to teen-agers — no bangs.

Earle Gister went to Carleton College, Northfield, Minn., the finest in the mid-west. During his junior year he first met Bob Corrigan who was professoring there. After graduating Earle went to Indiana U. for graduate work.

Then came the Korean War. And student Gister became a draftee stationed in Augusta, Ga. In the two years there, many things happened. Especially one. The nurses of the town arranged weekly dances for the army boys. For $1 admission they could have danced all night. But there never were enough girls for the guys that jammed the hall.

That's when soldier Earle — smart fella — used the wisdom of Solomon. He figured he'd wait til the last dance of the month — before pay-day. By then the other fellows would be stone broke. Meantime, of course, holding on to his own dollar.

That night only six guys showed up. And there were gals aplenty. His first dance was with lovely nurse Glynda Oglesby. You guessed it. One date followed another. When Uncle Sam discharged him, Earle went to New Orleans. Bob Corrigan was teaching there at Tulane U. and asked Earle to become managing editor of Tulane Drame Review. Swell. But without Glynda much was lacking. So one fine day he sent her a message which read: "Meet me in New Orleans." And they soon became Mr. and Mrs.

Three years later Corrigan joined Tech and brought Earle along as his assistant. Meantime something new had been added. Two lively sons, Carey and Brian. Their third son, Andrew, is Pittsburgh-born.

As to Tech plays which coach Gister will produce the coming season they will be varied and stimulating. Like for instance, George Feydeau's "Hotel Paradise." And "Don Juan or the Love of Geometry" by Max Hirsch. And others equally interesting.

But the most significant thing that has happened in the Drama Department since Gister came is the establishment of the American Conservatory Theatre, called ACT for short. Tech and the Pittsburgh Playhouse have joined in this exciting experiment — there are only three or four in the entire country.

ACT is also concerned with training actors and technicians who in turn will create new companies. This immediately means jobs. Formerly they had to go to New York for work since there was no ready market here. New York City drains actors waiting for jobs. This is a six-month venture with a budget of $400,000.

With a grant of $115,000 by the Rockefeller Foundation and also additional amounts from local foundations, ACT is "in business" as the saying goes. It offers a great range of plays. As for instance "Tartuffe" which reviewer Harold V. Cohen calls "a treasure". And "Tiny Alice" he says has a shine to it. "Six Characters in Search of an Author," "The Rose Tattoo," "Antignone" and "Noah" are also getting enticing reviews. It's a milestone in Pittsburgh's theatrical achievement, bringing to our city professional excellence to be envied by the world.

What do our neighbor's three youngsters think of their dad's exciting program?

Well, they don't understand as yet what it's all about — and couldn't care less. You see, Carey is just five and is thrilled about starting at the Minadeo School. Andrew has just turned 1½ and ain't talkin'. And as to Brian, who is four and enjoying the Y-IKC Nursery School, it's like this. It's not that he loves his pop less, but he likes Popeye more.

Does Earle Gister have any other interest? Outside interests? Who needs them? All he wants is work. And with such enthusiasm he can't miss. Our community wishes the Gisters well.

Janis Ilene Glick
Local Miss Enjoys Japan Visit

How would you like being just 20, beautiful, unusually bright and the recipient of a Watt Scholarship to visit Japan for 2 months? Not as an ordinary hum-drum gawking tourist but to live in the home of a wonderfully hospitable Japanese family. And learn about that fascinating country through the eyes of its own people. That deserving girl is Janice Ilene Glick, daughter of Mrs. Esther Glick, our neighbor at Phillips Ave. Now in her third year at Chatham majoring in Psychology, she hopes to attend a Graduate School to study Psycho-Linquistics.

The Scholarship is an experiment in international and educational exchange since its founder Donald Watts first introduced a group of American youths to their French and German-speaking counterparts in Switzerland in 1932. Now it's the best-established program of its type in the world. With representatives from over 60 countries involved in the annual exchange of some 5,000 young men and women between our country and those around the globe. It's non-profit, with headquarters in Putny, Vt. The Experiment recognizes that communication is the key to understanding another people and its culture.

The co-ed group of 40 from U. S. met in Oakland, Cal. last June 30. Janis herself paid for her flight that far. From then on, all her expenses were "on the house." Their first stop in Japan was in the Hachioji Inter-University House near Tokyo. There Janis and her group of 11 girls studied Japanese 8 hours a day, 7 days a week — enough to somehow get by with. The first few days, what with the trip's excitement, the new environment and food, several got indigestion. And hurried to the corner drugstore. To help describe their need they pointed to their tummies. Guess what the smart clerk sold them? Birth-control pills! At their House they soon learned of the misunderstanding. Bowing apologetically the clerk quickly made the exchange.

Later the visitors divided into 4 groups, traveling together but staying separately with a Japanese family for a whole month — like with their own. Janis helped cook, went shopping for groceries on their bicycle. Okaasan (mother) taught her Japanese cooking. Their food is healthful, with plenty of vitamins and a minimum of fats and sugar. She went with her "sisters" to take flower arranging, dancing and koto lessons. Once, to surprise her "family" she wanted to bake American chocolate-chip cookies. It took her 4 hours and $5 to get the ingredients. Only to find they had no oven!

So she fried the stuff in sesame seed oil. "Mother" made 5 kimonas for Janis to bring home. She herself brought back dried foods that can be made into hot Japanese menus. Locally the ingredients are hard to come by. From here Janis sent her host family the following: "Sisters" Kazuko and Keiko (12 and 21) got a jump-suit nightgown and a pair of wooden clogs. "Brother" Tooru (16) received an I.D. bracelet. Their parents were sent a book titled "The Family of Man" with pictures of peoples around the world. She also sent them jello custard, Lipton chicken-noodle soup, popcorn, canned potato chips, to name a few.

Their last two weeks were spent sight-seeing throughout Honshu, the central Island of Japan. Janis would have preferred staying with her host family — she had grown to love them so much. But sight-seeing in other places other than where they stayed was a must on the Experimental program. They went to Ise, Nara Osaka Kyoto. Janis even had to spunk to climb Mt. Fuji. There she met climbers from around the world. They shared foods, experiences, scenic beauty. Between travels she accepted the chance to teach English in a Middle-School and work in a Hospital Children's Ward.

Our young neighbor writes regularly in Japanese every two weeks to her much-loved far-off family. And gets interesting letters in return. Will they visit here, as they've been invited many, many times? Without being able to speak English and lack of financial funds, it's regretfully doubtful, at least for now.

Mom Ester Glick, aren't you proud of your lovely daughter? Our entire community is too.

Dr. Herbert S. Gochberg
Pitt Professor Writing a Book

Our neighborhood personality of the week is a tall, easy-to-look-at professor of French literature in our University of Pittsburgh. He's young — scarcely 35 — and remarkably brilliant. He is Dr. Herbert S. Gochberg, called here from the University of Chicago, and honored with an Andrew Mellon post-doctoral fellowship. His family consists of his interesting wife Carol and three lively boys. They live at Beeler St. David, 8 is in his third year at Wightman. Jonathan, 6, is enjoying his first year there. Little Joel is only 2 and hasn't decided yet.

Dr. Gochberg received his Bachelor's degree from the City College of New York; got his Ph.D. at Brown University in Providence, R. I.; spent two years teaching French at Northwestern University, Evanston, Ill. and has been on the faculty of the University of Chicago since 1958.

As a Mellon Fellow, Professor Gochberg has been spending a year at Pitt working on his own project. He is writing a book on plays of Alfred de Musset. He says no other university offers such an ambitious program in giving young teachers and scholars time off to write. During the summer he will be teaching two graduate courses at Pitt.

The Gochberg's have no special hobbies. Mom Carol enjoys being "just a housewife." And what a housewife! She makes her own clothes and has been sporting a beautiful winter coat she made for herself. She is an expert craftsman in leather goods. And you know what lovely things can be made out of leather — when you know how. Also, she has gone in for the new crewel work that is gaining in popularity. This work is of Elizabethan origin and has currently become big news among needleworkers.

And listen to this — Carol Gochberg joined a group of Pitt professors' wives in cooking demonstrations, organized by the current Fannie Farmer (Wilma Lord Perkins). Each wife specializes in a dish of some foreign country. In a recent demonstration Carol prepared Chinese egg fu-yung, chicken velvet and Chinese vegetables. The group looked on, tasted and liked. She also specializes in Italian cuisine. And believe it or not, even her boys like it.

Our professor likes Pittsburgh — its hills and landscapes. He believes our schools are superior to Chicago's. He likes living in Squirrel Hill, but thinks the parents are too good and over-protective of their children. Instead of letting them have the healthful benefit of walking to and from school — and coming home for lunch — too many mothers chauffeur them. He thinks there is an excess of group activities for children with not enough chance to develop personalities.

Doc Gochberg sometimes gets involved with baby-sitting at home. Like most he-men he doesn't like the idea. But when in it, he gets a feeling of great satisfaction and enjoyment at sharing an entire day with his boys.

Our young professor says if he were now graduating from college he would join the Peace Corps. He calls it the most exciting challenge to young people which has come along for many, many years.

Does he favor teenage steady dating and early marriage? Of course not. And particularly not for boys. He himself was "an old man of 23" when Carol said "I do" eleven years ago. David, Jonathan and Joel — Let that be a lesson to you!

Dr. Gochberg will return to the Windy City next September to continue at the University of Chicago. He'll teach French Literature and give a course in General Humanities which includes readings in history, philosophy, world literature and literary criticism. We'll be sorry to lose them as neighbors. But Chicago, too, must live. Meantime, it's nice to have them as neighbors. Come next September we shall wish them God-speed and the best of luck.

Lee Goldman
'Pro' in Field

A funny thing happened to a talented and interesting neighbor on his way to Carnegie Tech (now Carnegie-Mellon). He was made Associate Professor of the Department of Design. That was in 1961. Since then he advanced to Acting Head of Arts, Painting Design and Sculpture. And currently — since 1967 — he is Professor and Head of the Department of Design.

So who is this smart fellow holding so many important jobs at our famous University? Neighbor Lee Goldman, that's who. And in private practice at home is a Graphic and Industrial Designer. Goldman shares one of the Hamilton Cottages on Beacon Street with his lovely sister Lois. She works for the well-known Lando Advertising Agency, Downtown.

To get where Goldman got takes a fine educational background, much experience and plenty of know-how. He has all these — and more even. So let's take a look into his personal life.

A native Squirrel Hiller, young Goldman attended Colfax, graduated Allderdice and Carnegie-Mellon. Then went for further study at the University of Tampa. During WW II Lee soldiered for Uncle Sam for nearly three years in the Field Artillery and Infantry, travelling all over northern and western Europe. At war's end he returned for another year at Carnegie-Mellon. Then off he went to New York as a Designer for Corning Glass Works, staying ten years during which time he became Director of Design. Later he did free-lance work and traveled in many middle eastern countries — Greece, Israel, Iran, India, Burma, Thailand, Cambodia and Japan. Even Vietnam (before the war). And Hong Kong (before the flu). Then to Singapore and western European countries. To this day he still retains some of his German and Japanese clients as consultant for the production of glass and ceramics.

Our neighbor has been interested in so many professional activities that limited space doesn't permit listing in full. But we'll name just a few. For two years Goldman was on the Exhibition Committee of our Pittsburgh Playhouse; on the Design Committee of the Three Rivers Art Festival, and Chairman of the Film Committee. He's Design Consultant for the TB League of Allegheny County. His published articles also are too numerous to list completely. But he wrote "Doing Your Own Thing" in the Year Book Clinic of Pitt. He's editor of "Flim Flam" Survey of Motion Films which were screened at the Three Rivers Arts Festival.

Goldman's hobby is his work to which he brings enthusiasm and intelligence. As they say, when you love your work you have it made.

Lee is one of 3 brothers only one of whom is married. His brother Robert of Montreal (a bachelor) is president of Clairol Corp. of Canada. His dad, spry at 80 lives in the Manhattan apartment Lee and Robert lived in while in New York. He lives alone and likes it. Every day, weather permitting, he walks eight miles to keep fit. When "the boys" come to New York there's plenty room in dad's "hotel." And the price is right. Eldest sister Sylvia is married to well-known Samuel Stern of our neighborhood. Lee is an uncle four times and a great-uncle once.

An uncle, great-uncle, and lives with his sister? How come? Well, we may as well tell it like it is. Although an easy man to take a shine to, our neighbor is a bachelor. He's had a few "close calls" he'll tell you. Maybe next time the "calls" will come so close that he'll find himself saying so-long to bachelorhood and I Do to some beautiful woman.

Meantime he just returned from a trip to the University of Texas to lecture on "Movies & Animation." And a stop-off in Florida for some sunshine.

Let's wish our nice neighbor a happy and meaningful New Year.

Dr. Joel W. Goldstein
Prof Answers Drug Questions

Watergate rather than drug usage has taken over front-page news coverage. But don't get complacent about the latter; it has not gone away. And if there are things you always wanted to know about drug usage but were afraid to ask, speak up. A brilliant fellow equipped through vast education and experience has many answers. And he's not an old behind-the-times graybeard, but only 33. What's more, he's easy to look at. Say hi to Dr. Joel W. Goldstein, our Forbes Avenue neighbor. Dr. Goldstein is assistant Professor of Psychology and Industrial Administration at C-MU. He has answered countless questions and given insight into drug use during speaking engagements here, there, and everywhere. Let's list a few "heres," as follows: First Annual Meeting of the B'nai B'rith Hillel Foundation Board; School of Medicine Western Psychiatric Institute and Clinic; Squirrel Hill-Shadyside Mental Health Team; Pittsburgh School Teachers; a Special Program on KDKA-TV; "Newsroom Drug Use and the Media" on "WQED-TV, and "Drug Use and Youth" on WTAE-AM. Were you listening? He has written countless papers on drug use and drug education. In addition, our neighbor has earned research grants from the National Institute of Mental Health and the Maurice Falk Medical Fund. He has taught so many courses on drug usage and belongs to such a variety of professional organizations that listing all in limited space is prohibitive. So let's now learn a little about his educational and personal background.

Born in Chicago, Joel graduated high school in the suburb of Highland Park. Then he had a year at Purdue. His BA degree was earned from Grinell, and his Ph. D from the University of Kansas. While at Kansas he needed to visit one of his professor's office. And who do you think was there? - lovely Marcia Gray. They had both attended Purdue at the same time, but never met (the student body is so vast). Marcia recognized him. Soon steady dating followed, and in 1963 they married. While the youthful husband finished graduate school, his BW became Assistant to the Dean of Women at Kansas. They came to our city in 1966. Their Pittsburgh-born children (Lauren 6 and Daniel, 4) both go to C-MU Children's School. When they are older their mom plans to resume outside work. Meantime she enjoys caring for the family, keeping their 7-room home charmingly comfortable, and playing the guitar. When first married, Joel presented her with a cheap guitar. When she improved, he got her a brand new one, which inspired her to take lessons. Gratifying results were achieved. Last summer the family went camping at interesting spots in Pennsylvania, Maryland and West Virginia. When Marcia's brother was stationed in Panama, they had a family reunion, including a trip to Columbia, South America.

Dr. Goldstein believes that if alcohol and drugs are compared, the former is without question the most serious problem in this country. It is strongly associated with violent crime, auto accidents, deaths, suicides, broken marriages, and job absenteeism Heroin, he says is also a serious problem because it is so strongly habit-forming; it is attractive to youth and people who are unhappy. It often leads to thefts, burglary, drug-pushing or prostitution as a means of paying for expensive drugs. Marijuana, he feels is virtually harmless to the casual user and to American society. He has found that most students don't go in for heavy drugs, and that those with no professed religion are the biggest users of psychoactive drugs.

The Goldstein youngsters love watching "Sesame Street," "Mister Rogers Neighborhood" and "Zoom". Their lovable pet kitten Sugar sits alongside but soon gets bored curls up and takes a snooze. She knows nothing about drug usage. And doesn't ask.

Mrs. Louis E. (Bickie) Goldszer
'Kovad' Understandable For Dedication Woman

As this is being written, our personality of the week is in Israel for ten days. With her husband and two sons (Richard 16 and Franklin, 13 both Allderdice students) she is visiting their eldest, Robert. He is taking a pre-Med course at the Hebrew University in Jerusalem. Here the Abominable yet beautiful Snow Man is already in full force. In Israel it's California weather. By the time you're reading this, they'll be back home Then, should you want to know what's the newest news in that fascinating, dangerously-surrounded yet courageous little country, give her a call. And don't forget to greet her with the beautiful Hebrew word "Shalom" which means peace — for which Israel and the entire world is hoping.

Meantime, let's learn a little about our remarkable neighbor of Ferree St. She's Mrs. Bickie Goldszer, charming missus of Dr. Louis E. Goldszer, a well-known and experienced Optometrist. They first met where most often boy meets girl— at college. Our University of Pittsburgh, to be exact. After months of steady dating, they married and started housekeeping in a small 3rd floor walk-up apartment in Oakland, right across from St. Paul's Cathedral.

The former Bickie Feldman was born in Woodbine, N.J. At Pitt she finished its Graduate School with an M.Ed. degree and a Restoration Certificate, qualifying her to help all types of handicapped children. In between being a housewife and rearing her three boys, she worked for 20 years with children and adults who had reading problems. Now, with the boys grown and a full-time housekeeper in their 12-room home, she is devoting her time to many other interesting and important projects. She's Education Specialist for Action Housing. Inc., a non-profit Agency trying to improve the neighborhood through better housing. Bricks and paint, she says don't make a neighborhood. People make it. The schools determine the kind of neighborhood. She helps the community make the schools a place for children to reach their fullest potential. Mrs. Goldszer is also Education Specialist for School Volunteer Ass'n. of Pgh. She prepares the reading material and trains the tutors (volunteer men and women from our entire city). These volunteers teach reading during school days in public and parochial schools.

And as if this were not enough to keep her out of mischief, she does writing too. Her recently published "Primer for Perception" is used by para-professionals, tutors and parents to help children "learn to learn." It's used throughout the U.S. and abroad. The Department of Health, Education & Welfare considers it the most effective teaching tool for youngsters who can't make it in school. Also, Bickie travels all over the U.S. as consultant and teacher of teachers. And to top it off, works with her Optometrist husband on children's perceptual problems.

The Goldszer cluttered home is filled with antiques, pictures and with what Bickie laughingly calls "trash." (We all should own such interesting trash).

Our neighbor is treasurer of History & Landmark Associates; past president of penn's Optometric Auxiliary, and ditto of Gerald Yoakam Reading Council of the International Reading Ass'n. Her favorite charity is Yeshiva Achei Tmimim. She feels education has been and is our only hope for survival.

For their visit in Israel, pop and the boys took along a Nickon F. and a Hasselblad for picture-taking. She herself brought an ordinary Brownie Instamatic. And that self-confident gal is certain her pictures will come out the best of all. Should you have a chance to see their pictures, you will judge which are the bestest with the mostest.

Mrs. Goldszer feels the "kovad" (respect) she receives from her family is her most valuable asset. They admire what she's doing. So does our entire community. "Shalom" and a Happy New Year to neighbor Bickie, her family and all the many others dear to her.

Mrs. Benjamin Goodman
Movie Writer Doesn't Forget Mom

Wasn't it Lincoln who once said: "All that I am or hope to be I owe to my mother." So it could be that a neighborhood boy who made good feels the same about his own mom. And dad, too.

The parents are Benjamin and Rebecca Goodman, our neighbors at Beechwood Blvd. Their son, Abraham, writes under the name Abby Mann. And has become famous not only throughout Hollywood and New York but around the world. As you may already know, he won an Academy Award for his first screen play, "Judgment at Nurenberg". It was translated for showing in Germany, Italy, Sweden and at the Moscow International Film Festival.

Abby Mann did an adaptation of another Stanley Kramer picture "Ship of Fools", which has already won raves along the preview circuit. Recently he has been signed to write three movies — and produce them too. But first he wants to finish the "Andersonville" script for Kramer.

While writing "A Child is Waiting" — about retarded children — Abby lived in a retarded children's home every moment for six weeks. He caught the atmosphere alright. He also caught the mumps! But mumps, schmumps — he got $250,000 for that movie. And is paid similarly for every one he writes.

Abby's parents have been married 51 years and our neighbors for 22. For 40 years they've been in the jewelry business in East Pittsburgh — working together hand in hand. They always dreamed their son would learn all about jewelry and take over when the time came. A natural, human hope all parents have. But their son had other ideas.

Days and many nights he sat upstairs writing, writing. Lonely work. But they were wise enough not to fight talent. For that their son has been ever grateful. When the parents wrote him congratulations on "Judgment", he replied in part, "The things I was able to write were philosophies and attitudes you have taught me through the years."

The Goodman's famous son is now 39. And in spite of all the beautiful girls in Hollywood and elsewhere, is still a bachelor. Well — married he can always get.

He constantly sends his mother flowers. And phones at the drop of a hat. Recently, calling from Hollywood, who did you think also said hello? Irvin Berlin. When in Beverly Hills, Abby lives in the home originally built by Frank Lloyd Wright for Joan Crawford. A swimming pool? But of course.

Rebecca and Benjamin Goodman are also proud of their daughter, Dr. Ester Sack, a skilled optometrist in East Pittsburgh. Her husband, Dr. Nathan Sack is also a well-known optometrist in Braddock.

The Sacks have four children: Joe, 18, recently a high honor graduate of Allderdice, is entering John Hopkins Medical School come September. Trudy is 16 and a senior at Allderdice. Sari is 10 and Jackie, 8. Both attend Colfax.

What do you think, neighbors? Is it just sheer luck to have such remarkable children? Or is it inherited intangibles, not seen but there just the same? Or both? Whatever it is, our community is proud of the Goodman Family. And particularly of the fabulous Abby Mann.

Rabbi Robert Goodman
Brilliance Behind Whiskers, Foliage

Today you'll meet a youthful neighborhood newcomer. But don't let his longish hair and chin foliage fool you. They are backed by a brilliant mind, the finest education, and a personality that wins you over in a minute. Say hello-welcome to Rabbi Robert Goodman, scarcely 29.

Born in Chicago, at age 7 he moved with his parents to Great Neck, Long Island, N.Y. After grade and high school there Bob entered the University of Cincinnati, at the same time attending the Hebrew Union College — a joint program. In 1964 he graduated Phi Beta Kappa with honors from the University.

A year later found him in Israel for an intensive Hebrew program at the Hayim Greenberg Institute in Jerusalem. There, studying similarly was another student. A girl. Beautiful Haydee Roitman, a Hebrew teacher from Buenos Aires, Argentina whose dad is a men's clothing merchant there. Before she learned English and Bob Spanish, they courted in the language both knew — Hebrew.

After 9 weeks they were married by an Orthodox Rabbi in a small town near Jerusalem. July 3, 1966 to be exact. Following their honeymoon in romantic Tiberias they went housekeeping in Flushing, N.Y. After 3 years Haydee received her BA degree with honors in Political Science from Queens College, N.Y. When her husband was ordained they moved to Parsippany, N.Y. where he served as Rabbi of Temple Beth Am. At the same time attending New York U, working toward his Ph.D. in Jewish History.

Soon Rabbi Goodman's capabilities began showing and he was invited to our city. July 1st of this year he became Director of Reform Education, heading a program for the School of Advanced Jewish Studies. Under the direction of the well-known learned Dr. Aharon Kessler. With headquarters at the Y-IKC, Bellefield Ave. Currently the Rabbi is completing his thesis dealing with Latin-American Jewry. He became fascinated with that subject during his various visits with Haydee's family.

Several weeks before arriving here, guess who came to dinner? The stork! Because Argentina is world-famous for its fine beef, here's how the parents announced his arrival: "The Argentine-American Alliance for Progeny proudly announces a new beefy product, CRAIG ADRIAN, weighing 5 lbs. 7 ounces. He is available for public display as of June 16 at Birchwood St., Pittsburgh. For further details please contact the directors of this enterprise."

The Goodman's rented new house is on the very tip of narrow, hilly Birchwood St. To reach the living quarters you walk up two flights of green carpeted stairs. The five cheerful rooms contain a minimum of furniture as yet. But their cellar looks like a mini Carnegie Library with wall-to-wall shelves jammed with books. From their patio you look down on long rows of lovely trees and other mountain greenery now gently turning to red and gold. Craig's young-looking grandma flew in from Buenos Aires for a look-see. It was love at first sight. She remained a while to help out.

Currently Haydee is concentrating on being a housewife and mom. And is proficient in international cooking. Like for instance Israeli fallasel, Spanish empanadas, Jewish gefillte fish and American menus too numerous to list. Baby Craig couldn't care less for any such, and makes his wants known in a language all his own. Sometimes with a good healthy yell. Later — much later — his parents plan to teach him no more than 3 languages.

How does our neighbor feel about the World Series? As a life-time New Yorker he naturally owes loyalty to the Mets. But as things look now he feels they can't BUC the Pirates. (Keep your fingers crossed).

Our community wishes our new neighbors the best of everything now and in the years ahead. P.S. — And who do you think is a 'round-the-corner neighbor of the Rabbi's devoted parents (Abe and Marian Goodman) — and a life-long friend of the family in Great Neck, Naomi R. Blum, the writer's sister.

Mrs. S. H. (Esther) Green

Quite A Personality

Remember those articles in Reader's Digest entitled "The Most Unforgettable Character"? Well, we have one in our very neighborhood, at Riverview Apartments to be exact. Say hi to Mrs. Sydney H. Green, with the queenly name of Esther.

Mrs. Green has been Social Chairman of Riverview, on a volunteer basis, since Phase One of this remarkable facility was built seven years ago. And at age 77, with an enviable alert mind, is continuing as such now that the beautiful Phase Two is built and completely occupied. Her duties, which seem to have no end, we'll not enumerate. Let's just learn a little about her personal life. But you should know that the most often-heard expression around the place is "Go see Mrs. Green".

The former Esther Shapiro was born in Poland where she graduated high school, and worked in her dad's general merchandise business and wine factory — "doing everything." Her brother, who already was in America, brought the family over when Esther was 21. They were located in the Hill District on Overhill Street. She got a job as cashier in a kosher butcher-shop on Center Avenue and during the three months there she went to night school at Fulton High. After 42 evening sessions Esther got a diploma! No longer a "greenhorn", she became an interpreter in the foreign department of Kaufmann & Baer's (now Gimbel's).

Her fluency in Polish, Slavish, German, Russian and Hungarian was invaluable. When foreigners came to the store she'd take them to the various departments and interpret their needs. She'd scan the marriage announcements in the dailies, then contact the foreign parents. One such family came to the store and asked for "Mees Estter Sapirro" and purchased merchandise totaling $2,300 for the newlyweds. Esther received a bonus for the most sales - $10!

She was introduced to an interesting fellow working in the Foreign Department of Mellon Bank, fluent in the various languages she herself spoke so well. He was Sydney H. Green. With so much in common, Cupid soon stepped in and eight months later he became her devoted husband. And now get a load of this. Esther was so bashful that she never kissed her sweetheart until they were under the Hupah. (teenages: take note). The marriage knot was tied by Rabbi Sivitz (of blessed memory). Their's wasn't a stylish marriage but it "took". They moved to Uniontown where the young bride worked at the Fair Store owned by the late husband of a new Riverview tenant— lovely Dora Davis. And Sydney became a traveling salesman.

Later they returned to our city. The husband worked for the Historical Society of Western Pennsylvania during which time he got a citation "For extensive research work in the library archives — and as an accomplished linguist." The Greens were blessed with four children. Jerome, now an engineer for General Motors; Margaret (Mrs. Kalvin Tannenbaum) of Eastmont; Harry, an executive in Baltimore, and Thelma (Mrs. Harry Michaelson) of Detroit. There are 12 grandchildren. Here's a partial quote from Thelma's originally-composed Mother's Day message to her mom: "God only made One Mother for me. THANK YOU GOD."

Eight years ago sadness struck. Their father had a stroke and was taken to the Jewish Home & Hospital for the Aged. That's when his devoted wife moved into Riverview nearby to the Home so she could be with him as much as possible. Four years ago the inevitable happened and Esther was widowed. She continued living at Riverview, making use of her ability and leadership which she has in large supply.

Mrs. Joel (Virginia) Greenwald
'Neighbor' Heads 'Playhouse Plus'

You know of course that our Pittsburgh Playhouse has a brand new artistic director. With a famous name (John Hancock) he comes from that fabulous city of little cable cars — San Francisco. Chock-full of creative brilliance and simply bursting with new ideas, he has caught the imagination of everyone.

Especially "Playhouse Plus" — a group of civic-minded and theater-loving Leading Ladies of our city. And where do you think their capable president lives? You guessed it. In our very neighborhood. So let's meet and learn a little about Mrs. Joel (Virginia) Greenwald of Maynard St. Everyone calls her Ginger.

Husband Joel is also a president of Wayne & Weil Carpet Co. In 1961, when he opened a new branch store in Monroeville, he asked his missus to help out the first week. She stayed on for two years.

The Greenwalds have two interesting and talented girls. Julie, 11½ is in the 7th grade at Allderdice. She's a gifted artist and an excellent horse-back rider. Lucie is 10 and goes to Wightman, 5th grade. She twangs and plunks a guitar. And ever since they put in their own swimming pool several years ago, she's become an expert swimmer. Both attend the Rodef Shalom religious school.

Then there's Alice, their capable full-time housekeeper. And Carrie, a Kerry-blue terrior. And honeybun, a Shihtzu. That makes 6 females in the household. Do they spoil their one man with too much attention? Ginger says No. He spoils them. The Greenwalds are the reading-ist family ever, with TV taking a back seat.

Ginger Greenwald is a sun-tanned blue-eyed blond, with a figure that looks good even in stretch pants. Born and bred in Buffalo, she came to our city 14 years ago. And taught at the Playhouse. She was in a show titled "Remains to be Seen." Then went on TV for several years on "This Time Next Week." For a few years she wrote and did a radio show. And a couple of shows and reviews for the United Jewish Fund— wrote, directed and been in them. Also for the Council of Jewish Women and for Ort.

The purpose of the Plus women is to supplement the Playhouse and aid in presenting it to the public. Originally a small group, but with the advent of the Hancock know-how and understanding of what the public wants, it has grown by leaps and bounds. But of course more women are always needed.

These women do everything, from having the director or an actor at their home for dinner, to hunting around for furnishings for the cast's temporary homes. They also arrange the "Twelfth Night" parties, held on the 12th performance of each play. To give the audience a chance to meet the cast and the actors a feeling of belonging to the community. The audience gets a kick out of meeting the performers personally. And listen to this, The Playhouse restaurant furnishes sandwiches and coffee "on the house." But should you thirst for anything stronger — well, as the saying goes — a drink is a drink is a drink.

The Playhouse is the first live theater to provide a drive-in box-office for its patrons. Chaired by Mrs. Richard R. (Anita) Morganstern, the drive-in "Subscription & Ticket Center" was officially opened several weeks ago. At the Mellon Bank's University drive-in office, Fifth & Craig St., Oakland.

Mrs. Greenwald's capable co-chairmen are Mrs. W. Pierce Widdoes and Mrs. Robert L. Kann also Squirrel Hillers. And incidentally, so is the above-mentioned Anita Morganstern.

With all the exciting plans afoot, it looks like there'll be a hot time on Craft Avenue in the cold months ahead.

Aaron Gross

He's Played to Royalty

You've heard the old saying poets are born, not made. The same is true with teachers.

And it's particularly true of Aaron Gross, our neighbor at Hobart St. He's a teacher par excellence — of the piano. The flood of letters he constantly receives from former pupils throughout the country attests to that.

They all carry the same theme: "You have given me life's most precious gift — music, and all the joys that come with it." And they in turn are sending their own children to Teacher Gross to continue the tradition.

They know he has the rare gift of musical talent and teaching know-how that few possess. and teaches with a heart that cares.

Let's learn a little about our dark-eyed, dark-haired neighbor whose pupils adore him. First off, although his background is fantastic and reads like a "Who's Who in Music," he's the most modest fellow you ever met.

That's how it sometimes is. The one who has the mostest brags the leastest.

At age eight, Aaron Gross was a "vocal prodigy." He began studying the piano in order to play his own accompaniments. Soon piano became his major interest. Since then he has studied with the foremost teachers of the world.

A graduate of Grove City College before he was 18, young Aaron became a protege of Dr. Herman Poehlman, director of the Royal Conservatory in Dresden. Then followed study with internationally-renowned concert pianists Joseph and Rosina Llevinne of the Julliard School of Music.

He studied composition under Gustave Mehner and attended master classes of Arthur Friedheim, a pupil of Franz Liszt!

When quite a young man, Mr. Gross performed at Syria Mosque as guest pianist for Prince William of Sweden who was in our city on an official visit.

After touring the country as soloist, ensemble player and accompanist, and being heard over NBC, WEAF and WNYC, Aaron Gross came here to open his own piano studio. That was 27 years ago. Born in noise-ridden New York, he likes the comparitive quiet of good old Pittsburgh.

And now let's meet his missus, the former Rosalie Sanders — a five-foot, brown-eyed blond bundle of dynamic charm. She too is talented. For 12 years she wrote a column "Madelon's Mirror" for the former Sun-Tele. Then did free-lance writing. And until very recently was Woman's society editor for the Jewish Chronicle.

When Aaron was a bachelor (28 years ago) Rosalie came to interview him for a Sun-Tele article on music.

But it wasn't love at first sight. Their love, like Topsy, "just growed."

The Gross home which they own is alive with excitement. The pupils feel free to come and go any time.

Aaron and Rosalie are a most happy couple. But as in every life, some rain must fall. Not long ago a typical American tragedy struck. Their pet cat Willie Schubert by name, outlived all his nine lives and breathed his last. He used to supervise all music lessons by jumping on the piano, saying nothing, just listening.

The memory of Willie is slowly fading but his scratches on the piano linger on.

Dr. Franz B. Gross

Graduate Dean Has Repository of Knowledge

Are you a Ron Jay "Hot Line" fan? Or Marie Torre's "Contact"? Either way you've heard each interview a most fabulous fellow. He's none other than Dr. Franz B. Gross, recently appointed Dean of the Graduate School of Liberal Arts and Sciences at Duquesne University. Also Professor of International Affairs and African studies. A newcomer, he had the good judgment to come live in our very neighborhood, buying a pleasant home on Plainfield St. So let's welcome and get acquainted with our pipe-smoking neighbor.

Takes a brilliant mind, complete educational background plus vast scientific experience for his important job. Dr. Gross has them aplenty. But limited space prohibits going into complete detail. So we'll skip the whole thing except a few highlights. Then snoop a little into his personal life. Might be more fun.

Born in Vienna, young Franz attended the University there, going on to the University of Rome. Later he transferred to Harvard. There he earned his M. A. degree in 1943, and finally his Ph.D. He studied and lectured throughout the world: South America, Europe, Asia, Middle East (Beirut and Israel), Africa, India, Asia — you name it and interviewed key personalities there. Our neighbor was a Fulbright Fellow at the University of Mysore, India. And is listed in Who's Who in Education and in Science. He was Editor-writer for the "Des Moines Register" and "Tribune." Also the Sunday edition of the "New York Times".

But it wasn't all work and no play. Handsome Franz found time to do what comes naturally. Fall in love. While a G.I. student in Geneva he met lovely Margaret Chappel, statistician with the U.N. there. She was transferred to our New York U.N. about the same time Franz entered Harvard. Four hours apart in travel-time, they kept the mails busy and the phones buzzing. In 1952 Franz and Peg said "I Do" to a Unitarian minister. And started housekeeping in Forest Hills Gardens, N.Y. When the young husband became a Distinguished Professor of Political Science at PMC Colleges in Phila., they lived in suburban Wallingford. His bride worked with the Population Studies Center at the University of Penna. In due time son, Christopher John, arrived. Now 15, with shoulder-length hair, he's a Junior at Allderdice. He had a year's schooling in Dakar, Senegal. Chris loves skiing and swimming. And, of course, is a rock music fan. (Don't tell the neighbors, but so is his dad).

On the right-side of the Gross 9-room home is a large lovely swimming pool. It may become an ice-skating rink this winter. In front of their garage is a basketball and badminton court. Living with them are two fascinating personalities: a tan beagle named Sir Winston. And a lovable kitten, Twilight. Winston has about reached his golden age while Twilight is young and playful. He prefers taking a snooze on a cozy chair while she tantalizes him with gentle pats. When he growls a little she simply jumps on the lap of whoever happens around, knowing full well she's loved and welcome.

Mrs. Gross has very little outside help in her home. With all the modern time-saving electrical appliances, pop doesn't even need to do the dishes. Their home is cheerful, lovely to look at, filled with artifacts and pictures collected from their world-wide travels.

Our community wishes our new neighbors the best of everything now and in the years ahead. May Sir Winston continue enjoying his golden years and Twilight keep happily purring throughout all her nine lives.

Father John Guiniven
Shake Hands With A New Pastor

It's always a joy to tell you about an interesting new neighbor, but when that personality is someone extra special, it's a privilege as well. Shake hands with Father John Guiniven, new pastor of St. Philomena's Parish, Beechwood Boulevard and Forward. His Provincial (Major Superior) chose him to head the Redemptorist community of Squirrel Hill. The appointment, approved by Bishop Leonard, became effective July 17.

Like for ministers and rabbis, years of learning, vast preparation and imaginative leadership are also "musts" for priests, so let's look a little into Father Guiniven's background. Born in the City of Brotherly Love, his mother died when he was a little tyke of not quite five. Like most little fellas, he wanted to be many things - a policeman, even. But the time he reached the eighth grade, it was a priest - nothing less.

He entered the Redemptorist Minor Seminary (equivalent to four years high school and two of college) at North East, Pennsylvania. A year at the Novitiate in Maryland followed, at the end of which he pronounced his religious vows of Poverty, Chastity and Obedience. Then he went to the Major Seminary in N. Y. State where, at the end of five years, his dream of the priesthood came true.

After three years at the Catholic University of America, he received a Doctorate in Canon Law. During WW II, the young priest served Uncle Sam as an Army Chaplain in France, Germany and Austria for 29 months, and received a Bronze Star.

At St. Philomena's, Father Guiniven hopes to concern himself not only with Catholic problems, but with those of our entire community. He lives in the church rectory with five other Priests, namely: Fathers Charles Guttenberger, Frank Nelson, William Jacob, Charles McLaughlin and James Kerr; also two religious Brothers, Rupert Morgan and Gerald McNamee. By the way, Father Jacob (listed above) is not Jewish!

A housekeeper prepares lunch and dinner; at breakfast, they fend for themselves. With such close proximity to Murray Avenue, it's likely bagels and lox are often found on their breakfast table.

The rectory is furnished simply, but books line the walls. It was originally built as a convent for the Sisters who taught in the school; now they have their own convent at the other end of the Church complex. The school, convent and church are all under one roof, and currently there are 261 children in the school. Father Guiniven says a priest's vow not to marry is "one of the most difficult sacrifices," and, of course, he's against abortion.

Mass is celebrated weekdays at 7, 8 and 11:15 a.m.; Saturdays, 6:30 p.m.; Sunday, 7:30, 9, 10:30 a.m., noon and 5:30 p.m. The Mass dialogue is in English — not Latin as in the past. All are welcome.

Our neighbor likes music — classical as well as popular; and tho' he can't read notes, plays the piano by ear, if you please. He enjoys movies. His favorite? Along with "Song of Music," it's "Fiddler on the Roof" at our nearby Manor. His out-door color indicates love of golf, but he says Jack Nicklaus needn't lose sleep worrying. Nothing gives him a bigger laugh than humor between priests and rabbis — more so, if the joke's on the priest.

Our entire community wishes Father Guiniven and his dedicated, devout Family the best of everything now and in the years ahead.

Mrs. William Hackney

On a Clear Day You Can Enjoy Forever!

Been to the Pittsburgh Playhouse Lately? Of course you have. But if not, you'll be rarin' to go see "Complaisant Lover" which premieres there this Saturday. Not just because it was a hit on Broadway for several seasons. But also because a talented neighbor is in it.

She's none other than the popular Doris Hackney of Fair Oaks St. Doris plays "Mrs. Howard," the banker's wife. And as the saying goes, it's like having money in the bank.

The former Doris Fast is the lovely missus of Lawyer William P. Hackney of Reed, Smith, Shaw & McClay. But before going further into the low-down on her personal life, you'll be interested to know she also was in many other playhouse hits.

Like "Voice of the Turtle" in 1952, "Take Her She's Mine"; "Critic's Choice," "The Pleasure of His Company," last season's hit comedy "Mary, Mary," and recently "Rhineoceros." Doris also starred in the Playhouse production "Angel Street" on KDKA-TV and on its medical series, "With These Hands."

And now listen to this. Doris first met Bill Hackney in nearby Uniontown where both their families — lifelong friends — lived. In kindergarten, of all places. At that time she was several inches taller than Bill and actually looked down on him. As to future husband material, she couldn't care less.

But wait! By the time they attended Sunday School together, went through the grades and graduated Uniontown High, Bill had grown tall, straight and handsome. And you guessed it. Romance took a turn for the better. Then parting became love's sweet sorrow.

Bill went on to Princeton, later graduating from Harvard Law School. Doris entered Carnegie Tech Drama School where she graduated. During World War II Bill served two years in the Army Air Corps. Doris went to Europe as a civilian actress technician. Then, in 1947, Cupid won out and they said "I do" in Uniontown's First Presbyterian Church.

The Hackneys are blessed with three lively, interesting children. Penn, 12 is a talented pianist. (Pssst, listen. Dad plays the piano too). He is active in basketball and club work at our neighborhood Y-IKC where Mom Hackney takes figure-trimming exercises. He attends Allderdice. So does kid brother Peter, 10. Sis Jeanne is seven and goes to Wightman.

Doris Hackney thinks of herself as a professional, but a house-wife and mother first and foremost. Husband Bill enjoys her avocation and cooperates in every way. When they entertain at their home after shows — he becomes the town's most hospitable host with the most.

A member of Junior League, Doris works as a volunteer for the Crippled Children's Home. And does tutoring for the underprivileged youngster on the North Side. She's on the boards of Pittsburgh Plan for Art and Family & Children Service. She also belongs to "Playhouse Plus".

The women members of the latter group find lodging for the New York actors and arrange many dinner dates for them at various homes. They've also recently inaugurated what is called a "Twelfth Night Party." For all actors and whoever in the audience wants to join the fun after the show — and meet one another. The Playhouse restaurant furnishes sandwiches and coffee on-the-house.

But if you thirst for anything stronger, as the saying goes — a drink is a drink is a drink. The initial party was during "Rhinoceros." And the specialty was "rhinoceros" sandwiches.

For "Virginia Woolf" was it maybe wolf meat? No, but the table was covered with a wolf rug — or a reasonable facsimile thereof. For the "Complaisant Lover" party, who knows? Could be lover-boy sandwiches.

The Hackneys own their lovely nine-room home. Their Television room walls are decorated with the children's hand-drawn pictures. Doris does her needlepoint work — mostly between acts. And catches up on letterwriting.

Should you be invited to our neighbors' home for tea, their capable housekeeper Edith Dorsey serves it in charming blue decorated china, steaming hot. And delicious home-made cake that melts in your mouth, not in your hands.

Honestly — at the Hackneys, on a clear day you can enjoy forever.

David Halliday, Jr.
Student Shows Skill in Shop

Today it's accent on youth. You see, our neighborhood personality is just 18 years of age. A likeable teenager with an unusual talent. Say "hi" to David Halliday, Jr., of Bennington Ave. He's a senior at Allderdice. His dad is Dean of the Faculty of Arts & Sciences at Pitt. And mom loves her garden. But mostly in the summer.

While most high school workshop students are building tie racks and small jewelry boxes our youthful David is building a $20,000 organ. After nearly a year of work during class hours — 35 to 40 minutes a day five days a week — the organ console is nearly done.

David decided to build a musical instrument about a year ago, after finishing his required woodshop project. "I've been working on the whole idea for five years," he said. "And have collected all the parts I need." He got a lot of pipes from churches and the foot pedals from the Pittsburgh Musical Institute. The generator came from West Virginia. And a wind-chest was furnished him by the Asbury Methodist Church (of blessed memory). The constructed plans call for $300 to $400 in materials. The completed organ will be worth $20,000 to $30,000.

Under the direction of his shop and "Audsley's Treatise on Organ Building" the youth went to work on the project last year. And says it should be finished in February. The console he'll put in their living room and the pipe work in the basement. Already their basement is filled with nearly 1,000 organ pipes; ranging in length from several inches to 16 feet. It's in such clutter that for every three people who go down to see the organ, only one can find his way up. His parents are wonderfully tolerant and David has full sway of their home.

Young Halliday graduated from St. Edmonds and Shadyside Academies. He studied piano with Mrs. Mihail Stolervsky and the organ with the late Marshall Bidwell. Then continued with the well-known Robert Lord and Stanley Tagg.

David will graduate Allderdice this June and hopes to go on to Goddard College in Vermont — a liberal arts College — on a work-study program. January and February students work in whatever field they wish. He will be an apprentice to an organ-builder. In four years, when he graduates there he will work for a factory to buy out or start one of his own. Money? He'll borrow from dad and the bank, and get the few people together to go in with him.

Last summer our David played at St. Bartholomew Church in Colorado, performing a Solemn Mass. Four of the top hierarchy there and a large audience listened to his concert with genuine admiration — even though the player was nervous as all get-out. He also played at the neighborhood Church of the Redeemer. And for 10 years sang in the choir in that church, under the direction of Dr. J. Vobert Izod.

Young David does a lot of skiing in Hidden Valley. And helps mom with the dishes. If he gets callouses from that job, it's only from turning the knob of their dish-washing machine, he tells you.

Our youthful neighbor has shaved only once. But now the bit of fuzz on his upper lip that is beginning to sprout he plans to keep. And maybe let his hair grow. You see, he plays the piano in a Shadyside Coffee House — "The Word" — two evenings a week. And the year prior he helped run the "Rising Tide" there. If he continues to look clean as now, someone may wop him with "Are you a nut or something?" As to smoking, you'll never believe it. He doesn't. As they say in the commercials, he can live without it.

Peter Hamilton
Shall We Dance?

The stock market is erratic, cost of living higher than the temperature and our Pirates, as of this writing, are win-hungry. So let's dwell on happier things. Like those ever-lovin' Civic Light Operas that brighten the summer. You've seen some of them before — perhaps several times — and are familiar with their lyrics and haunting melodies that grip and won't let go. But do you remember the choreography — the dancing — that brings to the musicals that extra touch of class? Well, today you'll learn a little about a fantastic fellow who creates and directs the dancing. He's Peter Hamilton, choreographer - director par excellence.

Hamilton was born in Trenton. Even as a little tyke he danced in vaudeville. His folks, with a Pennsylvania Dutch background where they speak no evil, hear no evil, see no evil wanted him to forget theatre and become a school teacher, so in due time shooed him off to Lafayette College, Easton, Pa. where he earned his BA degree and taught school in Trenton. But wait! Talent will come out. Each day after school he took a train to New York City to study dancing, under world-famous Doris Humphrey and Martha Graham.

His first job was with a modern dance co., making costumes, sets—everything. And of course dance. Salary? $30 per week! Soon followed commercial theatre, musical comedies. Progress came fast. He was star dancer and choreographer on the Fred Waring Show for three years, and on Ed Sullivan's Big Revue. He danced for famous industrial and fashion shows throughout the country with such stars as Maria Callas, Margaret Leighton, Andy Williams, Arlene Dahl, Faye Emerson, to name a few. Let's quote some newspaper reviews following 150 musicals Hamilton choreographed in New York City and around the country: "Absolutely first rate, humorous and highly imaginative"; "Choreography so exciting it could stand alone as an evening's entertainment", "Mr. Hamilton is not only a brilliant choreographer but a miracleworker".

Here Peter works his miracles— ably assisted by Lenore Nemetz of nearby Green Tree — on between 32 and 50 dancers, adding more when a Show requires it. Their ages range from 18 to 30.

Hamilton lives in New York City in the section where the theme for "West Side Store" originated. He shares his five rooms with a lovable dark-brown poodle. Charley Brown by name. Where Peter goes so goes Charley. What does Charley think of the dancing? He doesn't say, just quietly watches the rehearsals from the side-lines in the brightly - lit wall-mirrored room in Heinz Hall. And cuddles up with joy to the many who pat and embrace him.

The Operas? Starting July 9 they're as follows: West Side Story, South Pacific, Brigadoon, Student Prince, Gigi, The King and I, in that order.

Choreographer - Director wears no shoulder-length hair. Nor does he have chin foliage. He's clean-shaven, sandy-haired, blue-eyed, gracefully streamlined, handsome. And a bachelor! Ladies, how would you like having him as a partner for the Last Tango — even if not in Paris?

See you at Heinz Hall.

Hilda Hammerschmidt
How To Succeed By Trying

Some people, they say, succeed in business without really trying.

But not Hilda Hammerschmidt. Her life-time hobby, Contract Bridge, developed into a success because she tried—really tried. And loved trying. Also because she has the will and energy and intelligence to make a go of whatever she sets her mind to. Even when she first met handsome Dan Hammerschmidt, she made up her mind he was her man. She chased and chased after him, she boasts, until he caught her!

Hilda has played bridge as long as she can remember. In 1958 she became a life master—the highest one can go in the bridge world. At the American Contract Bridge League regional tournament held in Pittsburgh recently, she won two section tops. Thus, even though the names Goren, Jacoby, Fishbein, Silidor, Sobel and other international bridge experts were flashed across the front pages of our newspapers, many Squirrel Hillers made names for themselves.

Thirteen years ago Hilda started teaching Contract Bridge as well as holding Duplicate Bridge games in her home, Shady Ave. Because of her know-how and natural flair as a "hostess with the mostes", bridge players from everywhere have flocked to her hospitable home.

She has an average of 100 "bridgers" every week. They not only enjoy playing among Pittsburgh's best, but love the deliciously brewed coffee (and what goes with it) made and served by the efficient and likeable houseman, Clarence Moore.

The planning and arranging are Hilda's, of course — aided and abetted by husband Dannie. The latter prefers good reading to bridge, but often is inveigled into playing when someone is minus a partner. Those who come for bridge, whether they end with high or low score, leave with the feeling that they have had a delightful afternoon or evening at the Hammerschmidt's.

Dannie for many years was purchasing agent for American Bridge Co.—a subsidiary of U.S. Steel. He retired 10 years ago. He and Hilda have two sons, both married. Jack, a free lance advertising man, lives in New York; Lee resides in Churchill Borough and is a factory representatives for several steel firms. There are four grandchildren.

Aside from Bridge, Hilda has a remarkable educational background—self-propelled, one might say. In 1958 she graduated cum laude from the University of Pittsburgh. She was the first woman with grown children (and without having graduated high school) to have entered Pitt. She went for 5½ years and earned 81 university credits. Fifteen years later she returned and earned her Master of Letters in English.

Hilda has a garden where she collects and raises Pennsylvania Wild flowers. Dannie prefers reading to gardening, so she lets him get away with merely mowing the lawn. She also collects Pine and Deer patterns. And those who were ever dinner guests at the Hammerschmidt's agree that Hilda's cooking is the greatest.

They recently celebrated their 50th wedding anniversary. Unlike Jack Benny who clings to his 39th birthday, they are proud of their years, so full of interesting activity.

We'll end with a humorous little poem which Hilda composed:

An Amoeba counted its vowels one day
And discovered an amusing fact:
The a and the o and the e were there;
It was the I and the u it lacked.
It laughed so hard that it split in two
Could that partly account for the I and the "you"?

Dr. Moo-Young Han

Korean Professor's Family Are American As Hot Dogs

Koreans — bless 'em — are such likeable people. And wouldn't you know it, and interesting professor from Korea and his little family live right in our very neighborhood.

In a furnished duplex on Raleigh St. Furnished because he's been here for just two years. And will be leaving us in September for greener pastures. So before they move away, let's get to know them a little. Better late than never.

Our neighbor is Dr. Moo-Young Han, assistant professor of Physics at Pitt. During the Korean War, Moo-Young was a high school student in Seoul — too young to serve his country. And went on to the National University there. At war's end, scarcely 21 he came to the U. S. to continue studies at the University of Wisconsin. In three years he received his BS degree. And went on to the University of Syracuse, N.Y. for his Ph.D. Since all work and no play often makes a fella dull, he accepted an invitation to a student picnic. And what do you think happened? Something, in his modesty, he thought incredible, unbelievable and plain sensational. A beautiful co-ed from Korea was also there. Her name, Chang-Ki was music to his ears. And his heart melted like a snow-flake in the Sahara. She was taking a librarian course at the same University. It took a year of wooing and winning. They became Mr. and Mrs. in 1959 and have been living happily ever since. Because graduate students receive a nominal salary and since the young husband helped out in the University's Science department, they were able to start housekeeping in a furnished flat. When Moo-Young got his Ph.D and Chang-Ki her MS in Library Science, he was called to Pitt to start his professional career in earnest. That was in 1965. He is now working in theoretical nuclear physics— different from experimental.

Their little girl Hewon (American name Grace) was born in Syracuse. She's three now. Her future career? She hasn't decided yet. Too engrossed in TV. She's fascinated by the Monkees the Moppets and the Puppets. And is simply ecstatic over the commercials. She's even sympathetic toward the weeping plumber who cries because a certain bathroom product works — and he's losing his customers. Some day, in a home of her own Hewon will definitely give him a job. By then she will have become a discriminating shopper. Or a confused one. As to their baby son Su-Young (Christopher) all of 1½, what are his plans for later? He ain't talkin'.

Wife Chang-Ki goes for American clothes but she's no mini-skirter. Half-and-half, whatever that means. On special occasions she dons a traditional outfit, distinctly Korean.

Dr. Han's parents were MD's in Seoul. So was his wife's father. His mom writes that Korea is importing a lot of things from far and near and is on its own feet. But not yet prosperous. Korea's population is around three million. The country is surrounded by beautiful mountains and the climate is similar to ours.

Before the children were born, Han and Chang-Ki would enjoy movies. Now they take the kids to the zoo.

Meals at the Han home are mostly American. But they have their favorite Korean dish every now and then. It's called Pulkoke, made of beef, soy sauce and all kinds of exotic herbs. Our professor, being a mere man, doesn't know exactly how much of each ingredient. So better ask his capable missus.

Dr. Han has been called to Duke University at Durham, North Carolina for a better position. Better in terms of research opportunities. He feels good about it. But what's so bad about feeling good? He's sorry to leave Pitt and our city — especially the friendly neighbors.

The Hans started learning English in Seoul and now speak it perfectly. Little Hewon is catching on fast. Baby Chris can't say a word in either language yet but understands both. Let's wish our erstwhile neighbors the best of everything in the Sunny South Sept. 1st and in the years ahead.

William Hansen

Awaiting Hot Time at Craft

You already know of course that our Pittsburgh Playhouse has started the new sea-son in great style. The seats are newly and comfortably upholstered, the accoustics improved and the carpeting lovely to look at and tread upon. But most important are the tantalizing plays coming up. And the great actors who'll be delighting you time and time again. And another nice thing is that some of them are Squirrel Hillers. Like for instance William Hansen who had the good judgment to lease an apartment in our very neighborhood.

The opening play at the Craft Theatre is a revival of George M. Cohan's comic melo-drama, "The Tavern". And who do you think is the Tavern's innkeeper? Neighbor Hansen, no less. And what happens there to a variety of guests including the Governor, his wife, their daughter and her fiance shouldn't happen to you. Throughout the play you are holding your breath wondering what happens next. And when it does happen you are convulsed with laughter.

Bill Hansen has a wealth of acting experience under his belt. He has been delight-ing audiences for almost 30 years. After a liberal arts course in the University of Wash-ington at Seattle — majoring in Drama — he came direct to New York. There he had further training in the Ouspenskaya School for Theatre and private class lessons with Morris Carnovsky. His first acting job was in 1935 in summer stock in Peterborough, N.H. Then he tried for work in New York, but no sale.

So off he went to Hollywood. There he did 9 bit parts in 9 pictures in 9 months. But, as he says, "it was all for the birds — and best forgotten". Then back in New York where he struck gold with his first Broadway job in the Group Theatre production of Saroyan's "My Heart's in the Highlands". Then followed 19 Broadway shows — out-standing hits like "Twelfth Night" with Maurice Evans and Helen Hayes; "MacBeth" with Judith Anderson; "Member of the Wedding"; "Waltz of the Toreadors". Finally, in "Tea House of the August Moon". And "The Visit" with Lunt and Fontaine.

While touring in "MacBeth" in 1942 they played at our old Nixon Theatre. After the show the popular actor hurried to his hotel. In the lobby the night clean-up crew was busy with mops, brooms and such lying around. Hansen tripped and kerplunk, boom, down he went. And broke his leg in 3 places. One wasn't enough! He was in the Mercy Hospital for 1½ years. The nuns there treated him like a king. And many prominent personalities visited him — even Gladys Schmidt among others. He made a decision then and there never to act again. Not with a limp he wouldn't. But it's funny. Adversities often bring blessings. He got more opportunities to act in plays — with his limp — than before without it. When you see him in "The Tavern" hobbling around, it's a natural for that character. But you will know it's for real.

Before coming here Hansen worked 6 summers in Williamstown, Mass., under the world-famous Greek director with the teeth-breaking name of Nikos Psacharopoulos. He gained much experience there. Also in regional theatres in Houston, Atlanta and now in Pittsburgh.

Our actor neighbor has no family at all — except one kissin' cousin. And he doesn't know how to cook. But he prepares his own breakfast, and says he makes the best coffee in Squirrel Hill. He just puts a spoonful of the powdered stuff in some boiling water and swoosh — coffee is served.

Bill says he loves Pittsburgh — its lovely hills and trees. And especially the interest-ing friendly people.

You know what they say — There's no People Like Show People. In their acting they are some one else. Off stage they are themselves — warm, friendly, delightful. That's our neighbor Bill Hansen.

It looks like there'll be a hot time on Craft Ave. in the cold months ahead.

Milton Harris

CLO Enthusiast

Summer time and the livin' is easy. Especially in July. Oh, not only because there's a long week-end coming up. But those Civic Light Operas — remember? This season, instead of seen-before offerings strung out during the entire summer, there are just three — each Pittsburgh first-timers. In July only. The CLO Board decided to make it quality instead of quantity.

And speaking of the Board, it will doubtless interest you to learn that a prominent and dedicated member lives in our very neighborhood. He's Milton E. Harris of Darlington Rd. His home, built ten years ago is a stone's-throw from the Schenley Park golfing area. Already his deep tan is showing, accentuating his silver hair. He also golfs at the Westmoreland Country Club of which he's a member.

But our neighbor didn't always have it so good. Took a lot of doing and hard work to climb the success ladder. Let's take a look into his personal life. Born in the East End 63 years ago of non-affluent parents (Who had big money those days!) he managed to graduate Peabody Hi. Then worked his way through college (University of Pittsburgh) selling shoes. In 1926 he received his BS degree and an LLB three years later.

Successfully passing his exams and admitted to the Bar, the young attorney started Law practice in the Berger Bldg., downtown. This was right smack in the middle of the Depression. Some 15 years later he gave up his practice and became affiliated full-time with Continental Transportation Lines, Inc. Starting as Executive Vice President, at year's end he became its President. After the merger of his firm into Werner Continental Transportation Lines, Inc. Starting as Executive Vice President, at year's end he became its President. After the merger of his firm into Werner Continental, Inc. March of last year, Harris became its Chairman of the Board.

Many years prior there was a merger of another kind. When a handsome bachelor, young Harris took a trip to New York. There, on a blind date, he met lovely Ruth Kerstein. A year or so later he and Rabbi Rothchild, former Associate Rabbi of Rodef Shalom Temple, made a trip to the big city together. Milk quickly contacted Ruth. During that visit he proposed to her — in the presence of the Rabbi! Ruth must have figured that a close friend of a brilliant Rabbi couldn't be all bad. So guess what? She said yes. And in due time they merged into marriage. They started housekeeping in a small kitchenette apartment in the Morrowfield. In 1946 to be exact.

Time marched on. Today, their son Milton, Jr. is 22 and just graduated Brandeis University. Richard 20, will be in his 3rd year at the University of Pennsylvania come September. Dad and mom took the boys on a trip to England, Scotland and Greece several summers ago.

Mr. Harris is interested in so many worthy projects that limited space prevents enumerating all. So let's just name a few. Harris served as State President of the Penn's Motor Truck Ass'n. for two terms. He's Past Master of Fraternity Lodge No. 705 F. & A.M. Also a Rotarian. And was National President of his college fraternity Phi Epsilon Pi. Currently he's Director of the Pittsburgh Federation of Jewish Philanthopies and the Montefiore Hospital. Also a Board member of the Better Business Bureau.

As President of the Jewish Chautauqua Society and the National Federation of Temple brotherhoods, his hobby is Brotherhood.

Milt's lovely missus does volunteer work in the X-ray Department of Montefiore Hospital and has served on its Board. As to cooking, get a load of this. Milt says when they first were married she didn't know how to boil water. Now — you'll never believe it — she's the best cook ever. Especially gourmet dishes. If you're invited there for dinner, come just as you are — hungry. And be convinced.

P.S.— The three CLO Pittsburgh first-timers are: Ray Bolger in "Happy Times"; Tony Randall in "How Now, Dow Jones", and Rowan & Martin with their Sock-it-to-me Gang. See you there.

Ross Harris
Diverse And Exciting Life

Summer is long gone, autumn past and winter is in full swing, with snow already. So let's warm up a little by meeting a most interesting neighbor. His life is filled with so many varied activities, it's tough sledding—in limited space— to tell you all. But it's worth a try. So who is this smart neighbor, expert in so many interests?

Ross M. Harris of nearby Wightman St.— that's who. Our neighbor is a youthful-looking recent retiree from a retail food business whose late dad founded and the son conducted successfully for many years.

Harris was born in our North Side. At the ripe age of seven he moved with his parents to Squirrel Hill. After graduating Wightman and Schenley Hi, he went on to Pitt's Business Administration.

He was on the University's first boxing team and at the same time a band leader, playing the sax. His orchestra played at college and high school dances. (Recently he played that instrument at Syria Mosque). After Pitt he went to work in his dad's business, learning all about foods. Meantime he became interested in ballet, taking lessons from Karl Heinrich. With his teacher he formed the Pittsburgh Civic Ballet and became its first president, and performer too.

Then guess what? The ballet dancer started racing motor boats on the Allegheny between Highland Park Bridge and Oakmont. His trophies for racing and other hobbies currently adorn the mantels, tables and cellar of his beautiful 12-room home. At least 106 of them.

During WW II Harris became Chief of a gun anti-aircraft crew at Camp Davis, N.C. There he wrote and started an Army show, "Scotch & Sofa" for the purpose of selling war bonds. After only two performances they sold a half-million. People of that small Southern town brought merchandise which was raffled off to the highest bond bidders. A youngster came on stage with a little pup (cocker spaniel)—the only thing he had to offer to the cause. Someone bid $50,000 and the boy handed him the pet, but not before tearfully kissing it good-bye. The audience too was in tears. The bidder, without hesitation said: "This puppy means more to you than to anyone. Take him home—he's yours."

Soldier Harris then left for Europe with the 9th Army. At war's end there still were several million troops remaining. The Army asked him to form a band to entertain them. Called "The Top Hatters" they played at shows and dances in Antwerp, broadcasting over radio to Brussels and Paris. January 1946 Ross was honorably discharged. And resumed his food business. He joined the Zionists and worked for Israel bonds and the Jewish National Fund. He's a member of Rodef Shalom Temple.

In 1950 our neighbor married, but 17 years later it ended. He got custody of their two daughters. Bonnie, now 15 goes to Allderdice. Georgia is 10 and attends Wightman. Ross makes it his business to always know where they are and with whom. The kids say even tho' pop is considered a swinger, he's old-fashion strict. And they love him for it.

In 1960 he started racing cars and became Western Pennsylvania's auto-cross champion. Five years later he went on the national road-racing circuit with the Sports Car Club of America, becoming regional champion and a director. He formed its announcing staff which covers their races. Several years ago Ross joined the "Single Parents" Club (3 women to every man!) and became its v.p. A year later he joined "Guys & Dolls." Again fewer guys than dolls. After selling his food business, his efforts include real estate, securities and orchestras. Now he plays the sax with the Don Charles Orchestra at Country Clubs. This year he was appointed to the Pittsburgh Area Community Advisory Council of the Small Business Administration. It was confirmed in Washington. He's listed in more "Who's Whos" than you can shake a stick at.

The Harris home is cared for by a full-time live-in housekeeper and outside help three days a week. Ross brings in the groceries.

Neighbors: by now wouldn't you consider Mr. Harris the Catch of the Year? But he insists "no second time around." And to play it safe, dates 5 different women. Let's see. Didn't King Solomon change his mind at times? Should that ever happen to Ross, may the best gal win.

Mohamad Hassibi

Love Conquers All For Young Marrieds

This is being written on a lovely day, a few snowflakes falling here and there, gently hinting that winter is on its way. And what neighborhood personality do you suppose you'll learn about today? A most interesting one, be assured of that.

Meet Mohamad Hassibi from far-off Iran, for centuries known as Persia. Married to American-born Naomi Foote the Hassibis are our neighbors in a rented duplex Alderson St.

In his native country young Mohamad graduated from the University of Teheran with a BS degree in mechanical engineering. And a thorough knowledge of English with a British accent don't-you-know. Then, together with 5,000 others he tried for a scholarship offered by the Iranian government to 100 deserving students. He was a lucky winner.

In 1958 Mohamad came to Washington. There he entered the American University in its language center. His main purpose was a cram course in English with emphasis on Americanization. In three months student Hassibi shed his British accent and acquired perfect Yankee English. Then to our city with his Iranian scholarship. And entered Carnegie Tech's Printing Management Dept. After graduation he was hired by Herbick & Held Printing Co. as production engineer. A year later he was promoted to assistant plant engineer. Now he's plant engineer.

Wife Naomi, before marriage was a nurse at Shadyside Hospital. A dance was being held there. And tall, dark, good-looking Hassibi with another fella sauntered in. So did Cupid. Soon the machinery of fate began to chug. After two years of dating, Methodist Naomi Foote and Moslem Mohamad Hassibi became Mr. and Mrs. Five years ago, to be exact. During that time the many problems engendered by their diverse religions have been somehow resolved. They've been blessed with two beautiful little girls.

Shereen (Persian for sweet) is all of 20 months. Laleh, meaning red tulip is 2½ months. When they are old enough, the parents say they will be given the privilege of choosing the religion they prefer.

Meanwhile the Hassibis don't go to any church as yet. If and when they do it will in all probability be the Unitarian. The household language is English. But they will teach the youngster Persian, too. Just now, the girls ain't talkin' any language, although they seem to understand both.

Mohamad's parents were against the marriage, not through religious prejudice but because it meant he would settle here instead of in Teheran as they had hoped. Parents are like that the world over.

Our neighbor doesn't want to go back to Iran because it's a dictatorship country. Since he himself spoke on TV for our newspapers against dictators, being there would be unsafe. The secret police would forever be watching his every move and his family put under constant pressure.

Mohamad says he owes a great deal of adjustment and learning from belonging to the International Samovar Club of Pittsburgh. Of the Club's 120 members 30 different countries are represented — Iran, Arabia, Israel, Turkey, India, Sweden, Poland, Brazil, to name a few. The Club tries to create an atmosphere free of prejudice — racial, cultural, political. About half of the membership is American. For two years Mohamad was vice president. Now he's the Club's president. The members are students, professors and professional people — age 18 to 50.

The meals at the Hassibi household are mostly American with an Iranian menu once a week. Mohamad's mom (first name Aziz) visited them for two months last summer. And taught Naomi a famous Persian dish — Khoreste Bodemjan. It's lamb with eggplant and rice, seasoned with all sorts of exotic herbs. Wish there was space to give you the complete recipe. Regretfully there isn't.

Rev. Lewis S. Hastings

Area's Rev. Civil Rights Worker

After telling you about all sorts of fascinating neighborhood personalities, somehow the theologians have been overlooked. Mostly because we have many various denominations.

And it's not easy to determine who is the bestest with the mostest. However, risking the warning that "fools rush in where angels fear to tread," we'll give it a try. And choose at random Rev. Lewis S. Hastings, pastor of the closeby Ashbury Methodist Church. It's located right smack at the corner of Forbes & Murray.

The random choice proved a lucky one because Rev. Hastings turned out to be a most colorful fellow — not only the church but in his personal life as well.

Our neighbor's church has a membership of 250. Asked why not more, Rev. Hastings says simply "We're in a predominantly Jewish neighborhood. And Methodists don't pray in synagogues."

However, listen to this. Until the Forbes Avenue Temple Sinai was completed, the Jewish members held their services at the Methodist Church. On Friday evenings. This made for warm friendships between the two faiths.

And now let's get down to brass tacks. This is Rev. Hastings' third year as minister here. Previously he served in Aspinwall, in which area his forebearers were pioneers several hundred years ago. He completed four years at Allegheny College in Meadville, getting his B.A. degree.

Then three years at the Boston University School of Theology. And did graduate work there for two years. While at Allegheny he did volunteer youth work at the Bethany Church. One of the many "youths" was Phylle Boyle. Lovely to look at but too youthful for our serious-minded minister.

One spring evening he was caught in the rain —without an umbrella. Who came along but Phylle with a large one. And invited him under it. No, they didn't sing in the rain. They just walked and talked. Well, a fella has to show his appreciation somehow. So he invited her to a community concert at the high school. A year later they were saying "I do" in Neville Island, Pastor Edwin S. Wallace now of blessed memory, tying the knot. And where do you think they went on their honeymoon? To New York City. Because they had never seen the Statue of Liberty or the Empire State building.

Today the Hastings have two lively children: Stewart, 11 and Holly, 9. Both attend Regent Square School, cata-corner from their home. They were born of all places, in Hawaii. A Japanese doctor delivered them. The newlyweds had been sent there as missionaries and remained five years. They converted many youthful Buddhists to the Methodist Church. The priests had no objection, saying "We have the old folks. You get the kids."

Ever since boyhood our neighbor has earned extra money as a folk-singer, twanging on a guitar. He knows some 500 songs — some in French. He entertained groups here, there, all around. Eventually his bank-roll was sufficient for a trip to Europe with Phylle. But they had to budget themselves on $5 per day — no more, regardless.

In Paris they paid $1.80 daily for their hotel room on the Left Bank. They could see Notre Dame Cathedral through their window. They cooked their own meals. Often they were seen carrying groceries, with a long loaf of French bread under their arm. Their neighbors never took them for Americans who spend money like mad. They thought they were British who always manage to get the most for the least. Before their trip they studied French, German and Italian — enough to keep them from getting stranded.

Last summer Rev. Hastings, with a group of other ministers, was sent to the Communist countries on a peace mission — Czechoslovakia, Poland, Russia and into Tashkent in Central Asia. And returned through Scandinavian countries.

Things there appeared freer now than before de-Stalinization. But compared to us, the people are still greatly restricted, especially as to religion. The children are taught godlessness in the schools. The state feels when the old people die out, religion will die with them. The greatest sufferers are the Jewish people.

He saw evidence of anti-Semitism. A book, published in the Ukraine and translated for the visitors by a man in the U.S. Embassy contained much anti-Semitic propaganda. The book is now out of circulation.

Our neighbor went to Mississippi during the Civil Rights marches and to Selma. He was cursed at, called "a white nigger" and suffered other indignities. But he came back more alive than ever — and kicking.

Like other dedicated theologians, Rev. Hastings believes that families who pray together stay together. And are happy together.

Roland W. Hawkins

Aviary Leader Near Neighbor

Been to the beautiful new AVIARY yet? You know — the million addition to the Northside Conservatory - Aviary? It was made possible by a city fund of $125,000 and a $960,000 grant from the generous Scaife family. Opened Memorial Day, already thousands have flocked to the exotic Bird Paradise and been refreshed in heart and spirit. And because you too will be going there, you want to know a little about the remarkable fellow who has charge of it. Meet aviculturist Roland W. Hawkins, our almost-neighbor. He lived in an apartment above nearby Arts & Crafts Center, Shady and Fifth.

Born in Alberta, Canada, and when a youngster of 6 a neighbor became "more like a father" to him. And took him on long walks — 16 to 20 miles on Saturdays — to study birds, trees, flowers, mammals. An ideal foundation for his later profession. At 19 Roland graduated from Alberta High. This was in 1939 when Germany declared war on France. So he volunteered in the Canadian Army. He spent that Christmas on the high seas on the way to Britain and landed in Scotland New Year's Eve. After 5½ years over-seas duty he got his first home leave. By the time he reached Alberta the war had ended!

So the ex-soldier enrolled at Alberta University. About that time Dr. Arthur C. Toomey — that handsome fellow who heads the popular Travelogues at our Carnegie Art Museum and so charmingly introduces the various photographers — was leading an expedition in Alberta for the collection and study of birds. The trip was sponsored by the late Thomas A. Mellon. Roland, having studied with Toomey before the war under the same naturalist — and even went duck and pheasant hunting with him — joined the expedition. They traveled by pack — 27 horses. And Hawkins even had the experience of being bucked off his horse.

In 1946 he joined the staff at the Ottawa National Museum as a Taxidermist. And later an Ornithologist in the Dept. of Birds. And as Curator of Mammals. May 1947, at the invitation of Dr. Toomey, Mr. Hawkins came here as Preparator in the Bird section of Carnegie Museum. And later became Toomey's assistant. He joined in numerous field expeditions throughout western U.S. and Honduras, Central America. In Honduras, guess what? Bachelor Hawkins met beautiful Maria Helena Bario. She spoke no English. He no Spanish. Aided and abetted by the language of love — and a dictionary — he soon knew she was his kind of girl. A year later, while the man-in-love was still with our Museum, Maria Helena came here as his bride.

While still on the Museum staff, the young husband worked part time in the original Aviary first opened in 1952. A year later he left the Museum to join the Dept. of Parks & Recreation, taking full charge of the Aviary.

Their daughter Linda, now 19, is an art student at the Edinboro State College. And James Roland, 17, goes to Peabody High. They speak Spanish a little but understand more. Same with dad. And mom? You'd swear she's a born Yankee.

The Hawkins built a small cottage near Lake Ontario and go there on vacations. They all enjoy fishing and swimming. At home there's Ginger, a yellow-headed parrot; Cheery, the canary. And their lively dog Laddie who loves everybody. Even the mailman.

Mr. Hawkins' recent hobby is taking slide pictures of wild flowers from the U.S. and Canada. He does some sculpturing of birds. Also oil painting and murals. It's he who painted the Aviary's scenic background— mountains, valleys, waterfalls, providing birds and visitors with a panorama of breath-taking beauty.

Neighbors, gather up the wife and kids into your jalopy. Or your Cadillac mebbe? Or better yet, JOG over to the Northside. You'll be glad you did.

Sara Henderson Hay
Composer's Wife True Poet and Music Lover

Winter has just begun so spring, the poetic season, is pretty far behind. But who waits for spring when we have in our neighborhood a fabulous poet whose fame has already spread far and wide. Our neighbor with that certain something called talent is Sara Henderson Hay living at Bartlett Street. Her husband is Nikolai Lopatnikoff, distinguished composer and professor of music at Carnegie Tech.

Miss Hay, born in our city but reared in Anniston, Ala. began writing poetry as a child. At ten her poems were published. In 1933 her first book of poems, "Field of Honor" won the Kaleidograph Book Award. For several years she worked in the Rare Book Department of Charles Scribner's Sons, N.Y.; and edited the Stevenson Home Book of Quotations. She also reviewed poetry and fiction for various periodicals. And still does.

In 1939 came her second book of poems, "This, My letter" published by Alfred A. Knopf. Of it the late William Rose Beret wrote in the Saturday Review; "In a day of so great confusion it is good to come upon verse with clean line and penetrating thought precisely expressed..."

In the spring of 1951 came her third book, "The Delicate Balance published by Charles Scribner's Sons. It received the Edna St. Vincent Millay Memorial Award. Then followed a fourth collection of poems, "The Stone and the Shell" published by the University Pittsburgh Press. It too got rave reviews. Her fifth volume, "Story Hour" was published by Doubleday and came out this past September.

Are Miss Hay's poems the "rose is a rose type? The answer is no. They rhyme perfectly - all of them - in traditional sonnet form. "Story Hour" reflects humorous and sometimes poignant commentaries on the bewildering complexities of human nature. Sara herself says, though the poems are based on nursery tales, "they definitely are not for children."

At a luncheon in Harrisburg Oct. 17 Governor Scranton made Sara Henderson Hay one of the Distinguished Daughters of Pennsylvania. She has given, and continues to give many readings from her poems over TV, radio and from the lecture platform.

Sara and Nikolai met 13 years ago at the world-famous exclusive McDowell Colony, Peterborough, N.H., where artists of exceptional talent are invited. The Colony is huge, with studios in the heart of the woods - a most peaceful atmosphere for creative work. They married a year later. Every summer they take a two-month "working vacation" at the Colony. Sara already started work on her sixth book. They both are interested in what the other accomplishes - but they don't compete.

Our neighbors' Bartlett St. home is tastefully furnished. Added to its charm are two beautiful Siamese cats named Igor and Nadia. These seemingly are unimpressed by the talent surrounding them. At the sound of a lovely concerto or a sonnet recited aloud, Igor hops on an easy chair and takes a snooze. And Nadia likewise curls up into a furry ball and catnaps nearby.

Dr. Samuel P. Hays
Our Neighbor Who Resembles JFK

They say brains and looks seldom go hand in hand. Yet in rare instances they do.

That's how it is in the case of Dr. Samuel P. Hays, chairman of the department of history at the University of Pittsburgh. He not only is brilliant but good-looking as well. In fact, he resembles JFK so much that he could pass as his twin brother. Except, of course, he doesn't own a rocking chair!

The Hays family came here from Iowa City in the fall of 1960. They occupy an interesting 70-year old house on Wightman St. Besides Dr. Hays there are his interesting and charming wife Barbara and four lively children: Peter 10; Polly 8; Michael6 and Becky 4. The older children go to Wightman School. Little Becky attends the nursery school at the Y-IKC. Peter takes ceramics there and Polly completed a course in ballet. And all enjoy the Settlement's swimming facilities.

Dr. Hays is a typical small-town-boy-makes-good. From his birthplace, tiny Corydon in southern Indiana where he even worked on a dairy farm, he made his way to Swarthmore College; and graduated there in 1948. Four years later he got his M.A. and Ph. D. at Harvard. He taught a year at the University of Illinois and seven years at State University of Iowa.

Wife Barbara is from New Haven, Conn., daughter of a famous pediatrician formerly at Yale Medical School. The father, Dr. Daniel Darrow, discovered a cure for infant diarrhea.

The Hays are Quakers. Barbara Hays is chairman of the local American Friends Service Committee. This committee specializes in arranging week-end work camps and seminars for high school and college students. These camps are in the Homewood and Manchester districts. The students volunteer their services.

Dr. Hays is steeped in historical knowledge — particularly American history since the Civil War until the present. He does research and writing on the subject. Two of his published books are "Conservation and the Gospel of Efficiency" — a history of the conservation movement in the U.S. from 1890 to 1920. And "The Response to Industrialism" — a history of the U.S. from 1885 to 1914. Sounds like heavy reading? Not at all. It's fascinating, not only to students of history but to readers in general.

Our professor is also studying the history of Pittsburgh and collects manuscripts and books relating to our city. And particularly on the history of Squirrel Hill and its ethnic groups. He is looking for old books about Pittsburgh for use of his students at Pitt. He wants, especially, reports of various religious organizations such as the Holy Name Society, B'nai B'rith, Y-IKC and any other groups. Take a look — all of you — in your attics, cellars and files. Maybe you have something interesting for him on the subject.

Dad Hays, Mom Barbara and their four youngsters go on hikes and week-end camp-outs together. They love sleeping in tents, and have discovered some ideal camp sites along the sky-line drive of Shanandoah Valley. How lucky the children are, to have parents young enough and who care enough to share in their fun.

Dr. Hays, with all his educational background and degrees modestly says: "Just call me Mister." Nuthin' doing. You are DR. HAYS to us and we are fortunate and proud to have you and your interesting family as neighbors.

Mrs. Reuben Helfant

'Woman of the Year'

Recently a pleasant voice on Radio Station WRYT made an announcement. It said: "We choose as the First Lady of the Day — Mrs. Reuben Helfant." Such an honor isn't given to just anybody. You have to be someone extra special. Mrs. Helfant, our neighbor at Woodland Road, is all of that. And much, much more.

She is now serving her second term as president of the Ladies Hospital Aid Society, an auxiliary of the Montefiore Hospital. A voluntary service it is. And an overwhelming one. Mrs. Helfant has the know-how, temperament and devotion that it requires.

First let's learn a little about her private life. The former Ethel Blumenfeld is a graduate of H. C. Frick Training School for Teachers and the University of Pittsburgh. For six years she taught music at Dilworth School and supervised Pitt, Tech and Duquesne music students who did practice teaching.

Then — wouldn't you know it — Ethel began going steady. And before long became Mrs. Reuben Helfant. Husband Reuben is president of the Thrift Drug Co.

During the 23 years that followed, good things happened. They were blessed with two lovely daughters. Carol Lee, 21, just graduated the University of Wisconsin, majoring in French. Last summer she studied in Paris with the Sarah Lawrence College session. She attended McGill University in Montreal, studying and conversing French. Come September Carol will pursue graduate studies for her master's degree.

Sister Sherry, 19, is now summering at the University of Wisconsin. And will enter her junior year at the University of Pennsylvania this fall.

The Helfants' lovely home is flooded with sunlight, surrounded by beautiful trees and radiant flowers. And a garden in the back. Inside you get a feeling of relaxation and ease. Until you take a peek into Madam President's bedroom. Near her bed is a desk piled high with correspondence, notes, records. And a closet chockfull of files.

In between, though, Ethel manages to prepare meals, play golf and the piano. Her devoted secretary is none other than her likeable Mom, Mary Blumenfeld who lives there. Mary handles the constant phone calls far better than telephone - answering service.

The Ladies Hospital Aid Society has approximately 3,000 members, several hundred of whom are volunteer workers. It's now in its 67th year. It provides medical, social, educational and financial services and also volunteer personnel for Montefiore Hospital. And to the Pittsburgh community as well.

The society pledged to raise $350,000 over a 10-year period. And you know women — they are raising it. Their Gift and Coffee Shop in Montefiore has become "big business." And the annual charity "Montefiore Ball" at the Hilton is the talk of the town. Because of these "Ladies," Montefiore has acquired new equipment in its Radioisotope Laboratory. This equipment has already demonstrated its value in picking up early tumors.

Their Service-to-the-Blind Committee has received the Lane Bryant Citation. Hundreds of other services are too numerous to mention. All is accomplished through the combined efforts of hundreds of dedicated women — officers, board members, volunteer workers. And their president is proud of each and every one of them, has made friends of them and is grateful to them.

The Helfants went to Europe in May. Ethel had hesitated because of her LHAS responsibilities. But husband Reuben — smart fella — insisted. After her term expires they plan to travel more widely and often.

Mrs. Helfant is interested in dozens of other civic and charitable organizations. And has served on their executive boards.

Station WRYT called her "Lady of the Day." We'll go one better and name Mrs. Reuben Helfant "Lady of the Year".

Theodore P. Hipkins
"Little Warm Springs" Right Here

Today let's learn a little about our neighborhood Home for Crippled Children. And its capable executive director, Theodore P. Hipkins, who likes to be called Ted.

For those who may not know, the Home's main entrance is at 1426 Denniston St. It occupies the entire area surrounded by Northumberland St., Wilkins and Shady Avenues. As you saunter along outside you see the low rambling red brick building that looks like a long cluster of small cottages.

The expanse of velvety grass and young trees bursting with spring blossoms give the place an atmosphere of peaceful quiet; as if nobody lived there. But once inside you'll become breathless with wonder, admiration and pride at the activities going on.

And your heart will melt with sympathy toward the youngsters each seriously handicapped. Struggling to improve through rehabilitation, along with readin', writin' and all kinds of fun things. Go through it farther and you'll understand why cripples from two years of age to late teens and early 20's are brought there.

Founded in 1902 as a voluntary non-profit organization the home has served the handicapped ever since. There is room for 150. Some are amputees. Others learning-disorder children.

None can romp and play like normals. But they are told, regardless of race, creed or color: "You belong, you are wanted. Much we can do to help you." The staff of 130 comprises dedicated professional workers and teachers.

To tell you more would fill a book. Maybe a library. Better take a good look-see yourself. Or if you're pressed for time, ask Mr. Hipkens to show you their 19-minute movie. You'll be glad you did. And you'll be proud that this fabulous place called "The Little Warm Springs" is in our very neighborhood.

Mr. Hipkens? Oh, yes — the home's executive director — Ted. The brains and pulse behind all the goings on. He and his interesting family live on the premises, in an old-fashioned 15-room house. His capable missus, the former Norma Hitchings from Syracuse, is a full-time librarian at Taylor Allderdice.

Son, Robert, 23, graduated there and is now a graduate student at Syracuse University. Anne is 18 and graduated Allderdice last June, and is a student at the University of Lausanne in Switzerland majoring in languages. She's coming back to continue at Barnard College in N.Y.C.

While at Allderdice Anne was assistant editor of "The Forward," the school's paper. The youngest is 11 and his name is Henry. He attends Linden School. The children's grandma, Fannie, lives with them. So does great-grandma Libby — 98 years young.

Mr. Hipkens graduated Syracuse University, originally in forestry. Then taught science, math and military subjects in upstate New York. During World War II and the Korean War, he served seven years in the Marine Corps and 14 more as a reserve officer.

He was attracted here by a Squirrel Hiller — Dr. Leslie A. Falk of Bartlett St., area medical director. He became administrator for the United Mine Workers Welfare & Retirement Fund. Nine years later our neighborhood "Little Warm Springs" called him.

In addition to his constant duties with the home, Ted travels all over the country as consultant and adviser to other rehabilitation centers. Even to Warm Springs, Ga.

With so many responsibilities in their respective jobs and their personal family, Ted and Norma hardly have time to sit down and talk with one another. For diversion, do they ever do anything gay and mad and daring: Sure. On Tuesday evenings they hop in their car and drive to North Hills. And do their shopping!

Mrs. Sophie Hoechstetter

82-Year Old Widow Bursts With Enthusiasm

Halloween is already past, and the trick-or-treaters are home watching TV — or with luck, studying their lessons. So now we can give ourselves a treat — learning about a most remarkable neighbor — Mrs. Sophie Hoechstetter living on Beacon Street.

We all know people not yet 40, and though physiologically living, are not really alive. The fire is gone from their eyes; their imagination dried up, and like old soldiers they just fade away. How different is Sophie Hoechstetter. At 82 she's vibrant, radiating enthusiasm and warmth. Always she's been like that. And during passing years even more so. She's a true example of a real young-at-hearter.

Our neighbor was born in Frankfurt-am-Mein, Germany. Her father was a rabbi. during her teen years a friend from Braddock, Pa. visited them. And told Sophie "how wonderful" America is. So at 20 Sophie came to Braddock to return the friend's visit. In no time she met the latter's bachelor cousin. Four weeks later she said "I do" and became Mrs. Leopold Hoechstetter.

The happy couple started housekeeping in Wilkinsburg. Fifty-two years later they celebrated their Golden Wedding anniversary.

The Hoechstetters were blessed with two sons: Lionel, an aeronautical engineer for Fairchild Air Co., Hagerstown, Md.; and Dr. Stanton Hoechstetter, Chief of Radiology of the Rutland Veterans Hospital, Rutland Heights, Mass.

There are four grandchildren (two boys, two girls) and two great-grandchildren. Then tragedy struck. Son Lionel, at 35 — in the prime of life — passed away. And a few years later Mrs. Hoechstetter became a widow.

Some women, confronted with similar life's eventualities, would spend the rest of their lives crying the blues. But not Sophie. She continued, even to a greater extent, her lifetime community service. They have added up to a treasure-house of worthy deeds. Wherever you go — at meetings and affairs of charitable groups, there you see her, smiling and veritably bursting with enthusiasm. Forty-three years ago she was one of 30 women who founded the Lillian S. Davis Chapter of B'nai B'rith Women.

She is the only survivor of the Founders' group. For 42 years she's been active in the National Council of Jewish Women, and has done 55 years of "do-gooding" for the Rodef Shalom Temple Sisterhood.

In 1905 she completed a Red Cross course in elementary Hygiene & Home Care. Her certificate was signed by President Wilson.

Sophie has never dropped out of her many activities. She's been blessed with good health and considers it a joy and privilege to be interested in everything worthwhile.

Sophie belongs to the Y-IKC Choral Group. She got first prize and a loving-cup for singing "Bless This House, O Lord, We Pray." And listen to this: Sophie plays the zither.

At the Jewish Rosh Hashona Services recently at Syria Mosque, who do you think was the proudest — and most devout — worshipper? Sophie. You see, her devoted son, Dr. Stanton Hoechstetter, was at her side. He came all the way from Massachusetts to see her. Such a busy doctor, you may ask. How come he traveled so far just for one day to be with his mother? It's obvious he is proud of his mom. So is our entire community.

Lew Horn

Hey, Mr. Lahr! Please Move Over!

Oh, for laffin' out loud! That's how it is during "The Mad Show" currently wowing them at the Pittsburgh Playhouse.

The five zany characters creating the fun are all top-notch. But today you'll learn about one in particular because he had the good sense to come live in our neighborhood.

Meet comedian Lew Horn, enjoying a room with kitchen privileges at the Home of Mrs. Lawrence Cuneo, Dalzell Place. And because he comes from that place where a tree grows — Brooklyn — most likely he makes the best bagel and lox breakfast in Squirrel Hill.

When Lew Horn played in "Where's Charley?" in Kansas City last year, he was hailed as a "young Bert Lahr." He also appeared in New York in "The Fantasticks," "The Days and Nights of Beebee Festermaker" and "Telemachus Clay", giving a personality-packed, energetic performance.

And sharing the fun with his audience.

He also made a comedy album called "I Never Let School Stand in the Way of My Education" with Sandy Baron, star of the new NBC-TV series "Hey, Landlord." He has made several commercials and has appeared on major New York and West Coast television stations.

Our current neighbor is a graduate of U.C.L.A. where he ran off with the Best Actor Award. And has as yet to return it.

Born in Manhattan, Lew spent most of his younger years in Brooklyn. His widowed mother still lives there. After five years on the West Coast, he now resides in New York City. He has two sisters and one brother. And is an uncle nine times.

The other talented members of "The Mad Show," besides neighbor Horn are Betty Aberlin, Jay Devlin, Ted Schwartz and Fiddle Viracola. The revue is produced by the Establishment Theatre of New York and is based on Mad Magazine. It lampoons everything from television to cereal ads to sports broadcasting.

Opening night three weeks ago was auspicious but sedate. You see, that night come mostly regular Playhouse subscribers. So there was a minimum of teenagers clamoring for autographs. But things livened up each succeeding night. What with performances every Tuesday, Wednesday and Thursday nights; two on Friday, Saturday and Sunday evenings; and, by popular demand beginning July 31, Sunday matinees — the place is humming.

In addition, the "Twelfth Night" party after the show August 9, when the audience is invited to come back stage for sandwiches and coffee and to meet the cast, will likely teem with shriekers and screamers.

During the cast's first week here, they were on a 12-hour-per day rehearsal schedule.

What do actors do after the show? Martin Pochapin, Playhouse manager, gives them conducted tours to interesting night spots in and around our fair city. At the B & M Cafe recently they were served a delicious meal — southern style.

Sleep? Who needs it? But actually they can snooze until 11 the next morning.

So what else is new? Here's what.

Tall, handsome Lew Horn with that mischievous come-hither look, is a bachelor But don't let it get around.

Mrs. Pearl Kantrowitz

Too Many Cooks Won't Spoil This Fair!

Remember the all-day March of Dimes Telethon you watched on television one Sunday last January? When gifted entertainers had you glued to your screen? And reported collection totals from minute to minute— for the fight against polio?

Well, you'll see another Telethon come next January. And as you doubtless know, wonderfully dedicated workers are already planning and arranging the campaign.

One of the various ways and means to raise funds is the ever-popular Food Fair. It will be held at the Civic Arena Oct. 27 and 28. And who do you think is chairman of the fair? A squirrel Hiller, naturally.

She's none other than Mrs. I.Henry Kantrowitz of 5351 Fair Oaks St. First name Pearl. And a pearl she definitely is. Husband Henry is a successful CPA. And actually he's the one who got her interested in the cause. Twelve years ago, to be exact.

It's like this. Henry Kantrowitz was on the board of the National Foundation of the March of Dimes. For 14 years. He was a board member when they brought Dr. Jonas Salk to our city. Now he's Allegheny County chairman. And you know how it is when a husband is the nicest fellow you ever want to meet. His missus soon falls in line.

Their son, Kenneth, 25, is an architect. Richard is 23 and a graduate accountant. And pssst! listen but don't let it get around. Both are unattached. The family is close-knit and cooperative and dinner is always ready. Pearl's household is so well organized that she's practically a full-time Food Fair worker.

Pearl knows only too well that polio isn't completely licked in spite of the Salk and Sabin vaccines. The American Medical Association warns that two-thirds of the nation's pre-school age children have not received full protection through vaccination. And while polio is primarily a childhood disease it also can strike adults. And in addition to polio the Salk Institute in California is carrying on research on the ever-widening birth defects. So the battle must go on. And with her brand of magic, imagination and energy she's accomplishing wonders.

Chairman Pearl sits at the phone for hours on end, contacting food brokers, bakeries, chefs restaurants. Her pleasant telephone voice has sales appeal and has brought remarkable response. Baked goods, delicious foods, candies and all such will be flowing to the arena at the proper time. For instance, Polis of our neighborhood will donate shrimp steamed in beer.

Weinstein's will send its various specialities. And our neighborhood bakeries will contribute all sorts of delicious cakes and breads. And listen to this. The students of the South Side Vocational High School will bake all kinds of cakes and bring them down to the Arena to compete with artistic decorations. Also Rankin High and Allderdice.

All the chefs whom Pearl contacted will prepare exotic foods and auction them off at the fair.

Nationality groups will bring their specialty foods. Like for instance Ukrainian perogies, Serbian stuffed cabbage, Syrian boklawa, Lithuanian ausukes. The Scotch group will send their famous meat pies. And there will be Lebanese, German English and Russo-Carpathian foods.

And Pearl herself will bake her mouth-watering strudel. And speaking of foods, she says if you ever want to lose weight, be a chairman of the Food Fair. She's already shelved 15 pounds.

Our neighborhood chairman was a nurse's aid at Aspinwall's Veterans Hospital. Also Magee Hospital for five years. And what was her salary? One dollar a year! When she first started it was in the middle of the year. So her pay came to all of 37 cents. We wonder if Henry made her report it to the Internal Revenue?

Do the tantalizing foods mentioned above make you hungry? Do this: On October 27 and 28 head for the hills — leading to the Arena. And "break a bagel with all your friends. You'll be glad you did.

Mrs. Isadore (Lillian) Karelitz

'Tree Lady' Devotes Hours to Major Love

When a personality in our midst has devoted years and years for extra special causes and done them quietly and modestly, she herself is someone extra special. So today you'll learn about her. She's Mrs. Isadore (Lillian) Karelitz of 'way down Murray Ave. Mrs. Karelitz whom everyone calls Lil, became interested in Trees for Israel before it became a State. In 1948 she was appointed Tree Chairman of her then Hadassah Group 1 (now the Henrietta Szold) and 5 years later headed the Hadassah Chapter for the same project. It became her life, spending days and evenings phoning and selling trees. Now, so well known, people contact her. But she still phones before special events like Birthdays, Bar-Mitzvahs, Mother's Day, In Memoriam, Anniversaries, Weddings, Father's Day — you name it, she sells trees for it. Affectionately named "The Tree Lady" her Hadassah group presented her with a gold pin with 7 branches, each encrusted with shimmering stones. And the Jewish National Fund gave her a silver Bible "The Five Books of Moses" in Hebrew & English.

Prior to Trees, Lil worked for various other worthy causes. But first a bit about her personal life. Born in Homestead, the former Lillian Eskovitz married Isadore Karelitz in 1921. They were blessed with 2 sons: Edwin, now a successful CPA in Braddock; and Morton, an electronic worker in Monroeville. There are 7 grandchildren. After 30 years of a beautiful marriage life's eventuality struck and Mrs. Karelitz was sadly widowed. Did she start crying the blues with "Oh, why did this happen to me?" Not Lil. She went to work for son Edwin, continuing for 14 years. A trained wiz at mathematics she became an asset to his business. When WWII came along and Ed joined the Army, his mom joined the USO, making sandwiches for the boys. And three days a week went out for blood donors. The American Red Cross presented her with a Citation for exceptional volunteer work toward the Blood Donor Service. Dated May 30, 1945. Three months later the U.S. Treasury Department honored her with a Certificate for cooperation in behalf of the War Finance Program selling War Bonds. It was signed by the then Secretary of the Treasury, Henry Morganthau, Jr. Also she was made a Brigadier General for selling War Bonds and received a certificate from the Blue Star Brigade.

For her Henrietta Szold group our Lil has served as partial-payment chairman, treasurer, business-ad chairman and auditor. Currently she's Blue Box chairman for our whole District and of course still Tree Chairman of her Group and of Chapter. Also Chairman of B'nai Emmunoh Synagogue. As of November 30th, 1972 she sold $40,000 worth of Bonds and 45,740 Trees for Israel.

Our neighbor's personal joy is her weekly Sabbath dinner with son Edwin, of Darlington Rd., his charming wife (the former Bess Rosenbloom) and their 4 children. The best linen, silver, dishes — and the best kosher meal ever. Ed makes "Kiddish", recites the prayer over the wine and all sing grace after the meal.

Another pleasure is taking her French poodle Pepi walking. What does Pepi think of trees in Israel? He likes them better on the street where he lives. Be that as it may, 25 million more trees are needed in Israel. To enlarge the John F. Kennedy Peace Forest; those memorializing Eleanor Roosevelt, Winston Churchill and of course Harry Truman. Also the Martyrs' Forest for the 6 million Jewish victims of the Nazis, and the Freedom Forest for Soviet Jewry. And now a hillside as a living memorial to forever recall the 11 Israeli athletes killed in Munich.

A mere $2.50 will plant a tree. Call the Jewish National Fund Office (521-6866). The Tree Lady will follow through.

Mrs. Ilse Karp

Has Few Dull Moments

We have as our neighbors at 5467 Bartlett St., "Mr. Opera" and family — the Karps.

Richard Karp, as we all know, is the famous director of the Pittsburgh Opera Co. He's also professor of musicology at St.Vincent College, and evenings he has classes at Pitt.

But director Karp is written up often in all the newspapers, especially when there's a famous opera in town. So we'll let him rest on his laurels today and tell you a little about his interesting family. And particularly his wife Ilse.

The former Ilse Klein was born and reared in Berlin and was veritably steeped in musical education.

In her early 20's she was about to audition as clarinetist in Berlin for the Frankfurt Kultur Bund Symphony Orchestra. Their new conductor was a bachelor — handsome Richard Karp.

He frowned a bit and remarked that women had no place in a symphony. "Besides, what woman could play a clarinet?" He lived to eat those words because Ilse won the audition — and him for a husband. Served him right, she now laughingly reminisces.

The knot was tied — but good — with two weddings: a civil ceremony in Frankfurt and a religious one in Berlin.

Their happiness was marred by the Hitler menace and life became unbearable. In 1937 the Karps fled to New York.

A year later our city welcomed them with open arms. German's loss has become our gain.

Ilse Karp is organist and musical director at the Tree of Life Synagogue.

She teaches piano, some clarinet and guitar and other instruments at the Y-IKC. She has taught there for 25 years, starting when it was the Irene Kaufmann Settlement on Centre Avenue.

Ilse also teaches instrumental music at the Falk School. And at home there are classes at all times — seven days a week.

"Mrs. Opera" also is ardent in sports. She excels in swimming and tennis. As to the latter sport, her only objection is that in tennis there's no "love" after 40.

Son Steven, 18, attends the Georgetown University School for Foreign Service in our nation's capital.

His hobby is art. Barbara, affectionately called Bobbi, is at that most interesting age — 16. And she's chock-full of talent.

Bobbi has appeared on television, radio and was soloist of the Symphony Youth concert. She has also played for the Pittsburgh Concert Society.

And now listen to this. During a performance of "Aida" at the Mosque recently, Ilse's husband conducted on a chair. He had a bout with the flu and a 102-degree temperature.

As the curtain rose on the third act Tenor Flaviano Labo tripped on his way to the stage and fell down the back stairs. Followed 20 minutes of darkness, breathless anxiety and "a doctor in the house."

After tourniquets and bandages "Aida" was completed and our good old sympathetic Pittsburgh audience gave tenor and conductor a thunderous standing ovation.

Singer Labo, after several days at our Presbyterian Hospital, has already thrilled the Met in "Don Carlo." After a few days of warmth and care from his devoted family, he's now fit as the best fiddle in his orchestra.

We'll end with a sigh of sadness. Angelita, the Karp's beloved pet dog, recently breathed her last and has gone to her reward after 13 years of TLC — tender loving care. Our community extends its deepest symphathy.

Dr. Richard Karp
"Mr. Opera" Raises Baton

Opera lovers, pull up your chairs. And listen. For today you'll learn about a most fabulous fellow. A neighbor, of course—at Bartlett Street. He's none other than Dr. Richard Karp, famous Director of our Pittsburgh Opera Company. Before the curtain rises for the various beautiful operas and the symphony musicians have taken their places for the overture, there's thunderous applause as "Mr. Opera" appears to raise his baton. And even at the end of the performance the applause doesn't cease until he joins the cast for their final curtain bows. And don't tell the neighbors but often he even gets a kiss from the prima donna.

Dr. Karp reached the ladder of success in spite of the greatest kind of handicap—Hitlerism. Born in Vienna, after elementary and high school and State University in Dresden, he went on to their State Conservatory of Music, graduating in 1924. Immediately it was one important musical position after another, finally becoming Conductor of the Dusseldorf Opera. When Hitler became German's "hero," Karp went to Czechoslovakia to conduct the Prague Symphone Orchestra. Then was called back to Germany to conduct a "non-Aryan" orchestra. Even that wouldn't have happened if the American Government hadn't commanded forming it. The Orchestra was complete except for a clarinetist. So he went to Berlin to audition for one. Among the Jewish applicants was a lovely young woman—Ilse Klein.

A woman clarinet player? Nothing doing! But after hearing her play he changed his tune and she joined the Orchestra. They played in Frankfurt and throughout West Germany. When conditions worsened Karp decided to make it to the U.S. An American cousin arranged for his affidavit. But guess what? He had meantime fallen deeply in love with his first clarinet player. So the affidavit was changed to "Mr. & Mrs. Richard Karp." The newlyweds arrived in New York Armistice Day 1937. And started housekeeping in two furnished rooms. In no time the Karp talent began showing and they went on a U.S. country tour, he substituting as a quartet violist. Auditioned by the late famous Fritz Reiner, he joined our Pittsburgh Symphony as violist. And four years later became Conductor of the Pittsburgh Opera Society. Then developed it into our professional Opera Company.

Prior to then (in 1950) Pitt asked him to give courses in Music Appreciation. That started the ball rolling. Since too much red tape was needed to get his European credits evaluated, he entered Carnegie Tech (C-MU) where he got his American Masters degree in Musicology, in 1952. Six years later he received his Doctor of Music degree. Dr. Karp taught music at PCW (now Chatham) and returned to Pitt for evening courses. In 1956 he was Associate Professor of Music at St. Vincent College. Then became Professor of Music History at Seton Hill College—a position he still holds.

Between the season's five Operas, Dr. Karp is Adjunct Professor of Fine Arts at Point Park College and Music Director of the Westmoreland Symphony in Greensburg. Our neighbor was chosen "Man of the Year in Music" in 1966 and is listed in "Who's Who in Music."

Since 1958 he has been guest Conductor of the Philadelphia Lyric Co.; the Baltimore Civic Opera; International Season Opera de Bellas Artes, Mexico City; RAI

Symphony Conductor in Milan, Turin and Rome. Also guest Conductor of the Frankfurt Opera Festival in Belfast, Ireland.

The Karp's son Steven, 24 and married is on the staff of the Portland Oregon State University. Barbara (Bobbi), 20 is in the Graduate School of Boston University. There are two beautiful grand-children.

Years ago in Germany our neighbor met another music personality, William Steinberg, now world-famous maestro of our Pittsburgh Symphony. They have been good friends ever since.

As to Dr. Karp's lovely and talented missus — you learned about her through your NEWS several years ago—remember?

Isn't it great, having such wonderful neighbors!

Hyman I. Katz
Accepts Hospital Chairmanship

You know of course that Judge Samuel A. Weiss has had to cut down on his many— too many— civic and philanthropic activities. Doctor's orders. An important post he had to relinquish, among others, was his chairmanship of the local Committee of the National Jewish Hospital at Denver. You know — the Hospital with the world-famous motto "None May Enter Who Can Pay — None Can Pay Who Enter".

The Judge had served faithfully and well for 14 years. To replace the popular and beloved Sammy took pondering and some doing, you may be sure. But at long last the Committee — aided and abetted by Director Frieda Wechsler — came up with another great guy. He's the well-known Hyman I. Katz, executive vice-president and director of Papercraft Corporation. And where do you think he lives? In our interesting neighborhood, naturally. At 1 Hydin Road bordering Schenley Park. Luckily Judge Weiss will continue to serve as honorary chairman.

The new NJH Chairman is a graduate of Peabody High. Not a college degree to his name. Just a bright unassuming fellow who learned early in the school of life that you can't succeed in business without really trying. As a youngster he delivered newspapers in his neighborhood. And at foot-ball games was star salesman of pennants, mums and other novelties. His most valued asset were three devoted brothers—Joseph, William and Emanul. Some people see faster, better and farther into the future than others. The Katz boys did. Thirty years ago they started Papercraft. Brothers who work hard together, get along together — succeed together. Now Papercraft Corporation is known the world over. Its main factory, administration building and national headquarters are in nearby Blaw-Knox. Other factories are located in various cities of the U.S. And one is in Brussels, Belgium.

Mr. Katz is married to lovely Dinie Cooperman. And listen to this.

Her sister Elinor had become the wife of Hy's brother William — with one of those large beautiful weddings. So what do you think happened? Dinie up and married the Best Man—Hy. Time marches on. Hy and Dinie have been blessed with two handsome, lively sons. Harry Alan is "16 going on 17". James Richard will soon be 15. Both attend the Mercersburg Academy. And honestly, they are the luckiest kids ever. Their beautiful home is spacious and the parents are hospitable. Weekends holidays and summers their school friends flock to the Katz home. And the place becomes alive with Juke-box music and dancing. Sometimes there are 50 or 75 teenagers. When they tire of doing the frug, the jerk and other gyrations they can play pool, pin-pong or have a game of basketball in their lit-up court. Often mom and pop join in the fun. So does their devoted housekeeper Evora and husband Lucius. And no one goes to bed before the ball is over and the kids depart.

In their pond with a graceful water fountain happily live 22 colorful fish. And three turtles named Ike, Mike and Louie. They quietly mind their own business. But a household member who likes to be in the midst of everything and thinks she owns the place, is their Shetland collie named Heather. She loves people—even the mailman. But woe be to a prowler who may lurk in the shadows. Her bark is healthy.

Our neighbor soldiered for Uncle Sam during WW II for 5 years. Now he's a member of the Board of Trustees of the American Jewish Committee. He served as director of the YM & WHA and B'nai Israel Synagogue. Also of Technion. He's a 32nd degree Mason and a member of the Shriners. Hy's capable missus is V.P. of the Women's American Ort. And works in their shop called "Act II" in Shadyside. She's also chairman of the premiere performance of "Camelot" at our Squirrel Hill theatre come November 8 — for Ort's benefit.

The officials of NJH and the patients in Denver are all happy with the new Chairman. And wish him and his family the best of everything. So does our entire community here.

Saul L. Katz
His Goal Is Helping Others

Today you'll get an up-side-down article. That is, you'll learn about an extra special event first — then the fellow who made it possible. So stay with us. Don't go away.

The event was a matinee performance of "Bye Bye Birdie." The place, Civic Arena. The date, Saturday, August 26. In an exclusive section of the orchestra were special guests: patients from the Veterans Hospital. Some were vets from World Wars 1 and 2, of the Korean War, and a few from Vietnam already. Their faith, creed, color all varied. Their type of life is identical. All spend their days and nights at the Hospital.

In our civilian world are those who, in pursuit of happiness for themselves, pursue it also for the less fortunate. An outstanding example is our personality of the week — Saul L. Katz, past Commander of the Jewish War Veterans of the USA, Post 49. He's also Chairman of Programming. Himself a vet of five years' service in WW 2 and Korea, he's grateful to have made it back home alive and well. And because fate was kinder to him he spends most of his waking off-hours towards making life a little brighter for the others.

When Chairman Katz plans for the Vets, he plans in style. His committee includes the present Commander, Clarence Gomberg. And women too — of the Post's Auxiliary. Like for instance President Margaret Schwartz and V.A.V.S. representative Sara Goldenberg and Ruth Reznik.

The Vets arrived at the Arena in a huge chartered bus. And in 4 smaller buses driven by volunteer Red Cross nurses. "Birdie," as those of you who saw it will agree, was simply charming. During intermission what do you think happened? The Auxiliary women — bless 'em — came in with large boxes of sizzling hot-dogs, individual cartons of orange juice and ice-cream sandwiches. The guests were served where they sat. Arena concessionaire Herman Rosenberg, himself a Post 49 member, arranged for the food. At show's end they lined up for picture-taking. Gretchen Wyler and Dick Patterson, "Birdie's" headliners came down to autograph their programs.

If you studied the faces of the veterans you saw very little animation. Patients who spend many years in a hospital don't animate much. Outwardly they don't. But inside their hearts must have danced. Because the Hospital's nurses were greatly gratified with the therapeutic value gained. Last June the JWV of Allegheny Council arranged a Boat Cruise on our three rivers for 400 vets. With dancing, entertainment and enough soft drinks to float a battleship. They also hold a Goodwill Dinner annually for the patients and hospital officials during Brotherhood Week. And in American tradition the Post members put fresh flags on the graves of Soldiers in 33 Allegheny County cemeteries — twice a year. Before the Jewish High Holy Days they blend patriotism with religion and replace the flags on graves of the Jewish war dead. They also have given five scholarships to high school students with outstanding interest in American democracy and special emphasis on its history.

Chairman Katz in private life is Sales Manager of the Vinyl Wall Covering division of the Peerless Wall Paper and Paint Co. After attending David B. Oliver High he graduated Connolley Vocational School. And was president of the school and his class as well. At a dance long ago he was introduced to a pretty girl, Phyllis Nemster. Since dancing often leads to marriage, that's exactly what happend. The Katz's have been blessed with two wonderful children. Sue, 19, is in her third year at Boston University, preparing for an interesting career. Son Neil is 22. He graduated Civil Engineering at Pitt and is now attending the graduate school of Clemson University, N.C. He was recently commissioned a Lieutenant in the Air Force. And did what comes naturally — got himself engaged. To lovely Sharon Turk, a senior at Pitt. Mom Katz is full-time secretary for Railway Maintenance Corp., Aspinwall. And pop often helps with the housekeeping. But there's always time found for "Post" doings because both appreciate its deep meaning. They call it a labor of love.

Leon Katzman

Life Begins At 84

You constantly read about the golden age of retirement. How to fill in your unaccustomed leisure boredom; how to keep from being lonely; suggestions on how to be happy and make those about you glad you are around. Everyone is interested in the subject because so many are already in that group. And the others will be — sooner or later.

Our community is proud of its many interesting and active golden agers. But there's one personality in Squirrel Hill who is so extra special that he deserves special recognition. He is an outstanding example that "life begins at 84". Our man is Leon Katzman. Yes, he's 84 years young and we do mean young. He's tall, straight and youthful in appearance and shakes hands with the grip of a wrestler. And best of all — he's young at heart.

As second-term president of the Lounge for Senior Citizens, Mr. Katzman is an inspiration to the 75 or 100 members who attend daily. The Lounge, located at 5824 Forbes Ave., was opened 13 years ago by the Pittsburgh Section National Council of Jewish Women, with capable Mrs. Irvin Somerman as director.

Its service is non-sectarian and it is a bee-hive of interesting activity. The presidency carries with it many responsibilities but Leon takes them in stride. In addition, he takes part in their plays, concerts and charity affairs. He entertains with Scottish songs. And if you coax him a little, he will dance the Highland fling — Tam-O-Shanter and all.

Having lived in Glasgow, Scotland for many years, he still retains a bit of the Scottish brogue, which adds to his charm. The men admire and are inspired by him. The women adore him.

Leon Katzman, a widower, lives with his married daughter Edith (Mrs. Philip) Nesvisky on Melvin St. She teaches in the public schools and her youngest son Matthew David (Mat) attends the University of Pittsburgh and is editor of the Pitt News.

Mr. Katzman has three married sons, all graduates of the University of Michigan. Son Harry is now deputy chairman, Probation Dept., City of New York.

Alex, also in New York, teaches French.

Nathan, the youngest lives in Pittsburgh and is vice president of Adams Hats, Inc. That accounts for dad Katzman's nattiest head gear in town. And it's possible he gets them wholesale!

He has 4 grandchildren and one great-grandchild — all boys.

An incident in Mr. Katzman's life proves that truth is often stranger than fiction and is worth relating. His son Alex, while studying at the University of Paris, accidently happened across a circular letter from an import and export firm in Buenos Aires, Argentina. The letter was signed by its president, Nicholas Katzman.

The name intrigued the son and correspondence followed. It turned out that Nicholas was Leon's youngest brother —born after they had moved to Glasgow. The brothers had never laid eyes on one another. Nicholas long ago had become one of the many "wandering Jews" and contact between the brothers was completely lost.

It didn't take long for Leon to get an invitation to visit his newly found brother. A flight by jet brought the brothers together at the Buenos Aires airport, amid embraces and tears. He stayed four months and was shown every nook and corner of South America.

Mrs. Vigdor W. (Mina) Kavaler
Duties, Chores No Problem

The swallows have returned to Capistrano and spring — the season of joy and melancholy intertwined — is here. We'll concentrate on the joyous by telling you about an extra special neighbor who deserves admiration aplenty. Say we're proud of you to Mrs. Vigdor W. Kavaler of Fair Oaks St.—the former Mina Serbin. Husband Vigdor is Executive Secretary of Rodef Shalom Temple and was recently appointed to a three year term on the Board of Trustees of the Pittsburgh Ballet Theatre.

Mina Kavaler is VP of the National Council of Jewish Women in charge of fund raising. This May she'll take office as president. She's VP of the United Jewish Federation Women's Division; ditto of Brandeis Women's Organization; a Board member of the Ladies Hospital Aid, the Jewish Family and Children's Service, of NAACP, the American Jewish Committee, the ADA, and a Committee Woman of the 23rd Dist. She's on the Education Committee of the Y-IKC. And you've been hearing of the upcoming Israel Bond Fashion Show and Luncheon May 25 at the Wm. Penn. Well, Mina is Chairman of that fabulous affair. She's also active in Hadassah, Pioneer Women and Bickur Cholim Society. Are you out of breath?

Before marriage Mina Serbin taught public school and continued for several years after becoming Vigdor's charming missus. Currently she does subbing when called. She teaches Ethics at Rodef Shalom Religious School Saturday mornings. Week-days from 4 to 6 p.m. and Sundays 10 to 12 noon she tutors youngsters with special reading problems. And for the College Boards. Joining a car-pool, one day each week Mina picks up the neighborhood children to and from their respective schools — in her roomy station-wagon.

Now let's go back a little. When Vigdor returned from the Navy after WW II he entered Pitt as a senior. Mina was a freshman there. You know how it is at college — boy meets girl. They said "I do" June 18, 1950 — the first Sunday after her graduation. And now listen to this.

Fourteen years later, not having added to the population explosion, they adopted a pair of twins—boy and girl— 2 months young. Marti, now 8½ goes to Winchester-Thurston and John David (same age, of course), attends Wightman. They know they are truly wanted, are raised in an atmosphere of love, respect and responsibility. A spacious game-room for the twins and their school friends is now being added to the Kavaler 10-room home which they own. With outside help just one day a week, how does their busy mom keep their home so charmingly in order and get the meals? Here's how. She arises 6 a.m. weekdays. Saturdays and Sundays she "luxuriates" til 7. Goes to bed late. Sleeping pills? Who needs them! And budgets her time very carefully.

Mina and Vigdor have been in Europe 5 times and to Israel 3 (before the twins). She loves to help people. Her devoted mother Mrs. Fay Serbin of Darlington Rd. recently had a stay at the Shadyside Hospital. Instead of going to a nursing-home afterwards to convalesce she was welcomed with open arms to the Kavaler home, getting TLC (tender loving care). She'll soon be returning to her own apartment happy to report.

Between Vigdor's various evening meetings and her own, they somehow manage to attend the ballets, the theatre and you won't believe it — get fun out of jazz concerts. Mina is a photo-bug and loves snapping the children.

Compare and marvel. Beautiful neighbors — the Kavalers.

Thomas Kerr Jr.
University Instructor Is Avid Canoeist

You've heard the pun "I can row—caneo?" Well, an interesting fellow in our neighborhood can truthfully answer "Yes, I can. So can my children. And the missus too." And since we've recently celebrated Father's Day it's nice to get acquainted with this youthful-looking dad of five, and his various accomplishments. Meet Thomas Kerr Jr., our neighbor at Shady Ave.

Canoeing is just his hobby. So let's first learn about his important profession and interesting background.

Neighbor Kerr was born in a small New Jersey town. He graduated Lafayette College at Easton, Pa. with an AB degree in Economics. In 1956 he came here and worked in the Legal Department of Westinghouse for eight years. Now he teaches Law and Government at Carnegie-Mellon University. He's chairman of the Pittsburgh Chapter of American Civil Liberties Union — an old organization interested in continuing the rights set forth in the U. S. Constitution. These rights include freedom of religion, free speech and press, due process of law and equal rights before the law. He worked on many lawsuits to protect and expand the rights of Negroes. He's also on the board of trustees of Point Park College.

During World War 2 Tom Kerr was an officer in the Marines. So what did he see besides the sea? He saw lovely Jeannette Carey who was serving as a navy nurse. And married her post-haste, before someone else would, he says. And for reasons known mostly to women, she was glad he did. Soon he was sailing over-seas and the young bride went home to Montana to continue her profession as a nurse.

When marine Kerr was honorably discharged he enrolled in the George Washington University Law School in our nation's capital. He figured if the town was good enough for Harry and Bess Truman it was good enough for him and Jeannette. There his young missus exchanged her nurse's uniform for an apron and began keeping house. In due time she became a mother to baby Michael. And later David. The Kerrs must have been reading the Old Testament, giving their first two sons Biblical names. And their youngest daughter they named Sarah. Their two in-between girls got modern names.

Michael is now 20 and goes to Tufts University in Boston. David, 18 is a Vista-worker in the Community Action program in Baltimore. He works with people who need help — mostly in the slums. Ellen is 17 and a senior at Allderdice. Marian, eleven goes to Linden school. And the above-mentioned Sarah attends Homes school. She's all of 8.

Mrs. Kerr is on the board of trustees of the First Unitarian Church and a member of the Civil Rights committee of the downtown YWCA.

And now for the piece de resistance — canoeing. If you phone the Kerr's home week-ends and there's no answer, sure 'nuf they're out paddling their canoe on either the Allegheny, Youghiogheny, west branch of the Susquehanna — or you-name-it rivers. The waters are highest and at their best from early April till late June. Their canoe is 15 feet long and made of aluminum.

Dad Kerr takes along just one or two of the children at a time on trips. They bring a picnic lunch. If they go for an overnight trip they bring camping equipment and spend the night closeby. Mrs. Kerr chauffeurs them to the shore and meets them on their return. Many times they've rocked the boat and fallen overboard. But being excellent swimmers they clamber back in. And should it happen that someone gets a bump or bruise, or overeats or even worse, no one is panicky because mom is a nurse and mends them good as new.

Nice, isn't it — having such an all-American family in our neighborhood.

Elizabeth Schrader Kimberly
Affectionately Called Lady in Hurry

The long hot summer is gone. October's coolness and beauty are welcome. So let's also welcome a most interesting neighbor—Elizabeth Schrader Kimberly, of Forbes Ave. Affectionately known as "Bes" (just one "s" please) she's been called A Lady In a hurry. And small wonder — when you consider what she has accomplished in the past, what she's doing now and the many plans for the years ahead.

Last June our neighbor completed 40 years of teaching in the Drama Department of Carnegie-Mellon University. And received the title Associate Professor Emerita. She taught theatrical costume design, history of costume and make-up. Traveling extensively in Europe to study theatrical and period costumes helped make her a real pro in supervising the costume for all those delightful Drama Department plays from 1928 until now. And that's not all. Two years ago she journeyed around the world to learn evey more. In 1961 she was presented the Alumni Service Award and a year later was named "The Great Teacher on Campus."

The June parties given "For Bes with Love" by the faculty were to honor her retirement. Retirement? From teaching — yes. But for her it was Commencement. The beginning of meaningful things to come. Currently her title at C-MU is Special Assistant to the Vice President for Development. And she's a member of the National Society of Arts and Letters. As well as the National Fashion Group.

And now for a bit of back history. The former Elizabeth Schrader is a native of Massilon, Ohio. Before coming to Tech as a student she taught in country schools in Ohio for four years and another four in the Massilon schools. She met and married George Byron Kimberly ("Kim"), an alumnus and a member of the Drama Department faculty, where he was technical director and lighting expert. Bes herself is a 1928 graduate of the Drama Department. After eight years of a happy marriage, "Kim" passed away. Did his widow start crying on people's shoulders for sympathy? Not Bes. Instead she dried her tears, pulled herself up by her bootstraps and kept on with her work. She has taught and befriended hundreds of "dramats." These are scattered all over the world. Many have made their mark in films, TV, radio, and on stage. She has kept track of 1100 Drama alumni and is compiling a History of the Drama Department.

Through the years Bes was always close to her students who wrote her of their joys, their sorrows. Then 18 years ago she began to publish an annual Newsletter about their activities. She also arranges reunions for the Drama alumni in the form of cocktail parties. Twelve were held at Hotel Plaza, New York City; eight here at Carnegie-Mellon in connection with a theatre party. Four were held in Los Angeles.

Two of our neighbor's former students (Mrs. Benson G. Henderson and daughter Helen of our city) recently established The Elizabeth Schrader Kimberly Design Award for drama students. To be given annually to a student showing the most promise for a professional career in the field of Design. The first Award was given to a 21 year-old student from Massachusetts.

They say Guy Lombardo plays the sweetest music this side of Heaven. So what! Our neighborhood is the home of the sweetest gal this side of Forbes Avenue.

Barbara Klee
Young, But She's Oh So Talented

Teenagers — poor misunderstood darlings — are panned so often these days.

By the newspapers, speechmakers, critical neighbors. And by the cops even. Fortunately, at times it's gross exaggeration. We all know countless young people who are a credit to our community. So you'll doubtless be delighted to learn a little about one of these.

And may even find yourself envying her parents for being so lucky.

Meet Barbara Klee, all of 18 years our neighbor at Pocusset St. She's a piano wizard no less. And has given joy to listeners everywhere. Now sit back, kick off your shoes, and relax. And read on.

Her dad, Emanuel Klee, is Sales manager for Associated Hardware Co. Mom's name is Jessie. And sister Renee is married to Richard Goldman. Both teach in Pittsburgh schools.

Then there's their lovable dog Prince. No relation to our Pirates' broadcaster. And he has no aversion to the mailman.

First, let's find out what our neighborhood teenager is NOT. While she gets a kick out of the Beatles. Herman's Hermits, The Animals, The Lovin' Spoonfuls, The Yardbirds, they don't make her "feel funny all over." She hasn't joined the shriekers and the screamers.

Neither has she had her dress torn from pushing in a desperate effort to touch them. Actually she's too busy to go where the boys are. They come where she is. When there's time, she dates. But no one steady. No thigh-high skirts. No false eyelashes. Nor other "falsies." And her hair doesn't fall over her face. She must see where she's looking. Piano keys, remember?

Barbara's dark brown hair is cut gracefully short. She's 4' 11". Her clothes are young, attractive and seldom frowned upon by oldsters. She just graduated Allderdice High. Come September she'll start at Tech, majoring in piano under teacher Harry Franklin. And you may be sure she won't be selling magazines to pay her way through.

When only 11 Barbara was winner of a Pittsburgh Concert Society audition. A year later she was classical piano guest soloist with the Pittsburgh Symphony. To this day she plays as if she were operating with 176 keys instead of the standard 88.

Our neighbor teenager also sings, writes, performs. And once did a complete score for a children's opera.

What's Barbara doing now, you want to hear? She's traveling here, there everywhere. With a man. And the guy is married! And a Squirrel Hiller yet. They even cross state lines at times. And the authorities look and say nothin'. Before you start raising eyebrows, the fella is none other than the fabulous Don Brockett who, among other things, does industrial shows.

Naturally his cast travels along. It often includes his charming wife, Leslie. And always Barbara. Because Don must have the best pianist ever. Locally they performed for Duquesne Light, H. J. Heinz and H. K. Porter Co.

Out of town, for Clairol, Wearever Aluminum and the Association of National Advertisers to name but a few. When these firms have their conventions it's their way of introducing their products — via comedy sketches and song. However, don't confuse these with commercials.

When Barbara played for the Brockett zany skit "Stage Struck" at the Rabbit Run Theater last season, the Cleveland critics flipped over her performance.

Again, when she played at Don's spring tonic "The Great Society Dropouts" at Beck's Patio Theatre, the papers called her "A Squirrel Hill piano wizard."

So there you have it — a lovely teenager in our neighborhood. With quiet charm, intelligence and great, great talent — who is definitely "going places."

Henry Koerner
Squirrel Hill Artist Commissioned By Time

You've heard the expression "There's gold in them thar hills." We have it in Squirrel Hill, too. Not gold actually but something more precious, more lasting - interesting, gifted people. Right in our very neighborhood.

Take for instance Henry Koerner, Who is Koerner? Why, one of the nation's best living painters - that's who. To enumerate Mr. Koerner's artistic accomplishments and describe his background would fill a book. Maybe a library. So we'll give you just a few highlights.

But first let's take a look at our artist-neighbor as a person. Henry Koerner has reached that interesting age- 47. Of medium height, his sun-tanned outdoor look accentuates deeply expressive brown eyes. Coupled with a bit of grey at the temples and a charming Viennese accent to his English - well, honestly, it's enough to make one sorry he's married.

His charming wife Joan was studying violin at Chatham College when they first met. He was Art teacher at the same College at the same time. You guessed it. They fell in love and married. That was ten years ago. Now Stephanie, 9 and Joseph Leo, 5, complete an ideal American Family.

Artist Koerner has been commissioned by TIME magazine to paint prominent personalities for its weekly covers. He has painted JFK, Nelson Rockefeller, Maria Calla, Leonard Bernstein, Orville Freeman, George Sells, Harry Bellefonte, Leontyne Price and even Sir Henry Moore of England - to name a few. His paintings and drawings have been shown at the famous Midtown Galleries, New York and at the Maurice Sternberg Galleries, Chicago - with rave reviews from newspapers and magazines throughout the country. Locally they were exhibited at Kaufmann's Auditorium as recently as last month. Wherever you go at art exhibits you see Koerner masterpieces.

The Koerner home at Murrayhill Ave. is unimpressive from outside. But inside — it's a viewer's paradise. The huge picture windows are unhampered by curtains, letting in light and more light. The spacious floors are uncarpeted, their hardwood gleaming and cool. All the furniture, formerly shabby and scratched with age, has been beautifully decorated by hands that care. But the unforgettable part of the house is the studio on the second floor. The huge walls of each room are lined with an array of drawings and paintings that only a master has the words to describe. To an unschooled layman who enjoys just looking, they're refreshment to the eyes and enlightenment to the mind.

We'll end with something that should cause our community to simply burst with pride. Artist Koerner is doing a painting of a lovely Squirrel Hill brunette. She's Donna Frank of Forward Ave. - a hair stylist in a downtown beauty shop. While having dinner at a popular Murray Ave. restaurant our artist looked across the crowded room. There in a booth with her escort was beautiful Donna. Her lovely bouffant hair-do and perfect features are the makings of a modern Mona Lisa. She granted permission to be painted. Since then, every Monday evening when the restaurant is closed to patrons, art is being made in air-conditioned comfort.

The painting will be completed any day now. Where can you see it? On a wall of a restaurant, of course. Which restaurant? Weinstein's.

How lucky can a community be.

Beatrice Krebs
To Sing At Scholar Benefit

The Ides of March gloom is just about behind us and spring is already peeking around the corner. What better time to tell you about a talented neighbor with a golden voice and a million dollar smile. She's Beatrice Krebs of So. Negley Ave., Associate Professor of Voice at C-MU.

And herself a singer par excellence. A mezzo contralto, to be exact. A professional, she's performing for free at the annual Scholarship and Music Education Benefit next Tuesday, March 30 by the Tuesday Musical Club at the Le Monte Restaurant. So is her accompanist Ruth Perry Topping, also on the C-MU faculty and organist at the 6th Presbyterian Church, Forbes and Murray.

Both are dedicated members of the Club. Named "Opus 1971" the affair starts at 11:30 a.m. and includes a delicious luncheon; Beauty and Spring Fashion Show.

And, of course, songs and arias by Miss Krebs. (Her most recent performance here was last January with the Pittsburgh Opera in "Boris Godunov"). The Benefit's theme is "Old Music - New Style".

The Tuesday Musical Club was founded in 1889. Its first meeting was in the home of Mrs. Christopher Magee on the site which is now Magee Hospital. Growing. it kept moving — to the old German Club (now our Pittsburgh Playhouse). Then to Soldiers and Sailors Memorial Hall. Since 1935 its permanent home is in the Stephen Foster Memorial Hall on the Pitt campus.

Funds from the Club's benefits go toward music education and scholarships for the talented young. An example is the now already prominent youthful violinist Danny Phillips.

And now about our lovely singer, Beatrice Krebs. Born in Cleveland she earned her BM degree from the Cleveland Institute of Music. And immediately left for NYC. For ten years she was with the N. Y. City Center Opera. And performed on NBC-TV Opera. For 3½ years she was soloist of the Riverside Church and 5 years at the Fifth Avenue Presbyterian Church. Also 4 years at the Central Synagogue where its director taught her some Hebrew. That's why, three years ago — at the last minute— she was able to pinch-hit at our Rodef Shalom Temple for the Yom Kippur Services. In New York Bea sang Handel's Oratorio "Samson" at Carnegie Music Hall. In Yiddish, if you please! She toured with the National Company of "Sound of Music", giving over 1,000 performances. At the Jones Beach water-lagoon stage performance, the audience was record-breaking.

During our 1963 Summer Opera season Beatrice sang in "Carousel". And lost no time in buying a small house in our neighborhood to share with her parents Albert and Florence Krebs. Dad is semi-retired. And since mom is now an invalid, he enjoys doing the cooking. Bea says he cooks better than she. His beautiful dahlias brought from Cleveland are the pride of their neighborhood. Their pet cat Mushie can't cook at all, and what's more she doesn't know one note from another.

Wish there were more room to list the great Symphonies in which our neighbor sang throughout the U. S. Also, Europe. Under world-famous conductors, including our wonderful William Steinberg. And the numerous Grants, Scholarships and Awards earned from U. S. Foundations, Trust Funds and such. Also her recordings for Columbia, MGM, Victor, etcetra, etcetra.

Our community is proud of Beatrice Krebs and wishes her the best of everything now and in the years ahead. This goes also for the Tuesday Musical Club. Oh yes, you'll doubtless want to attend their Le Mont Affair next Tuesday. Mrs. Melvin G. Thomas (341-2466) will take your reservation. Have yourself a ball.

Mrs. Karl Kritz

Lovely Ballerina

Remember those summer evenings of outdoor Opera, before the Civic Arena? When you were at times rained out? Well, one of those seasons, rain or shine, a beautiful romance budded, blossomed and ended happily for two awfully interesting people.

Symphony-goers and other music lovers will recall that Karl Kritz was Associate Conductor of our famous Pittsburgh Symphony. He also conducted and still does, the orchestra for all our summer operas. And that's how he met Gloria Cutting, the talented and lovely ballerina performing in many of the productions.

Mr. Kritz now conducts his own orchestra in Syracuse, N.Y., and maintains a home there too.

Now let's learn a little more about the lovely missus. Gloria Kritz is the daughter of J. E. Cutting of New York City who was a well-known musical conductor with NBC and many Broadway shows. She received her training at New York's School of American Ballet. Soon she entered into a versatile dance career which ranged from Broadway musicals and TV to performances as soloist with opera companies throughout the nation. She also was a member of a Ballet Trio for which she created the choreography.

Three days a week Mrs. Kritz teaches ballet at the Laboratory School of Music at our own Chatham College. She is a firm believer in ballet training for a child. It builds graceful physical strength. However, the molding of a child in the technique of an art so physical is a great responsibility. Knowing that artists can't be mass-produced, she treats each child individually. And gets fantastic results. Maybe too, because the kids love her.

Should you happen in at her home unexpectedly, you'll find her intently listening to classical recordings and creating ballet routines. Her two Siamese cats — Sir Henry and Lady Pooh — have long since overcome their puzzlement.

Gloria has choreographed shows for United Jewish Fund, ORT, the Council of Jewish Women; as well as for the Concordia and Westmoreland clubs. She is now choreographing and designing costumes for an evening of dance with her pupils in May. She's also preparing the ballet program for three seasons for the Children's Concert Series of the Pittsburgh Symphony.

Not long ago she performed the dancing role in Stravinsky's "Histoire du Soldat." It was held at Carnegie Tech under the direction of William Steinberg, famous Music Director of our Pittsburgh Symphony.

Gloria plays the piano, speaks French and a bit of German. She's an excellent horse-woman, figure-skater and swimmer.

Karl Kritz

Leaving Pittsburgh for Syracuse

This summer's Civic Light Operas are ending. Before they become a pleasant memory let's concentrate a little on a very important personality associated with them for the past 15 years — Orchestra Conductor Karl Kritz and our neighbor at Beechwood Blvd.

Mr. Kritz was born in Vienna. At 7 he was already training to perfect his boyish coloratura soprano voice. In no time young Karl became a member of the world-famous Vienna Boys' Choir. Then, at around 14 when a fella's voice begins to turn that-a-way, he concentrated on the violin, piano and organ. Almost at once he won a 10-year scholarship for study at the Vienna Academy of Music. His training was so thorough that he became equally proficient conducting Symphonies, Operas and Musical Comedies. His classmate for 7 years was the great European conductor von Karajan. Karl's last position in Europe was with the Berlin State Opera House.

In 1937 Mr. Kritz came to New York, taking a complete "see-America-first" tour of the States as piano accompanist for famous Metropolitan and radio stars. After 7 years conducting the well-known Cincinnati Zoo Opera, 16 seasons with the San Francisco Opera, 4 years directing the Fort Worth Opera Association and 5 years with the Metropolitan Opera, he had gained national fame. Then our city claimed him. He became Associate Conductor of our famous Symphony. For eight years he worked hand-in-hand with Dr. William Steinberg, whom he greatly admires — and don't we all? Three years ago he was called to Syracuse, N.Y. to build up and conduct their New Syracuse Symphony.

Karl Kritz is not only a great Director of music but a sportsman as well — and has the physique to prove it. He has done much mountain-climbing in the Austrian Alps, the Colorado Rockies and the California Sierras. He is the dad of two very interesting children. Eric, 20, a motorcycle enthusiast, is studying languages at New York University. Daughter Susie won a 2-year Fullbright scholarship in Bonn, Germany. She'll return to New York this September to find a job there. And who knows, she may even do what comes naturally — start going steady.

And now about another important part of our musician-neighbor's life. His lovely missus. Gloria Kritz, a former ballerina, teaches ballet at Chatham College. And believe it or not, she's the best cook ever. She even can prepare a few famous Viennese dishes, taught her by you-know-who. It's no wonder, then that each week the stars of the Operas love to come to the Kritz home — for dinner, lunch and even breakfast some times. The late Saturday night after-theatre get-togethers are high-lights. In the pleasant atmosphere of the Kirtz home the performers easily shed their built-up tensions. They may take off their coats, shoes even. And let their hair down.

Two interesting onlookers at the Kirtz household are a pair of proud and beautiful Siamese cats — Sir Henry and Lady Pooh. Sir Henry shows his approval of the celebrities by brushing up against their ankles. He has even played footsies with Hugh O'Brian of "Music Man" fame and "Carousel's" Robert Horton. Lady Pooh, however, being faminine and a bit shy, mostly sits there — and purrs.

Dr. David H. Kurtzman

Like Fellow Next Door

Today you're going to learn about a most fabulous neighbor. He's Dr. David H. Kurtzman, Acting Chancellor of the   University of Pittsburgh. He lives a stones-throw from Forbes & Murray. In Maxon Towers, to be exact.

Of course, you've read about him and his remarkable accomplishments almost daily in our newspapers. And by now are pretty familiar with his outstanding educational background, experience and know-how. So you'll get here just a few highlights in that direction. Then have a peek into his personal life. So don't go away.

First off, Dr. Kurtzman got his B.S. degree from Temple University. His M.A. and Ph.D. in Political Science he received from the University of Pennsylvania. He taught that subject at Temple between 1931 and 1933. Then followed 26 years as Assistant Director of Research of the Pennsylvania Economy League's Western Division. In 1938 he came to our city and 21 years later was called to Harrisburg as Secretary of Administration in Governor Lawrence's Cabinet. After four years he left for the Fels Institute, a part of the University of Pennsylvania where he worked for 2½ years.

By then he had become well and favorably known by all of Pitt's board members and many other prominent individuals. Thus, when Chancellor Litchfield suffered a heart-attach and resigned, Dr. Stanton C. Crawford became Acting Chancellor. And because Pitt was in great financial stress, Dr. Kurtzman was asked to take over as Vice Chancellor of Finance. That was in 1965. Last January Dr. Crawford passed away, and our neighbor succeeded him as Acting Chancellor.

And now let's go back to around 1925 when something interesting happened. Young Kurtzman fell victim to the sweet mystery of love. And several years later he and beautiful Celia Buchdrucker became Mr. and Mrs. He was a Junior at Temple University then; she was attending Philadelphia Normal School. They set up housekeeping in the City of Brotherly Love. And get a load of this. Baby Rochelle was born— not the first year but TEN YEARS later. And was just a year old when the Kurtzmans came to our city. Now 29, she's married to a former Squirrel Hiller, Dr. Joel D. Weinman, an Optometrist. They live in Kutztown, Pa. and have three lively boys.

Son Marshall K. is 27 and married to Elene Moretsky, also from our neighborhood. He is doing Operations Research for Esso Research and Engineering Co. in Percipanny, N.J. They have two beautiful girls. So our neighbor is a grandad five times. And only 62 years young himself.

His charming missus belongs to Hadassah, Technion and B'nai B'rith. But mostly, she's busy with her husband's social duties. She's honorary president of the University Women's Association — wives of faculty and board members. The Century Club whose members each contribute $100 or more annually to the University, hold a dinner for the alumni every year. The Kurtzmans constantly take visiting guests to football games. The guests enjoy the hospitality of the Chancellor's suite in Bruce Hall. And there are always receptions and dances. And like LBJ and his Lady Bird, Dr. Kurtzman likes having capable Celia around.

Our neighbor recently was given the Emanuel Spector Award by our UJF. The plaque is presented each year to an outstanding member of the community in recognition of a significant contribution to educational and philanthropic development. He also received "The Man of the Year" award from the Oakland Chamber of Commerce. Couldn't have happened to a more deserving fellow.

Dr. Kurtzman predicts an eventual Pitt enrollment of 30,000 full-time students which means 40,000 or 50,000 students of all kinds. He wants to continue building up the University academically and find enough funds to do it with. Thanks in large measure to the efficient manner in which he has brought wide experience and economic expertise to bear upon the University's affairs, Pitt is back on the track and once more solvent. So long as he is on the job there is reasonable expectation of maintaining that blessed condition.

Pitt is fortunate to have him. And our community is proud as punch that the Kurtzmans are our neighbors.

Alvin L. Kushner
TV Moderator

After a 3-week "vacation" at the Montefiore and doctor's orders to "take it easy for quite a while", let's give it a try at the typewriter to tell you about an outstanding personality. Meet Alvin L. Kushner, Director of the Community Relations Committee of the United Jewish Federation (CRC-UJF), successor to the old JCRC. Every other Sunday at 9:30 A.M. on Channel 4 he is moderator on the informative program "Community Perspective."

He interviews and gets answers from brilliant persons on all kinds of vital subjects pertinent to what's going on in trouble spots here, there, everywhere. Tune in. You'll be the better and wiser for it. But first here's a secret which please don't tell the neighbors.

Mr. Kushner is not a Squirrel Hill-er. Lives in Mt. Lebanon, no less. And shame on him! However, his accomplishments are of such importance to every community and ours in particular, that all is forgiven. He came here March 15, 1969, after many years in the Detroit metropolitan area, including 11 in Mt. Clemens. In that city he was chairman of the County Art Show. He ran for City Commissioner, losing by 22 votes out of 5,000. And wound up asking for, and getting, the first re-count the city ever had. And guess what? No errors.

With Kushner came his lovely wife Ruth, their three interesting children: Gary, Blanche and Joel. . . 14, 12 and 9½. Also a lively little pup Brindle purchased at a White Elephant Auction sale. For 25 cents! Brindle loves everybody. Even the mailman.

They live in a 7-room home. Dad enjoys working in the yard, and even washes windows on occasion. He likes reading and swimming. Says he likes women, too, (but don't let it get around). His charming and capable missus is active in the National Council of Jewish Women and is co-chairman of the Senior Citizens programs. Mom and pop both smoke but since the children heckle them to quit, they are cutting down.

And now more about Kushner. Born in N.Y. a mere 44 years ago, he received his B. A. and M. A. Degrees from New York University, completing additional graduate courses at the University of Michigan School of Social Work. During his first job as head of a Settlement House in N. Y., the former Ruth Kaiser attended Queens College and worked part time at the same Settlement. When the handsome bachelor started feeling that-a-way about Ruth, he thought it wouldn't look good for the boss to romance the help. So suggested she quit her job and go full time at Queens College. She up and did, and graduated. A year later they married.

Since then Kushner's career and experience zoomed like a Who's Who. He was Associate Director of the Jewish Community Council of Metropolitan Detroit. Then District Executive for its Civil Rights Commission. Followed as Secretary to the Michigan Committee on the Human Rights and Genocide Treaties. He has lectured on community relations concerns, primarily before religious oriented groups, on local and statewide levels.

And now a bit about the CRC-UJF. In 1939 when Hitlerism was rife in Germany and its satellites, evidences of anti-Semitism in the U.S. through the Nazi Bund, occasional crossburning by the KKK attacks on synagogues and even incidence of violence against the person of Jews, deeply shook our people's security. Headed by the late Edgar J. Kaufmann and representatives of the Jewish War Veterans, the American Jewish Congress, the B'nai B'rith Anti-defamation League and the American Jewish Committee, the Council was formed. Its aim: (a) to protect the status of the Jews in this area; (2) to create better understanding between Jews and the general community. In the years that followed and for the last ten years CRD-UJF has helped improve the lot of all minorities, especially the blacks in our city and in America generally.

In our beautiful but tormented world, it's nice having a fellow like Alvin L. Kushner around.

Drs. Robert B. and Barbara Lane
Husband and Wife Anthropologists

Anthropology—what a high-sounding word! The average person knows nothing about it. Some just a little.

A chosen few are steeped in it, have found it fascinating and have made it their life-time profession.

Dr. Robert B. Lane and his lovely wife Dr. Barbara Lane are in the latter category. Pittsburgh has been benefitting by their being around and we are particularly happy they are our neighbors. The Lanes live in a duplex on Bartlett St.

Now let's see — just what is anthropology? Dr. Lane describes it in a few simple words: "It's the study of the physical and cultural attributes of man." But of course it's not quite as simple as that. It goes into the characteristics of man in relation to his origin, environment and social aspects. And because it includes peoples of the entire world, the subject is deep and boundless.

Bob and Barbara Lane both graduated from the University of Washington, in Seattle. In fact that's where they met and later married. Dr. Robert Lane went on to the Australian National University of Canberra, Australia. Later he did research in the Hebrides Islands located in the southwestern Pacific.

By then he was fully equipped to teach his subject at the University of Hawaii in Honolulu. At a later date he did research in that city's famous Bishop Museum which specializes in oceanic culture of the Pacific area.

Four years ago the Lanes were called to our city. Wife Barbara started teaching anthropology at Pitt University — and still does. Dr. Robert Lane taught the same subject at Margaret Morrison College for three years. A year ago he received the much-coveted Mellon post-doctoral Fellowship at Pitt. Here's how it happened:

When our university started its new development program, it set up what is called Mellon Chairs in the various sciences. This of course included anthropology.

Each of the Chairs is occupied, figuratively speaking, by an outstanding scholar in that department. Along with these chairs they also have in each department several Mellon Fellowships. These are given to younger scholars.

Dr. Bob Lane was young enough and brilliant enough to qualify for that honor. He was awarded a Mellon Fellowship in the department of anthropology.

These Fellows do no teaching but concentrate on research. Their intention is to introduce new ideas and to broaden the interest of the faculty and students.

Because of this program, scholars from countries throughout the world are learning of the exciting developments in our university. The Fellows, in turn, gain from contact with their colleagues. And our university, as well as our city, gain in prestige.

And now we come to a most interesting part of their personal life. Bob and Barbara have a son, Ian, 6. And they have adopted two little girls, in truly democratic American tradition. One, Laurie, is an American Indian. She is now 5 and goes to the Davis School. The other, Mara, is a little Hawaiian. She is 3½ and attends the Y-IKC kindergarten, and the Morewood nursery school.

"Big brother" Ian is in his first year at Falk School. Not all adopted children have the good luck to get such ideal parents.

The Lanes are members of the Pittsburgh Playhouse and attend all the plays. They also have a family membership at the Y-IKC and enjoy the various activities there. But they have no hobbies. At least, not yet. Their ambition is to bring up their children in the best possible way; and to further their fascinating profession.

Some married men, when they want to discuss their business problems with their wives are frustrated because the little woman knows hardly anything about business. With the Lanes it's altogether different. They actually enjoy "talking shop" because each one understands completely the other's experiences.

As the saying goes, they both speak the same language. Theirs is indeed an interesting and meaningful life.

Our community wishes this remarkable family good luck, good health and much, much happiness.

Esther Lapiddus

Humor Gal Realizes Value of Laughter

Anyone who hasn't laughed at or with our today's personality of the week — Esther Lapiddus — hasn't really lived. So live a little and learn about "the female Myron Cohen with Fanny Brice thrown in"—our neighbor at Bartlett St. Her husband is the well-known Saul Lapiddus, manager of the Forbes Travel Service, just around the corner.

The former Esther Schwartz was born in Donora. They moved to our city when she was two. Here she attended and graduated Allderdice, always managing to get into the school plays. She was voted "The Girl with the Best Sense of Humor". Humor, she now says has carried her through life's complexities.

Years ago Esther's brother Sammy Schwartz had a hand in all the plays at the Bellefield YM&WHA. And she used to trudge along for the try-outs. To get rid of her, director Moll gave her a part in "Arsenic & Old Lace". Barely 15 she played the part of a 70-year old lady. And was a sure-fire hit. She has continued to be that for 30 years. She's been in 5 different plays at our popular Pittsburgh Playhouse. Was in several Civic Light Operas. And a laugh-riot at Club Ankara and Gammon's Theatre 19. At

Beck's Patio Theatre she rolled them in the aisles. And ditto at Kramer's Back Room. Encouraged by our famous neighbor Don Brockett, Esther has been entertaining women's and men's groups throughout the Tri-state area, with her one-woman show titled "A Housewife Looks at Humor". When called upon—for free— our talented neighbor entertains at the Y-!KC and the Anathan House. And has delighted the dear hearts and gentle people at the Jewish Home and Hospital for the Aged. Also at the Riverview Apartments. Currently she's with Joe Negri and Bob McCully in an act called "The Ecumenical 3".

How did Saul and Esther meet? On a blind date. But get a load of this. Tall, willowy herself, with an enchanting smile, she expected a Rudolf Valentino, no less. She dressed up in a gown and a fancy fake fur coat. And hoped to be taken to the then popular Chatter Box at the William Penn Hotel. When she opened the door — oy vay!! There stood Saul.

Instead of a tuxedo he wore an old sports coat and sweater like for going hunting or fishing. And drove her, not the the Chatter Box but to Joe Mazer's on Washington Blvd. — a dinky night-club. From then on they got lost from each other for a whole year. Then one fine day they accidently bumped into one another. By then Esther was a bit wiser, and invited him to her home. Their courtship lasted 4 whole years, with no sign of marriage. Then the talented Esther was called to the Concord hotel in the Catskills as a social director for 6 months. Who do you think took a vaction there four times during her stay? Saul. When it looked as if he was going to lose her for good, what with so many other guys buzzin' around, he up and proposed. So they were engaged— sort of.

But when she returned home, Rabbi Benjamin Lichter (of blessed memory) tied the knot - but good. After eight years of marriage, a miracle — like the coming of the Messiah — happened. The stork delivered baby Sally. She's now 11 and attends Colfax. Four years later Maxine came along. At 6½ and a graduate of its kindergarten, she proudly marches off to Colfax grade 1.

An amateur decorator buff, Esther remodeled completely their 12 - room Bartlett St. house. She has outside help but one day a week. Daughter Sally likes to cook and experiment in the kitchen, like mom. Saul's weight, thanks to their cooking, is a healthy 225 lbs. — give or take a calorie or two. He and his lovely missus have traveled around the world. And three years ago mom took the girls on a 21-day Caribbean and South American cruise. Esther's greatest inspiration is sister Lilly June of Maxon Towers. She taught her the value of humor and the gift of laughter. Her nephew Merle Pollis is an announcer with WJAS.

Esther Lapiddus spoofs without ridiculing. She's a joy and delight. Harold V. Cohen once called her "A comic gem of pure platinum".

Mrs. J. H. (Lois) Lebovitz
Mrs. D. S. (Rose) Plung
Lois and Rose Co-Chairmen

To date, through your "News" you've already met 167 interesting neighbors. Anyone who thinks there are no more such should be asked to leave town. And to prove the point, today you'll learn about not just one but two wonderful neighbors. A doubleheader, our Pirates would call it.

Meet Lois Lebovitz and Rose Plung of Hobart and Northumberland Streets, respectively. These lovely young women are having an AFFAIR. Oh, not an "affair" with another woman's husband. Who needs it. Each has a handsome husband of her own. The former Lois Levy, a born Squirrel Hiller, is married to Joseph H. Lebovitz, a well-known food merchant. And the former Rose Weisenbaum's better-half is Donald S. Plung, a successful CPA. She too has lived in our neighborhood since infanthood. Each is a life-member of Hadassah, a past President and Donor Chairman of Hadassah Group 2. And they've been close friends all their lives.

Currently both Lois and Rose are Chairmen of the AFFAIR in question. It's an extra special event with the intriguing name "7 Come 11." Saturday evening, October 18, at the Westmoreland Country Club. It will include a late buffet supper and added attractions. Funds derived from this exciting Happening will go toward Hadassah's Youth Program, "Hashahar" which in Hebrew means "The Dawn." And will help finance a Youth Camp in the Catskills — Campt Tel Yehuda — for eastern regional youths. As mothers they couldn't come up with a better cause.

Lois and Joe have 4 children; the Plungs 3. Boys and girls— all interesting. They hob-nob together. When they reach that romantic age they'll hardly need a "Fiddler-on-the Roof" matchmaker to get them acquainted.

Both their moms are also members of the Renaissance Chapter of B'nai B'rith, the Ladies Hospital Aid Society and the Jewish Home & Hospital for the Aged. Their dads too are active in all important Jewish and community affairs.

And now back to that extra special AFFAIR. When Saturday, October 18, comes along, get a new hair-do or put on that lovely wig. Pick out your prettiest dress. And fill up your car with sisters, uncles, brothers, aunts and whoever. To join the other Beautiful People at Westmoreland Country Club. And have yourselves a ball. P.S.— And don't for goodness sakes, forget your husband.

Earl Leeder
Traces Heritage To English Royalty

As you know, our neighborhood is filled with countless outstanding, interesting and unusual personalities. Today you'll learn about a neighbor who is descended from royalty—on both sides of the family, if you please. And some day in the distant future will be entitled to share in a huge fortune left by a titled ancestor. At present, our neighbor is just an average likeable fellow trying to get along. He's Earl Leeder of Minnesota St. Let's learn a little about him.

Born in our city, young Earl graduated Allderdice. Six months later he enlisted for active duty in the Korean War. He served in Germany near the Russian border from 1955 to 1957, working as a tank mechanic. The heavy physical duties affected his heart. After an honorable discharge he went into his dad's construction business, but found the physical labor too taxing.

So he opened a filling station on the Boulevard of the Allies in the Soho district. After 6 months—wouldn't you know it— the State Department closed the Boulevard for two years of construction. And our ex-soldier's business went kaput. His mother Ruth, having been a beautician in her younger years, encouraged him to enroll in a Beauty School.

So Earl went on to hair-styling establishments throughout the country learning different styles from different teachers. As he now says—one never learns enough. He opened a small room in the back of a barber shop on Greenfield Ave. Every year or so, as his business prospered, he got larger quarters.

One June day lovely Anna Marie Benes, a secretary for Newman's Ready-Mix Cement Co. across the street, came in for a hair-cut during her lunch-hour. Between snips Earl served her coffee. Before long steady dating followed. When he asked her father's permission for Anna Marie's hand in marriage, her dad said: "You are of a different religion than we are. But you're the nicest fellow my daughter ever went out with. So I consent, but remember: Your children must be reared in their mother's faith." Anna Marie continued with her job, both saving their money. And eight years ago became Mr. and Mrs. The young wife still works, now as secretary in the neighborhood Marcus Optical Co. To date the devoted couple have not added to the population explosion. So the religious problem with youngsters of an inter-marriage is absent.

And now about that legacy. Earl's great, great, great (many more greats) grandfather was Lord Woolsley of England. When he died in the year 1610 he left no will. You see, his only son had married a commoner so he was disinherited. And instead of his father's fortune going to grandchildren, it reverted to his remaining relatives scattered here, there, everywhere — many of whom have since passed away. The Woolsley money, then worth about quarter of a million pounds, is lying in a bank in England, constantly accumulating interest. If you have a computer, you figure out what it's worth by now, after more than 3 centuries.

Earl's dad, looking up their family tree, has traced it back to the year 1066. And has sent for their family crest and coat of arms to show their heritage. Their geneology report is on record in the Toronto and Salt Lake City libraries. Two generations of Earl's family have been working on it. At first the relatives didn't have enough money to hire lawyers for tracing the geneology and pay for court costs.

Twenty-five years ago his aunt in Canada finally got the remaining family together to pool resources—a total of $200! That's why it's been taking so long to get the family geneology. The only surviving relatives known living number 150 legitimate ones. Illegitimate relatives —if any — are completely out.

Meantime our nice neighbor is minding his business and doing well. Every month he puts up pictures of new hair styles on his walls. Two years ago he won a Loreal hair-coloring Trophy in competition with 75 others. And another for permanent waving skill. And his lovely mom who doesn't look a day over 39 is taking a refresher course in beauty work and will help out in Earl's House of Beauty on Greenfield Ave.

If and when Lord Woolsley's legacy is untangled and our neighbor gets his share, what does he plan to do with the money? One think is certain. He will not buy a Greek Island.

Joyce Levenson

Spotlight On Joyce

Neighbor Don Brockett, that clever zany whose shows have kept them laughing here, there, everywhere—has opened "The New Amen Show", a religious musical revue at the Ben Gross Restaurant. We'll leave it to the drama critics to review its laugh-provoking charm. This column is primarily about a new charmer Don has added to his talented cast. Say hi to Joyce Levenson, also a neighbor. Her dad Irvin takes time out from his business for many civic activities. Mom Shirley does art-painting in addition to keeping their eight room house which they own, spic and span. No outside help. And you'll never believe it—Joyce gets a kick out of pitching in with the chores. Sister Donna is Mrs. Howard Wolfson of Monroeville.

Our personality is scarcely 20. When a baby they owned a collie named Tommy. He kept chewing off the netting from her baby-carriage. It became a toss-up: Get rid of Joyce or Tommy. The former won out. But she now says her dad sometimes thinks maybe they made a wrong decision.

After graduating from Allderdice Joyce entered the Cincinnati Conservatory of Music on a scholarship, then transferred to Pitt as a Theatre student where she'll graduate in June. She has studied voice and piano with Betty Dugan of Brentwood since age four, and took dancing at the Pittsburgh Playhouse Drama School. At eight, she made a film for National Library Week on Channel 2. A year later she did a Hospital Benefit Show on the same channel, and was on the John Reed King Show when 11. More recently she played in "It's About Time" at Stouffer's Oakland restaurant. In a show "Starlet on Parade" which Ed Schaughency mc'd, Joyce bounced on the stage with such vigor she fell kerplunk in front of everybody. The show went on, creating more fun than originally intended. Joyce has done industrial shows with Brockett; acted at the White Barn Theatre six weeks; was in "Three Penny Opera" at Pitt, and in "Jacques Brel is Alive and Well and Living in Paris". Now she has her own nightclub act.

This itty-bitty five-foot good-looker wears her black hair neatly short. Her speaking voice is velvety but so low you can scarcely hear. But on the stage singing— wow! You hear her 'way 'way back. Intermingled with the other fine talents (Earl Moore, Dave Dreher, Phyllis Stern, Michael Douglas and John Malone) it all adds up, as it says in the commercials.

A steady boy-friend? Not yet, she smilingly tells you. Planning to go to NYC after graduating Pitt, she doesn't want to have to "break away" from anyone. But get a load of this. Later, if and when she settles down and marries, she wants to have a lot of kids. Seems like she hasn't heard of the population explosion.

The songs with humorous religious dialogue of the Brockett Show — well, you gotta hear to appreciate.

A good suggestion is: Get out your car, gather up the wife, friends and neighbors. And have yourself a ball at Ben Gross. And save gas in the bargain.

Mrs. Samuel Levinson
Her Life Is Shared With Many

Widows — bless 'em — often prove themselves the salt of the earth. Particularly those who, when life's eventuality strikes, don't cry why-did-this-happen-to-me?

But instead, after time eases their heartaches somewhat, pull themselves up by their boot straps. They dry their tears and look about. And before long find there are countless others who are bearing even greater burdens. By helping these they often find a measure of happiness for themselves. And add luster to their lives.

Our community has countless such courageous women. An outstanding example is Mrs. Samuel M. Levinson of Forbes Avenue. As most everyone knows, her late husband was founder and later board chairman of the Levinson Steel Co. With a warm outgoing personality he was a part of our city's history and a vital force in its civic, cultural, religious and charitable activities.

During their 51 years of devoted life together Rose Levinson was in the environment of constant welfare doing. Thus, long before she had to go it alone, it came naturally to her. And her selfless activities are almost beyond counting.

Now let's go back somewhat. The former Rose Reuben graduated Fifth Avenue High. Evenings she taught there and during the day was secretary. She met young Sam, a handsome athlete, at a basketball game. They married in 1913.

At once Rose knew what she wanted: four children before she would reach 30, and to become the best wife and mother possible.

She took courses in home economics, first-aid, home nursing and pre-natal care. Also nutrition and child psychology. By age 30 she almost had it made. But not quite. Instead of four children the stork had delivered three.

Son Aaron P. Levinson now capably heads his dad's steel firm. Daughter June is Mrs. Louis Siegel and lives next door to mom. Netta is married to Rabbi Earle Grollman in Boston. There are eight grandchildren. Already one of them has made headlines. Grandson Jimmie, a '64 Harvard graduate and distinguished pianist, is with USAID in New Delhi, India.

Recently, there was a flurry of excitement among the Levinsons. They received an invitation from U.S. Ambassador to India Chester Bowles and wife to attend a piano recital at the Roosevelt House in Chanakyapuri. Followed by a dinner and reception at the Embassy. To hear and honor pianist F. James Levinson — Aaron's boy.

When her youngsters started school, Rose Levinson got a project of her own. Piano and voice, specializing in nursery songs. She directed the Eastern Star choir for 24 years. And 27 years ago organized the first Mothers' Club — the Alpha Epsilon Phi, in which she's still active.

Our neighbor worked in the Red Cross Blood Bank for three years. And she reads to the blind hours at a time. And now listen to this. She has given 15 years of uninterrupted service as teacher in our neighborhood Home for Crippled Children.

In the classroom she aids teacher Lorraine Briskman. In fact, she's often referred to as Lorraine's right-hand. The children idolize her and call her Aunt Rose. So does everybody else there. Through the James — Rachel Levinson Foundation a piece of equipment has been presented to the school's education department for the children's use. Every year it's something different.

Our neighbor deserves much praise but she'll have none of it. Her manner is quiet and unassuming. Her clothes unostentatious. No puffed-up hairdos. No spike heels. She doesn't even wear a wig. Just a lovely neighbor with a natural school-girl complexion — who knows what's to be done, and does it.

Gives you a warm feeling, doesn't it, having Rose Levinson in our neighborhood.

Dr. Gordon H. Lewis
Sociologist Proves Good Neighbor

Grandpop, as you may know, likes to reminisce about those absent-minded professors during "the good old days." Well, there are none such these days. The current profs are not only educationally distinguished but very much alert. And what's more, some are comparatively young. As for instance Dr. Gordon H. Lewis, our Beacon Street neighbor.

And don't let the facial foliage fool you. He's only 34. In 1969 Carnegie-Mellon appointed him assistant professor of sociology and industrial administration in its School of Urban and Public Affairs and the Graduate School of Industrial Administration. August 1970 (at age 32) he was promoted to Associate Professor. In addition, he's editor of the Journal of Mathematical Sociology.

Our youthful sociologist is a Phi Beta Kappa, having earned his A.B., M.A. and Ph.D degrees from Stanford U. between 1960 and '66. He taught 4 years at Yale and a year at Santa Clara U. And was honored with a Woodrow Wilson Fellowship. And another from the National Institute of Health Traineeship.

Our neighbor was born in Wenatchee, Washington. After High his life continued with constant serious study, resulting with accomplishments mentioned above. However the handsome student somehow found time for other things. Like for instance girls.

At Stanford U. trips to the library were daily musts. And there's where he met a girl-student, lovely Pamela Payne of Liberty, N.Y.—a small town near Grossinger's of all places. Looking so beautifully young he took her for a freshman. And he a lordly senior! Turned out she was a graduate student in English and a choir singer. Be that as it may, in no time steady dating followed. Their first date was dinner. But you'll never believe it. No sooner had they eaten when he drove her home, said "be seeing you" and left. Much to her surprise and disappointment. But before you jump to con-clusions, the truth is he simply had a stack of studying to do. And that, at the time, was awfully important. A year later—June 1961—they married and went housekeep-ing in Palo Alto near Stanford U. Gordon continued toward his Ph.D and his lovely bride taught 8th grade English. When he went to teach at Yale, Pam taught English at Southern Connecticut State College.

Since coming here she taught voice at Duquesne U. for a year and is now pursuing her master's in Opera at C-MU. She sings in a quartet at our Forbes-Murray Presby-terian Church. And if you happened to attend the High Holy Days Services at Rodef Shalom, you heard her beautiful mezzo soprano voice in the Temple Choir. March 3 and 4 she'll be sharing the role of Dame Quickly in "Falstaff" at C-MU. Of course, she and husband attend the Heinz Hall Operas.

Our neighbors have two lively youngsters. Peter Harriman, 5, goes to C-MU Children's School. So does Kevin Armitage, 3. Dad's office, some of mom's classes and the kids' school are in the same building. All leave home together. Dad tries to find time for writing. Son Peter likes fixing scrambled eggs. And gets a kick out of riddles. Ask how to catch a squirrel and he'll tell you to go climb a tree and act like a nut. And Kevin? At age 3 who needs hobbies? He just enjoys kindergarten — and that's it.

Last summer the family vacationed in a cabin-on-the-lake in Washington State. They traveled round trip by train (Canadian Pacific and Canadian National). An unforget-table experience for the youngsters. Now they think flying is for the birds.

How's that for beautiful neighbors?

Mark William Lewis
Playhouse Director Imaginative, Talented

Many are asking — so what's with our Pittsburgh Playhouse? You'll be delighted to learn that it's open, working and going. And the fellow who's keeping it that way is its live-wire Managing Director, Mark William Lewis. And where does this Lewis fellow live? In our Neighborhood, of course on Beacon Street.

The total season's selections of plays are still under discussion but will be announced soon. Meantime "The Odd Couple" is bringing them in. And "The Little Foxes" now in rehearsal will follow. They're importing a local girl who made good in New York for the Tallulah Bankhead role. The Playhouse Junior productions are in full swing. "Alladin" is delighting the small fry Saturday and Sunday matinees. So will "The Mystery at the Old Forest," "The Nutcracker Ballet" and "Rumplestiltskin." At chil-dren's reduced prices. And if mom or pop comes along the price is the same. Then there's the Repertory Film Festival — 17 motion picture classics of yester-year by the world's greatest directors — already started. "Wild Strawberries", "Ballad of a Sol-dier", Charlie Chaplin's "Gold Rush" to name a few. And of course the Stage Door Club is serving top-notch meals.

What does it take to guide a theater back on the track after a series of detours? Plenty. First, the backing of a reliable sponsor to put the breath of life into it. This time its Point Park College. Then it takes imagination, talent, experience and confidence. Director Lewis has all these. And more. He and his enthusiastic staff are working 8 to 14 hours a day, seven days a week.

Let's learn a little about this fellow who is superbly equipped for such a Herculean job. A native of Churchill Borough, young Mark up and earned his Bachelor of Fine Arts degree from Carnegie Tech (now Carnegie-Mellon of course). And his Master of Arts from Stanford University. But it wasn't clear sailing. His college years were interrupted to serve a four-year hitch in Uncle Sam's Air Force during WW II. There he took part in Army shows with soldiers. And became interested in the theatre.

Upon discharge, in between college training, he worked in summer stock in New Orleans with the Gallery Players. And as manager with the Potomac Playhouse in Washington, D.C. By then he was well-known and our Playhouse called him here. This was in 1954. His first area here was audience development. Two years later he took over the Playhouse School of the Theatre. And he's still with it.

During his Tech years our handsome bachelor did what comes naturally. Fell in love. And married beautiful Mary Elizabeth Kane, a life-long Squirrel Hiller. Also a Tech drama student, she was in various Playhouse productions. Now she's full-time housewife, concentrating mostly on husband and their three lively children. And teaches at the Playhouse School only several times a week. Daughters Mary Ann, 8, and Therese Marie, 7, attend St. Philomena School. Baby Mark, Jr. is all of four. He's sure his dad owns the Playhouse because he spends so much time there. But they're together every moment at breakfast and dinner. Young Mark gladly breaks away from "Popeye" to be with Pop.

Our neighbor is well-built with dark hair and eyes. And you'll never believe it. He has no bangs, no side-burns nor mustache. And not a sign of chin foliage. Just a clean-cut likeable guy who considers his Playhouse work a labor of love. So do the members of his capable staff. And although the actors are mostly local performers they're plenty skilled.

Already our Playhouse is going great guns. See you there.

Dr. Norman C. Li

Chemistry Professor Not to be Sneezed At

This is being written as snow is gently falling and the outdoors is a Winter Wonderland. A pleasant day to learn about an interesting personality. Especially since he's originally from China—the country that daily heads the front pages of our newspapers.

Meet Dr. Norman C. Li, our neighbor on Beacon St. However, don't let his title "Dr." misguide you. If you have a code-in-your-nose with sniffles, call an "MD," not him. Dr. Li is Professor of Chemistry at our Duquesne University. Since 1952. And not to be sneezed at.

Our neighbor was born in Foochow. His father, after earning a BD degree from Kenyon College, Gambier, Ohio, became an Episcopalian minister in that Chinese city. When Norman was 13, his dad took him, his mother, two sisters and a brother to Victoria, B.C. in Canada to continue as a minister there. Norman quickly learned English in the grades and graduated Victoria High in two years instead of the usual three. And completed Kenyon College in just three years instead of four. With honors yet. During Kenyon his folks went back to China and Norman was completely on his own. Soon he was off to the University of Michigan where in just one year he earned his MS degree. And continued at the University of Wisconsin for his Ph.D. Again, he skipped a year. That was in 1936.

While in Wisconsin, a funny thing happened to this brilliant fella on his way to Chicago during his Christmas vacation. He attended a Conference of International Students. And there met a girl! Or rather two girls, Hazel Chou and her sister Louise. Both were students at Rosary College. Hazel, the younger — and you'll agree the smarter — invited Norman to the Rosary College Prom. That did it. For several months they dated until Hazel got her BS degree and sent back to China. A year later— you guessed it— Norman followed.

Having become a Catholic herself, Hazel in no time converted him too. They married in 1937. For four years, the young husband taught chemistry at the Yenching University in Peking; and six years at the Catholic University of China in the same city.

Their first blessed event was twin sons, Peter and Paul. Eight years later along came Johnny. And while dad was a professor at St. Louis University, Mary and later Cathy completed the happy family group.

The twins are now 29. Peter is an attorney in San Francisco; Paul is advertising manager of a publishing house in Dayton. Both are married to American girls. John, now 21, is a senior at Georgetown University in Washington. Mary is 17 and a freshman at University of Michigan. Cathy, 15, is a junior in Sacred Heart High. Both teenagers like mini skirts. There are four grandchildren, and Dr. Li is the youngest-looking grandpop you ever saw.

February 1964 our neighbor spent six months in Taiwan as international atomic energy technical expert. He also served as visiting professor at the National Tsing-Hua University there. His research team at Duquesne come from Australia, Sweden, Japan, China, Israel and of course U.S. Dr. Li hopes to attend a conference in Jerusalem in 1968. Because of his many Jewish friends and neighbors here he has become interested in Israel more than ever.

Our neighbor plays tennis and he and Hazel often take pleasant walks in Schenley Park. They have two cars, but walking is more fun. Both play the piano. Hazel also plays the cello. Through the week she prepares strictly Chinese meals — chopsticks and all. But Sunday mornings there is the traditional American breakfast — bacon and eggs. But no coffee. They like tea better.

Any word on the conflict in China? Before his parents died last summer Dr. Li used to hear from them often. His one sister in Peking and another in Shanghai last wrote their sister in Washington, saying: Don't write us. It will only get us involved and create trouble with the Red Guards." So all he knows is what he reads in the papers— just like the rest of us.

Mrs. Irwin J. (Henrietta) Littman
Meals On Wheels Chief Booster Is Extra Busy

You've read, heard and been thrilled with a humane program called Meals-on-Wheels. It's the brainchild of the Lutheran Service Society of Western Pennsylvania and has caught the imagination of countless communities, and of course ours. So let's meet the fantastic gal who heads the Sinai section of the Squirrel Hill-Greenfield branch of which Ron Sancini is overall chairman. She's none other than Mrs. Oliver R. (Minnie) Litman. Husband Oliver is a successful dentist with office in Greensburg. They live in nearby Maxon Towers.

The former Minnie Lencher is Pittsburgh-born and the baby sister of Honorable Benjamin Lencher, long-time Allegheny County Judge, now retired—partially. More about our neighbor later.

The Meals-on-Wheels program is sponsored by neighborhood churches, synagogues and non-sectarian social service agencies. Top-grade nutritious meals are brought to shut-ins, who are alone and not able to shop and cook for themselves. Total charge is $8.50 for five weekly deliveries (hot lunch, cold supper). Approved applicants unable to pay the set fee are charged whatever their income can sustain, and no one is refused for lack of funds.

Strictly kosher meals come from the spacious kitchen of the Jewish Home and Hospital for the Aged, arranged by B'nai B'rith women. Non-kosher ones for various religious and ethnic groups are prepared in the well-equipped kitchen of nearby Temple Sinai. The only paid worker at Sinai is Sue Emanuel, full-time professional cook. All others are volunteers. For information on non-kosher meals, call Jackie Unger of the Anathon House (421-2550)

Mrs. Litman for the past 25 years has worked for Temple Sinai, as president of its Sisterhood, vice president and secretary of the Congregation, as well as administrator.

She herself rebuilt its beautiful garden containing a pond with gold-fish, water lilies and lotus blossoms. She's worn out many a pants at the knees and you-know-where else. Her great grandparents were vineyard owners in Russia, so she inherited a love for the good earth as an organic gardener. She hopes, when Oliver retires they will buy a trailer and drive from one golf-course to another where she can do her thing: pull out the weeds.

Since being involved with the "Meals" she's averaged four hours sleep, lost weight without dieting and is thrilled with her slimmer figure. Often she's called "Mrs. Sinai", and small wonder. Much credit for her being able to make exemplary use of her boundless energy is due her devoted housekeeper of 30 years—Mrs. Addie Rodgers. Affectionately called "Rodge", she's like a member of the family.

Our neighbor loves travel, and has been to Mexico five times. On one of those trips she drove all the way, to and fro. There were four trips to Hawaii and of course others to Israel. The Litmans are the happy parents of Mrs. Tim (Barbara) Bornstein, Amhurst, Massachusetts and Mrs. Donald L. (Marilyn) Gartner, Minneapolis. Their five grandchildren are all old enough to tie their own shoe-laces.

Additional funds are much needed for those wheeled meals. Look under your mattress for some bills. Checks are even better, payable to Squirrel Hill-Greenfield Meals-on-Wheels and mailed to Temple Sinai, 5505 Forbes Avenue.

The young grow old; the old, older with all dear ones gone. Visits of the friendly volunteers delivering the meals are the only human contact the shut-ins have with the world outside. The feeling that someone cares about them is as important and dramatic as the meals themselves. A word to the wise, as the saying goes. And a Happy Jewish New Year to you even if you aren't.

Mrs. Oliver R. (Minnie) Litman
She Combines Marriage and Career

Constantly, it seems, bells are ringing.

In December it's jingle bells. At its end are Happy-New-Year bells. In June it's wedding bells. And the minute you step under the shower it's telephone bells.

Today, however, it's "The Three Belles".

These Belles are three local housewives — all mothers, all charming, talented singers, and all music-makers in between their homemaking.

They are Jeanne Baxter, Dorothy Latterman and sister Henrietta Littman. But because we must be partial to our neighbors we'll concentrate on just one of them — the last named — a Squirrel Hiller since a tot of five.

Henrietta Littman is married to Dr. Irwin J. Littman, a successful New Kensington dentist.

He's somewhat overweight, a bit grey at the temples, but tall, dark and handsome for sure.

Son Richard, 21, goes to Pitt and is giving dentistry a try. William is 18 and a Penn State student. Young Jeff, 15, goes to Allderdice.

The Littmans live in a large four-bedroom house on Ridgeville Street. With day help twice a week Henny does the cooking and the boys, when home, help with the chores. In between she works on her part-time singing career. Now let's see how it all started.

In 1934 B.I. (Before Irv) the then Henrietta Rosenberg joined her lovely voice with two others and "The Three Belles" trio was born.

Immediately they began singing on WJAS, continuing for two years.

Then on KDKA. Fan mail poured in from here, there and everywhere — even from ships at sea. Lonely sailors just about went "overboard" for the feminine voices.

And the late Rosey Roswell, in California broadcasting the ball games, tuned in, heard the Belles, got homesick — and sent them a letter.

Then followed television. When they sang "Eili-Eili" and "I Believe" — the first time heard in trio form — the fan mail snowed them under.

Through the years they changed their names with every changing sponsor. Soon they were "Those Three Girls", then "Sophisticated Ladies".

And what sponsor do you suppose changed them to "The Better Light - Better Sight Girls"? You guessed it. For the past eight years they have clung to "The Three Belles."

Currently Henrietta does radio broadcasting. She's also working with another vocal group doing commercial jingles and background music on pop records.

The Belles entertain shut-ins in hospitals. Recently they delighted the senior citizens at the popular Murray Avenue Anathan House.

Amusing things often happen to song-singers. Once Benny Goodman took Henrietta dancing at the old Harlem Casino on the Hill. When her best fella Irwin sauntered in, the orchestra struck up "Love in Bloom."

Another time she "fell" for the inmates of the Western Penitentiary. She had come there with the Kay Kyser group to entertain during Christmas week. Looking up at a movie that was then going on, she tripped — and ker-plunk! boom! landed at the bottom of the stairs, right smack in front of the startled prisoners.

Later Horace Heidt offered to take the Belles to Hollywood to star in "Pot of Gold" with James Stewart. But Henny had been promised to Irv. Two weeks later they married.

Silly girl? Anything but. Now — 24 years later — many would consider her A Woman Who Has Everything. Everything worthwhile, that is.

Professor Nikolai Lopatnikoff

Distinguished Neighbors Grace Squirrel

They say it's a mad, mad, mad world. Yet there are wonderful people in it. And many of them live in our very neighborhood. Take for instance the Nikolai Lopatnikoffs. Their buff-brick house on Bartlett Street looks pretty much like the others on the block. But inside — well, that's a different story. Immediately upon entering you think "Someone lovely lives here." And you are absolutely right. Someone musical, poetic, artistic. These neighbors are extra special for still more reasons — reasons that will become clear in a minute.

Nikolai Lopatnikoff is the distinguished composer and professor of music at Carnegie Institute of Technology. Last month he was elected to the National Institute of Arts and Letters — the only musician among twelve persons eminent in the arts to be named to the Institute.

Prof. Lopatnikoff came to Tech in 1945. His compositions have given pleasure to thousands locally. They have been featured by our Pittsburgh Symphony lead by its popular Director, Dr. William Steinberg. Next season our neighbor's "Concerto for Orchestra" will be performed here by the Symphony.

Nikolai Lopatnikoff was born — you guessed it — in Russia, 60 years ago. His whole life was music. From the Conservatory of Petrograd he continued his studies in Finland. Then in Germany where his family had moved after the Russian Revolution in 1917. Fifteen years later he left Germany and moved to London. In 1939 he came to New York and a few years later he became an American citizen. In addition to English and the universal language of music, he speaks Russian, German and French fluently.

His many compositions have been performed by famous symphonies throughout the U.S. under the batons of Bernstein, Kussevitsky, Ormandy, Reiner, Stokowsky, Bruno Walter — just to name a few. And also throughout all of Europe.

And now listen to this! His lovely and talented wife is the well-known poet, Sara Henderson Hay. She has written four volumes of poems. The fifth book will be published in September. Her poems have freshness and sparkle not always found in contemporary poetry.

Composer-musician Nikolai and poet Sara Henderson Hay were married 12 years ago. They met at the world-famous and exclusive MacDowell Colony in Peterborough, New Hampshire. This art colony was founded and organized by Mrs. Edward MacDowell, wife of the famous composer. No artist lives and works there except by personal invitation that must be merited through exceptional talent. The colony is huge, with the studios in the heart of the woods — a most peaceful atmosphere for creative work.

The Lopatnikoffs share their charming home with two interesting personalities; a pair of proud and beautiful Siamese cats, named Igor and Nadia. Do these compose music? Write poems? Naw! They don't even "plant 'taters." But they have the run of the house and are masters of all they survey.

Nikolai and Sally will spend two months this summer at the MacDowell Colony. It will be a "working vacation". What about Igor and Nadia? They weren't invited. They will be boarded out in the luxurious manner to which they are accustomed.

John Lowenthal
Teaches Bridge, and Made A Name for Himself

You've heard it said you can learn dancing from Arthur Murray "in a hurry". Contract Bridge takes longer. To become a Life Master, that is. For many it takes endless years. Some suggest you should start in kindergarten. Others say it's just for those with "card sense". They turn to Poker instead — and often wish they hadn't.

So it might be a good idea to discuss this with bridge champion John Lowenthal, local-boy-made-good. At 24 he's the youngest — and only — Pittsburgher who has won national fame. During the recent five-day regional Contract Bridge Tournament at Webster Hall, the world-famous Oswald Jacoby had him as his partner. And in national tournaments John has been the partner of Fishbein, Moyse, Landy, Solomon — you name them.

First off, John picked brilliant parents — Alex and Anne Lowenthal. His lovely wife, Linda, a Pitt graduate, is daughter of Ben Paul and Lillian Simon, well and favorably-known Squirrel Hillers.

John first learned bridge casually as a student at Harvard, in 1957. His classmates wanted to see how fast a beginner could learn the game using their own strange system. No good. Four years ago he tried again. He learned the Goren system but didn't start playing seriously until last year when he was adopted by a championship group in Columbus.

He started going to tournaments almost every weekend, during which time he really learned to play bridge. He has since won so many sectional tournaments that you can't begin to count 'em. A year ago John Lowenthal became a professional bridge player. He went to four major national tournaments and finished 5th place or better. Thus, in only one year, he became one of the youngest Life Masters in the world. In the first seven months of this year he won another 300 master points. Usually it takes many years to accomplish this.

And listen to what happened at a national championship tournament in Lexington, Ky. in March last year. John came out second place over all national men's pairs championships. But when the scores were reviewed he found that they have been fouled up. Had he kept quiet no one would have been the wiser. But he pointed out the error. This cost him second place, but it won him national reputation in ethics. Now everyone wants him as a partner.

John Lowenthal teaches Bridge — one of only 200 in the U.S. who makes a living teaching the game. He makes the lessons lots of fun with a minimum of memorizing. He teaches at Horne's in the form of afternoon bridge teas; at the Chartiers Country Club, and has two groups at the Y-IKC. He has approximately 350 students. John says success in bridge is 60 per cent concentration; 20 per cent pure logic and 15 per cent psychological. Luck? Only 5 percent.

John attended Harvard for two years. Then on to Pitt where he graduated. He majored in physics, chemistry, creative writing and political science. His brain, he says, got such a whirl that there was room only for bridge.

The Lowenthals enjoy classical music. John plays the violin. He has written many bridge articles for the "Bridge World Magazine" and the "Bridge Journal". He is responsible for integration of races in all local tournaments, including Pittsburgh Bridge Assn. games. He campaigned for it. And listen to this. His hobby is gourmet cooking.

Wife Linda is John's business agent, manager and operator. Does she play bridge? No. But she enjoys watching her husband win. If you're bored with Canasta, Mahjong or Gin Rummy and are looking for a new exciting interest, give Bridge a try—and have yourself a ball. It's a diversion par excellence.

Kotu Lulla

Rice Curry Leads To Romance

This is being written during our Big Snow Blitz. But don't get scared. It's not about the Abominable Snow Man.

Rather it's to tell you about our new neighbor — a young brilliant atomic scientist. He's Kotu Lulla, living with his lovely wife Anita in a furnished duplex at Wilkins Avenue.

They came to our city last September for a two-year stay on a student visa. What happened before, and what is planned for after, will become clear in a minute.

Kotu Lulla was born 28 years ago in that part of India now known as Pakistan. His father was a building contractor.

When Kotu was three the family moved to Bombay. At college age he entered Bombay University. By then his dad had become a successful banker and student Kotu didn't need to "work his way through college".

Using full time to great advantage, he graduated in 1957 with a BS degree. Immediately he went on to New York for higher education. He got it after six years at New York University.

Somewhere along the line, to the surprise of no one, Kotu fell victim to the sweet mystery of love. He met Anita in a restaurant specializing in Indian cooking.

Over delicious rice curry he learned that she too had come from Bombay. Neither knew the other existed until then. One date led to another and in 1961 they married.

Their religions differed. He is a Hindu; she a Zoroastrian. Took a bit of adjusting but you know how it is — love conquers all.

For their honeymoon they motored through beautiful New England, ending with several weeks at Hyannisport. But wait. Last summer they took a second honeymoon— in Bombay, to meet all the in-laws. As it is here on similar occasions, there were luncheons, dinners, parties — and presents.

Young Lulla is at Pitt as a NASA post docutral fellow. NASA pays him $9,500 annually — their standard salary. He is working on atomic collisions in Pitt's large Donohue Laboratory studying the forces between different atoms.

And he's also helping other students in the Laboratory toward their Ph.Ds in the same scientific research.

Nice work if you understand it — and can do it. He does and can.

Anita completed nursing studies at Columbia University. Then she worked for two years at the Cancer Memorial and the Jacoby hospitals. Another year she nursed in the Sick Children's Hospital, Toronto. For six months after marriage she was a guide at the UN.

At home Anita wears what other Squirrel Hill housewives do — shorts, slacks and leotards even.

But in public it's strictly Sari. The way she drapes six yards of 45-inch-wide colorful silk or chiffon around her graceful form is enough to make even a Cassini stop and ponder. There are curves where curves belong — and hints of inner beauty that challenge the imagination.

With her black shiny hair smoothly drawn into a chignon, and in silver sandals, she's a vision of feminine loveliness. Under the Sari? In the words of Eddie Cantor, "don't ask."

Several times a year our neighbors go to New York for the plays, skiing and ice-skating. Meantime in Pittsburgh, in between his important work, Kotu is an excellent duplicate bridger. Anita is in the learning stage.

At the end of their two-year stay this charming couple will return to Bombay. Kotu plans to continue work in physics research there — and teach.

Like the familiar saying, half a loaf is better than none, so we're happy with having them as neighbors for just two years. Our community wishes Kotu and Anita Lulla the best of everything - now and always.

Milton Lyon

Former Area Resident Makes It To 'Big Time'

Weary of the many ills constantly facing our society? Well, there are good things too. The Civic Light Operas—six of them—will brighten the summer like a gleam in the dark. At Magnificent Heinz Hall, of course.

And who do you think is musical conductor, as well as stage director, both at the same time—a unique talent belonging to none other in this country? A former Squirrel Hill boy who has made it big throughout U.S. and beyond.

He's Milton Lyon, whose credentials are so impressive that it's a privilege to have him back if only for the summer.

Some of you may remember him as Milton Levine (show-biz, you know) who at age six months, resided on Phillips Avenue, later moving to Wightman Street near Darlington Road.

In 1939 Milt graduated from Allderdice. At 20, he served Uncle Sam in the Air Force. His great-great grandfather's picture hangs in Soldiers and Sailors Memorial Hall, as one of the veterans of the Civil War. The Honorable A. L. Wolk, retired Judge, is his uncle. His devoted mom, Mrs. Rose Wolk Levine, still lives in our city— in Chatham Center.

Our former neighbor earned his B. A. degree from Carnegie Tech (C-MU) and did graduate work at the University of California. He was on the faculty of Columbia, Princeton and Texas Universities, all between 1960 and 1973. His appointments include executive director of the Foundation for the Extension and Development of the American Professional Theatre. He was on the Advisory Board of the Maryland State Arts Council, Missouri State Arts Council, and Chelsea Theatre Center.

An excellent cellist and pianist, our talented fella has directed ten one and a half hour Specials for NBC, and staged Musical Productions in South America for our State Department.

He directed over 100 shows and had charge of Light Operas in Boston and Detroit. Music Circuses and off-Broadway Shows. He also was Vocal Director of Roxy Theatre.

In 1957, Milton met lovely Elaine Perry in New York City and did what comes naturally — fell in love. The marriage knot was tied two years later. Sad to say, it was dissolved after three years. Now he's batching it "above a garage on a 43-acre estate in Princeton, complete with deer, pheasant and glorious nature and privacy."

With him is a black-white kitten called Beau, and a similarly-coated mutt named Brummel. Beau-Brummel—get it? Milt loves tennis and more tennis. But this summer will be completely devoid of it. No time, plus the arm won't take tennis and conducting in one day. Will there be a second-time-around marriage? Too busy, he says; However, he's comparatively young yet, and there's lots of time. With his outstanding talent and personal charm, married he can always get.

Our summer Civic Light Operas? They start July 13 with "My Fair Lady" starring Edward Mulhare & Margot Moser; "Kiss Me, Kate" (Inga Swenson and Stephen Arlen) "Show Boat" (Ray Walston); "Music Man (Gary Collins and Betty Gillette— Bill Thurhurst's talented missus); "Applause" (Lisa Kirk); and "Sound of Music" starring Penny Fuller. It might be good to get tickets before the Sold Out sign is put up. And here's good news: Curtain time is 8 p.m.; so you'll get home earlier.

Rev. John Sherrill McCall

New Young Pastor 'Broad of Vision'

When you pass the stately Sixth Presbyterian Church at nearby Forbes and Murray, do you know that its Pastor is newly-arrived? And since it's always good to welcome new neighbors— especially important ones— let's extend a friendly hand to Rev. John Sherrill McCall. And learn a little about him. He was installed as Pastor of the Church January 4th. The installation ceremony, conducted by our city's outstanding religious leaders was most impressive.

Rev. McCall is only 32, but with his broad vision, educational background and neighborhood experience he has achieved maturity beyond his years. Born in nearby Bellevue, John's high school years were spent in Youngstown, Ohio. In 1960 he graduated magna cum laude from Westminster. And who do you think also graduated that College—a year later? His B. W. (beautiful wife), the former Ann Boardman.

They said "I do" to their preacher at a church wedding in her home town of Monongahela, a year after her graduation. In 1962, to be exact. The young bride began teaching school in Kendall Park. Her youthful husband received his bachelor of divinity degree from Princeton Theological Seminary in 1963, and a year later his master of theology. Since 1964 he was Assistant Minister of our city's Third Presbyterian Church. He has had experience as Moderator and Adviser to the Board of Deacons; done home and hospital calling; conducted services at the Negley House Nursing Home, and preached in churches of the Kiskiminetas Presbytery on a monthly basis.

He also participated in the organization of the Shadyside Planning Forum and served as its Vice President. Theologically Rev. McCall believes "the Christian faith is most meaningfully communicated today as the Gospel of Reconciliation. To make this reconciling love a reality is the challenge facing the Church." His sermons are rooted in the Bible and directed to the personal needs of the congregation and their questions about the world. He wants to get to know his people well and to establish a solid rapport with them through a vital program of support and comfort to all who are oppressed.

McCall was attracted to Sixth Church because of the congregation's interest in relating their church to our community. Especially the Hobbit Hutch Coffee House run by teenagers. It meets at the church every Friday night. The church recently purchased the lovely house next door owned by the late Robert L. Cook. It will be used in various ways to benefit the community. The Korean Christian Fellowship is now meeting at his church for worship services and other activities. Both Sixth Church and that group hope to develop closer ties one with the other.

Our neighbor is delighted with Squirrel Hill. He's intrigued with the shopping area, its diverse and unique stores. And because it's a cosmopolitan community he hopes Sixth Church will help maintain good lines of communications between the various groups. He was greatly pleased to receive a letter of welcome from the well-known Rabbi Ilson of Temple Sinai. He had participated in the Temple's Annual Institute on Judiasm for Christian Clergy. He's also happy that capable and loyal Corrine Smith is still the Girl Friday of his church.

McCall's lovely missus is currently teaching a Title One pre-school and kindergarten program in Verona. Morning only. While mom teaches, son David Bryant, 4, attends the Shadyside Presbyterian Church Nursery School. And a babysitter comes in to keep a watchful eye on Christopher Marshall, all of 1½ years young. What do these handsome kids think of their dad's ministerial doings? They couldn't care less.

as to David, it's not that he loves his pop less, but he likes Popeye more. And baby Christopher? He ain't talkin'.

Our community wishes the McCalls the best of everything now and in the years ahead.

Rev. S. D. McWhorter

New Rector, Spouse Find Home In City

Our neighborhood personality today is a tall, streamlined, handsome fellow just 29, whose modest charm wins you over in a minute. A movie star mebbe? Not at all. He's Rev. Stephen D. McWhorter, the new rector of the Church of the Redeemer at 5700 Forbes Avenue. And chaplain of St. Edmund's Academy next door.

He and his vivacious wife, the former Nancy Campbell, occupy the Church's rectory back of it, facing Darlington Road. Formally, Rev. McWhorter is addressed as Father. But he speaks of himself as just "mister." And many of his parishioners address him thusly. However, some even call him Steve. And believe it or not, he prefers it. That's how unassuming and informal he is.

And now let's learn about his background, education, experience—and snoop a little into his personal life. Born in Charleston, W. Va. where his dad was an auto dealer, Steve graduated from Parkersburg High and in 1963 received his A. B. from West Virginia University. Then went to the University of Mississippi for graduate work. In 1967 McWhorter earned his B.D. from the Episcopal Theological School, Cambridge, Mass. June of that year he was ordained a deacon. Six months later a priest.

While in Cambridge Steve made many visits to patients in the Recovery Room of the Massachusetts General Hospital. As you know, in hospitals is where beautiful nurses are. Nancy Campbell was one of them. It was love at first sight. During the year and a half they dated, the man-in-love was trying to decide about his future: Medicine or the Ministry? Finally the latter won out. And now both are glad it did. August of 1969 his Bishop pronounced them Rev. and Mrs. Before coming here, Rev. McWhorter began his ministry as Episcopal Chaplain of Marshall University, Huntington, W. Va. serving three years.

There he was inducted as a member of the National Honor Society ODK and served on the Planning Committee of "Impact." The chaplain's lovely missus sang in the church choir. Here she does part-time nursing at the Presbyterian University Hospital. But should husband Steve get a "code-in-his-nose," with sniffles yet—no problem. He has the comfort of full-time nursing service, with TLC (tender loving care) in the bargain. And the price is right. Nancy also enjoys housekeeping and in the summer will tend the beautiful flowers and greenery that surround and almost hide the rectory.

Because Rev. McWhorter loves people and in addition to his pastoral ministry he feels strongly about personal counseling on marital problems, loneliness, death, grief. He thinks our greatest problem is the population explosion. And believes in planned parenthood. He is confident his parish is healthy, with good attendance. There are three services Sundays: 6, 9:30 and 11 a.m. Also Tuesday evenings at 8 and Thursday mornings 11:45. Stop in sometimes, regardless of your own religious faith, and take a listen to his meaningful sermon. Might brighten your day.

Our neighbor swims every day at the Downtown Y. The youngsters of his church and St. Edmund's Academy splash in the Y-IKC pool next door. And the latter's kids join in the athletics of the newly-built Academy Field House which beautifies the neighborhood. A living example of good-neighbor policy. Or better yet, as it says in the Good Book, "Love Thy Neighbor."

Steve and Nancy have been here about 12 weeks and are so adjusted and acquainted they feel like they've lived in our city 12 years.

Our community is proud of the new young Rector of the Church of the Redeemer
and wishes him and Nancy the best of everything now and in the years ahead.

Mr. & Mrs. Lincoln Maazel
Prodigy's Parents Also Talented

Today you'll meet the interesting parents of world-famous maestro Lorin Maazel.
They're Mr. and Mrs. Lincoln Maazel, for years our neighbors on Darlington Rd. and
now living on Fifth Avenue, Shadyside.

You know, of course, that Lorin was a child prodigy and now, at 41 was named
Music Director of the Cleveland Symphony Orchestra to succeed the late George Szell.
On a 5-year contract beginning next September 1. And you also know that last month
(Nov. 9) he appeared at the magnificent Heinz Hall to conduct the new Philharmonic
Orchestra of London.

It was a benefit concert for the Pittsburgh Youth Symphony Orchestra. He received
a standing ovation not only from the wildly enthusiastic audience but the musicians
themselves. The Youth Orchestra is a training-ground for serious students, many of
whom later attain solid positions in the music profession. Lorin's concert helped make
possible sending the Orchestra to Luzanne, Switzerland in 1972 for the International
Youth Orchestra Festival. Other such Orchestras from throughout the world will be
there.

And now who do you think is Managing Director of said Orchestra — with a private
office in Heinz Hall? Lorin's mom! So let's learn a little about Mrs. Lincoln Maazel,
the former Marion Shulman. New York born, she graduated from the University of
Southern California as a pharmaceutical chemist. And studied piano privately. She
taught piano and theory all her adult life and is listed in "Who's Who of American
Women." Associated with the Symphony for 20 years and a former V.P., she's now a
board member of the Advisory Committee. And founder of the Symphony Silhouette.

Another plus is dad Lincoln Maazel — talented in his own right. During the past 15
years he's played important roles in over 50 productions at our popular Pittsburgh
Playhouse, doing character parts ranging from farce to drama. At one time he had the
unique distinction of being in three plays the same evening: Act 1 of "The great
Sebastion"; Act 2 of "Oh, Dad, Poor Dad, etc." and the last act of "The Inspector
General." Took a lot of know-how and running to and fro. And remember "Tevye and
His Daughters" at the Playhouse Upstairs — the fore-runner of "Fiddler"? He was the
Rich Man. Also the Rabbi.

We could go on and on but space must be reserved for a bit more about their fabulous son. Lorin was born in Paris. His absolute pitch and photographic memory were
discovered when he was 4. At 5 he began violin lessons privately. Two years later the
piano. At 8 he was tutored in violin and conducting by Vladimir Bakeleinikoff. Six
months later, a full-fledged conductor, he directed the University of Idaho Orchestra.
At 10 the child prodigy was invited by Toscanini to conduct the NBC Orchestra.
Honors have crowded his colorful career ever since.

Lorin attended public school in our city (Peabody Hi) and entered Pitt to study
languages, mathematics and philosophy for 4 years. And played the violin in our
Pittsburgh Symphony while a student. The dark-eyed maestro is married to Israela
Margarlit, a beautiful pianist from Israel. Their daughters are Anjali, 9 and Daria, 5.
Son Ilann Shean is 3 months young. Currently they are home-based in London.

What do you think, neighbor? Is it just luck that brought so much talent to this amazing family? Or is it inheritated intangibles from 'way back? Or both? Whatever it is, our community is proud of the Maazels — and particularly their world-famous son Lorin Maazel.

Lorenzo L. Malfatti

He Describes Operas

Bored with TV westerns? With wrestling? And you don't give a hoot who robbed which bank? Try radio for a change. Try WWSW. Every Sunday afternoon at 6:30 you'll hear a world-famous Italian opera. On hand to interpret Italian into English is our own Lorenzo L. Malfatti. He is a faculty member of Chatham College. His voice is warm and wonderful. He tells you about the opera's composer. Its plot. Names the famous Italian performers. Describes in English who's in love with whom, who's jealous of whom, which lovers embrace and who gets stabbed.

Now let's learn a little about this talented and charming man. Lorenzo L. Malfatti (affectionately called Larry) is a Pittsburgher, born of an American mother and Italian dad. At seven his mother took him to Italy to visit his grandparents — in the little town of Tuscanny, near Florence. There, in two years, he learned the pure Tuscan Italian. Upon his return to Pittsburgh, he had forgotten English! But you know how it is with bright youngsters. In just two months he was speaking perfect English again.

Lorenzo went through Knoxville Junior High and graduated from South Hills High. Right off his teachers knew he was a born singer. He received free voice lessons for 1½ years on a scholarship. Then, after enlisting in World War II, he had opportunities to perform with Lili Pons and Andre' Kostolonitz in India. At war's end he attended the Julliard School of Music in New York. Was auditioned and won a Fullbright award taking him again to Italy to continue studies in the conservatories of Florence, Rome and Siena. Followed five wonderful years making concert tours to Rome, Switzerland, Belgium and France. He sang in "Don Giovanni" and dubbed in the Italian voices for MGM's musical films.

Upon his return to the states he did a daily show on WATV in New York, singing Italian, and Chatham College "grabbed" him. The College wanted a voice teacher who sang "now" — not in the past. He was hired for one year and has been there seven. He gained added reputation training the 40-member Chatham College Choir which just returned from a successful tour through New England and New York City.

His voice students come from all over the U.S. — as far west as Oregon. They arrive as teenagers and, at graduation four years later, emerge as beautifully trained, poised women. Lorenzo tells them how much sleep to get, what foods are healthful, how to protect their throats. And, when asked, which boys to date. To sing well, he explains, you have to be well physically and emotionally. No wonder the girls call him "dad." In class he's called "Mr. M." and on the outside — socially — they call him Larry.

What's Lorenzo Malfatti like? Personally, that is. Well, he's above average height, he-man build. Has those flashing Italian eyes. Smiles easily and seems to love life. He's 39. Not the Jack Benny 39, but for real — going on 40. And listen, everybody: Lorenzo is a bachelor, but don't let it get around.

Mrs. Philip (Harriet) Mallin

Soprano With a Guitar

You've heard it said — if winter comes, spring's not far behind. This bit of hopeful philosophy brings us to a most remarkable neighbor. A sudden affliction could have made life one long winter for her. Instead, she up and turned it into spring — for herself and those about her.

Meet Mrs. Philip Mallin, the former Harriet Rosenberg of Forest Glen Rd. Harriet, as most everyone knows, was stricken with polio in the prime of life — ironically, shortly before the Salk vaccine became available. Unlike LBJ's operation scar which is covered except when he humorously bares it for picture-taking, her leg braces are visible. And she gets about on crutches.

At first you feel sorry. But soon you find yourself envying her. For her attractive and sparkling personality, her yes-I-can spirit, her lovely soprano voice. And what's more important — the insight and understanding of her family.

Formerly in the jewelry business, husband Philip now owns the White Cross Visual and Hearing Aids in Eastland Shopping Center. As to their three children, they have become self-reliant. No one needs to pick up after them.

They delight in helping Mom run the home normally, cooperatively, beautifully. Harriet has only part-time help and does the cooking herself.

Let's see now. Our neighbor is a graduate of South Hills High and Pitt University. For five years she taught English and history. Between times she studied voice and appeared in Pittsburgh Playhouse musicals. While singing in a concert at Carnegie Music Hall, bachelor Philip Mallin was in the audience. Greatly impressed, he maneuvered an introduction.

In no time they started dating and continued for several years. Then Harriet got the wonderlust and off she went to California. There she worked in the CBS recording studio and rubbed shoulders with many celebrities. Even Gregory Peck. After five months she became homesick for-you-know whom. And came home. Before you could say Jack Robinson she and Phil became Mr. and Mrs.

A year later daughter Dorie was born. Now "16-going-on-17" she's in the 11th grade at Allderdice. An accomplished pianist, she often accompanies her mom's singing rehearsals for entertainment at Hadassah, B'nai B'rith, ORT, the Lions Club, the United Nations dinner, to name a few. Then along came Sammy. Age 15, he's now in the 10th grade. And was Bar Mitzvah at the Young Peoples Synagogue. Summers he goes to camp in the Catskills. He loves the theatre and had the lead in the camp's play "Damn Yankees." And wowed them.

Thirteen years ago Harriet and Phil, together with another couple went to the Tanglewood Music Festival in Boston. There she enjoyed swimming, played tennis, danced a lot and was having the time of her life. Suddenly she became ill. Maybe not enough rest. Phil placed her in a Boston Hospital.

The doctors diagnosed it as polio. After several weeks she entered our local Children's Hospital at Shady Avenue. Then went to Warm Springs, Ga., the polio rehabilitation center made famous by President Roosevelt. There she learned self-reliance and kept busy studying Spanish, and teaching the Spanish patients English. Her pupils idolized her.

When she returned home permanently, their lovely ranch-style bungalow was organized for her comfort and convenience. Phil had an automatic elevator installed, running from the garage to up-stairs. The children decorated it with home-drawn pictures. Their car was equipped with special hand-controls. Now she drives like a house on fire! — Well, not quite! And loves it.

Then, guess what? Little Monte was born. Now five and a half he proudly attends Hillel Academy. And has also been studying French, and more recently took up the guitar — to strum during her folk-singing. Her most ardent fan is her beautiful little mother — Mrs. Elsie Rosenberg of Maxon Towers.

It's like they say — into each life some rain must fall. And when you're good sports about it, sunshine creeps in. That's how it is with the Mallins. Aren't you proud they're our neighbors?

Frank Marcosky
Retirement Hours Dwell on Hobbies

They say it's better to be young at 75 than old at 40. Our personality of the week belongs in the former category. And dat ole debbil boredom stays away from his door. Say a friendly hello to neighbor Frank Marcosky. Years before retirement he planned things to do later in life. And now, at 75 — by gum he does them! And is the happiest man in town.

First let's learn about Marcosky's early life. Born in Russia, his parents migrated to the U. S. when he was a little tike of seven. Dad started a grocery store in Duquesne. It was open for business 24 hours a day. Young Frank became star salesman and door-to-door order-taker for groceries. In that polyglot neighborhood he learned five different languages. Up at 4 a.m. he did a man's work before reporting to school at eight. Often he fell asleep at his desk.

But the teachers were sympathetic and he learned quickly and well. Later, being needed in the store full-time he quit school in the 7th grade. Time marched on. In 1914 he went into a newspaper agency in Shadyside as manager with his eldest brother. After two years he moved to Detroit. There he became interested in upholstery design and soon got a job with Fisher Body Corp. to work on interior design for their cars. He continued for eight years. During a vacation he came home for a visit. And something wonderful happened. He met a girl. Beautiful Helen Kramer. And like smart girls often do, she invited him to her home. Her parents, also smart, were hospitable. After a few dates he tore himself away and returned to his job in Detroit. But he continued his courtship through the mails. One fine day in June 1923 they became Mr. and Mrs. and started housekeeping in the motor city. In due time daughter Angie was born. She's now Mrs. Benton Pumpian living in Baltimore.

Meantime business conditions began changing. Automation set in and women did such jobs as his for half the pay. So he came back to our city. Here the young husband became manager of a Home Delivery Service in the Squirrel Hill district. He ran that business for 35 years — until retirement in 1963. Frank and Helen were blessed with two more wonderful children. Son John, now 34, is a professional engineer for General Motors. Their youngest daughter, Phyllis Klein lives on Beacon Street. There are nine grandchildren.

And now for the piece de resistance — our neighbor's hobbies since retiring. Mr. Marcosky owns the most modern tape recorder. With it he goes to lectures, book reviews, concerts. And records them. Later he plays them off at the weekly Summer Lecture Series for Older Adults at our Y-IKC. Or wherever they are wanted. For free, mind you. Included in his repertoire of around 16 recordings are Rabbi Poupko's report on his recent trip to Russia, his many wonderful book reviews. And a concert by a rock'n'roll Chassidic Rabbi who composes and sings his own songs and plays the guitar.

And that's not all. Our neighbor has a top-notch camera. He takes pictures of anyone anywhere, individually or in groups. Then puts the picture on a charming key-ring made of colorful plastic. They go like hot cakes. As a Thanksgiving gift for the patients at the Home for Crippled Children, Mr. Marcosky took a picture of each child. And encased their pictures in plastic key chains. The youngsters were thrilled and will not soon forget their friendly neighbor.

The Marcosky 11-room home looks like an interesting workshop — with his pictures, recordings, gadgets, samples everywhere. His hobbies require three things: Good eyesight, a clear mind and steadiness of hand. He's been blessed with all these. And has an extra special bonus besides — his devoted missus. She lets him use the entire house as he wants. And loves him for it. She herself has a hobby too — knitting and sewing dresses.

Frank Marcosky is a living example of the human spirit and a most happy fella.

Dr. Hershel Markovitz
Prof's Off to Israel, Sans Topless Suit

Have you already been in Israel? Or are you going there soon? Or is visiting that fabulous little country just a dream for the future?

Whichever it is, gather 'round and learn about a brilliant Squirrel Hiller who is sailing for Israel August 10. On the S.S. Shalom.

He's Dr. Hershel Markovitz of Solway St. However, our important neighbor isn't just an ordinary tourist on his way to Israel for a routine look-see. He's going there to teach rheology and do research work at the Weizmann Institute of Science. Not for just a week. Not for just a month. But for a wonderful, meaningful year starting September 1 on a Fullbright Fellowship sponsored by our U. S. government.

It's a Sabbatical granted by Mellon Institute where he has been a senior fellow in fundamental research since 1949. At the end of the year he will return to Mellon.

Just what and where is the Weizmann Institute? This world-famous science research center is named for Chaim Weizmann, Israel's first president — himself a renowned chemist.

It is surrounded by magnificent gardens in the lovely little city of Rehobot, a stone's throw from Tel-Aviv. There they do research in mathematics, physics, biology, biochemistry.

There our neighbor - professor will teach rheology. But don't confuse it with theology as some people do — and think he's a rabbi! Rheology is the study of the deformation and flow of matter, like for instance rubber, molten plastics and such. He will teach in English. But of course he speaks some Hebrew and is studying to improve it.

Dr. Markovitz was born in McKeesport 42 years ago. His proud mother still lives there and just celebrated her 80th birthday. Son Hershel did undergraduate work at Pitt and in 1942 went to graduate school at New York's Columbia University.

For two years the Doctor worked on the Manhattan Project (making the atom bomb).

Then in 1949 he did two other important things — got his Ph. D. and got married. To the former Marion Lamson of Hartford, Conn., his Columbia school-mate and herself a chemist.

Marion is active locally in various organizations like the Labor Zionist Movement, the Chay Commission for Habonim Youth, the PTA of the Hebrew Institute and the UJF.

There are three promising children. Naomi, Joshua and Sarah — 11, 9 and 4, in that order. The elder two attended Wightman School and our neighborhood Hebrew Institute. They both can carry on a conversation in Hebrew — a great asset for their year's stay in Israel.

Our professor is past president of the Young People's Synagogue and is a board member of the American Technion Society. And he's in the process of making an educational movie on theology for use in universities and engineering schools.

His hobby is Biblical studies and archaeology. In Israel he will view many archaeological sites.

Golly but this article is high-sounding and serious. How about a bit of mischief? Let's see now. Does the professor by any chance have an opinion on the topless bathing-suits?

A bit of hesitation. Then: "They won't go over. Not in Israel they won't." You know, he could be right!

Dr. Sidney P. Marland, Jr.
A Connecticut Yankee in Pittsburgh

This is written mostly for you students attending public school. Teenagers and youngsters alike. So put away Ringo's picture — with or without his tonsils — and pull up your chairs.

Oh, yes — call mom and dad. And your Aunt Minnie too. For today you'll learn about an outstanding personality. And because he's a closeby neighbor living scarcely a mile beyond Forbes and Murray, you'll simply ooh and awh with pride.

So who is this fabulous neighbor of such vast importance? Dr. Sidney P. Marland, Jr., superintendent of schools. That's who.

A six-foot athlete with an engaging smile and much charm, he wins you over in a minute. Add to this a brilliant mind. An extensive educational background plus vast experience and you have the ideal man for a herculean job.

A Connecticut Yankee with experience in West Hartford and Darien, Dr. Marland has been serving our schools since early 1963. In that time you've read about him constantly in the newspapers. You're hearing him on television and radio. And on the lecture platform. So you know what? Let's skip the heavy stuff and snoop a little into his personal life.

His comfortable home at Briar Cliff Rd. is graced by his lovely wife, the former Virginia Partridge. Where did they meet? In Connecticut — where else? That was 25 years ago.

She was instructing physical education and he was a high school English teacher. Their son Sidney III, 22, graduated from Harvard last June in anthropology and geology. Now he's an ensign in the Naval Reserve.

Pamela is 18 and a graduate of Allderdice. Currently she's a freshman at Wheaton College, Norton, Mass. Kid sister Judith, 14, is in the ninth grade at Allderdice.

With dad the school superintendent there are problems galore. Regardless what they do in school, it's either the teachers were "too tough" because of their dad; or their school mates think they receive "special advantages." So no matter what, his children can't win. He quickly adds, however: "Our children have been happy and successful in school — in spite of their dad. In fact, their teachers have leaned backwards to ignore me."

And he continues: "No man could ask for more genuine good will than I have found in Pittsburgh — from teachers, parents, organizations and the world of business and labor."

What does Dr. Marland hope to accomplish in our schools?

He wants to provide truly equal educational opportunities for all boys and girls — especially those who live in our deprived neighborhoods. And to continually aspire toward excellence that will satisfy the intellectual needs of our ablest children."

He is dedicated to winning back from the suburbs the families we need in the city.

The Marlands, as a family, love the wilderness. And go canoe-camping in Canada. And you'll never believe it. Dad does the cooking.

Now isn't it nice your superintendent is a real guy — far, far removed from the kind grandpop brags about? In the days when a professor was so absentminded he'd put his umbrella in bed and himself in a corner.

Mary Shaw Marohnic

Artist of the Year

Recently — January 4 to be exact — a pleasantly modulated voice on radio station WYRT made an announcement. The voice said: "We choose as the First Lady of the Day — Mary Shaw Marohnic."

Then, just a few days later, this First Lady was named "1963 Artist of the Year" by the Board of the Arts and Crafts Center.

Such honors aren't heaped on just ordinary folks. You have to be someone extra special. Mrs. Mary Shaw Marohnic is that — and much, much more.

Mary Shaw (everyone calls her that — she's so refreshingly informal) was given the one honor for her outstanding contribution to the cultural, social and civic progress of our Greater Pittsburgh area. The second, because as an artist and teacher of art you have to go far to find her equal.

To give her life history, educational background and describe her paintings would fill a book. Besides, she's been written up — with raves — so often in so many newspapers and magazines that anything more would be repetitious.

Therefore — what's Mary Shaw Marohnic like? As a person, that is. Well, let's see. She's much taller than average, and graceful. Statuesque would best describe her. And she has the laughingest blue eyes you ever saw. She seems to burst with enthusiasm and love of life. You enjoy being with her. Her pupils idolize her. Doubtless that's why she gets such fantastic results.

Pupils? She has 300 of 'em — in Gibsonia, Pleasant Hills, Washington, McKeesport, Greensburg and surrounding areas. And of course her popular pair of classes at the Arts and Crafts Center here. Every week she covers some 500 miles in reaching them.

People wonder how she found time to paint 82 pictures exhibited at the Center galleries January 7 through 27. "River Symphony," "Tree House," "The Web," "Eye of Summer," "Farewell, Rocks" and "Industrial Lace," to name a few. She shows the earth, fields, woods, the affinity to the country. At her exhibit thousands of viewers flocked from everywhere — art lovers and laymen alike. All lingered. All left with a feeling that they had just experienced pure delight.

Mrs. Marohnic is a mother and thrice-grandmother. Daughter Jean (Mrs. Joseph D. Pascarella) lives in Fox Chapel. Son Louis is with the First Boston Corp. in New York.

We in Squirrel Hill are particularly proud of this talented woman. You see, she is a descendant of a pioneer Pittsburgh family with their homes mostly in our community. As a little girl she attended the Sixth Presbyterian Church at Forbes & Murray. She had to walk through empty fields to get there. Now she knows almost every other person she meets. Mary Shaw occupies an old historic house called Oak Nest. It was built by the old Harvey Childs Family after the Civil War.

Victor A. Martuscelli

Central Grad Back After Viet Service

What a thrill it is to tell you about a young soldier recently returned from Vietnam.

Deeply tanned, fit as a fiddle, he was wearing an Army Commendation Medal on his dark green dress uniform upon arrival. He earned the award for 13½ months meritorious service as a generator mechanic with Headquarters Detachment, Signal Support Agency, Saigon near Tan Son Nhut. A hearty "Welcome Home" to Victor A. Martuscelli, our neighbor in Hazelwood. Twenty other lucky buddies arrived with him at Fort Dix, New Jersey where it was 70 degrees compared to 120 in Saigon, and it often felt like 200. All left for their respective homes.

Victor (his folks call him Marty) graduated Central Catholic High in Oakland. Evenings and weekends he worked in the corner Drug Store. You'd hardly have called him a drug-store cowboy as he had no time for standing on the corner watching all the girls go by. Fact is, he had a girl of his very own — lovely Mildred Litsko, an Allderdice graduate. They married June, 1968 and lived with his devoted parents, William and Adelaide Martuscelli, Greenfield Avenue.

The young husband had a job as mail clerk with Blue Cross and his bride worked for Bell Telephone—the "Dial O Girl" for long-distance calls — a job she still holds. Six months later Uncle Sam called Marty to Fort Jackson, South Carolina for Army training. June 3, 1969 he left for Vietnam. In the Signal Support Agency where he was stationed, he heard many secret messages.

But, of course is not talking about them. He admits he was scared and against the War when he left but while there he found out what it's all about and felt it necessary to serve. And proud and happy he could. However, he thinks it will be a long time before the War ends. His group of 28 all felt the same way. May their predictions prove wrong!

For recreation the soldiers had a day off once a week and could visit Saigon.

Beer and sight-seeing were plentiful. But dancing with the local girls was not permitted. Any girl seen walking hand-in-hand with a fella in public would be considered a prostitute by the local government. Their laws are very strict. Soldier Martuscelli was fortunate — he received three, four and often five letters a week from home. But others were not so lucky and very, very lonely. So guess what?

They went to the zoo! Oh, not necessarily to see the interesting animals; but that's where the girls went too. And no government officials around. The beautiful animals could look on doubtless in puzzlement — at the hanky-panky going on in the surrounding park. But bless 'em — they never talked!

Upon his return from Vietnam, Blue Cross promoted the ex-soldier to a file clerk. He plans to finish a course in computer management and get his degree. He and Mildred have their own apartment now on Hazelwood Avenue. And have invited a handsome soldier buddy who lives in New Orleans to visit them this month. He will sleep on their livingroom comfortable studio couch. And psst! listen! They already have a beautiful date lined up for him.

Thank you, Marty, for serving your country — and ours — so well. Our community is proud of you. The best of everything to you and those dear to you — now and in the years ahead.

Dr. Nahum Z. Medalia
Chatham Professor To Visit in Taiwan

This is being written on a day when the rains in Spain are falling mainly in Squirrel Hill. So let's put a bit of sunshine into it by telling you about a most interesting neighbor. He's Dr. Nahum Z. Medalia of Murrayhill Ave. Dr. Medalia is Professor and Chairman of the Sociology-Anthropology Department of our famous closeby Chatham College. He was called here when Dr. Mabel Elliot retired after her long and successful regime as Chatham's Sociology Chairman. Three years ago, to be exact.

How did Dr. Medalia come by his interesting name? Quite naturally. His venerable dad was born in Tel Aviv, Israel. However, he himself was born and bred in Boston. And his charming wife, the former Ruth Rosenberg was born in Germany and came to Boston at age 12. Nahum and Ruth met, fell in love and said "I do" in 1945. Now they are the proud parents of three lovely, lively daughters. Suzan and Alice, 16 and 13 respectively, both attend Ellis School. Eldest daughter Elizabeth works for the Polaroid Corp. in Cambridge, Mass. in an experimental photography unit.

And now some highlights on our professor's educational background. After attending public schools in and around Boston Dr. Medalia received his A.B. and Ph.D. (Magna cum laude) from Harvard in 1940. Then came WW II and the Japanese surrender. Young Nahum served Uncle Sam in the Military Government Office in Japan for a year. Upon honorable discharge he finished in Harvard's Department of Social Relations. Then worked in Seattle in Human Relations Research. There he studied the effects of isolation on men stationed in outlying radar sites. Afterwards he taught at Georgia Institute of Technology in the City Planning and Social Science departments He was living in Atlanta when the schools weren't going to be opened from one day to the next because of the crisis surrounding racial integration. After 8 years he decided to come North. In Washington he worked in the U.S. Public Health Service. There he studied the social aspects of air pollution control, particularly concerning the annoyance suffered by small-town residents from pulp-mill fumes in the northwest Washington areas. Partly as a result of these studies the Government held hearings which led to strict controls of factory exhausts. Later he took leave from the Government for several years to teach at Smith College and lecture in the Sociology department.

In addition to his air pollution studies Dr. Medalia has published articles in scholarly journals on "Morale and Efficiency in Military Units," "Race Relations in the South" and "Problems of Adjustment to Stress Among College & University Students." A recent definitive collection of essays on "The College Student and his Culture" published by Houghton-Mifflin contains an article by Dr. Medalia as well as an essay by Chatham's president Dr. Edward D. Eddy titled "Student Culture."

For diversion our professor is a member of the Carnegie-Mellon Explorers' Club. The group goes on hikes in the spring and fall, walking along the Youghiogheny River. And he does a bit of winter skiing in Hidden Valley near Somerset. His lovely missus, in addition to being an excellent housewife is taking a course at Pitt in Remedial Reading so as to teach elementary school children.

This summer Dr. Medalia is going to Taiwan on a fellowship from the Pittsburgh Regional Council for International Education. He'll be making a study of social and intellectual organizations of the Taiwanese students. Let's see now. Maybe we can cook up a bit of mischief here. Our professor is 48 but doesn't come close to looking it. And he's tall and handsome. Will there be student riots in Taiwan? Among the girl students, that is? With a smile, he doubts it. And so do his women at home. Evidently they know their man. Be that as it may, let's wish our interesting neighbor and his family the best of everything now and in the years ahead.

Mario Melodia

Humble Beginning Winds Up Success

Of course you gathered up the wife and kids recently and went down to the Three Rivers Arts Festival. And took along umbrellas, raincoats and boots. But only the first day. After that it was sunshine and roses. With thousands of others you oohed and ahhed at the countless exciting exhibits. And even bought.

And early evening you sat down to enjoy a varied assortment of thrilling live stage entertainment. Let's discuss one of these. The Mario Melodia Dancers. They had so much vitality and grace that the entire performance was later repeated several times on WQED. And another thing — the talented fellow responsible for the dancing has his studio in our very neighborhood. He's none other than Mario Melodia, Choreographer.

Also director, actor, singer, dancer. His Mario School of Dance, with the motto "Professional Training for Sincere Students" is at 5824 Forbes Avenue. He has approximately 250 students from age six on up through professionals. They come from all over the Tri-State area. And you'll be delighted that the little ones are mostly Squirrel Hillers.

Our neighbor's dancing experience is fantastic. But first about his personal life. He is married to the former June Spurrier of North Hills, his life-time sweetheart. They steady-dated through high school. Then he left for New York to study and dance professionally. During his five years there, dating was a commuting basis. Then May 1952 he married June. And started housekeeping in the Big City. After two years the young husband decided he wanted to teach as a steady livelihood instead of traveling here, there, everywhere.

So they left for Colorado College for a year's study of choreography and teaching. Then he returned to our city where Mario started his Dance School — first in Oakland, then in East Liberty and finally in Squirrel Hill. Soon baby Mark arrived and a year later sister Stacy followed. At first it was touch and go to meet the bills. June worked as his secretary and Mario took on odd jobs between teaching until his School got under way. He even drove a truck for his dad.

Now, after only five years in our neighborhood he has a waiting-list. And is so much in demand for choreographing shows and to dance in them that he's constantly on a merry-go-round. And loves it. At age 38 he looks like a teenager — energetic and handsome.

Our neighbor is active in all community civic affairs. In addition to the Festival he was choreographer and fellow dancer for our Civic Light Operas two seasons. And also for our Pittsburgh Operas for three seasons. Did you hear Roberta Peters in "Lakme"? Mario directed the ballet. He's guest lecturer on "Dance" at Pitt. And choreographs for WQED's educational programs for the Dance. Last winter — on Sundays only — Melodia flew to eight different states for Dance Educators of America, to teach teachers. In July he will instruct approximately 400 teachers at the Dance Congress in New York.

The Melodias live in a 2-story eight-room colonial home in Ross Township — far re-moved from dad's professional work—the way he wants it. His capable missus is a full-time housewife and takes care of his phone calls. Son Mark is now all of five and at-tends Sewickley Academy. Sister Stacy, 4 will start in the Nursery School come September.

And now get a load of this. Producer John Kenley of the Kenley Players in Warren, Columbus and Dayton, has leased for the Melodias a lovely ranch house completely furnished for all summer. Near the lake, with a pool, too. Rent free. So Mario could be on hand, without commuting, to choreograph all the Kenley Players shows and direct the musicals. Shows like "Call Me Madam," "Take Me Along," "Good-bye, Charlie," "Can-Can," "The Great Sebastian" — to name a few.

Starring, respectively, Ethel Merman, Arthur Godfrey, Martha Ray, Joey Heatherton and Van Johnson. And that's not all. Five of his exceptional students will also be there. To dance in the chorus. At a generous salary. A nice start toward their college education.

For a fellow who started at the very bottom, his success in such a short time is pretty sensational. And he's humbly grateful.

Phillip S. Merrill
Rich In Artistic Talent

You've heard the expression, "There's gold in them thar hills." We sure have it in Squirrel Hill. Not gold exactly but something more precious, more lasting — gifted people. Right in our very neighborhood. An outstanding example is artist Phillip S. Merrill, our neighbor on Woodwell St. And his talented wife, the former Ethel Mae Michael.

Often a fella wants to talk shop with his missus but the little woman knows from nuthin' what he's saying. Which is frustrating. But artist Merrill has no such problems. He and Ethel speak the same language, as the saying goes. They constantly learn and improve through mutual understanding and cooperation. Both love their work. And when you enjoy what you're doing, you have it made. But they didn't "make it" the easy way. The success ladder was a long one to climb. Especially during the corrosive years of the depression. Let's see now.

Born in Jackson, Miss., Phillip's first effort toward education was to a Friend (Quak-er) school. Then to public and High School in Atlantic City. They were normal, un-eventful years — an average student with a leaning toward the Arts and Philosophies. In 1929 his family could support only one son for higher education. But Phillip managed, with a scholarship and work the school gave him, to complete a year at prep school and another in Architecture at Carnegie Tech (now Carnegie-Mellon).

Financial trouble still plagued and off he went to New York and got "mixed up" with WPA work doing research in Lithography and Etching. Soon his talents started showing. And Albert Herter, the then world-famous mural artist asked him to come to Palm Beach and work for him. There young Phil had another "in." His cousins, Addi-son and Wilson Misner were famous architects who practically built all of that fash-ionable resort city. After six years he opened his own studio, primarily as a decorator.

Then Mrs. Lorenzo Woodhouse, a very wealthy New Yorker, learned of the promis-ing artist. And sent him to the Pennsylvania Academy of Fine Arts in Philadelphia, paying for his tuition and maintenance for the first three months. In no time the Academy, wanting to support his talent gave him a scholarship. Then along came

World War II. Uncle Sam quickly had a job for him — to design, build and operate the War Rooms. And later sent him to India for 2½ years in the same capacity. During that time he had a chance to travel throughout all of Asia.

At war's end he became a resident instructor at the Pennsylvania Academy of Fine Arts in Philadelphia. Among his many students was the beautiful and gifted Ethel Mae Michael of that city. Before long she was "teacher's pet." And then guess what? She became his bride. That was in 1946. After their honeymoon they spent two years in Europe among the art centers of the world. In no time the young bride got herself a job with world-famous Christian Dior in Paris as fashion illustrator. And the husband opened his own studio in the French city. By the time they returned to the States and he was close to 40 — what do you think happened? Son Johnny was born. He's now 14 and a student at Peabody High. Dad says he's handsome, likeable and "all man." The parents are grateful for having him.

To evaluate artist Merrill's hundreds and hundreds of fabulous paintings only a master critic has the words. They are on display in New York and other large cities throughout the country. Their prices range from $250 to $3,000. Portraits cost $1,200. Merrill is tall, friendly, easy-to-look-at. And you'll never believe it but he wears no beard. Neither does his hair fall in curls. And he doesn't walk barefoot in the park to attract attention. His works do it for him. Aside from being a master artist he's master of himself. Four months ago he stopped smoking. Quit — period. And the nice part he doesn't bore you with bragging about it.

Mr. Merrill calls himself an "honest" painter. As he puts it — "What I do I feel is right for me. I am myself." At 54, getting older holds greater promise. He says the longer his type of artist lives and works the better he becomes. So, for our talented neighbors it could really be a case of "You only live twice."

Robert Mervick

Manager has role at theatre

While enjoying a live play at the theatre, do you ever think of the manager? Probably not. You're too engrossed with the plot, the performers. But he's there just the same, lurking behind the scenes — watching, caring. So today let's concentrate on this season's brand new Manager of our 37-year-old Playhouse — Robert Mervick. The opening play (Cole Porter's "Anything Goes") is already in full swing and a big hit. The others will be listed later in this article.

Mervick was born in Etna and attended St. Mary's High in Sharpsburg. At the tender age of 14 he joined the U. S. Air Force, continuing for 25 years. During several years off-duty in the States, at 19 he met and married a lovely young Montana girl, setting up housekeeping in Utah. Later he resumed war service, traveling with his bride practically all over the world.

Even India and China. In 1954, sad to say their marriage was dissolved. However, get a load of this. During their life together Robert became a dad five times. All daughters. Like Tevye, in "Fiddler." But unlike Tevye's, all but one of Bob's girls married without benefit of a match-maker and are living happily in various cities throughout the States. Now a youthful-looking fellow of 52 and built like a football guard he's a grand-dad "12 or 13 times — forgot exact count." He batches in a four room apartment right smack across the Playhouse. And does a swell job of meal-making — when there's time.

During the past summer Mervick and his gang worked like mad to renovate the Playhouse. Oh, not like Heinz Hall, but beautiful. New comfortable chairs, better acoustics, nicer lobby, a prettier Lillian Russell Room, improved bar and the best meals ever in the Stage Door Club Restaurant downstairs. Bob's in charge of the three theatres within the Playhouse operation, plus the summer Film Festivals.

And now let's go back a little. In 1968, unattached, fancy-free but seriously ambitious, our "bachelor" enrolled in Point Park College and by the end of last semester earned his B.A. degree in Economics and a Bachelor of Science in Business. "In fact," he says, "the young students really dug an old guy like me entering college." Later a group of them threw a party in his honor to give him a new image, presenting him with bell bottoms, wide buckle belts, body shirts, fringed vest — the works in mod. Before graduation Arthur Blum, Point Park president, recognizing in Mervick vast capabilities offered him the Playhouse managership. The Playhouse is affiliated with Point Park.

The Playhouse is combining the talents of a resident company of Equity actors (many from New York) together with experienced local performers. Thus becoming a fully professional theatre. Already familiar to theatre-goers include Betty Aberlin, Alan Clary, Ken Costigan, Will Disney, Val Mayer, Lenora Nemetz, Helen Wayne Rauh and Tom Thomas. New talents are Earl Boen, David Emge and Doris Hackney. Greats like Gene Kelly, Shirley Jones and Frank Gorshwin got their start on the Playhouse stage.

After the current 'Anything Goes", our Playhouse will bring you: "Boys in the Band"; Noel Coward's comedy hit "Blithe Spirit"; "My Daughter, Your Son"; "Cactus Flower"; "Little Murders"; "Never Too Late'" and "Man of La Mancha".

Does Bob smoke? After a life-time of chain-smoking he quit cold five years ago. But shhhh, don't tell anyone — he started again during the summer. Maybe the pressure of work. Second-time-around? Too busy now but he doesn't rule it out completely if and when there'll be time to fall in love again. Meantime his chief love is work and the people connected with it.

Mrs. Hyman (Pauline) Milch

Able, Willing 'Leader'

A funny thing happened to an outstanding neighbor on her way to a Hadassah meeting last spring. She was asked (urged is a better word) to be president of their Business & Professional Women's Group 8. And graciously accepted. She's none other than the well-known Mrs. Hyman Milch of Douglas Street.

Everyone affectionately calls her Pauline. So what's so unusual — and such a big deal sacrifice — taking on Group 8's presidency? After all, there are many larger groups, and other important charitable organizations. And a vast number of Paulines in Group 8 all have done magnificent jobs. Well — there is a difference in her case. Just read on, compare and ponder.

Let's first learn a little about our neighbor's background. The former Pauline Hirsch was born and reared in the old Hill District on Centre Avenue. Her dad owned a Jewish book store. Through the years she attended the Hebrew Institute, after regular school. The Institute was on Wylie Avenue then. After graduating Fifth Avenue High she went to the H. C. Frick Teachers Training School to become a public school teacher. And to the Sol Rosenbloom Hebrew Teachers Training School for teaching Hebrew.

Then she began teaching in our North Side Manchester School. Her closest friend was another teacher — Clara Milch. One enchanted evening Pauline attended a meeting at Clara's home. And who sauntered in but Clara's good-looking brother Hyman. He had gone to the same school with Pauline, but in those days who looked at girls! Pauline maneuvered another invitation to Clara's Home. No other women. Just Clara, Hyman — and Cupid. The rest is history. They married in 1938. Hyman was teaching at South Hills High while the young bride continued at Manchester.

Soon a blessed event was on the way and Pauline took a leave of absence from teaching. The stork delivered son David shortly after Pearl Harbor.

And dad took a job with IBM in Baltimore. Before Jerome, their second son was born the family returned to Pittsburgh. The boys later attended Colfax and after school went to the Hebrew Institute now on Forbes near Shady. And who do you think was their teacher? Mom, no less. Pauline became Program Director of their Day Camp. The boys later transferred to Hillel, the all day Hebrew School on Beacon Street, from which they both graduated. David, now 25 was with Uncle Sam's Defense Department in Arlington, Va. Now he's attending Duquesne University here. Jerome is 22 and a graduate of M.I.T. where he received a degree in Life Sciences and another in Political Science. Dad is a social worker at Schenley and Washington Vocational High Schools.

For over a year our neighbor taught Hebrew on station WQED — 7 to 7:30 evenings. Thousands benefitted from her program. She now teaches at Hillel—full time. For the past ten years Pauline had charge of Group 8's monthly Wednesday evening Study sessions. They studied the Hebrew bible, Jewish literature, Great Ages and Ideas of Jewish History. Now the group is studying History of the American Jewish Community. She attends all the monthly board meetings, also their regular meetings — plus committee meetings. She's active and publicity chairman for Histradrut and Ivrit of Pittsburgh. She even goes "collecting" for various other charitable causes. Her phone rings constantly.

The Milch's Douglas Street home has six rooms — with a basement yet. Pauline has cleaning help but once a week. She herself does the washing, ironing, cooking and baking. Incidentally, her chiffon cakes and fudge tarts melt in your mouth, not in your hands. She looks forward to Friday evenings — the beginning of the Jewish Sabbath— to enjoy the peace and quiet of undisturbed family life. And to catch up on reading.

Organization women — bless 'em — are the salt of the earth. But when one's time is so completely jam-packed, taking on added responsibilities of another presidency makes our neighbor Pauline Milch just a bit saltier.

Charles Werner Moore
Tech Has A New Drama Professor

In Squirrel Hill anything can happen. Especially good things. So what happened? Two awfully interesting people were married. A year and a half ago, to be exact. What's so unusual about people getting married? Well, you see, these are talented, gifted, outstanding personalities — a credit to our community.

The most happy fella is Charles Werner Moore, associate professor of drama in the College of Fine Arts, Carnegie Tech. The young missus is one of his drama students— beautiful and talented Marjorie Battles of Philadelphia. Recently returned from a half-year study in New York, she has re-entered her professor-husband's class and will graduate this January.

Professor Moore (not the absent-minded type) received his B.A. degree from Williams College and his M.F.A. from Yale University. Following completion of his graduate work at Yale, he joined the faculty of the University of Kansas City as assistant director of the theatre, a position he held until joining the faculty at Carnegie Tech eleven years ago.

At Tech he has directed many of the productions, including George Bernard Shaw's "Mis-alliance." Had you seen this play you'd have sensed immediately that someone with theater know-how directed it. Marjorie, a bundle of dynamic personality, had the leading feminine role. The entire cast brought out Shaw's richly humorous satire in gay abandon. Other productions our professor directed were "Anything Goes," "The Rehearsal" and "The Ghost Sonata" to name a few. He has also done directing in summer playhouses at Provincetown and Sharon, Connecticut.

Recently, the Press Club held its annual Gridiron Show, written by some of the members. It was a Review titled "A Funny Thing Happened on our way to Oblivion" — a humorous satire on our city's gradual loss of business. Director Moore had the exact ability and finesse to make it a howling success.

Wife Marjorie recently starred in Tech's Greek drama 'Bacchae." playing the difficult role of Agave. New York Time's drama critic Howard Taubman rave-reviewed it in his famous newspaper with her picture, no less.

Were you among the thousands who thronged Gateway Center recently during the Three Rivers Festival? Then you saw "Don Juan in Hell" presented by four faculty members of Carnegie Drama School. Charles Werner Moore was Don Juan. His deep rich voice and perfect enunciation did full justice to Shaw's philosophical humor. Now, Hell doesn't seem such a bad place to go to, after all.

Until a month ago Charles and Margie had been our welcome neighbors at Fair Oaks Street. Now South Aiken Avenue claims them. Their charming apartment is shared with a proud and disdainful black cat, Latunda by name. He's not pedigreed, but is loved just as if. Recently Latunda (African name for witch doctor) came near losing two of his nine lives. Twice he was almost run over by cars. So now, right after breakfast he is gently placed on the third floor roof. The neighbors speak of him as "Cat on the Hot Tile Roof." But alive and safe he is, at the end of the day when the Moores get home.

Prof. Moore and Marge are spending the summer at Sharon, Connecticut — seat of the well-known Sharon Playhouse. Both will star in "Time of the Cuckoo" and "Our Town."

What will be done about Latunda is anybody's guess.

Mrs. Anita Morgenstern
Culture Her Forte

No, this is not about The Week That Was. It concerns The Week That Is.

This week, filled with interest, wonder and excitement.

Of course it's the Three Rivers Arts Festival attracting thousands of visitors from here, there and everywhere. And while you're under its spell you'll be proud that one of its important planners is a Squirrel Hiller.

Meet the festival's promotion chairman, Mrs. Richard R. Morganstern, the former Anita Freund — our neighbor at Fair Oaks St.

To list Anita's fabulous background and accomplishments would fill a book. Maybe a library. So let's see just some highlights.

Anita's well-known husband Richard is head of Morganstern Electric Co. Daughter Judy is wed to Robert Licht, now at St. John's College in Annapolis, Maryland, completing a liberal arts course.

Son Jim is 28 and working on his doctorate in history of art and specializing in Byzantine architecture. Incidentally — but don't let it get around — Jim is a bachelor! Now back to Mom Morganstern.

Her most important contribution to our community was organizing the Pittsburgh Plan for Art — a project financed by the A. W. Mellon Educational and Charitable Trust and the Rockefeller Foundation. It's to help our city culturally as well as physically.

As to the festival, as early as last October Anita organized its committee of 32 men and women. She divided the work, publicized the event on radio, television and in 225 local and national publications.

She's been snowed under ever since. A full-time job on a volunteer basis.

As musician of the family, Anita studied piano at Tech. Later, of all things, she turned to sculpture. And all because of smoking! In the good old days when smoking was taboo in Tech's College of Fine Arts, smokers could sneak off to another room.

The Mud Room it was called. The plaster, wood, clay and other indescribable objects that go into sculpturing fascinated her. Soon she was studying drawing, design and other subjects in preparation for her new interest. Even went to New York to study privately.

Now Anita is a seasoned sculptor. Her "Grieving Woman" — a wood carving — won a prize at an Associated Artists Show. The wood she uses now comes from apple trees on the Morganstern Laurel Mountain summer retreat near Somerset.

The more gnarled the wood, the more fascinating. And when it's worm-infested, Anita simply takes it to an exterminator.

Their Fair Oaks Street home, filled with paintings, sculptures and modern furnishings, has that "lived-in" look. Members of a group known as "The Experiment in International Living" they have hosted visitors from the far corners of the world.

In turn, on their many trips to foreign lands, they have been welcomed into all types of interesting homes. This has cemented friendships and developed Anita into an exotic cook.

Our interesting neighbor takes her causes seriously but herself lightly. And now listen to this: recently Anita attended Pitt's Anti-Smoking Clinic. From a daily pack-and-a-halfer most of her life, she has emerged a complete non-smoker.

And will never smoke again, she says. She has also stopped coughing.

Mrs. Ronald E. (Shirley) Moritz

Teen Worker Has Talent, Knowhow

To date, through our NEWS, you've already "met" 144 interesting neighborhood personalities. Anyone who says there are no more such in our neck of the woods should be asked to leave town. Actually the surface hasn't been scratched yet. So today meet another outstanding neighbor — Shirley Moritz of Eldridge St. The former Shirley Karpas is the capable young missus of Ronald E. Moritz, well known wholesale salesman.

Shirley Moritz works in the Teen Department of our neighborhood Y-IKC. There are around 800 teenagers constantly coming and going to and from the popular Center. Often with spirited youthful whoops and hollers. Takes a lot of experience and understanding to keep them busy and happy. Shirley has the know-how. She helps plan their club programs. There are 33 different clubs each with an adviser. She hires the advisers and supervises the club activities. In addition to her daytime responsibilities at the Center she is available two evenings a week when the kids are around having meetings.

A graduate of Allderdice with high honors in 1959, Shirley received her B.A. degree in Social Science from Pitt — cum laude. But it took her seven years instead of the usual four. How come? Well, it's like this. At age 18 Shirley said "I do" to Ronald E. Moritz, her childhood sweetheart. And in her senior year at Pitt, guess what? The stork came a-hovering. Nowadays such an event wouldn't even stop traffic. But six years ago it created a flurry of excitement. Everyone was solicitous and worried. When she missed class someone immediately phoned the hospital. Exactly one week after final exams were over and the semester ended, baby Faith arrived. Henceforth Mom Moritz became a Pitt day-time dropout. But needing 20 more credits to make up for her degree, she started going to night-school. During the long 4 years Dad Moritz must have done a lot of baby-sitting.

Little Faith is now 6 and goes to Colfax, first grade. She likes swimming and dancing. Opportunities for these are many where mom works. Meantime something has been added. A boy. Stephen is all of 3 and attends the Y-IKC nursery school. At their modest six-room house Shirley does the cooking. Faith helps with the dishes and makes the bed — when she must. Stephen couldn't care less about household chores. He prefers watching the TV cartoons. And is simply ecstatic over the commercials. What does he want to do when he grows up? Run a gas station!

Before graduating Allderdice Shirley was chosen "Teenager of the Week" in 1959— "an active class leader with a long and varied list of activities."

Shirley is treasurer of B'nai B'rith Women's Gabrielle group. Also belongs to the Children's Aid Society of Jewish Women. These women support a pre-school class for mentally-retarded children. They pay the teachers and for the equipment. Class is held in the Regent Square school and the classroom is provided by the Board of Education.

Our neighbor is expert at knitting. Recently she completed matching outfits for herself, Faith and Stephie. In Fisherman's design — pure white. Where did they first show off their outfits? At the Passover Seder held by the children's grand-parents— Pearl and Jules Karpas. They too are Squirrel Hillers.

The Y-IKC is a non-sectarian center for everything worthwhile. It's a bee-hive of activity for pre-schoolers on through to senior citizens. Shirley says she loves her work with the Teens. When you enjoy what you do, you have it made. More than likely her teenagers will become fine mature adults and happy senior citizens in the years ahead.

Mead J. Mulvihill, Jr.
School Director — A Family Man

They say it's a mad, mad, mad world. Yet wonderful people live in it, and, of course, in our neighborhood. An example is a fantastic fellow who, over and above his private professional practice, is giving extra time to benefit others. And for gratis yet. Say "We're proud of you" to Mead J. Mulvihill, Jr. our Fair Oaks Street neighbor. Last March, he was named the newest member of our School Board of Public Education, and sworn in by Common Pleas Judge Henry Ellenbogen. His appointment brings the total membership to 15.

In private life, Mr. Mulvihill is Deputy City Solicitor, having worked in the City Law Department since 1958. He began Law practice 16 years ago. What with the controversies over school re-organization; budget-trimming without omitting essential programs; keeping taxes down so that people will remain in our city instead of moving out; racial integration without the need for busing, and a raft of other problems, the responsibilities of a board member are herculean. But Mulvihill considers them a challenge. And now in the limited space remaining, let's learn a little about our neighbor's personal life.

He was born in Salt Lake City and when a little tyke of three, his family moved to our neighborhood Hobart Street. He went to Davis School, Colfax and Shadyside Academy. His BS and JD degrees were earned from Pitt and Duquesne University, respectively. He was a popular newscaster and announcer for KQV. Remember "Music for Reading" and "Request Matinee"? Mead announced both.

Somewhere along the line, something exciting happened. The quiet-mannered bachelor fell in love with KQV's lovely secretary, Peggy O'Brien. After two years of dating, they became "Mr. and Mrs."; that was 22 years ago. Their marriage turned out like it was made in heaven. It's been filled with love, respect and responsibility. They are the happy parents of three lively, interesting children. David, 16 is an Allderdice senior and an editor of its newspaper "The Forward". He's also in the Allderdice Scholars Program. Bobby is 13 and in its 9th grade Scholars Program. He's a photo buff and the proud owner of a good camera, purchased out of his allowance money and earnings from miscellaneous jobs. Susie is a 6th-grader at Wightman. Dad says (quote): "She's pretty, cute, bright, nice and has a natural talent for writing stories". Well — creative writing at 11 is the stuff authors of "best sellers" are made of. Then there's "Snoopy," their pet poodle. His boundless love for all — even the mailman — is a genuine morale-booster for the family. And he gets plenty of affection in return.

Mead's charming Peggy is past president of Wightman PTA and PTSA of Allderdice, and was a parent representative of the latter school. She enjoys school kids — in fact, adores them. And the feeling is mutual. Peggy is unusually well-read and loves writing poetry. Their summer place in Jennerstown, with its beautiful natural surroundings, inspire her poetic instinct.

Mead served in Uncle Sam's Air Force for 13 months during WW II. His hobbies are being with his family and enjoying things together. A licensed pilot, he flew his own plane until he sold it a few years ago. Now he has a sailboat, and is learning to maneuver it. His youthful-looking mom, Lahela Mulvihill is the best gardener on Bellerock Street — her flowers are radiant.

And now guess who's Mead's sister? Leslie Brockett — Don's lovely missus — that's who. At Darlington Road.

Honestly, ours is the luckiest neighborhood.

Mrs. Joseph (Edith) Muskat
Outstanding Nursery Teacher Has Many Accomplishments

You've heard about April in Paris. Miami Beach is better. Healthwise especially. By then the weather is settled. The days are flooded with warm sunshine. The ocean is like a caress. Soon you are suntanned, refreshed, relaxed. And by May lst, guess what. You don't want to go home. But you do return, for many reasons. Foremost is to continue introducing you to our interesting neighbors.

Today meet Mrs. Joseph (Edith) Muskat of Melvin St. She's an outstanding nursery teacher at Hillel Academy. There are 39 lively tots in her class, from 3½ to 5. And she has other accomplishments, too. But first, where and what is Hillel Academy? Located at 5685 Beacon St., it's a private Hebrew day school sanctioned by the State Board of Instruction. Named for Hillel, one of the greatest sages of the Talmud, living in the first century. The Academy is alive with teaching and learning in an atmosphere of dignity, devotion and joy. Its teachers all have a lot of educational background and know-how. And Edith has aplenty. In addition she comes from a musical family. Her father was a musician and composer. Mother a violinist. Two sisters play the piano and cello, respectively. And Edith herself is a violinist and violist.

Our neighbor is a graduate of Radcliffe and the Hebrew Union College in her native Boston. When a Freshman, one hot August afternoon she and a girl-friend went walking in the park to cool off. Soon they were joined by handsome Joseph Baruch Muskat, a Yale graduate and graduate student at M.I.T. The temperature immediately went up — not down. Right off Edith thought to herself: "There's a fellow I'd like for a husband." But nothing happened until October when she was invited to a meeting of the Jewish Student Group. There — big as life — was Joe. That night he was elected president and asked her to be on the Board. Later, pssst! listen! They began studying books of the Bible. Together, mind you. So what happened? You guessed it. June 28, 1959, they became Mr. and Mrs. On his parent's 25th wedding anniversary. Said the happy groom: "I gave mom and dad the best anniversary present of all." Now he's associate professor of Math and Computer Science at Pitt.

Edith teaches from 10 a.m. to 1 p.m. Her cherubs eat lunch at noon and play afterwards, thus learning to live with each other. They quickly pick up Hebrew words and learn the background of all Jewish holidays. Also the songs appropriate for each. And while teacher Muskat plays the piano they learn rhythmical activities along with the singing. Afterwards there's always rehearsing. Edith plays the violin in the Tuesday Musical Club Instrumental Ensemble. And the viola in the Carnegie Tech College Community Orchestra. She's also a top-notch folk singer in Hebrew and Yiddish, and has entertained widely in the Boston and Pittsburgh areas.

For the High Holidays they both go to Marietta, Ohio — Joe's hometown. There he serves as cantor, reads the Torah and blows the shofar.

At home their pet project is extending hospitality to out-of-town Jewish students. Hardly a holiday or Shabbot but what they have several students for the entire time. Pesach and Succot they often have as many as five for kosher meals. During meals they discuss Jewish traditions and practices. And sing Zemiroth (Sabbath table hymns).

It's good to be back to tell you about our interesting neighbors. But honestly now, don't you wish there would be a bit of the Atlantic Ocean at, say, Forbes & Murray?

Moshe Nahir

Newcomer 'Typical' Of Israeli People

Today you'll learn about a tall, dark-eyed easy-to-look-at neighbor who came here from Israel. He's Moshe Nahir, living at the Morrowfield Apts. Typical of the Israelis, he had the necessity for solidiering and a deep love for study and learning. And since he's been in our city scarcely more than a year, let's say hello-welcome and get to know him better.

At the ripe age of one year, Moshe, his parents, two brothers and a sister migrated from Czechoslovakia to Israel where they settled. In no time — so it seemed — he embarked on study and learning. And before long began the serious business of being a soldier. At age 14, before Israel became a state, Nahir started serving in the famous Haganah — the Jewish secret Underground Army of Palestine. And at 17 joined the Nahal Unit of the Israeli Army — a volunteer unit. There he served two years. Part of his army duties included building a Kibbutz (a collective settlement) near the Jordanian border. And living there. At the same time he received military and agricultural training.

And now listen to this. After the Six-Day War an Egyptian secret document was found. The document called for the annihilation of everybody in his Kibbutz! As well as another village town near Jerusalem. Doubtless the God of Israel planned otherwise. During and after his army days Nahir continued his studies and before anyone realized it, the ambitious student graduated with a B.A. degree from Bar-Ilan University in Ramat Gan.

At 22 he started learning English and mastered it to such a degree that before long he was teaching that language in a high school in Tel-Aviv. Also Hebrew of course. There he continued for eight years. Then was made the school's Principal. In Tel-Aviv he lived in a house bearing the number 11.

In Jerusalem, also in a house No. 11, lived beautiful Tsipora Haya Guttman. So what happened to Nahir should happen to your handsome sons. He fell victim to the sweet mystery of love. She was 18 and about to go into the Israeli Women's Army. But Moshe won her as his bride. And instead of a lovely girl-soldier she became his devoted wife, setting up housekeeping in Peta Tikva. And what do you think was the number of their house? You guessed it. No. 11. Unplanned, merely a coincidence. Their lively son, now 5 and attending Hillel kindergarten, was born there. His Hebrew name is Menachem, but in Israel they soon took to calling him Mickey. And that's what he answers to here.

And now let's go back to Tel-Aviv when Nahir was a happily-married school principal. A college in Manchester, England, invited him to come there to teach Hebrew. He loved his work in Tel-Aviv. Yet he had always dreamed of seeing England. So Manchester it was. During his two years of teaching there he saw much of England. And even took on a bit of the British accent. Then his love for more learning brought him to one of the best schools in the U.S. The University of Pittsburgh, of course. Currently he's a graduate student at Pitt. And teaches Elementary Modern Hebrew in its School of General Studies. One evening a week (Thursdays) from 8:15 to 9:45. Meantime working toward his Ph.D. He hopes to receive his M.A. there in Linguistics (comparison of languages) during the coming summer. In addition to Hebrew and English, Nahir speaks Hungarian, some French and German. After university hours, at 4 p.m. he is on the faculty of our neighborhood Hebrew Institute.

Nahir's lovely wife, a graduate of Teacher's College in Jerusalem, now teaches kindergarten at the Hebrew Institute. And Jewish History at the Sunday School. She's currently studying Sociology at Pitt. Always interested in Art, she studied at the Arts & Crafts Center as well as Carnegie Museum.

Our neighbor's two brothers live in Haifa and Jerusalem, respectively. They too are working toward their Ph.D. In Israel they're waiting for Moshe to come back. A teaching job at a Haifa University awaits him.

Aren't you glad you met our likeable neighbors? Our community wishes mom and dad Nahir and little Mickey the best of everything now and in the years ahead.

S. Joseph Nassif
Playhouse Exec Looks To Big Season Ahead

With the hazy, lazy days of summer quietly edging toward autumn and later snowflakes, people are asking: What's cookin' at our popular Playhouse? The answer is: Plenty.

Executive Director S. Joseph Hassif, his dedicated staff and big-name actors have been knee-deep for months planning and rehearsing, to make the coming season even more delightful than last year's. So let's learn about handsome Nassif, who's the split-tin' image of Omar Sharif, only younger and not a master bridge player. Sharif, as you may know is of Egyptian background; Nassif's is Lebanese. Both countries are closely Mid-eastern — maybe that accounts for the resemblance; but Lebanon is far more democratic politically than Egypt.

S. Joseph Nassif is also chairman of the Department of Theatre at Point Park College, executive producer of the Pittsburgh Ballet Theatre, and has just been named a member of the board of trustees of the Piscator International Theatre. Preceding his Playhouse position, he was called here in 1968 as producer-director of Channel 2 KDKA-TV, producing the enjoyable Marie Torre syndicated "Talk Show" for a year. It took a lot of artistic skill to get that far up the success ladder, so let's go back some and climb a little with him.

Nassif was born in Cedar Rapids, Iowa some 33 years ago. After High, he went to Grinnell College, earning his BA in Chemistry in 1960. Three years later, he received an MFA degree from Yale. In that college town, he opened his first theatre while teaching English and Drama. His director was Ken Costigan (now the Playhouse artistic director).

Then guess what? The young bachelor met lovely Michelle McKenna, an apprentice there; and fell victim to the sweet mystery of love. A year later they married in Washington, C.D., her home town. They went housekeeping in Denver, where the young husband finished his Ph.D. at Denver University. Michelle took several courses there in Children's Theatre, and taught at a private school. Later Joe became a visiting professor of the theatre at the University of Montana. Then it was off to L.A., where he taught dramatic literature and English at U.S.C. His additional academic, administrative and professional publication honors are too numerous to list in limited space.

Now get a load of this:- Before the Nassif marriage-knot was tied, Joe's parents made the couple promise, should there be children, they would go to a Lebanese church, even though Michelle is Irish Catholic. The promise was made and kept. Jonathan, four and Alexandra, two, both go with Pop to St. George Orthodox Church. Mom attends St. Paul's Cathedral. The kids like Irish stew and Lebanese kibbee.

The Nassifs bought a big, big battered-down barn of a house in nearby Shadyside, with six bedrooms. They themselves plastered, painted, papered, floor-finished, and landscaped it; with furnishings from garage sales and second-hand shops. Joe does the gardening and Michelle, without outside help, keeps the place shipshape and does the cooking. When the kids grow up, she'll become a women's libber. Meantime, she's a devoted wife, mother, hostess. Show people have countless friends, so often it's "Guess Who's Coming to Dinner?"

The 1972-73 list of Playhouse performances? Starting September 9, it's "Fiddler On the Roof", followed by: "How the Other Half Loves"; "Original British-USA Premiers"; "Who's Afraid of Virginia Woolf?"; "Last of the Red Hot Lovers"; "Forty Carats"; "You Can't Take it With You"; "A Street Car Named Desire"; "Child's Play", and "Carousel" - all with big-name leads.

Joe will be reading this at Chatauqua, where they holiday for a month each summer. The place is exciting culturally, and the air is clean; the water pure.

George Neiman

Shipwrecked Couple Active on Land, Too

Remember? Not long ago all about the luxury liner "Shalom," Israel's newest and finest merchant fleet. Bound for the Caribbean on her maiden cruise, and scarcely three hours out of New York, she collided with a Norwegian tanker.

You will also remember that among the ship's 616 passenbers were our neighbors, Mr. and Mrs. George Neiman of Beechwood Blvd. They were photographed and quoted everywhere. So by now most details of the incident are well known and nothing further need be added here.

But you should know more about them personally, for many reasons. Including one in particular. Please read on.

Let's start with husband, George. A graduate of Fifth Avenue High and only a short evening course at Duquesne University, his college degrees are conspicuous by their absence.

Not a Ph.D. nor an M.D. to his name. Just an average fella, he says of himself, trying to get along. But those who know him consider him the greatest guy ever.

Mr. Neiman's success as a special agent for a widely-known insurance firm is due mostly to his friendliness, dependability and sincerity. And of course hard work. But his love of people — not necessarily clients — and his readiness to help others in any way any time, often inconvenient to himself — this gift was endowed him by nature, not college.

Vowing to remain a bachelor, do you know what happened at age 26? He up and got himself married. To the former Freda Martin, a five-foot-two with eyes of blue. And to Niagara Falls for their honeymoon. Now their son Harold is 28 and an accountant representative with Cal-Pacific Leasing, Inc. Wayne, 24, is in personnel work with an engineering firm in L.A. Both are bachelors. But you know what happened to their old man. Sanford — affectionately called Sandy — is 18 and a freshman at Kenyon College, Gambier, Ohio.

And now for the piece de resistance of this article. Please, please read on.

Several years ago, at a B'nai B'rith "Cafe Tel-Aviv" affair a group of women came without escorts. You know — men shortage. As the orchestra struck up for dancing, one of the women was invited to join in the Twist. The Watusi, the Frug, the Alley Cat and the Monkey were as yet unheard of.

At going-home time, hurrying to get her wraps, her heel tangled with the carpet and ker-plunk, boom — down she sprawled on the floor. Her arm started swelling. What to do? Call a cab? Not with the Neimans around.

Although they had an early morning appointment and already it was 2 a.m., they drove her to Montefiore Hospital for emergency first-aid. During the several hours of waiting for X-rays and things, George helped her morale with humorous stories and hilarious jokes. Many unprintable.

It was 5 a.m. when they brought her home, bandaged arm and all.

The broken arm has long since healed and is forgotten, but the Neimans' gracious friendliness lingers on. And who do you think the lady in distress was? The writer of this article.

Neighbor Neiman and his blue-eyed missus surely belong in LJB's Great Society.

Dr. Ezra (Ted) Newman

Relativity, Politics Among Chief Interests

Our neighborhood personality of the week is a nicely - built easy-to-look-at professor of Physics in our University of Pittsburgh. He's comparatively young — scarcely 38 — and plenty knowledgeable. So who is this smart youthful professor? Dr. Ezra Newman — that's who — living on Wilkins Avenue. Everyone calls him Ted.

His family consists of his talented wife Sally and two lively children. David 8, and his 6-year old sister, Dari both attend Wightman school. Their beloved household pet a mischievous hamster called Seltzer, is conspicuous by his absence. Several months ago he breathed his last, joined his ancestors and the critter is no more.

In addition to teaching Physics at Pitt for the past 11 years, Dr. Newman also does research on Einstein's Theory of Relativity. Relativity? What kind of a whoozit is it? Well, since that fabulous fellow Einstein who started the whole thing is no longer living, let's see if we can learn about it from our Pitt professor. Relativity, he explains, is a doctrine which says the velocity of light is independent of the relative velocity of the observer. That it is a maximum which the velocity of material can never reach. You understand? Neither does any other layman. So let's just skip the whole thing and learn, instead, a few things about our neighbor's personal life.

Dr. Newman, a born New Yorker received his B.A. degree at New York University and his M.S. Ph.D. from the University of Syracuse. His lovely missus, the former Sally Faskow, is a graduate of the Julliard School of Music. She too was born in New York. But their paths never crossed until each came to our city. He to teach at Pitt and she to start a music class in nearby Carnegie. And where do you think they met? Where boy usually meets girl. At the Bellefield Ave. YM&WHA. What with its concerts, lectures, educational courses, swimming and dances — fellas and girls find common interests — and find each other.

And that's what happened to Ted and Sally. Sally now teaches music — part time — at Mt. Mercy College in its campus school. Among other instruments she also plays the harpsichord. And what do you think Ezra plays? The recorder — that 15th century instrument with a plaintive sound — which the shepherds used to play while tending sheep. And as an extra hobby, he collects rocks.

They are rock crystals—semi-precious stones collected from hikes all over the country — in the mountains, valleys, deserts and far-off exotic places. Ted makes jewelry out of them. He has accumulated about 500 pounds of these rocks. They are all around — upstairs, downstairs, in the basement. But he has no rocks in his head!

The Newmans all love skiing. They've taken part in that sport in Canada, Austria, Switzerland and of course all over the U.S. The kids have long passed the "Look, ma — I'm skiing" stage. They are fast learning total harmony of the head, the body, the skis — with the snow. While dad was teaching Physics for a year at the University of London, they all traveled throughout Europe. Also Poland. Next July they are going back to London on Ted's sabbatical for a year. He has an invitation for a conference next September in the Soviet Union. The trip will be financed jointly by Pitt and London.

And now listen to this. Ted and Sally are seriously engrossed in politics too. They want Senator Eugene J. McCarthy, D-Minn. to be nominated for President. And they are on his band-wagon. McCarthy, as you know, calls himself a peace candidate and is challenging President Johnson on his Vietnam policy.

Whatever your political views, it's nice, isn't it — having such charming neighbors as the Newmans.

Rose Noon

Friendly and Busy

Of course not everyone in Squirrel Hill knows Mrs. Leo Noon. But those who do— even casually—are glad they do; and those who are lucky to know her intimately are even "gladder". Obviously, there are many reasons for it. That's why we are writing about her.

Rose Noon is recently retired president of the Business and Professional Women of Hadassah Group 8. Her two-year regime has been fruitful and successful. However, that is not so unique because many other women who preceded her as president of the same group, served equally well. What is outstanding in Rose's case is that her Hadassah duties had to be sandwiched in between many other responsibilities.

Rose is a devoted wife, an excellent home-maker (no maid) and has been holding down a steady position from nine-to-five every day and until noon on Saturdays. Her full-time job is a combination bookkeeper-secretary-switchboard operator-and-interviewer for a well-known Squirrel Hill real estate firm.

Rose and Leo Noon were married ten years ago December 7 and live in a pleasant-looking apartment building on Shady Avenue. Rose is fortunate in her Hadassah work because Leo appreciates Israel and what the Hadassah women do for that beloved country. Leo is a traveling shoe salesman. When home on week-ends, he often finds groups of women holding meetings there. He joins right in and helps being a gracious host. It would be interesting to measure the good that comes to Israel through understanding and cooperative husbands such as Mr. Noon.

Rose has attended approximately 36 regular Hadassah meetings as well as many board meetings. And dozens of special meetings to people's homes or in her own home. Seldom was there an illness or a death in the family of a member but what Rose was not on hand. She rarely made excuses but came and added her warmth and friendliness where needed.

Even though Rose is retired from the presidency, already she has been given — and accepted — another important job. When the Hadassah national convention is held in Pittsburgh in September, Rose will do a lot of planning and arranging. There will be a large luncheon in honor of the business and professional women delegates of the entire United States. Rose is the chairman of that affair.

Maybe now, at long last, Rose can enjoy her beautiful hi-fi classical and modern recordings which she loves but which have been so sadly neglected through the busy months. And perhaps she will find time for a game of Canasta, Bridge or Mahjong. In the meantime, Hadassah and her many, many friends wish Rose and her husband good luck, good health and much happiness.

Mrs. W. O. (Thelma) Parker
Wins Friendships With Ease

A-h-h-choo! Do you have sprig-has-cub sniffles (heaven forbid!)? If so, you and even our healthy neighbors will feel good when you learn about an interesting personality living right around the corner at Wightman Street, a minute from Forbes. She's Mrs. Thelma Parker, devoted missus of Dr. W. Oren Parker, Professor of Theatre Design at our Carnegie-Mellon U. The former Thelma Teschendorf is affectionately called Teschie by most everyone. However, husband Oren accidently-on-purpose often forgets and calls her honey. And actually, that's what she is. Both are now working on a book titled "Theatre Decor."

Our neighbor is a V.P. of the Greater Pittsburgh YWCA and currently chairman of its Festival of Nationals Fair coming up May 5 and 6. Her association with that project has given her a chance to meet visitors from around the world. So naturally her second love is travel. She works with the Y on the college level—the student portion of its program. And has served as Advisor to the Y's National Student Association.

A native of Detroit, Teschie graduated its City College with a BS degree in Occupational Therapy. Then worked on Decorative Design at the University of Michigan, where Prof. Parker was teaching Theatre Design. When she returned for her Bachelor of Design degree, guess what? She became the teacher's pet. And in April 1937 became his bride. Oren's minister from Rochester, Mich. came down to tie the knot and the young couple started housekeeping in Ann Arbor. The next year husband Parker received a Rockefeller Fellowship for Yale and they moved to New Haven. While Oren was working on his MFA Teschie got a job to organize a Rehab Center at nearby Bridgeport. That way she was able to help pay the bills. By the time her husband got his degree, what do you think happened? Teschie got pregnant (as they say in the sex books). They moved to Williamstown, Mass. where the soon-to-be dad connected up with Williams College. And the Stork brought Margaret Anne—the only New Englander in their family. Then came WW 2 and Prof. Parker became a Theatre Consultant for the War Department in Brookhaven, N.Y. Mom and baby went to live with her parents in Detroit. At war's end son Wilford was born and dad was called back to Yale where the family remained for 17 years. There Teschie became Director of the Area Rehabilitation Center. Soon CM-U called Prof. Parker here and they chose to live in the nicest neighborhood - ours.

Margaret Anne is now Mrs. Clifton V. Rice in Boston. Cliff is Public Relations Director of the New England Foundling Home. Son Bill has been serving Uncle Sam in Germany 2 years and in Saigon 6 months. He's scheduled to return home in July.

And now get a load of this. Two years ago the Parkers planned a trip to California. But for some unexplainable reason (ESP maybe) they went, instead to nearby California, Pa. To see a student play. Meantime a fire broke out in their house. When they rushed home, the firemen—bless 'em— had put out the fire, covered the furniture and china and everything with tarpaulin. No one was hurt. But their pet cat Spuminti (Italian for champagne) was gone. Of course they feared the worst. But cats are smarter than people. They don't wait for ladders to get out of a burning house. Four days later who do you think was peacefully snoozing on their daughter's bed? You guessed it. Spuminti is now living out her nine lives with Margaret Anne in Boston.

Before ending this article, our neighbor wants everyone to know she thinks the Squirrel Hill firemen are the greatest. Of course she's right. And our community thinks ditto of the Parkers.

W. Oren Parker

Professor Lurks in the Scenery!

When you see a play, attend an opera or watch a movie, do you ever think about the scenery? Hardly. You are too involved with the plot and the performers.

But the scenery is there. And it's very important. Good scenery, that is. So you'll be interested and pleased that in our neighborhood—where else?—is a fellow with plenty of talent, skill and a fantastic background in this interesting profession.

He's W. Oren Parker, professor of theatre scene design at Carnegie Tech, who lives on Wightman St.

Our neighbor designed the scenes for all our Civic Light operas during summer 1963. And he scored high. A herculean task requiring 12 hours work daily, yet the job was challenging, he says, and the experience invaluable.

Last fall Prof. Parker started teaching at Tech and has resumed again this season. Working with young students, he will produce the scene designers of tomorrow. He was lured here from Yale because of the new theatre being planned by Tech. Mr. Parker calls the proposed theatre "one of the best, if not the best in the U.S."

Our neighbor is soft-spoken and unassuming but the depth of his know-how has no bounds. Let's learn a few highlights.

For 17 years Oren Parker was technical director of the Yale Drama School. Prior to Yale he spent three months abroad studying continental and English production methods. Also he was staff designer for CBS-TV, for industrial shows like American Motors, Coca Cola and RCA.

With a fellow Yale teacher he co-authored a book titled "Scene Design and Stage Lighting." It was published and has become a best seller in the profession.

In 1937 at Ann Arbor, Oren did what comes naturally. Got married. To his favorite pupil—Thelma Teschendorf, affectionately called Teschie. For many years she worked with handicapped children — teaching ceramics, weaving, design and graphic work.

Their own daughter just graduated from Pembroke — a full-fledged artist. Son Wilford, 18, is a sophomore at Lafayette. Thinks he'll study architecture. An athlete, he plays soccer, baseball and loves to ski.

While at Yale, Prof. Parker designed scenery for all the Yale plays. One of them required a life-sized horse. His star pupil, Amon Adar — an Israeli — created one out of excelsior and wood. The Parker children breathlessly counted the days when the horse would become unemployed and be turned to pasture in their back yard. The great day finally arrived.

Dad Parker crowded the horse into his car and drove through jammed traffic, its huge head protruding through the window. A sight that attracted all the kids in town, not to mention a few suspicious cops. When it was permanently settled in the Parker yard, all the youngsters in the neighborhood converged, clamoring for a ride. And it continued thus until one sad day the horse fell apart and was no more.

Meantime the horse's creator returned to Israel and later married. Not long ago our neighbor received an interesting announcement from Jersualem. A son was born to Mr. and Mrs. Amon Adar. And what do you think they named him? OREN.

To the lively little sabra who will answer to the name Oren and his proud parents — the Parkers say SHALOM.

Mrs. Carl F. Patterson
Secretary, Teacher And Rose Grower

Because of the Ecumenical Council everyone thinks big, in terms of St. Peters in Rome, no less. St. Philomena at 6424 Forward Ave. is less pretentious. But if anyone were to take a look into its school he would see, with admiration, the teaching and learning accomplished there, in an atmosphere of quiet dignity, devotion and joy.

There are 325 children in grades from 1 to 8. The seven nuns who teach are remarkably capable and dedicated. But the business responsibilities fall on the efficient secretary and teacher when needed, Mrs. Carl F. (Rita Marie) Patterson. Having no children of her own she bestows much TLC (tender loving care) on the youngsters— which they spontaneously reciprocate. The highlight of the day is every morning at 11:15 when teachers and Rita Marie lead all the children to mass.

Mrs. Patterson is a graduate of St. Benedicts High School and Mt. Mercy Academy. She and Carl were married Thanksgiving Day 1941, during World War 2. They spent the first 23 months of their married life in Charlotte, N.C. where the young husband took his basic training as a pilot.

When he was sent overseas and stationed in Paris, young Mrs. Patterson went home to Pittsburgh. Carl remained there for two years, piloting small fighter planes (A-20 and B-26) in the 9th Air Force. Not once during the two years did he have a furlough home. Once his plane was shot down and he was reported missing. But the Lord was gracious and later his wife received the glorious news that he was safe.

Carl was honorably discharged and came home August 15, 1954 on Peace of Assumption Day. He established himself in business and now owns and runs Pat's Service Station on Route 60, five miles from the Airport.

Last August the Pattersons took their vacation in a most commendable manner. They drove Mother Superior (Sister Wilhelmina) and three other Sisters to St. Louis, Wilton, Conn. and Baltimore. At each of these cities is a mother house, the main one being in Baltimore. These are schools for the Sisters of Notre Dame who use them as retreat in the summer during their one-week vacation.

The Sisters enjoy lectures, prayer and rest. In St. Louis alone there were approximately 1,000 Sisters in the audience.

Rita Marie and Carl belong to the Mt. Lebanon Players and the Catholic Guild Players. They attended all the plays, among which were "Tea House of the August Moon," "St. Bernadette" and their most recent hit "The Housekeeper."

As a hobby Mrs. Patterson goes in for huge hats — the larger ("and the crazier," she adds) the better. Being tall, graceful and easy to look at, she is a natural for them. She makes them herself, having studied hatmaking at Carnegie Tech. The first thing they taught her in that class was that if a hat rates stares from men and they turn around for a second look, that hat is a success! They attend all the Mad-Hatters Fashion Shows. At the recent one, Hedda Hopper was the guest of honor. Rita Marie's hat got not only stares but whistles from the men guests — and out-hatted Hedda.

Mrs. Patterson was chairman of the Hat-o-Rama held very recently at St. Philomena Church. They sold 300 hats and raised a nice sum of money. The funds are used for repair and upkeep of their school.

Rita Marie also raises roses in her garden. They are called "Peace" roses and some are as large as dinner-plates. Next summer she hopes they will grow larger than her hats — and lovelier.

Charles A. H. Pearson
Yom Kippur . . . With Presbyterian Tones

Are you especially fond of organ music? And are you spiritually moved by the lovely choir voices that usually go with it?

Then you'll be pleased to know that a gifted organist of exceptional talent is our neighbor. He's the well-known Charles A. H. Pearson living at Barlett St.

Mr. Pearson is faculty member of the Department of Music at Carnegie Tech. In addition he's organist and choir director at Rodef Shalom Temple.

It takes a lot of doing to arrive far up the ladder of musical success. So let's learn how our neighbor got there — especially since his beginning was a humble one.

Born in the nation's Capitol, young Charles became fatherless at six. The widowed mother attended business school and worked as a secretary. Charles and kid brother Jay F. W. went to grandma's in Grove City, to attend public school.

Charles graduated high in 1915. The little family then reunited in our city. Mom Pearson worked here for various large firms, including Pittsburgh Coal and H. J. Heinz. Soon big brother also became a bread-winner.

For three years he worked at the Union Paint Co. and later attended Tech's evening school to study the organ. No one needed to prod him with "go practice."

Then came World War I. After serving Uncle Sam he started day school at Tech, graduating in 1921 with a B.A. degree. Then post-graduate work and an M.A. degree— the first degree in organ and the first masters degree in music ever given by Tech.

Winning the Russell Hewlett Memorial scholarship, off he went to France to the Fontainebleau Conservatory where he studied with Widor and Libert. Later he studied privately in New York under the great organist Lynnwood Farnam.

Soon Mr. Pearson was in great demand locally as organist for various churches, including four years at the Third Presbyterian Church. There he was assistant to the famous Charles Heinroth.

In 1924 he joined the faculty of the Department of Music at Tech, teaching History of Music. When Kaspar Koch (now 91) retired, our neighbor succeeded him as teacher of the organ. He also served as head of the department for 18 years.

Somewhere along the line — to the surprise of no one — Charles fell victim to the sweet mystery of love. And married the charming and talented Hortense Scannell, then supervisor of music in the Braddock schools. Later she taught short-hand and accounting at Margaret Morrison for 13 years.

In 1924 — 40 years ago to be exact — Mr. Pearson became organist and choir director of Rodef Shalom Temple, a position he still holds. Former Rabbi Goldenson and through the years the well known Rabbi Freehof guided him in the Hebrew Liturgies. And to perfect his pronunciation of Hebrew he took a course at the YM&WHA.

To hear Director Pearson pronounce the difficult Hebrew "Ch" you'd think he was a rabbi!

Our neighbor is a boy at heart. He still loves railroads and steam locomotives. Loves to ride them, watch them come and go. He collects books and pictures of trains. Airplanes? They're for the birds.

Brother Jay F.W. is now chancellor at the University of Miami. And Charles A. H. will be 66 this September. A Presbyterian, his birthday falls on the holiest of Jewish holidays — Yom Kippur!

Dr. Mark Perlman
Economic Historian In Talented Family

The war news is disquieting. The stock market erratic. The cost of living soaring. Football is long past and baseball hasn't started. And spring is not yet around the corner. So enough's enough already. Let's instead concentrate on pleasant things. Like for instance interesting neighbors. And get acquainted with Dr. Mark Perlman of Bartlett St. He is Chairman of Economics at our University of Pittsburgh. Dr. Perlman started at Pitt in 1963. An economic historian, he is interested mostly in the growth of population and its relationship to economic advancement. He not only teaches the subject but lectures and writes on it. His latest book (with Timothy D. Baker, M.D.) titled "Health Manpower in a Developing Economy" was published last September.

Our neighbor, comparatively young—scarcely 44 — is tall, grey-eyed, with a personality that wins you over in a minute. And he has much learning and experience under his belt. Born in Madison, Wis., he's the son of the late Selig Perlman, an Economics professor at the University of Wisconsin. Following in his dad's footsteps he received his B.A. degree there. And taught a year at Princeton. Then earned his Ph.D. at Columbia University. He did his doctoral dissertation in Australia.

Enroute to Australia he stopped off in Hawaii. And fell in love with the country — as who doesn't. In no time he was teaching Economics at the University of Hawaii, remaining there a year. Then on to teaching at Cornell in Ithaca, N.Y. Again he fell in love. This time with an interesting girl — a graduate economics student from Columbia University. Lovely Naomi Waxman. She was working at the U.N. as an economist. She too comes from a highly educated family. Her dad, Meyer Waxman is a retired professor from the Jewish Theological Seminary in Chicago. And is author of a 6-volume book, "The History of Jewish Literature."

Her brother is Mordecai Waxman, a well-known Conservative Rabbi of Temple Israel in Great Neck, N.Y. And who do you think pronounced Mark and Naomi man and wife? Dad Waxman. With the help of brother Mordecai and several other rabbis, they tied the knot, but good. The newlyweds went housekeeping in Ithaca. Then the young husband was called to Johns Hopkins in Baltimore where he remained eight years.

Meantime something wonderful happened. Baby Abigail was born. Her dad wrote many important books and became well-known nationally. And was asked to come to Pitt.

A year prior to coming here the Perlmans spent several months in England— on a Ford Foundation grant. And listen to this. It was so cold in London that it cost them $90 a month over and above rent, to keep warm. With electric heaters yet. Our neighbors spent a lot of time on the Continent. In 1962 Prof. Perlman was sent to Formosa for three months. Naomi and baby stayed home. An epidemic of cholera had broken out in Formosa and the Commissioner of Health advised his going alone. Incidentally, without family ties they were able to get more work out of him, he says. The end of April they will all go to Japan, Hong Kong and Australia.

Our professor's talented missus taught Economics at Duquesne University here for several years. Now she's devoting all her time on a new Journal to be edited by the Perlmans for the American Economic Association.

Dr. Perlman is a lucky and most happy fella. Some married men when they want to discuss business problems with their wives, are frustrated because the little woman knows from nuthin' what he's saying. With the Perlmans it's altogether different. They actually enjoy "talking shop" because each understands the other's experiences. As the saying goes, they both speak the same language.

Daughter Abigail — affectionately called Abby — is now 9 and goes to Colfax. Her devoted pet and friend is a miniature French poodle. He's registered under the name of a famous French economist — Leon Walras. But his close friends call him Joe. Abby worries about whether her family is "too educated." What's Joe's opinion on the subject? Joe ain't talkin'.

Danny Phillips
Fiddling Family Fits Well in Music World

Had you tuned in on "Week-end Two" on a recent Sunday afternoon you'd have heard a 13-year-old youth play the violin. Magnificently, like a master. And when questioned by TV personality Terry McGovern how the youngster became a virtuoso so early in life, the youthful violinist responded with unassuming poise and natural charm. The young prodigy in question is none other than the already well-known Danny Phillips. And of course he lives in our very neighborhood on Northumberland St., to be exact.

As you might expect, Danny comes from a long line of music lovers. His grand-dad is a violin maker. When a 2-year-old toddler, Danny took hold of a bow and "sawed" it across a violin. The sound fascinated him. So learning to play for real came naturally.

At 5 he was taking lessons. His teacher was his dad, Eugene Phillips, now a popular violinist with our Pittsburgh Symphony. Mr. Phillips teaches violin at home and at Winchester - Thurston.

In addition dad has a class at Carnegie-Mellon. He also teaches at The Center for the Musically Talented—a new project sponsored by the Federal Government. Ours is the only city in U.S. that has such a school. There are 200 gifted students from the 8th to the 12th grade inclusive. The lessons are free and the teachers the best ever. In addition Eugene Phillips composes music.

Mrs. Phillips, the former Natale Barnet from nearby Beaver, teaches piano at home. She received her B.F.A. degree from Carnegie-Mellon and her M.Mus. from the University of Michigan. In their ten-room house, four are studio rooms. She's so busy with teaching that she has taken on two assistants.

Danny's sister Amy, age 10 plays the cello and piano. And little Todd, all of 6 is engrossed with the piano and violin. Both attend Wightman school. At home neither has to be prodded with "go practice." Amy takes a lot of teasing from her brothers.

And now let's concentrate on Danny himself. Our youthful prodigy hops out of bed at 6:30 in the morning. And practices a full hour before breakfast. After that he continues practicing for two more hours. By then it's time for lunch, which he prepares himself. It consists of hot dogs or hamburgers. Or his favorite dish — a Chinese omelet. He mixes choy sauce, a bit of sherry, ginger and sugar. Then beats in an egg, adds a shrimp or whatever left-overs he finds in the frigidaire. Fries the whole concoction — and whoosh, lunch is ready. His favorite beverage is milk. At noon he leaves for school and remains 'til 4. He's in the 8th grade Scholars Program at Allderdice — a special class for bright kids.

Three times a year our young violinist goes to New York City to study with world-famous Ivan Galamian. And during the entire summer vacations he attends the Galamian Music Camp in the Adirondaks. The camp is exclusively for gifted violinists. The 150 campers come from all over the world. There he practices at least four hours a day. After his first summer at the camp he improved 100 per cent.

Danny is a concert-master of the All City Senior High School Orchestra. And a member of the Pittsburgh Youth Symphony. A 3-times winner of Carnegie Awards and winner of the Pittsburgh Youth Audition — on the violin at age 10 and the piano at 11. Last year he was violin soloist at the Pittsburgh Symphony Young People concert. And has appeared with his dad in double concertos with the Wilkinsburg and Carnegie Civic Symphonies, respectively.

Mom Phillips takes in household help three times a week. But Danny has chores too. He clears the table, mows the lawn. And since he's not on strike, takes out the garbage. Mrs. Phillips cooks just plain food. For gourmet meals pop Phillips takes over.

What a fiddler and what a family! Honestly, ours is the luckiest neighborhood.

Dr. M. Ley Piscator
Visiting Professor Directs Classic

Even though our Pittsburgh Playhouse new season doesn't begin till early autumn, its capable crowd-pleasing staff has arranged an extra special production of Shakespeare's "Comedy of Errors," May 11 to 19. And who do you think has been directing this world-famous classic? Dr. Maria Ley Piscator, distinguished visiting professor of Point Park College. Brown-haired, dark-eyed, graceful, Dr. Piscator has an international reputation as director, choreographer, instructor and playwright. And speaks with a charming European accent. So let's great her with "bon jour" and get acquainted with this outstanding personality.

Born in Vienna, the former Maria Ley was educated at the Vienna Academy, Columbia University and the Sorbonne, Paris. A concert artist in dance for ten years she choreographed Max Rheinhardt's "Midsummer Night's Dream", "Imaginary Invalid" and "A Servant of Two Masters" for the Vienna and Salzburg festivals. One enchanted evening Rheinhardt invited a famous guest — Director Erwin Piscator. Another guest— uninvited — also showed up. Cupid, no less. Soon as Erwin laid eyes on Maria, love stepped in.

They married in 1934, moving into her charming Paris home near the Arc of Triumph. After traveling through Europe and South America they came to NYC and founded the Dramatic Workshop of the New School for Social Research. Maria still serves as its president. As its teacher and director, let's name some of the famous actors their Dramatic Workshop led to stardom: Marlon Brando, Harry Bellefonte, Tony Curtis, Rod Steiger, Walter Matthau, Shelley Winters, Elaine Stritch. And a host of others too numerous to list here.

Since into each life some rain must fall, in 1966 Maria's beloved Erwin passed away. In his memory she established the international Piscator Foundation, serving as its president. Last September rain of another sort fell. At the Playhouse to make arrangements with film star Sylvia Miles for "Who's Afraid of Virginia Woolf?", rehearsals had started. A day prior she went to NYC to sign on the dotted line. And guess what? A taxi hit her! Result: A broken leg and two concussions. Since "the show must go on" Joe Nassif finished directing. After three months of healing, Maria snapped back, good as new. Adding to her other accomplishments Dr. Piscator has published Essays in Theatre History, Poetry, many original Plays and two Novels. One — "Lot's Wife" sold over 10,000 copies and was translated into Hebrew. And she a Catholic! Recently when Dr. Matti Megged, a Haifa professor was here to address our synagogues he learned the author of "Wife" is in our city. And paid her a personal visit. A beautiful fringe benefit!

While here Madame Piscator lives in nearby Fairfax Hotel. The end of May she'll return to her NYC duplex between Madison & 5th Avenues. Two MD's have separate offices beneath her living quarters. Do they make house calls? You better believe it.

By the way, the 1973-74 Playhouse season starts September 22 with the ultra smart musical "Company." Followed by "One Flew Over the Cuckoo's Nest"; "Our Town"; "Cyrano de Bergerac"; "The Killing of Sister George"; "The House of Blue Leaves"; and "The Boys from Syracuse" — a Rogers & Hart musical based on "Comedy of Errors." Easily the best schedule ever.

And isn't it nice meeting such a gracious visitor as Dr. Maria Ley Piscator?

Dr. Leonard Plotnicov
'Large Town Youth' Makes it

This is being written while it's June-in-January — a pleasant time to tell you about a most interesting neighbor. Say hi to Dr. Leonard Plotnicov of Beechwood Blvd. Dr. Plotnicov came to our Pitt University in 1963 as instructor of Anthropology. A year later he advanced to Associate Professor for 3 years. Currently he's a Professor in Pitt's Department of Anthropology.

But you can't speak of our neighbor as a small-town boy who made good. He's from a large town. None other than where a tree grows — Brooklyn. And he did it all on his very own — as delivery boy, cabby, truck-driver, you name it. Years ago he did caddying in the Catskill and also delivered bread to Grossinger's, rooming nearby. In the same house roomed a clever, humorous, loveable fellow who never knew when to quit horsing around — performing in summer stock. He was Zero Mostel, later the first Tevye on Broadway's stage "Fiddler on the Roof." The movie version, by the way, with another master actor from Israel is currently packing them in at our Manor Theatre.

And now more about our fantastic neighbor. After Boys' High School in Brooklyn, Leonard went to Cooper-Union Art School and Brooklyn College, N.Y. — both at the same time, days and evenings. From the former School he earned his Diploma in Fine Arts and his BA from the latter. All accomplished by 1934. Then on to the University of California and Graduate Studies in Anthropology. Sponsored by the National Institute of Mental Health, Plotnicov did research for his Doctoral in Northern Nigeria's City of Jos, for two years. He studied how its people adjusted to city life, their interests, problems, how to make a satisfying life for themselves. Some were extremely wealthy and highly educated. Others just the opposite. Like it sadly is all over the world. Even in our U.S.A. He returned to California to write his Doctoral Thesis. By then his vast experience began showing and he was called to Pitt (per above). Recently Dr. Plotnicov conducted an all-day seminar on Africa at Grace Hall, Carlow College — visiting classes and discussing various topics relating to African culture. And presented an illustrated lecture on "The Enigma of African Modernization."

At Pitt, a beautiful blonde, Katy Hager from Lancaster was majoring in French and later became interested in Anthropology. Prof. Plotnicov was her teacher. Before you could say Jack Robinson she became his lovely bride. They were married by a Lancaster Judge, a friend of her family. Now a graduate student at Pitt, her shiny blonde hair falls 'way below her shoulders.' And the husband's thick black hair is just below his ears. It would be much longer if Kathy didn't snip it now and then.

Their home is charmingly furnished, with art objects from around the world. No children. But who knows? Maybe next April they'll get to our Pittsburgh Playhouse to see "Never Too Late" and get ideas. Their cozy fire-place is enjoyed for snoozing by their three shiny black cats with pure white spots on their paws and elsewhere. Upstairs is a stray mother-cat with several kittens. They had been abandoned in a nearby cemetery. Kathy is caring for them until a good home is found. Darling, playful kittens, anyone? Our professor brings in the groceries and cat-food. His mother taught Kathy how to cook delicious traditional Jewish foods. And he himself reads, writes and speaks Yiddish so fluently that it's hard to believe he's American-born.

Our neighbor has many Research interests, Fellowships, belongs to countless professional Societies and has written numerous Publications. Wish there were space to list them. There's room for just one sentence: Ours is the luckiest neighborhood.

Mrs. Max (Dorothy) Podolsky
Mrs. Micha (Bonnie) Theiner
Mother and Daughter Will Warm Your Heart

This being written as snowflakes are gently falling and outside it's a Winter Wonderland. A pleasant time to tell you about two remarkable neighbors that will warm your heart.

They're a mother-daughter singing team whose voices harmonize like — like — well, like love and marriage for instance. Say "We're proud of you" to Mrs. Max (Dorothy) Podolsky of Forest Glen Rd. and Mrs. Micha (Bonnie) Theiner, Phillips Ave. These

"Singers in Service" are particularly interested in groups which stress education and support the State of Israel. They sing in Hebrew Yiddish, Russian and, of course, in English.

Their songs are Jewish-Israeli in content, esthetic and educational. And now listen to this. The pay-checks they receive for performing at various charitable and social affairs they immediately turn over to the Pioneer Women's Child Rescue Fund. And at times to Jewish National Fund. Nothing is kept for themselves. They don't even deduct the baby-sitter's cost for little Immanuel Hai age 2½. Beautiful!

March 8th they'll perform at the Poale Zedeck Donor Luncheon. And March 12, they'll attend and contribute to the Pioneer Women's "Spiritual Adoption" Luncheon, at the Beth Shalom Synagogue. The Pioneer Women have pledged caring for 300 orphan children in Israel. Cost per child is $300 per year.

And now about mom. The former Dorothy Hankin's husband, Max Podolsky, is a local businessman. They were Schenley High School sweethearts and married 36 years ago. Dorothy's father, the late Samuel Hankin was principal of a Hebrew School in the Hill District. He was a founding member of the Zionist Organization of Pittsburgh and a delegate to the World Zionist Congress in Vienna. Dorothy is a life-member and former V.P. of the Pioneer Women on Chapter and Council levels; is a life-member of Hillel Academy Women's Club; American Technion Society, and is active in Israel Bonds. JNF and American Friends of Israel. Also a board member of the Young Peoples Synagogue.

She was the first in our city to lead group-singing of Hebrew and Jewish songs. And has opened so many meetings with "Hatikvah" and our National Anthem that Bonnie calls her "The Marian Anderson of Pioneer Women." Last August Mrs. Podolsky was honored with a community-wide Tribute Luncheon at Beth Shalom, sponsored by the Pioneer Women's Council, and Israel Bonds.

Daughter Bonnie is the lovely missus of Dr. Micha Theiner, Assistant Professor of Biochemistry at Pitt's School of Dentistry. An Israeli, they first met on a blind date — which took. Mrs. Theiner attended Hillel Academy and graduated from the Hebrew Studies Department of the former College of Jewish Studies. She earned an AB degree from Pitt in Counseling and Guidance. After teaching Hebrew and Judaic Studies in Boston and here, she's now on the faculty of the School of Advanced Jewish Studies.

Although the age difference between mother and daughter is 28 years, if you would see them together in person you'd swear they're sisters. TWIN sisters. Fantastic.

You of course, know of the world-famous Harry Golden from North Carolina. He says amazing people and thing happen "Only in America." Correction: Only in Squirrel Hill.

Dr. Joseph Pois

Wife Find Pleasantry In India

When the Ford Foundation finances someone to New Delhi for 3 months as consultant to the Indian Institute of Public Administration, that someone must have know-how aplenty. This he has and it's a privilege to tell you about such a fabulous fellow. Shake hands with Dr. Joseph Pois of nearby Morewood Avenue. Dr. Pois is professor of Public Administration in Pitt's School of Public and International Affairs, having served as Department Chairman for ten years.

Born in New York, our professor earned his A.B. degree from the University of Wisconsin; M.A. and Ph.D., University of Chicago, and his J.D. from Chicago Kent College of Law. All between 1926 and 1934 when he was admitted to the Illinois Bar. Ever since he's been a board member of so many vital civic, professional and government organizations, and has written such a variety of publications that listing all would fill a book. So let's just snoop a little into his personal life, and then learn about some of his fascinating experiences in far-off India.

Dr. Pois met his lovely wife—the former Rose Tomarkin—when he was doing graduate work at Wisconsin U. She was a resident student there, taking a general course and working as secretary for that State. They married in 1928 and have been blessed with two very interesting sons: Robert, now 33 is an Associate Professor of History at the University of Colorado; Marc, 30, was in Israel for some time, came back and is now planning to return there — permanently maybe. There are two grandchildren.

Dr. Pois with his capable missus as his personal secretary found the three month stay in India exciting and rewarding. Not only did he serve as a consultant but had the opportunity to visit and lecture at various institutions of higher learning. He obtained many interesting insights into the culture, economy, government and problems of India. He and Rose visited a little synagogue in New Delhi which has limited congregants because there are so few Jews in that city. Most migrated to Israel. The Jews are Sephardic, speak English and Hindi. Sabbath services are held Friday evenings.

Their short stay in Teheran enroute to India was fascinating. They visited the ORT facility. ORT, founded by American Jewish women is a voluntary rehabilitation and training system for the deprived and dispossessed — with schools throughout the world. They also attended the Iraqui synagogue. Jews in Iran, they were told, feel secure under the present Shah. The Indian government has family-planning programs. Yet in Calcutta and Bombay, with poverty related to over-population, thousands live on the sidewalks. India represents overwhelming contrasts: The magnificent Taj Mahal on one side; ugliness on the other. The intellectual and the unschooled.

Dr. Pois also attended Parliament where Mrs. Ghandi was present. One couldn't help feeling the regrettable strain between their country and ours. Attending an Indian dance was especially enjoyable. They witnessed much student unrest and Delhi U. was closed for an extended period. On the same street one sees an auto, motor skooters, thousands of bicycles, carts drawn by bullocks (oxen) and — sadly — heavy carts pulled by men.

The two courses Dr. Pois is now teaching are greatly helped by much information and materials brought from India. For diversion he and Rose enjoy the symphonies and operas. Recently some sadness crept into their household. Sinbad, their loveable prize-winning Afghan, after a lingering illness breathed his last and left for the Great Beyond. Our community extends its profound sympathy.

Philip Polito
Nine-Year Veteran Mail Carrier

Did you get some interesting mail today? A love-letter mebbe? Thank the fella who brought it — your dependable mailman. Like it says — neither snow nor rain nor heat nor gloom of night stay him from the swift completion of his appointed rounds. And since we're smack in the middle of the snow, sleet and slush season, you'll appreciate him more if you learn a little about one of them personally. Especially since he himself is a Squirrel Hiller. In fact, was even born in our neighborhood.

So, give an appreciative pat on the back to mail carrier Philip Polito, Flemington St. Polito has been delivering mail for nine years — seven in our neighborhood. He is of course best known to residents where he brings it. Like for instance parts of Northumberland, Woodmont, Solway, Wilkins, Wightman and South Negley. From 6 to 9 a.m. he works in our Murray Avenue Post Office arranging his mail in proper sequence. Then, after his rounds are completed, he's back there from 2 to 2:30, getting the sequence started for the next day.

And speaking of our Murray Avenue Post Office, Phil says it's the greatest place in the world to work in because the workers there create so much fun. Often he starts his delivery rounds chuckling. If some of the people think he's laughing at them, 'taint so. There are no laugh-provoking "characters" in his territory, he says, but plenty of them in the P.O. Even if he were rich, he tells you, he'd work there anyhow. It's such a ball.

Our tall, lithe, blue-eyed nice-looking neighbor graduated Central Catholic High in Oakland. Instead of a mailman — or policeman even — he always wanted to be an athlete. He played basketball and baseball in the grades since nine. He tried out for the Pirates two seasons when 16 and 17. The coach even talked with his parents and wanted to give him a chance. But there was a war on in Korea — remember? And Phil joined the Marine Corps. In Korea he was a truck driver for 14 months. Drove ammunition and supplies from Inchon to the front lines or wherever needed. Then he was transferred to California.

On his first 30-day home leave his mom mom met him at the airport. Enroute she wanted to stop off at a Jewish Friend's home for something. The "something," it turned out, was her friend's lovely daughter Shirley Savage. In curlers, at the sight of a handsome soldier in uniform she fled upstairs in embarrassment.

But be darned if they didn't start dating. Upon return to California he asked to be transferred to an eastern base, boiled down to either Philly or Quantico, Va. Quantico, it was. This enabled him to come home weekends. Eight months later Phil and Shirley were married by a Justice of the Peace. That was 11 years ago, to be exact. He was 19, Shirley 16 and attending Allderdice. A year later baby Cindy came along.

When Phil's four-year service was ended they rented an apartment. And later, when Michael was born they bought their six-room Flemington Street house. In that home something new was later added — baby Daniel. Michael is now seven, and Cindy, 10. Both go to Minadeo School. In their mixed marriage Michael as of now wants to be Jewish; Cindy, Catholic. Later? Who knows. As to baby Daniel's religious affiliations, at age three months he hasn't made up his mind. Meantime Shirley who before marriage couldn't fry an egg, is a perfect housewife, Phil says. And the best cook he knows. And is still beautiful — even in curlers.

Polito plays softball for the P.O. teams in the summer, of which there are 16 over the area as far as the Airport. He helps manage them. He also plays basketball at the Y-IKC Adult League every Sunday. And golf at the Manor Valley Country Club. His hobby is sword-collecting. He has six on the wall on each side of their fireplace.

How about a nice long hike on his day off? No, thanks.

Dennis Portnoy

Wandering Youth Shuns Old Life

Dear parents of run-away teenagers: Don't despair and take heart. From one such neighborhood youth. After three years of complete absence from a good home, roaming throughout the U.S. and as far as India to "find myself," he finally returned. Now at age 20 he has buckled down to hard work. Better prepared, he feels, to face the world on his very own, with an improved sense of values. Meet Dennis Portnoy, the amazing youngster in question. And let's learn a little about him.

Son of William and Edna Portnoy, Dennis was born in Queens, N.Y. Later they moved to Mt. Lebanon and after five years came to our neighborhood on Valmont St. Sister Mickey lived in Rome two years. Sis Jyll has a master's in Archaeology and Greek History from Penn State.

At 15, long haired Dennis dropped out of the 10th grade in school. He was bored with the system, desperate with frustration. Barefoot, with one pair of jeans, only one shirt, and a few paltry dollars, he hitched all across the States to Haight-Asbury in San Francisco—that well known hippie haven. Limited space won't permit describing his travels and travails. So just a few highlights. Dennis experienced over 80 LST "trips" to put him on the road to the "real thing." So he thought. Now he's against drugs of all kinds. Won't touch them with a ten-foot pole.

After a month in San Francisco he hitched to the Big Sur in Central California. There he lived in an open trunk of a huge redwood tree for a month. Then, as a surprise to his parents, Dennis returned home. His mother fed him as if he were starving. Again wanderlust set in. So he hitched to New York City, begging for food and mostly for drugs. Then to Woodstock. Several weeks later he landed in Boston. There he "struck gold." Two women took him into their comfortable apartment. And someone gave him a large collie whom he named Princey. Again boredom. So he made it to South Carolina's "Center for MEHER BABA" (Compassionate Father). Baba's teachings fascinated him and changed his life. In Boulder, Colorado, he got his first job—an orderly in a Nursing Home. When the "Compassionate Father" called his "Lovers" to India, he flew there, stopping off enroute in Rome and Israel. Baba said one must find one's real self through infinite love and shedding one's false ego-self. At once Dennis saw the fallacy of drugs and painfully gave them up. In fact—don't tell the AMA—he won't even touch prescription drugs now. He became interested in natural organic foods. He studied all the books on the subject and met many food experts personally. After a close haircut and shave he settled down to the work best suited to him—health foods. At first he shared space and phone in a neighboring shoe-repair shop. Now he's full proprietor of a nice-sized Health Food Store—"The Good Earth," Murray Avenue. He's on the job daily 9:30 a.m. to 8 p.m. Sundays 'til 2 p.m. Once a week he drives to the airport to meet a plane bringing organic vegetables and fruits from California, not sprayed with DDT. Every dollar he earns, back it goes into the business. He himself eats no meat, fish nor drinks water. Lives entirely on nuts, fruits and vegetables—mostly raw. Says they contain 90 per cent water. Princey eats like his master.

His dad was recently transferred in his work to Philadelphia and bought a suburban country place. They doubtless will raise organic vegetables. Maybe their son will be their best customer.

Let's wait and see how Dennis turns out by age 39—and later. Meanwhile, toward young Portnoy, there's no complaint. Only admiration and best wishes.

Mildred Miller Posvar

Talent In Abundances

Dear neighbors: Stop what you're doing, pull up your chairs, kick off your shoes, relax and listen. For today you'll learn about a most fabulous personality. She's none other than Mildred Miller Posvar. Not only is she a famous mezzo-soprano of the Met but the beautiful missus of Dr. Wesley W. Posvar, Chancellor of the University of Pittsburgh.

Last October the famous singer was the flamboyant Carmen to the delight of a jam-packed Syria Mosque audience. In the words of Donald Steinfirst, P-G music critic, "she was consistently exciting both in sheen and clarity, elegant phrasing and full, round, rich tones." The leaders of the Pittsburgh Chapter of Hadassah, who know a good thing when they see and hear one, invited her to sing at the eagerly awaited Hadassah Spectacular February 28. And guess what? She agreed. So once again Miss Miller thrilled 2,000 Hadassah women, husbands and friends who packed Carnegie Music Hall. In addition to her magnificent voice, all were charmed with her beauty and grace. Even the colorful gown she wore was exactly suitable for the occasion. You'd have sworn it came from Israel.

Miss Miller rendered arias from "Carmen," "Samson & Delilah." Also some American and Israeli folk songs—the latter in Hebrew. Then "Rozenkas mit Mandlin"— in Yiddish, if you please. And she an Episcopalian! The Yiddish, she says, comes easily for her as she is fluent in German. But Hebrew? Maybe the fact that the Posvars live right near Rodef Shalom Temple helped.

Born in Cleveland, Mildred started voice in her senior high school year. Then the Cleveland Institute of Music. With a voice that "comes along once in a blue moon" she sang for Boris Goldovsky, Boston impresario and musicologist. And entered the New England Conservatory of Music in that city.

While in Boston, a fella from Cleveland phoned for a date. A test pilot in the air force — Wesley Posvar. They had gone to high school together but never dated. On that enchanted evening—their first date—each learned that the other had a scholarship for study in Europe. He as a Rhodes Scholar at Oxford and she to study voice on the Continent. So right off they had something wonderful in common.

Imagine how it must have been throughout Europe when they had each other to share numerous experiences. In Stuttgart in 1950 they did what comes naturally—got married. The young bride performed with the Opera companies not only in that city but in Vienna, Berlin, Munich, Frankfurt. Then Rudolph Bing discovered her. Her debut with the Met was in Mozart's "The Marriage of Figaro" in 1951.

She has completed one movie "The Merry Wives of Windsor" and was featured artist on "Encore from the Bell Telephone Hour." As a recording artist she was awarded the Grand Prix due Disque for a recording made with the late Bruno Walter.

The Posvars have three interesting children. Wes, 19, is a Soph at Harvard. Marina and Lisa, 15 and 9 respectively, attend Ellis School. There are two over-sized identical poodles—Chancy and Beau Beau. Mildred's 4th "child" is the Chancellor himself.

After nearly two hours of voice practice first thing each morning, she becomes the Chancellor's Lady. She has grasped more than 25,000 hands in reception lines; has personally served hot chocolate and cookies to hundreds of students; is on boards and committees; attends lectures by the scores. She has been hostess at brunches preceding each home football game; has entertained such notables as the late Dwight D. Eisenhower and Chief of Staff General William Westmoreland. And is on hand for all State and Official functions. The Chancellor likes having her around.

During the Posvars' first Christmas at Pitt (1967) she offered—on a rare impulse—to sing "Silent Night" to the humming accompaniment of the Pitt Glee Club. When she finished, one of the students ran up to her with "Gee, Mrs. Posvar" you should have tried for a career in Opera— or something." Our Hadassah women—bless 'em—are not so naive.

Dr. Hedwig Pregler
Dedicated Teacher Gets Best From Her Life

You've read recently in all our newspapers about a dedicated school teacher who retired from our neighborhood Colfax school after 42 years of teaching. Including 29 years as principal there. She retired last June 30th, to be exact. Because you, your children, and their children have greatly benefited from her teaching skill and generous love you naturally want to learn more about her. So gather around and say hello to Dr. Hedwig Pregler, teacher par excellence.

Hedwig was born in the West End. After eight grades at Birmingham School (no longer here), she went to South High School. Then to Pennsylvania College for Women, now Chatham. There she specialized in dramatics and, along with her degree received a certificate. The latter unexpectedly came in very handy during an interview with a personnel director. She was applying as elementary teacher. The director scratched his head, pondered and said: "Now, if you could teach dramatics I'd have a place for you." Out came her certificate! That September she started teaching dramatics at Lemington School.

At first the new teacher had no room of her own because the school was so crowded. So she was a "floater," going from room to room to teach. It was a wonderful experience. In the 2nd grade she met a well-known Squirrel Hill teacher, Sara Raphael. Sara later became Mrs. Michael Myers, is now retired and living with her husband in Florida. When Hedwig came to Colfax in 1937, Sara was teaching there. They've been friends ever since.

Every summer teacher Pregler went to various universities for further learning. In 1946, when she got her Ph.D. she had attended the University of California at Berkeley. Then Cleveland's Western Reserve University. Followed by consecutive summers at two different universities — Vermont and Colorado. She was specializing in teaching Gifted Children. And wrote many articles on the subject which have been published and widely read. She also lectured on it.

Thirty-five years ago Hedwig met an Allderdice teacher, Bertha Mitchell (now also retired). They became good friends and have made their home together ever since. Bertha takes care of the cooking. Hedwig does the dishes. She also drives their Olds, and takes a stab at gardening — when in the mood. She seldom remembers what she's planted. The next year, thinking they're weeds she pulls them out. But they have asparagus in their ivy patch and tomatoes in among the rose bushes. As to their strawberries, they're for the birds. Knitting she does to perfection. She's knitted tassel-caps, dresses, sweaters, coats, hats and hundreds of helmets and pull-overs for the soldiers during World Wars I and II. Their three-year-old mixed-breed dog, Bonnie, has no such chores. She just rules the household, barks at strangers, never takes a nip at the mailman and travels everywhere with them. She loves staying at a motel and prefers Howard Johnsons and the Holiday Inn. And is ecstatic in elevators. Hedwig got her from the Animal Rescue League of which she's a board member.

After 20 years of teaching, the Colfax PTA presented Dr. Pregler with a magnificent watch, bearing her name and years of service. Five years later they gave her a plaque which reads: "For outstanding service and guidance."

Last June the Squirrel Hill Kiwanis Club named her "Woman of the Year" at a fabulous program dinner at Poli's. But most of all she treasures the hundreds of letters received from former pupils and their parents. Wish there would be space to print some. They'd bring a lump to your throat and some tears even.

Mothers with children — compare and ponder. Have you done a better job with your life than our neighborhood school teacher? They say — it's not what Fate hands you but what you do with it that counts.

Our neighborhood wishes Dr. Hedwig Pregler the best of everything now and in the years ahead.

Dr. Ann Quattrocchi

Outstanding Educator at Allderdice

School teachers — bless 'em — are the salt of the earth. Kids could never get along without 'em. Neither could parents. And even the rest of us couldn't. So let's get our minds off the Pirates and state tax problems and learn a little about an outstanding educator.

She is Dr. Ann Quattrocchi, head of the Department of History at Allderdice High. Dr. Quattrocchi (affectionately called Dr. Ann by her many friends) is tall, graceful, warm, talented and energetic. She could look chic with her hair puffed high, wide and handsome. But she likes it in natural, unaffected soft waves. And we do too.

As a youngster Ann was called a book-worm, for the logical reason that she enjoyed an old-fashioned pastime — reading. She thumbed her way through thousands of books in the Carnegie Library ten blocks from her home. Ann graduated from Allegheny High with top honors. But she had talent in her fingers too. She made her own graduation dress. And her versatility didn't end there. Ann was on the Allegheny High Champion Basketball team. Top graduate, Top seamstress. Top athlete.

Later, Ann received her BA and MA degrees from our University. Then the greatest joy in her life was doing research for her Ph.D. in History. She took a cross-country trip, often camping out, and returned with a dissertation on a certain Thomas Hutchins who figured in the early history of our country. The research was done in the Clemens Library at the University of Michigan, the Congressional Library at Washington and a number of Historical Societies. Only original documents were used.

Although Pitt claims Dr. Quattrocchi as its graduate, she has also attended the universities of Michigan, Columbis, Chicago, Pennsylvania, Illinois and even the University of Mexico. She has traveled abroad through all of western Europe as far east as Budapest. Her heart was in the center of everything.

About her work at Allderdice Dr. Ann says, "My classes are orderly because the students are interested in what is going on in the class-room." Rumor has it that she's "tough" on the outside but surprisingly "soft" on the inside.

She inaugurated a testing program for History students at every grade level. No other school does this. Dr. Ann is the original teacher in the American History Advanced Placement Program in our city schools. Because of this program the students can take college courses for a year while in high. If they do well on a national Advanced Placement test, they earn college credits. Then later, at college, they thus have saved time for other courses they would otherwise not have time for — courses that will help enrich their lives. She has been guest speaker on the Advanced Placement Program at many conferences in and around Pittsburgh.

Last year Allderdice needed to raise funds. So a basketball game was held. The women faculty played the girl students. The girls got the surprise of their lives. The faculty, with Dr. Ann as Captain playing guard, won hands down. In fact, they never gave the girls a chance to get their hands on the ball!

Dr. Ann likes going to summer school and to travel. And she also — when possible— loves staying home, cut grass, work on her rock garden. And she delights in sewing, reading and entertaining.

You wonder how she finds time to accomplish so much. Doubtless she's grown accustomed to her pace.

Stuart Rabinowitz

Chess Champ In Own Right

Among the political headlines and TV coverage is also news about other important happenings. Like for instance the World Chess Championship challenge between U.S. champ Bobby Fischer and Russia's Boris Spassky— planned to start in Iceland and end in Yugoslavia, 24 games in all. Even if in your heart you don't feel the emotion "To Russia with Love," still you can't help admire Spassky's dependable conduct. He arrived in Keykjavick, Iceland on time, ready to play. As compared with Fischer's "I won't, I will, I won't unless . . . " etc., etc. It's been causing uncertainty for chess lovers around the world, embarrassment for the International Chess Federation, and headaches galore for the Icelandic Chess people.

So, it's a joy to tell you about a Chess Champ in our very neighborhood. He's none other than Stuart Rabinowitz of Beechwood Boulevard. Age 17, as compared to Bobby's 29 and Spassky's 35, he's anything but a prima donna with moods. Stuart recently won first place in the Pennsylvania State High School Championship. During the recent flood, no less. Because of high water the tourney was moved several times ending at Point Park College. He's being sent to Minneapolis, Minn. to compete in the U.S. Junior Championship being held July 31, and was asked to get there several days earlier for a warm-up tournament. Prizes are College Scholarships. Our community's best wishes go with him!

Our youthful champ is a June honor graduate of Allderdice. Come September, he will enter C-MU in Industrial Administration and Management Science. May 20 to June 5 found him and 15 other youths in our nation's Capital, selling souvenirs at Transpo '72. With a million visitors (mostly from foreign countries), business was booming. Earnings for college — remember?

Stuart is the youngest son of Louis and Maxine Rabinowitz. Dad is manager of Blue Ribbon Meat Company, and Mom teaches piano. She was just named chairman of the 1972-73 Tree Campaign for completion of the Freedom Forest in Israel for Soviet Jewry, succeeding Mrs. Herman (Evelyn) Engelberg in that vital and humane project.

As a kid, Stuart first gave his brains a whirl learning duplicate bridge at home. His parents always were good players. He watched, caught on and practiced. But his twin brothers (Marc and Leonard, now 23) played chess. Soon he became fascinated with that game, but didn't take it seriously till age 14. Brother Leonard is a board member of the Downtown YMCA Chess Club. For a nominal fee, Stuart went down every Saturday, made friends and got opponents. The games there are played faster— just for fun. At tournaments you take your time. The unaffiliated ones are small, short, quick; they have 30 moves in 30 minutes. The bigger games sponsored by the U. S. Chess Federation comprise 50 moves in two hours. Games take at least four hours of deep concentration.

The chess-board is black and white with 64 small squares. Each board has 16 upright figures called chessmen. Eight are named Pawns; 2 Rooks; 2 Knights; 2 Bishops; 1 Queen; 1 King. The idea is to CAPTURE THAT KING! If you make a bad move, you don't have a partner to blame (as in bridge). You're on your own against an icy opponent who's also intent on winning. Stuart's mother brought him a beautiful chess-set from England. He says it's "just for show," and likes his old beat-up one for practice.

In addition to sports, bridge and, of course, chess, our young Champ likes girls. But no steady girl. At least not yet. Mom Maxine: Are you worried already?

Jay Rice

Sees 'Iron Curtain'

Today's neighborhood personality is a teenager. A TEENAGER? A beatnik mebbe? Who won't take a bath, flaunts ethics, scorns his elders, rides a Honda and thinks the world belongs exclusively to his generation? Dispel your fears. Our teenager is clean-cut, handsome, with imagination and understanding of the problems confronting far-flung Jewry. Especially those from behind the Iron Curtain where there's suppression of Jewish social cultural and religious life — far beyond the restrictions of any other Soviet ethnic groups. He's none other than Jay Rice, son of Charles and Marjorie Rice of Pocusset St. Dad is a well-known pharmacist.

Jay was one of a carefully-chosen group of teenagers from throughout the U.S. who recently returned from a 6-week trip to Communist countries, to seek our fellow-Jews, learn their culture and to extend a friendly hand. It's the first youth group that has ever made such a pilgrimage. It included Leningrad, Moscow and Bucharest, culminating with two weeks in Israel. There were 11 boys, 10 girls and 4 staff advisers. One of the latter had visited Russia twice before and is a Russian Studies major at Columbia University. He familiarized the group with some basic Russian phrases and the amenities to be observed.

But first let's learn a little about our youthful neighbor and why he—the only one from Pennsylvania was chosen. Jay recently graduated Allderdice and the College of Jewish Studies. He's a board member of the United Synagogue Youth Organization (USY) with branches throughout the country. The local branch meets at our neighborhood Beth Shalom synagogue. To finance his trip, Jay used a $300 scholarship fund awarded him by Beth Shalom. And his dad chipped in the rest — $1,000 at least. He is now enrolled at Penn State University for a liberal arts course to pave the way toward his future profession — Medicine.

Enroute the group stopped in Paris. At the Rothschild synagogue they met Algerian and Tunisian Jews. In Amsterdam they visited the Anne Frank House, saw the tiny bedroom where she slept. And the bulletin board on which she kept her now world-famous Diary. Their nine days' experiences in the USSR would fill a book. So just some highlights.

Kosher meat being unobtainable, Jay's group ate mostly fish, dairy foods and vegetables. Nine days without meat! As visiting tourists they were permitted to wear yarmulkas. And silently recited their prayers at meals and other necessary times. The lone synagogue in Leningrad is attended mostly by the old. The young, instilled with Atheism in the schools, usually stay away. But word had gotten around that American youths would be there, so they flocked to the synagogue. One fellow from a distant province whispered "I am a Jew; I'll live a Jew, and die a Jew." The group gave him a pocket-size Russian-Hebrew dictionary and a "Star of David" pin. He said with emotion: "Who at home will ever believe that these were given me by young Americans!" Many quietly spoke of tragedies and anti-Semitism suffered. And all hope for the blessed day when they can get permission to leave for Israel.

In Moscow they met privately with the learned Chief Rabbi Yehuda Leib Levin. His words too were spoken guardedly. He had visited our neighborhood Shaare Torah synagogue not long ago and wanted to be remembered to his many friends made here. In Bucharest Chief Rabbi Rosen also greeted them with deep emotion. There too words were quietly and guardedly spoken. Secret police are everywhere. Before leaving for Israel they stopped off in Athens. There they attended a concert by the Israeli Symphony in a stadium facing the ancient Acropolis. And were invited to a

reception where they met leading Athenian Jews. Their 14 days in Israel are beyond words to describe. Unlike Russia, in Israel Freedom truly rings! While there Jay had a special stamp made up. He and his group use it on all their school and personal correspondence. It's in Russian, Hebrew and English and reads: "Remember Soviet Jews."
TEENAGERS? Lord bless 'em!

Mrs. Noel Riggs

No Stranger To Theatre

Dear neighbors and Playhouse watchers: You want to know what's new on Craft Avenue the coming season? The answer, in short, is PLENTY. With 8 wonderful shows coming up, the Playhouse will be swinging.

The new executive producer, S. Joseph Nassif, though only 30 years of age has a wealth of radio, TV and theatrical experience under his belt. And is simply bursting with enthusiasm and new ideas. And his Girl Friday, blue-eyed Noel Riggs, is working on audience development to give you the bestest with the mostest for the leastest. So today, because she's an outstanding personality and of course lives in our neighborhood, you'll learn a little about her.

The former Noel Mills, born in England and "brung up" in Quebec, is our neighbor at Forbes Terrace—a stone's-throw from Murray. She was married to the late Thomas Riggs. Remember "Tommy Riggs and Better Lou" — that famous coast-to-coast radio show? For years it was a household name. Makes you kind of nostalgic, doesn't it?

Living with her are two awfully nice guys: Her revered father-in-law James Riggs, 82 years young and son Jim, 19 years old. Jim's dad was a Navy man and taught him the art of keeping things in ship-shape order. This leaves mom free to do the cooking, which they say is top-notch. Jim is a sophomore at Carnegie-Mellon Drama Department. He wants to major in Lighting Design.

Noel Riggs is no stranger to the theatre. She began work as a radio actress in New York and Hollywood. It was in Hollywood she first met Tommy. Through the years she appeared in various plays at the White Barn Theatre, Civic Light Operas, and of course the Playhouse, which she calls "home." Formerly Group Sales Representative for the Playhouse, now she's Subscription and Membership Secretary.

You want season tickets? Call Mrs. Riggs, tell her where you want to sit, what evenings, etcetra, etcetra. And swoosh! everything will be arranged for you. However, should you desire individual tickets for separate plays, drop in at one of the 23 National Record Marts which are ticket agencies for the Playhouse. Yours is on Murray Avenue next door to the Waldorf Bakery.

You reserve your seats, then buy your bulkies and bagels. That's how easy it is. and oh, yes. For faculty members and student groups, our neighbor has arranged free tickets for the two preview performances of each play, prior to date of formal opening. She also works with Playhouse Plus of the Women's Auxiliary.

As to the plays being readied for you, Nassif has put together an appetizing season of community theatre. From musical "Gypsy" which opens October 2nd to dramatic "Joe Egg" to frothy "Irma La Douce" to melodramatic "Streets of New York," you'll find the new season spiced with a blend of deeply stimulating and highly entertaining productions.

With all the exciting plans afoot, and delicious dinners served at the Playhouse Downstairs Restaurant, it looks like there'll be a hot time on Craft Avenue in the cold months ahead.

Elayne Rosen
The 'Y's' Girl-Friday

They say looks and brains don't mix. Especially in women. A girl is either a brilliant ugly duckling or a beautiful-but-dumb blonde. But it ain't necessarily so. At least not in our neighborhood.

Take for instance Elayne Rosen, our neighbor at Beechwood Blvd. She's not only lovely to look at, delightful to know, but has a job that none but a clever girl could handle. And you know what? She doesn't think she's interesting enough to be written up. So she's modest too — an admirable quality in these sophisticated times.

Let's learn a little about our interesting neighbor. In her middle 20's Elayne Rosen is single. She's grateful her mother didn't encourage her into a teenage marriage as so many mamas do these days. So she's had an opportunity to complete her education, learn about people, see the world a little and find meaningful work.

For past five years she's been a program director of the Downtown Young Women's Christian Association—that fabulous Wood Street educational and social center for things worthwhile. Elayne's dad is Harry Rosen, well-known owner of the Allegheny Cigarette Service in Wilkinsburg. Her mom's name is Rose. Elayne has two sisters: Mrs. Henry (Roberta) Recht who has returned to Pitt for her degree. And Myra, a senior at Pitt doing practice teaching at Mt. Lebanon.

Their German schnauzer Pepper completes the family circle. Other dogs sometimes take a nip at the mailman. But Pepper — never.

Elayne got her BA degree from Chatham College, majoring in English. And taught that subject at Allderdice for one year. But how can a young attractive girl teacher be strict enough to discipline the lively, often pampered Squirrel Hill students? She wasn't. And left for a job in a department store. In a year she learned much about people and how to handle them. Her next step was at the YWCA — a natural for her kind of training and temperament.

At the "Y" Elayne organizes all sorts of club groups. Does anyone have a special interest in something? Or a need for it? Soon a group is formed. Her favorite one is "The Open Door for Handicaps." Many are afflicted with multiple sclerosis and can't use their hands. Nor can they walk and must be in wheelchairs.

Before the "Y" was erected that group influenced the architects to build all doors and elevators extra wide so they could wheel through. And to put special protective equipment in the wash-rooms and the swimming pool. The group is taught, among other things, art appreciation. They can't hold a paint-brush, so learn to appreciate paintings done by others.

Then Elayne arranges all-day bus trips for members to all sorts of fascinating places. The buses are filled with laughing, chatting women and an occasional husband or boy-friend. They've gone to "Falling Water," the Hershey Chocolate plant, to the Pennsylvania Dutch country, to all the summer theatre matinees, to maple sugar festivals, glass factories and even on nature hikes. And to Cleveland for the Mike Douglas Show.

Recently 200 went on the Gateway Clipper to Old Economy. Because the groups are large, the price per person is right. But they don't compete against professional travel agencies because the trips are just for one day. The Travel Bureaus plan much longer trips.

The four-day conferences Director Rosen is constantly arranging have helped make the "Y" famous. Problems of our society like unemployment, changing morals, teen-agers and of course sex are pondered over. Prominent speakers from far and wide bring their know-how to guide the discussions.

Elayne is expert in tennis and is third-ranking woman player in western Pennsylvania. Recently she started a knitting class. So she now knits her own sweaters. And get a load of this. Our neighbor loves to cook. When she knows you're coming she'll bake a cake.

And now the 64-dollar question. Does our charming neighbor go steady? No answer. Just a mischievous smile. So it could be yes.

Seymour Rosen

Plays Vital Role In Symphony Makeup

Our personality of the week is tall, easy-to-look-at Seymour Rosen of Alder St. He is our Symphony's new business manager — as of July 1st. Soft spoken yet built like an athlete he could easily qualify for the Pittsburgh Steelers. Fact is he did play football in his earlier years. But let's not digress from the business at hand.

Born in N.Y.C., Mr. Rosen graduated high school there. Later he received a degree in music education from the Julliard School of Music. A talented and outstanding double bass player, he joined—consecutively—the orchestras in Dallas, Minneapolis and St. Louis. Then was made manager of the Columbus Symphony and later the Buffalo Philharmonic. Somewhere along the line he became executive director of the American Symphony League in our nation's capital. It's the trade association for symphony orchestra. By then he had much experience under his belt — and it was showing. He became widely and favorably known. Our local board of directors, always alert and wise in such matters, invited him to come here as business manager. Mr. Rosen accepted — for obvious reasons. He knew that our city has one of the great conductors of the world and that our symphony is the greatest. Rosen was happy to become a part of it.

So what does a business manager do to keep out of mischief. Plenty. He does general planning for the Orchestra. Arranges the fund-raising and ticket-selling campaigns. He engages the guest artists and maps out the many tours. And his side duties are too numerous to list in limited space. Let's instead take a look into his personal life.

What seems like ages ago, young Rosen soldiered for Uncle Sam during WW 2 and was stationed in Germany. There he was taken a prisoner of war and kept in a Nuremberg prison for 6 months. After release and an honorable discharge the young soldier came home. To build up his health he went to a summer camp where in his earlier years he had been a counselor. There he found that something new had been added. A dance and swimming counselor. Lovely Bernice Malkind, a pupil of New York's famous Martha Graham. It's simply amazing how quickly Seymour regained his health! And started to feel thata-way about Bernice. What with the flowers and trees and moonlit nights, and Cupid a-buzzin', they became engaged. And in June 1946 did what comes naturally — got married.

The Rosens have been blessed with two handsome children. Judy, 17 attends the Albert Einstein High School in Washington, D.C. Son Jesse goes to Peabody High. Being musical like his dad, he plays in the school's orchestra and band.

And what do you think their mom does? She teaches modern dancing at Chatham College. The frug, the jerk, the monkey mebbe? Or the surf, the swim, the mashed-potato? No, not quite that modern. Hers is modern dancing suitable for the stage.

The Rosen's 3-bedroom apartment is kept in good order without any outside help. They don't even have a dish-washing machine. Son Jesse does the dishes and pop pitches in when occasion requires. A family that cooperates together is happy together.

Musuc lovers, gather 'round. When you're next at the Mosque and Maestro Stein-berg raises his baton for a concert by our world-famous Symphony. And you get that healing sense of good things to come — enjoy, enjoy. But later give thought to the important personalities behind the scenes. From the start he liked Pittsburgh and his work here. Now he definitely confirms it.

Our community wishes him and his interesting family the best of everything now and in the years ahead.

Samuel Rosenberg
Artist, No Beatnik

You've heard the expression "There's gold in them thar hills."

We sure have it in Squirrel Hill. Not gold actually but something more precious, more lasting. Outstanding, gifted people. Right in our very neighborhood.

On the top rung of the golden ladder is Artist Samuel Rosenberg, our neighbor at Mt. Royal Rd.

To describe Mr. Rosenberg's life history and accomplishments in the art world would fill a book. Maybe a library. To evaluate his hundreds and hundreds of fabulous paintings only a master critic has the words. To unschooled laymen who enjoy just looking, they're refreshment to the eyes and enlightenment to the mind.

His paintings have had rave reviews in all the newspapers and magazines here, there, everywhere. So for a change let's just take a peek into his personal life.

Artist Rosenberg received his B.A. degree from Carnegie Tech where he taught and painted for the past 40 years. Recently he retired and teaches there only one day a week. Public recognition of his painting, outstanding as they are, is far outdistanced by the admiration and affection he earned from his students, colleagues on campus and our community.

He has received more prizes at more outstanding exhibits than you can enumerate. Throngs have oohed and aahed — and bought.

So what's our neighbor like? Personally, that is? Does he hob-nob with the Shady-side beatniks? Naw. Does he wear a nest of robins in his hair? Of course not. He doesn't have hair. Not much, anyhow. No beard, and no long-flowing scarf non-chalantly slung around his shoulders. Neither are his pants skin tight.

Actually, you'd take him for a friendly doctor. Or a Forbes Avenue business man. He's soft-spoken and his unassuming manner wins you over in a minute.

Forty-five years ago bachelor Rosenberg was invited to a party. At a friend's home. Also invited was Libbie Levine whose dad was cantor at the Tree of Life Synagogue for 40 years. Sam had seen her hundreds of times when he returned books at the Carne-gie Library where Libbie was a librarian. They even had attended Forbes school at the same time.

But never, until that enchanted evening, had they been introduced. To the surprise of no one they started dating. Three years later they did what comes naturally. Got married. And to this day, he likes having her around.

The Rosenberg dark frame and concrete-block house, snuggled in among thick foliage, scarcely rates a second look. But inside it's a joy to behold. The walls are huge picture windows throughout, overlooking a view that resembles a bit of Grand Can-yon. Sam's studio is in the garage off the bedroom. It too is flooded with sunlight and an array of dazzling colors.

Should you be lucky enough to be invited to their home you'll dine on a long table covered with linens from India, china and silver from other exotic places. But the food will be home-made. Libbie, in addition to being Sam's secretary enjoys the house-wifely arts. He has at times gone on a diet, but he got "Thick and tired of it." However, he stopped smoking long before it became the thing to do.

Sam and his charming missus recently returned from a six-week trip to Europe. They saw the Prado Art Museum in Madrid. And enjoyed several relaxing weeks at a Portugal seaside resort. And guess what! They visited the Casbas and market-places in Morocco. As to modern art there's very little there, he says.

Our neighbors' one and only son, Dr. Murray Z. Rosenberg, is a pathologist in a Connecticut hospital. And has two art-loving children — Joel, 14, and Sue Anne, 12.

The Agony and the Ecstacy? Our community wishes the Rosenbergs a minimum of the one and plenty of the other — in the years ahead.

Mrs. Gabriele Rosenwasser
With Her, the Accent is No Accident!

"Parlez vous Francais?" Sad to say most of us don't. But happily many are learning that fascinating language. Mostly because of our capable and charming neighbor, Mrs. Gabrielle Rosenwasser of Douglas St. She's a French teacher par excellence at Allderdice High. More about that later.

Her husband Sigmund is a well-known lawyer. He and their many friends call her Gaby for short. Those who address her as mom are 17-year-old Marc, a senior at Allderdice. And Evelyn, 13, in the same school's eighth grade.

Their Boston terrier Comet doesn't call her anything. And what's more, he "no speek French." Nor English even. But he's the most important member of the household and loves everybody. Even the mailman.

Sigmund and Gabrielle first met 21 years ago in Oran, Algeria, when it was French-owned. She was born there. So what was a youthful snipper-snapper lawyer doing in Old Algiers, so far away from home? Uncle Sam stationed him there. World War II, you know. For four months.

At first it was lonely as you know-what. But one Friday evening something wonder-ful happened. He attended services at the synagogue. And a prominant local wor-shipper invited him to his home for dinner. He was Gabrielle's dad. Because of her perfect French and knowledge of English, she was interpreter for the American Army headquarters.

You guessed it. One date followed another. But no wedding as yet. Dad didn't be-lieve in quickie war marriages. When Rosenwasser was transferred to Burma, then to India and then to China, three years elapsed, but throughout all that time they kept the mails busy. After Sigmund's honorable discharge and return to our city, Gaby followed and became his happy missus. That was 18 years ago and they've been our neighbors ever since.

Our likeable neighbor started teaching French at Allderdice in 1960, after the chil-dren were of school age. First as a sub, then steady. Now she's entered Pitt University to work for her master's degree.

Three years ago she started a series on WQED Channel 13, teaching French conver-sation. During the summer she had a half-hour nightly show. And another series for beginner's French conversation. Then teaching at Pitt, beginners and intermediates. Now she's a full-time French teacher at Allderdice.

What's our neighborhood teacher like — personally that is? She speaks with an in-triguing French accent. Her hair is a lovely brown. And her hazel eyes crinkle easily in-to a pleasant smile. With a figure slightly rounded, she's entirely feminine.

Gabrielle loves teaching and "going to school" together with Marc and Evelyn. In their charming six-room home she and the children sit around the same table together, doing their home-work — while Comet curls up into a blissful snooze. It's a picture of family stability, closeness and warmth.

Gaby thinks teaching is wonderful for women — after the children grow up. And she encourages greater education for moms. She enjoys reading, music, the theatre. And letter-writing to her folks who now live in Paris.

The Rosenwassers wish their many friends and neighbors a Happy New Year. In French it's "Bon Anee." Our community wishes them the same — and many, many more.

Mrs. B. (Audrey) Roth
Shows Talents and Skills

This is being written on a shower-cooled day after those sizzlers. The foliage is refreshed and a-bloom and our Pirates won a double-header. A pleasant day to tell you about a talented neighbor.

She's none other than Audrey Roth of Wilkins Ave. Formerly from nearby Duquesne, Audrey is the lovely missus of well-known Bertram Roth. He is vice president and general merchandise manager of Horne's Home Division. And where do you think they met? At Gimbels! Bert was that store's assistant buyer then. And Audrey assistant fashion coordinator to the then popular Francine Blum.

One enchanted lunch-time Mr. Roth and Audrey sat down at the same table in the store's cafeteria. You guessed it. They chatted as they dunked. Steady dating followed and several years later they became Mr. and Mrs. Now they are the proud parents of three lively, interesting children. Gil, 24 is a junior in Pitt's Dental School.

A sports car enthusiast, he will race "Formula V" in the national sports car races. Holly is 19. She spent all last summer at the Mountain at Jennerstown and all winter with Margo Frye's Knickerty-Knockerty Players. Adair, 15 and a red-head, is in the 10th grade at Allderdice. Gil and Holly have an identical birth-date and each year they have a double birthday celebration.

And now more about their talented mom. Audrey attended Tech Drama School. Then went to New York in the singing chorus and as understudy in "Best Foot Forward." And on the road for a year. Then back to our city, modeling at Horne's, Gimbel's and Kaufmann's. After marriage she did free lance fashion shows, doing the commentary. She also filmed TV commercials and for over five years taught teenage charm classes at Horne's.

Audrey played wife Golda to Don Brockett's Tevia in his take-off skit of "Fiddler on the Roof." Together with Barbara Klee as daughter — and pianist — the three have entertained hundreds of organization affairs all through the Tri-State area.

She also was in Don's "This is our Generation" at Rodef Shalom Temple — with other "pros" like Helen Wayne Rauh, Esther Lapiddus and Betty Aberlin. Don is now preparing a package titled "The National Jewish Test." And as you already know, whatever neighbor Brockett creates, comes up roses. Audrey will be in that too. And when you're in a Brockett show, you have it made.

Audrey also designs the costumes for some of his shows. Her House is one mass of sequins, feathers, ribbons and bows. And glue. The Roth's furry black cat Sylvester looks on in puzzlement at the goings-on. And at times gets tangled up in them. But mostly he curls up on the floor and takes a snooze. Or just sits and purrs.

Our neighbor and daughters all wear mini-skirts. But not the "for goodness sake don't bend over" style. Moderation, you know.

Audrey likes to paint pictures — and even walls when in the mood. And she's an expert wall paper hanger. She does excellent needlepoint as wedding gifts. So what do her best friends do? They get married. As to cooking — you should pardon the expression. Brockett says Audrey is the only housewife in Squirrel Hill with frost-bitten fingers. From handling frozen foods.

Aren't you glad you met such a many-splendored personality? Honestly, ours is the luckiest neighborhood.

Norman E. Roth
Remains Single and Handsome

Our neighbor Don Brockett—that delightfully zany entertainer and gad-about— is constantly being written up in our press. So today you'll meet another clever fellow importantly connected with him. He's none other than Norman E. Roth, our neighbor at Inverness St. After working for Don six years as public relations man writing his press articles and many other valuable things, he's now Company Manager for the Don Brockett Productions. And "gads" with him.

For the past two years Norman has been helping write and produce the Canterbury Cabaret Shows at the popular Ben Gross Restaurant in Irwin. And wowing the crowds that come to eat, relax and laugh. Out loud mostly. Recently they wrote a new show titled "BEADS" which opened there September 30 and will run for 12 weeks. Already it's a smash. So gather up the wife and friends and come to enjoy, enjoy.

Two years ago Roth directed the Parkway Players "IN A VARICOSE VANE" by Brockett. In the Playbill program here's what our "modest" Norman, its director, wrote about himself (quote):

"Thirty years old, single, rich, devilishly good-looking. Won letters in Football, Basketball and Baseball. Writes satirical material for the Brockett Industrial Shows. He's also Equity Stage Manager for them. He directed HELLO, GOODBYE, I LOVE YOU! for Beth Synagogue. Also THERE'S A MORAL HERE SOMEWHERE for the Bob Locklin Singers. Born in Squirrel Hill, his home is now a national shrine and Pittsburgh's most popular tourist attraction. . . "

He ends with "Has Tux. Will Travel." And travel he does — here, there, everywhere.

And now let's go back a little. After going through Wightman, Norm graduated Allderdice. And later the University of Michigan. Too young to serve in Korea, he spent 6 months as a reservist at Fort Knox, Ky. Then 3 years in San Francisco as an accountant for an outfit we all thoroughly dislike—the IRS. He also took a Creative Writing course in that city's State College. Norman loved San Francisco but didn't leave his heart there. He likes Pittsburgh more.

Roth started a summer theater, the Odd Chair Playhouse, as one of the original investors. In no time they were in the black. Norm came to his love of the theater naturally. His late dad Morris Roth owned vaudeville houses, silent and sound movies all around. His mother has the queenly name of Esther. Sister Natalie Meyers and two brothers (Sam, an attorney and Charles, an English teacher) all are Squirrel Hillers.

Norm and Don write and produce all kinds of Industrial Shows. Recently they were in Milwaukee for the Bolens-Husky Tractor Co. September they entertained in Cleveland for Stouffer's Frozen Foods, at sales meetings for clients. Sometimes their Show has just two performers. Often as many as 30. Like for Baltimore's Bi-centennial

Anniversary of the Methodist Church, at that city's Civic Arena. They did an hour-long original drama depicting the history of the Methodists in America. They took sets and costumes with them. Next month they go to New York for Calgon Corp.

For H. J. Heinz they have been in Boston, Washington, New York and Chicago. With a cast of four. Don writes the Shows and Roth takes care of all details like travel arrangements, costumes, sets, rehearsal schedules. In Washington the Heinz manager hadn't informed Roth what hotel had been booked for them. Being Sunday, the Heinz fellow couldn't be reached.

So the group went from one hotel to another—six of them— before learning it was the Sheraton Hotel. They did a satirical political Revue for Milton Shapp at Carnegie Music Hall the first time he ran. And again there this month (Oct. 8). Whatever your political persuasion, be sure to vote. And may the best man win!

Our neighbor is now 32 and it's still "Look, ma — no wife!" But since he writes of himself (see above quote) as "Rich, devilishly good looking." And with the added gifts of talent and personal charm — married he can always get.

Arthur Rotman
Puts New Life Into Y-IKC

Honestly, ours is the luckiest neighborhood. Right smack close to Forbes & Murray is the popular Y-IKC. It's buzzing and alive with interesting activities. And the fellow who came here all the way from Canada to keep it alive — and even more so — is its new Executive Director, Arthur Rotman. Mr. Rotman officially took over his duties last August. And lives close by on Ferree Street.

In addition to the Y-IKC Squirrel Hill Branch, the new Director has charge of the YM-WHA Branch on Bellefield Avenue. also the East Liberty Branch. And there's the Emma Kaufmann Camp in Harmony, Pa., as well as the Henry Kaufmann Family Recreation Park and Day Camp Site in Monroeville starting this summer. Happy days ahead.

In case you don't know, the Y-IKC is a Jewish Center for every kind of worthwhile projects. It's a bee-hive of activity for kindergartners, tween-teens, teenagers, young and older adults. And of course senior citizens. They come to learn, to study, to socialize and to enjoy.

And now let's learn a little about our interesting neighbor. Born and reared in Montreal, Rotman's education background reads like a Who's Who and Why-Not. In 1947 he received his B.A. degree from Montreal's Sir George William University and two years later his M.S. in Social Administration from Cleveland's Western Reserve. For 19 years he worked for the Montreal YM-WHA, starting as a staff member and advancing to Associate Executive Director. Rotman has given lectures and workshop courses for staff members, community leaders and volunteers. And is a member of the National Association of Jewish Center Workers and the Council on Social Work Education. His informative articles have been published in leading magazines. Our neighbor is active in the National Jewish Welfare Board and the Association of Leisure Time Services. In 1958 he was an Advisor for the Jewish Community Center delegation. His delegation joined the first International Youth Conference in Jerusalem. Mr. Rotman was a board member and on the program committee of the Reconstructionist Synagogue in Montreal. As well as on the educational committee of the Jewish People's School.

By then Mr. Rotman's capabilities were plainly showing. And when former executive director A. J. Auerbach left for the West Coast to teach, the local Board knew whom it wanted. And invited Rotman here.

When Arthur Rotman was a handsome and carefree bachelor he met lovely Anita Schecter. At a party, 22 years ago. Steady dating followed and in due time a Montreal rabbi pronounced them man and wife. Ho-hum! That you call romantic? Arthur's dad and mom — THEY had the romance. In 1903 Meyer Rotman migrated from Czarist Russia. And settled in our city. About the same time a beautiful young girl from the same country also came to Pittsburgh. And before long Meyer and Mollie became acquainted. After six months of "going together" she moved to Montreal. And you know something? Meyer Rotman couldn't live without his Mollie. So guess what? He too moved to Montreal.

And before long Mollie became his adoring bride. So that's how it happens that our current neighbor is a Canadian. And so are his three interesting children — Stephen, Laurie and Carol. Time marched on. Stephen is now 18 and goes to Antioch College. Laurie, 15 attends Allderdice. And Carol, 10 goes to Hillel Academy.

The Rotmans think Pittsburgh people are the greatest — warm, friendly and hospitable. And they like it here. Our community likes having them, and wishes them the best of everything now and in the years ahead.

Mrs. Gershon (Ann) Ruben
Educational Talent Put To Good Use

Honestly, ours is the luckiest neighborhood. Where else are there so many remarkable personalities? Today you'll learn about a neighbor who has been endowed with many blessings. And has the wisdom to put them to the best uses. Not just for herself and family but for others as well.

Let's meet Mrs. Gershon Ruben, the former Ann Moliver, our neighbor at Fernwald Rd. In her teenage years Ann had lots of fellas but Gershon Ruben rated first. Not only was he a great guy himself but had the most wonderful parents (Jacob and Ida Ruben).

And pssst, listen! She lived next door to a rabbi — Benjamin Lichter of blessed memory. Although a bachelor himself he enjoyed nothing better than to officiate under a "hupa." So she couldn't miss. And at 18 became Gershon's missus. This was in 1943 during World War II. The husband, then a junior at Duquesne University joined Uncle Sam's air force and was sent overseas. His young bride went to live with his parents to replace, for the time being, their only son. Ann's sister Rose Egger was also a war bride. Later the two husbands, by coincidence met in Munich, Germany.

Time marches on. Mr. Ruben is currently a corporation executive with United Overall Service, Inc. in Lawrenceville. And now about Ann herself. During the war years she was a secretary in Pitt's School of Social Work, attending night school there. Later, after becoming a housewife and mother she continued night school "between children."

Upon earning her BS degree she taught elementary education for four years. Then became a community agent in the Poverty Program of our Board of Education. Her job was to select children for the pre-primary classes, choosing those who needed preschool work most — the 3 and 4-year olds. She followed the same program as was being used in Israel. Ann would visit the homes of public-assistance youngsters — kids who had no father. She continued for two years. During that time she set up a mental health program for mothers of these children. And when the Community Mental Health Program came into being our neighbor joined the Dept. of Social Psychiatry at Pitt. Now her title is Educational Consultant, if you please. Wanting to devote summers to her own children she signed up a contract for only nine months.

The Rubens have three handsome, healthy, lively sons. Stephen is 19. An honor graduate of Allderdice he goes to Bethany College. The parents haven't yet been told whether later they'll be introducing them as Our Son the Doctor, Lawyer, or Rabbi. He can't decide now. During the summer he was counselor at the Jewish Community Center Camp in Atlanta, Ga. His kid brother David, 14 was a camper there. Both came home with a trace of yo-all shugah in their talk. David goes to Allderdice and is president of the Y-IKC "Marquis Club." Richard, 16 is learning dad's business. He's also learning you have to work hard to pay the bills.

The Ruben 7-room ranch-style house is the answer to a home-maker's dream. Not lavish with costly interiors, but full of charm and elegant taste. Their housekeeper of 24 years keeps everything sparkling. As Ann has often told her, "Clara, part of my diploma belongs to you."

Ann's parents-in-law are celebrating their 50th wedding anniversary come Oct. 29. It's in the planning stage now. Not to be outdone, the Ruben's dachshund named Sebastian Cabot Lodge recently celebrated his first birthday. The boys brought him a bone done up in colorful wrapping and ribbon which he quickly tore apart and dug his teeth in. Among the many well-wishers was Bobo, the neighbor's French poodle. He dropped in to find out what all the fuss was about. And went home none the wiser.

Aren't you proud of such interesting neighbors?

Mrs. Jack R. (Mildred) Rubenstein
Her Singing Pleases Us All & Baky, Too

This is being written on a day to remember. It's warm and sunny outside, with spring blossoms bursting out all over. And the Bridge to Nowhere will be going somewhere. So lean back, relax, and learn about a well known neighbor with a beautiful voice.

Meet Mildred Rubenstein, talented wife of Jack R. Rubenstein of Hempstead Rd. Jack teaches commercial subjects at Braddock Senior High. Without having a million, his missus sings like it.

Mildred is from Boston. There she met Jack 23 years ago, during World War II. He was a Navy man on submarine patrol duty. She a hostess with the "mostest"at the USO. As a patriotic gesture — or was in maybe because he was handsome? — she invited him to her home for dinner.

On that enchanted evening, woe is me! she had a code-in-her-doze. And served him herring. But herring schmerring, Jack came again. With knapsack on his back he announced he had a 72-hour pass and would Mildred please have dinner with him. Playing it cool, she quickly answered "But of course."

Or words to that effect. At any rate, during his two long years of active duty they kept the mails busy. After being honorably discharged he asked her to come to Pittsburgh to meet his folks. You guessed it. A month later they both said "I do" to a rabbi in Boston.

They had no honeymoon. You see, Jack had to immediately start teaching. She did office work for the government. Years ago while a secretary in Boston her first pay was spent for voice lessons. It awakened in her a love for all forms of art. So that now they opened a music store in Swissvale and lived it for 13 years. Once, when their elevator broke down, she pitched his lunch down to him from the window. He caught it like a Roberto Clemente.

As a youngster Mildred started her stage career playing "Goldilocks and the Three Bears." And in the chorus of Gilbert & Sullivan operettas. Soon she worked up to the lead in "Iolanthe" and "The Mikado." To this day she's still studying voice. With Mrs. Grace Mansell of the Y-ICK Perlow Music School.

Our neighbor directs the Anathan House Folk Singers. While performing at the Wightman Manor and the Negley House, the Singers were taped for television later shown on Channel 4.

Our neighborhood songstress thrilled the hundreds of members of Hadassah Group 8 at its donor luncheon last year. She has sung for B'nai B'rith, Technion, and in the surrounding towns of Greensburg, Latrobe, Donors, Aliquippa and others. At the many Israel Bond and UJA dinners and other important affairs Mildred Rubenstein starts the program by singing our National Anthem and Hatikvah.

The Rubenstein apartment is inauspicious in furnishings but tastefully and artistically arranged. From their patio you look down on rows and rows of beautiful Homestead mountain greenery.

And now get a load of this. When Mrs. Bakalienikoff, widow of the late world-famous concert-master passed away she left Mildred a goodly heritage. No, not jewels. But something more precious. Her beloved parakeet named Baky, in the loveliest cage you ever laid eyes on. Radiant in his aqua-blue-yellow featters, Baky sings along with Mildred. But not with Mitch.

And if you listen closely you'll hear him say "give me a kiss," "I love you," "Please sing, Mildred."

The Rubensteins love the theater, operas and concerts. And the middle of June are going to Europe and Israel. Mildred is an expert swimmer. Those famous beaches in and around Boston — remember?

How about that for a neighbor who has made good? And hopes to make even better.

Mrs. Myer W. Rubenstein

She Savors Best of Many Worlds

You know what they say — the busiest people are the happiest. And when the busyness" is for the benefit of others — whole-hearted and voluntary — they truly deserve happiness.

That's how it is with our neighbor, Belle Rubenstein of Plainfield St.

The former Belle Barsky is the missus of Dr. Myer W. Rubenstein, well-known local dermatologist. He graduated from Jefferson Medical School and was a fellow at Mayo Clinic for four years. But wait. As a youngster he was considered a "child prodigy" of the violin.

At a wedding of mutual family friends he played "Oh Promise Me." And this will kill you. Belle was a flower girl! No, they didn't start dating then. Unlike current fashion, "steady dating" didn't start at age five.

Years passed. One enchanted evening at Syria Mosque each was seated for the opera at opposite ends of the second balcony. During intermission, whether accidentally or on purpose, Fate stepped in. Cupid followed.

Many years have passed. Son Mark is now 29 and a fellow at Mayo's in pediatrics. A graduate of Pitt Medical School, he was president of its Men's Glee Club, with the title "Mr. Pitt." For three years, during the Jewish High Holy Days, he was cantor at the Greensburg Temple.

Daughter Bonnie is married to Dr. A. Leonard Zimmerman, a former fellow at Mayo's. They live in Palo Alto, Calif. Bonnie and Mark each presented their parents with a boy and girl. That's four grandchildren, — just what the doctors ordered.

Their pet collie, Cleopatra by name, is the neighborhood's most reliable baby-sitter. She's loved by all and gets a free meal anywhere any time.

And now more about Belle herself. Small in stature, big of heart and boundless energy, she's a whirlwind of activity. When the kids were young she returned to Pitt to complete some "unfinished business" — a B.A. degree. She majored in languages, specializing in Spanish.

She and Myer belong to the Pittsburgh Council for International Visitors. Foreign visitors, especially of Spanish origin, come first thing to Myer's office. He brings them home where all converse in Spanish. Belle received her musical know-how from widely-known piano teacher Aaron Gross of Hobart Street.

For many years Belle was chairman of the YM&WHA Musical Society.

She introduced to Pittsburgh audiences the greatest artists for the first time. Now she's on the program committee of Hadassah. But her pet project is the Anathan House — that fabulous House for Older People, a stone's throw from Forbes and Murray.

For 14 years she's been its musical director, conducting classes in music appreciation and opera. She sees to it that her "young" students get free tickets to everything musical in our city. For their monthly birthday parties Belle brings in the best professional artists who perform gratis. She does the piano accompaniment for the musicians.

Our neighbor belongs to the Pittsburgh Association for the Blind. She helps test children's eyes at the public schools. And reads to a blind woman who is taking a course in English. She's also president of the Women's Division of Technion Society.

At home there's always music. The couple has two grand pianos in their living-room. Local and foreign artists flock there.

A family that enjoys music together, stays young together. And is happy together.

Harold J. Ruttenberg
From Union Man to Capitalist

You know those supermarket wire carts in which you load your groceries — and your kids when you have 'em? And those wire crates in which your dairyman delivers your morning milk?

Well, a closeby neighbor makes them. He's the well-known Harold J. Ruttenberg living at 5821 Aylesboro Ave.

Actually, though, he doesn't make them himself. His firm The United Steel & Wire Co. of which he became president last May. It's in Battle Creek, Mich. He's there most of the week and spends all his week-ends and holidays at home.

His wire products are used throughout the world and Harold has traveled there dozens of times.

But that's not all. This 50-year young dynamo with a brain has a fantastic background. Let's see now. A 1935 graduate from Pitt, Mr. Ruttenberg was one of the founders of the United Steelworkers of America.

He was the union's research director for 10 years when Philip Murray was its head. During World War II he was assistant director of Uncle Sam's War Production Board in Washington.

In 1946 he left the union to become executive V.P. of Portsmouth Steel Corp., Portsmouth, Ohio. Then became president of Stardrill-Keystone Co. in Beaver Falls. Recently he formed a consulting firm called Humanation Associates, with complete offices downstairs in his home.

Through the years he did much writing. His "Self-Developing America" and "The Dynamics of Industrial Democracy" are best sellers. The latter is being used in every American university and has been translated into several foreign languages.

This year he wrote a booklet "How to Save and Create Jobs in the Pittsburgh Area." It deals with solving productivity problems through collective bargaining.

Harold married 28 years ago. The former Kitty Monori, born in Budapest. At age 13 she came to the U.S. Where did they meet? At Pitt where both were students.

One day Harold was working at the blackboard. Wanting to attract a friend's attention he hurled an eraser at him. Instead it landed on Kitty. What she told him is unprintable. So — wouldn't you know it? — he asked for a date.

Soon they married and have been living happily ever since. And make no mistake about it, Kitty helped make Harold what he is today.

She even helped with his various manuscripts. Their huge house she transformed into a charming home — the kind in which you like to linger longer.

Harold flies to Europe and Israel at the drop of a hat. And Kitty enjoys going with him.

Many friends from foreign countries are often hosted at the Ruttenberg home. Recently, in Normandy they celebrated their 28th honeymoon. They drank champagne and were flown around in a private plane "Le Petit Prince" owned by a business associate. When in Budapest Kitty visited the apartment in which she was born. A moving experience, to say the least.

Children? Charles, 25, is an M.I.T. graduate and is finishing his Ph.D. at New York University. He edits a magazine for those interested in the social sciences.

James is 23 and also an M.I.T. graduate. He is working on his Ph.D. at Stanford University in mathematics. Also languages and music.

He endeared himself locally for his talent in blowing the shofar at Temple Sinai for the past nine years. Edward, 18, is at Antioch College studying business management. Daughter Ellen is 15 and a sophomore at Ellis School. She takes part in all Temple Sinai youth activities.

The proudest person in the house is Grandpop Emil, Kitty's venerable dad. He's 84 and unbelievably alert. Umbeschrein!

Their cocker spaniel "Buffer" helps deliver the mail. As yet he hasn't taken a nip at the postman. But he's thinking about it.

Dr. Esther G. Sack

'Contacts' Win Her National Recognition

Women — bless 'em — have been clamoring for Equal Rights with Men. Well, a nearby neighbor has received MORE than Equal Rights. And not by campaigning nor marching. But through sheer talent, ingenuity and her husband's implicit confidence and encouragement.

She's Dr. Esther Goodman Sack of Hobart St., Optometrist par excellence. So is husband Dr. Nathan Sack. With one difference: Esther specializes in contact lens work. And last April was chosen "Contact Lens Woman of the Year" by the National Eye Research Foundation. She and Nate practice together in their Braddock office — an ideal and satisfying partnership.

They were twice invited and twice attended the International Visual Congress in Tel Aviv, Israel. And two years prior went to a similar World Congress at the University of Rome, Italy. Both were on the Visual Panel which administered all the newest phases of eye care, theoretical as well as practical.

Now a bit of our "Contact" neighbor's personal life. The former Esther Goodman graduated High School in East Pittsburgh where her parents ran a jewelry store. Then earned her degree at the Penn's College of Optometry in Philly. She took a postgraduate course in Glacoma testing at Indiana University and another at Ohio State U. on child development and how their eyes function.

Now she's a charter member of the newest science "Orthokeratology" which deals with reduction of vision defects by adopting contact lenses. Her first patient' was almost blind in one eye. After contacts she could see with both. Her patients range in age from 8 to 75. After a cataract operation, contacts exclusively. Never those ugly heavy glasses. The kids look prettier and the oldsters younger.

And now let's go back some. Dr. Goodman first put up her Optometry shingle next door to her parents' jewelry store in East Pittsburgh. Since they owned the building, guess what they charged her for rent? Nothing! It was at the start of WW II. One day an Optometrist from Braddock phoned. Said he was soon leaving to serve Uncle Sam and his assistant also will be in the service shortly. Did she, by any chance, know of a newly graduated GIRL Optometrist? To take over his practice? Of course, he hoped she'd be the one — the sly fella! He was Dr. Nathan Sack of Braddock. She liked his voice first off but wanted to take a personal look-see.

They arranged to attend a professional meeting. Instead he took her to Bill Green's the then most popular dine-and-dance spot. They danced the night away. To make a long story short, they married August 1944 and he left for over-seas. The young bride took over both offices — his and hers. After 1-½ years he returned to his lovely missus — on Valentine's Day, no less.

Time marched on. Today our neighbors are the proud parents of: Joseph, 23, attending John Hopkins Medical School. Trudy, 21, just graduated the University of Wisconsin as a teacher. Sari, 15, is in the Scholars Program at Allderdice. She was in Israel's Kfar Silver all last summer. Jack is 13 and was recently Bar Mitzvah. He too is entering Allderdice Scholars Program. When the kids were young, Dr. Goodman made it her business to be home by 3:30. They never needed to ask "Where's mom?" They now ski, swim and go horse-back riding. An all-around athlete himself, dad took the older boys to Switzerland to ski during their Christmas vacation. His capable missus minded the office and home.

And now guess who Esther's brother is? None other than world-famous Abby Mann of Hollywood. He won an Oscar for writing "Judgment in Nuremberg" and the script for the movie. He also wrote and scripted "A Child is Waiting." And the movie version of "Ship of Fools" as well as "The Detective". Now he's writing a film titled "The Pied Piper". The movie industry is after him to do a special for TV.

And get a load of this. Last year, at the interesting age of 40, the famous and easy-to-look-at Abby Mann said so-long to bachelorhood and I-do to a lovely New York model of the Jewish faith.

If you were to ask him and his "Contact" sis who they feel deserve much credit for their achievements, they'd both say their devoted parents — Rebecca and Benjamin Goodman of Beechwood Blvd. Our community believes it. And congratulates them as well as their entire family.

Aaron Sacks

Need Help? Call Agency

Summer time and the livin' is easy, so the saying goes. But it ain't necessarily so for countless persons with problems too great to endure alone. But with flowers bursting out all over and the assurance that help is available, hope is in the air. And it's just great to tell you about an experienced, capable, dedicated fellow who heads an organization which aims to help those who need it. He's Aaron Sacks, our neighbor at Phillips Ave. Mr. Sacks is Executive Director of Information and Volunteer Services of Allegheny County — a United Fund-Community Chest Agency.

Let's first list a few of the many problems the Agency can help you with: get special care for a helpless person; find a nursing home for an aging relative; seek protection for an abused child; find assistance for an unmarried parent; meet special needs for a physical handicap; find ways to meet the demands of a long illness; work out a problem you are having at your job. In fact you name it. Simply call 261-6010 day or night.

And now let's learn a little more about this fellow Sacks. Born in our city's Hill District, he graduated from Pitt's School of Social Work in 1946. And immediately started as Group Work Supervisor at the Bellefield Ave. YM&WHA remaining nearly 5 years. Then went to Boston to direct a Jewish Center there. Later he returned to our city to work in the Health & Welfare Ass'n of Allegheny County. In 1957 Socks went to Israel for more social work, bringing back interesting slides to show to various local groups. Then guess what? A year later someone else returned from Israel with slides and also began showing them to groups here. Lovely Shirley Prizent, a born Squirrel Hiller. Needing new slides Aaron called her. Maybe they could combine their slides and show them together, he sort of hinted. A great idea, Shirley thought. So in May 1959 they got together with their slides and the following November they got together in another way. Got married. Next time they go to Israel it will be together, not separately.

and Joseph David...8 and 6. Both attend the Beacon St. Hillel Academy. Dad is also chairman of the B'nai B'rith Jewish Adult Education.

Our neighbors own their 6-room home. Everybody helps. And who do you think dries the dishes? Pop, of course. Shirley is V.P. of the Pittsburgh Pioneer Council, a group concerned with social services in Israel. She and Aaron were in Mexico, and last summer took the kids to the Cherokee, N.C. Indian Reservation. The boys danced on the streets with the Indians. They also took the youngsters to Plymouth Rock, Mass., and saw the Mayflower (restored and painted). Also the Plymouth Rock Plantation the way the Pilgrims lived at the time.

In addition to dealing with those who need help, our neighbor is in constant contact with those who want to give help. Last March he was guest speaker at Carnegie Music Hall on the subject "Volunteer Service — Give and Take". It was the Library's seventh Program Services Institute for club women throughout Western Penna. His talk emphasized woman-power in providing the community with services in the health and welfare field that add the touch of humanity and bring to the needy the help they otherwise could not get. Twenty-three community organizations sponsored the Institute, including the Pittsburgh Conference of Jewish Women Organizations.

Isn't it great having such good neighbors. and P.S. — don't forget the number: 261-6010. Someone is waiting.

Beverley Sacks

'Cleo The Clown' Makes World of Laughter

Oh, for laughin' our loud! That's what happens when "Cleo the Clown" entertains kids. Kids fromthree to 93, to be exact. And just who is this clown? Here's who I in poetry no less!

"Six yards of animated chintz. Three pompoms with bells that jingle.
A fuzzy-wuzzy hat with points that tingle.
Red velvet slippers piped in gold.
A painted face that's a sight to behold.
Bright red gloves — just think of that.
A bundle of crinolines to make her fat!
You think it's a couple of jumpin' jacks?
Naw, hidden inside — is Beverly Sacks!"

And the nice thing about it is she's our neighbor. Our next-door neighbor actually, at Forbes Ave.

Mrs. Beverly Sacks is tall, graceful and the youngest-looking mother you ever saw. Her sparkling blue eyes and easy smile tell-tale a great sense of humor.

Son, Ricky, 10, has been a day-camper at Camp Deer Creek. He is an avid numismatist and studies art at Carnegie Museum. This fall he looks forward to taking trumpet lessons. He thinks it's great fun having a mom who's "Cleo the Clown."

Beverly attended Hunter College in New York and came to our city in 1950. In addition to being a part-time clown, she is currently affiliated with the law firm of Rothman, Gordon and Foreman where she is a secretary.

In addition to many private and semi-private kids' birthday parties, this part-time harlequin has performed for several "Y" shows, Children's Hospital, the Holiday House, numerous church and synagogues benefit affairs, The Press Club, both Wightman and Liberty School Fairs, the Oddfellow's Home, North Side, American Legion, Sewickley, WQED "Children's Corner" and "Dimple Depot," Kaufmann's Spring Fashion Show for Children; and the St. Patrick's Day Parade — just to name a few.

At parties, "Cleo the Clown" pantomimes recordings of a circus routine which includes "Come to the Circus," "Be a Clown," Polka — Dot Polka, "Popcorn and Lemonade" — and a raft of others. Honestly, she should have a television show all her own!

Cleo's entertainment is a riot of fun. You'll agree when you, yourself, have a listen-and- see!

Mrs. Jonas E. Salk
Wife Of A Famous Man

As most everyone knows, Dr. Jonas E. Salk, world famous for his polio vaccine is leaving early in January for the West Coast. At LaJolla, Calif., he will set up his institute for biological studies. Next spring when his three sons will end their school year, they and his wife will join him there.

Because his family is still with us, it's a privilege to tell you something about them — especially since they have been our neighbors for the past nine years. They live on Bartlett Street.

Mrs. Salk, whose first name is Donna, is not only lovely to look at but brilliant as well. Her educational background is fantastic. Yet she is "down-to-earth." Asked how it feels to be the wife of a famous man, she answers: "It doesn't get my beds made, dishes washed nor the marketing done."

Peter, 19 is a junior at Harvard; Darrell, 16, is in his second year at Phillips Academy, Andover, Mass; and Jonathan, 12 1/2, is in the 8th grade at Falk School, Pittsburgh.

Summers they all go to their cottage at Deep Creek, Md. The boys love athletics and particularly go in for water skiing. Donna swims, of course, but leaves the more active sports to the kids, getting vicarious pleasure from "just watching."

While the Salks are primarily New Yorkers, they lived for five years in Ann Arbor. There Dr. Salk did virus and influenza research for the University of Michigan. From there they came to Pittsburgh where he continued his fascinating work at the Pitt Medical School. Later he continued on to polio research.

Donna Salk is a summa cum laude graduate of Smith College. She is a Phi Betta Kappa. After Smith she took a graduate social service in New York City. Before starting on her first professional job, she took a little vacation at Woods Hole, Mass., in the vicinity of Cape Cod. There, in 1937, she met Jonas who was doing research at the laboratory. Two years later they were married.

Mrs. Salk was a professional social worker until three days before her first son was born. Immediately she gave up her career to concentrate upon being a devoted wife and mother. Many women are apologetic at being "just a housewife." Donna loved it and was proud of it. She did not resume her outside career until after all her children were in school.

In 1954 she started to serve on the boards of various local social service agencies. Now she's on the board of the United Mental Health Service. She serves on the Community Chest's budget committee. And she is regional advisory board member of the Anti-Defamation League of the B'nai B'rith.

Donna is a trustee of Tuskegee Institute in Alabama. But her main field of interest is in the Mayor's Commission on Human Relations, of which she has been chairman since 1959.

The commission aims to make our city a harmonious place in which to live. They do it by education and by enforcing the law which makes it illegal to discriminate against people in jobs or housing because of race, religion or nationality.

She does a fair amount of public speaking. She plays the piano "but not well." She explains. And reads a lot. She speaks French, Italian and some German. She plans to study Spanish. Peter (her eldest son) spent 10 weeks last summer working on a Kibbutz in Israel. A kibbutz is a collective settlement in which everyone shares responsibilities, finances, and production. There he learned to speak the Hebrew language fluently.

Donna Salk was born 45 years ago of Jewish parents. Her husband is two years older and of the same religious faith.

A humorous incident in their family is worth relating. When the Salk vaccine story broke and all the papers flashed the news on their front pages, little Jonathon (then 4 years old) ran to the phone and called his buddy. "Billie," he said breathlessly, "I just got back from my vacation and want you to know that I'm famous. And listen, he added, "So's my daddy."

Jonathan, we have news for you: So's your mother'.

Lord Edwin H. Samuel
Temporary Visitor Fabulous Gentleman

Today you'll learn about a fabulous gentleman. In our city temporarily on important work at Pitt, he's staying near the University for convenience. But because he's scheduled to be guest speaker at a neighborhood synagogue and is someone extra special, let's adopt him as a neighbor — if only for the time being — and welcome him with a most friendly hand.

Meet Lord Edwin H. Samuel, renowned scholar, orator, author and academician. He's the eldest son of the First Viscount Herbert L. Samuel, British High Commissioner for Palestine (long before it became the State of Israel). When his venerable father passed away at 92, Edwin already had the vast educational background and experience to take over. Like father like son, as the saying goes. The British title "Lord" is that of a nobleman next above a Baron. Lord Samuel is 71 and looks 20 years younger — tall, graceful, with unassuming charm that wins you over in a minute.

About 52 years ago during World War I, Samuel was a dashing officer on General Allenby's political intelligence staff in Palestine. And met a beautiful sabra, Hadassah Goor. He was billeted in the Goor home, upstairs. Hadassah played the piano, downstairs. And Edwin listened. Soon — you guessed it — they met, dated and became betrothed. Edwin returned to London to earn his BA degree at Oxford and Hadassah went to Geneva to study. Several years and hundreds of love letters later the man-in-love came back to Palestine to claim his bride. They married in his dad's official residence on the Mount of Olives. And started housekeeping in Jerusalem. The couple also lived in Jaffe, Nazareth — all over — while he was in the Palestine government, a post he held for 28 years, ending as director of the State Broadcasting Service. They've been blessed with two interesting sons. David is professor of Isotope Chemistry at the Weitzmann Institute of Science at Rehovot, Israel. Dan heads the Shell Company in Belgium. There are five grandchildren. The oldest — a girl — is now serving in the Israeli army.

From January through April Lord Samuel is a Senior Mellon Fellow at the Graduate School of Public and International Affairs at Pitt, giving a seminar on the comparative administration of selected Welfare States. His lovely Hadassah is in Belgium with son Dan and his family. She's planning on coming here in March. At the end of April both will go to London for three months where Edwin will sit in the House of Lords (like the U.S. Senate). Then return to their apartment in Jerusalem. Next December — God willing — they hope to celebrate their Golden Wedding anniversary.

And now more about Edwin. In addition to Oxford he attended the Graduate School of Economics at Columbia University; was one of the military attaches to Dr. Chaim Weitzmann in 1918; a visiting professor on Middle East States at Dropsie College in Philadelphia, and a visiting lecturer at the University of Johannesburg. From 1956 to 1969 he was seminar lecturer in Public Administration and Comparative Government at the Hebrew University in Jerusalem. Lord Samuel has authored several books in English and Hebrew on Government Administration and Sociology in Palestine and Israel. Also five volumes of short stories. He's a director of the Jewish Chronicle in London, the oldest Jewish periodical in the world. In Israel he is a director of the Ellern Investment Corporation and the Moller Textile Company. In Britain he is a chairman of PATWA (Professional and Technical Workers Aliya to Israel) and a council member of the British Friends of the Hebrew University. You may relax now.

Lord Samuel will be guest speaker in the Horelick Hall of the Shaare Torah Synagogue, 2319 Murray Avenue, Tuesday, February 10 at 8:30 p.m. His theme: "War or Peace in the Middle East". You're cordially invited. You may even ask him questions. Honestly, ours is the luckiest neighborhood!

Mrs. Selma Sapira

Bridge 'Built for 2' at Sapira Home

You've heard the expression "If you can't lick 'em, join 'em."

That's what Selma Sapira, our neighbor at Plainfield St. did. She up and learned to play contract bridge. And learned it well. All because her husband Dr. Harry Sapira has been a top-notch bridger all his life while she herself didn't know nuthin' about the game.

Now, instead of sitting on the side-line wondering what the enthusiasm is all about, she smiles at him across the bridge table — and does a good of job of upping his score.

But wait. Sharing her husband's enjoyable diversion isn't the only satisfaction from having mastered the game. Now she teaches bridge! Teaches a large group of enthusiastic golden agers at the popular Murray Avenue Anathan House. For free — with the aid of another gracious volunteer bridge expert Mrs. Gertrude Schultz.

Now let's learn a little more about our lovely neighbor with sparkling dark eyes, easy smile and warm personality. And a slim figure yet.

The former Selma Mallin was a laboratory technician at Montefiore Hospital. One spring morning, while carrying a tray of medical oddities, a good looking red head gallantly opened the door for her, almost colliding.

He was Dr. Harry Sapira, a new intern starting his career of internal medicine. You don't believe in love at first sight? Well, now you can.

Although Selma had been dating another fella, this was it. In no time they became Dr. and Mrs. To this day she remembers the sun shining through his brilliant hair, and still calls him "Red". So do many of his patients.

During World War II Dr. Sapira was in Uncle Sam's Medical Corps. While stationed at McComb, Ill., wife Selma learned to keep house, cook and taught herself to sew. Needing a black blouse and not being able to find one in the small town stores, she bought a piece of black cotton material, a pattern and whipped one up by hand. Now she owns a sewing machine and makes many of her own clothes.

That's what happens when one has a natural urge to create.

The Sapiras have one son, 28-year-old Dr. Joseph Sapira, in Pitt's Department of Medical Research. He is married to the former Enid Gruskin of New York, whose father too is an M.D.

Joe and Enid presented their parents with a grandson, Lee Edwin, just 23 months young. And a few weeks ago baby Andrea Pearl came along. Just what the doctors ordered.

Selma gives all her spare time to the Anathan House. For two years she's been chairman of its entire program, introducing diversified interests such as mosaics, sewing and, of course, bridge.

Together with Mrs. Leonard Laufe — another Squirrel Hiller — she wrote "A Volunteer's Manual" — a guide-book for other volunteers. She's also a camera fan and has recently shown movies of her European trip.

As an end-of-the-term gesture toward her beloved bridge pupils, teacher Selma and assistant Gertrude gave a luncheon for their sweet girl-graduates — and one man. At the Anathan House, of course.

The long tables, decorated with fresh flowers, were laden with all kinds of delicious foods. Blintzes, blueberries, fish, salad and many kinds of cake to name a few. All baked, cooked and served by these gracious hostesses.

All this has made Selma Sapira a most happy woman. Bridge widows: — let this be a lesson to you.

Ronald Satlof

Director Utilizing Inventive Genius

While enjoying a live play at the theatre do you ever think of the play's director? Probably not. You are too engrossed with the plot, the performers. But the director is there, lurking behind the scenes — watching, caring. So today let's concentrate on this year's successful Artistic Director of our popular Pittsburgh Playhouse —

talented Ronald Satlof. Temporarily Ronald lives in Oakland near the theatre but hopes some day to become a Squirrel Hiller. So just for the heck of it — and because he's doing such a fantastic job for the Playhouse, let's pretend he's already our neighbor, and learn about him.

First off director Satlof is a handsome six-footer with dark hair and eyes. No beard. Just a whisper of side-burns. Scarcely 29 he has a carload of experience under his belt — and it's showing. Born in New York, after attending public school he went to the West Coast at the College of the Pacific to study drama for a year. At 17 he was already directing plays there. Then off to the Cleveland Playhouse as an actor, director and all manner of backstage work. For further study he came to Carnegie Tech (now Carnegie-Mellon) earning his B.F.A. degree. He worked his way through college, not selling magazines but singing in coffee houses in Shadyside and at women's and men's clubs.

Satof began his professional career in 1956 directing the off-Broadway production of "Rope". He also was director at the Holbrook Summer Theatre in Long Island and the Champlain Shakespeare Festival. From 1963 to 1965 he was managing director of the Tampa Community Theatre directing such hits as "Come Blow Your Horn", "Taming of the Shrew", "Bye, Bye, Birdie", "Take Her, She's Mine" and "Cat on the Hot Tin Roof". Also stage manager for the Zev Bufman touring production of "Porgy and Bess" and for Shelley Winter's "Who's Afraid of Virginia Woolf?"

Here, the last two seasons ago Ronald was production stage manager of the Playhouse. Then he also directed "The Knack" and "View from the Bridge" You've seen them. You've enjoyed them.

Director Satlof is married to lovely and talented Ginger Harmon from L.A. She too is with the Playhouse. Come April 20 you'll see her and a top-notch cast in "Galileo" which husband Ron is directing. And at this point meet also his capable and indispensable Girl Friday — Trish Pugh.

Ron and Ginger love skiing. Every Monday (their day off) during the winter they spent at Seven Springs, flying through the snow with the greatest of ease. But get a load of this. Recently big skier Satof — like Humpty-Dumpty — had a great fall, resulting in 3 bruised ribs. Then, wouldn't you know it, the very next night Harold Scott playing Hotspur in "Henry IV Part I" which Ron was directing, went down with the flu. So who do you think took over? Satlof. Hotspur, you may remember, was stabbed at play's end and rolled down a ramp looking dead as a door-nail.

Ron, with his painful bandaged ribs made it down the ramp all right, but looking "dead" without squirming was an agnozing ordeal. Then too the Satlofs enjoy sailing. The summer of 1966 in Seattle our director rented a boat to sail on Puget Sound. His pal Jack Axelrod owned a houseboat there and invited Ron to moor his boat at his Place. Then came another "American Tragedy" Ron's boat was just right but its motor was just wrong. Instead of a 15-minute sail to Jack's houseboat it took several hours of sailing in the hot noonday sun. So what happened? Ron and Ginger both got a beautiful sun-burn. With blisters yet.

Satlog's direction at the Playhouse is firm and imaginative. He is extremely inventive and adept at improvising in order to bring out the meanings and dramatic riches of his plays. With the aid of an able cast and back-stage assistants.

Ron says come enjoy a delicious dinner at the Playhouse restaurant. And have yourself a hilarious evening with "The Odd Couple". It starts April 3rd.

Mrs. Donald A. Sayles

Has Answers

Honestly, ours is the luckiest neighborhood, with the most interesting personalities. As for instance Mrs. Donald A. (Leah) Sayles of Beechwood Blvd. She's the new full time Marriage Counselor at Planned Parenthood of Pittsburgh. Its main office is 10th floor, 526 Penn Ave., Downtown, with branches throughout Allegheny County. Her husband is a chemical engineer.

Are you in love with a fellow and want to get married and your folks don't seem to like him? Or his family doesn't care much for you Or is everything hunky-dory but still you want to learn many things before taking the big step? Or are you already married and engulfed with problems seemingly beyond control? And you have no one to turn to? Well, you have now. Leah Sayles has the training, professional skill and experience to do her utmost to analyze your difficulties and help you cope with them. Her counseling (and of course planned parenthood) operates under a graduated fee system — say $15 an hour on down to zero, according to ability to pay or not pay. All services are available regardless of race, religion, income or residence.

And now let's learn a little about our interesting neighbor. The former Leah Siberzan is a native New Yorker. To work her way through Hunter College she clerked at Macy's. And worked at various Settlement Houses and Summer Camps. After WW 2 she helped plant, tend and grow vegetables in a Farm Camp garden. Graduating from Hunter she bought a one-way ticket to Los Angeles planning never to return to New York. But fate willed it otherwise, as you will soon learn. In L.A. Leah did graduate work in Sociology and Anthropology at UCLA. And earned a Ford Foundation scholarship to the University of Southern California. She did group work for B'nai B'rith Youth organizations and the Beverly Hills YWCA. Then taught elementary school During that time she applied with the government to teach in Europe And was accepted. By the time her contract came through the pretty schoolmarm met a fella! Donald A. Sayles. A Cornell graduate in Chemical Engineering and living in New York, he was in L.A. on business. And it turned out to be the nicest kind of business. Soon as he met Leah (through mutual friends) it was love at first sight — both ways. Instead of teaching in Europe she returned with Donald to — you guessed it — New York as his adoring bride. Later his work took them to Connecticut, Chicago, Philadelphia and Pittsburgh. Their boys — David now 11 and Michael 8 — were born in the Windy City.

During the five years in our city their mom got her Master's in Social Work at Pitt and used her know-how at the Penna. Association for the Blind.

Before closing you might like to get a few highlights on Planned Parenthood also. Fifty years ago Margaret Sanger, a professional visiting nurse, conceived the idea that babies should be born only if and when wanted. She traveled to Paris to study birth control methods. And returned to open a Birth Control Clinic in the Brownsville section of Brooklyn. Her unconventional ideas were termed pornographic and immoral. Eight times she was arrested and served 30 days in the Queens County jail. But she lived to see her fight taken up by the very forces that once opposed her — the church, the state and men themselves. Two years ago Mrs. Sanger passed away in a nursing home in Tuczon, Ariz., at age 82.

As to sex education in the schools, sons David and Michael couldn't care less. They learn at home. When they ask questions, mom and dad both know how to tell it like it is. No stuttering, no stammering.

Isn't it nice having the Sayles as our neighbors.

Monnya Schaff

'Woman Develops Varied Talents to Advantage

Everyone, they say, has talent of some kind or other. Only some can't be bothered to develop it. And end up with nothing. Today you'll learn about a neighbor whom nature endowed generously and who did bother. So that now you could really call her a Woman Who Does Everything. Or almost everything.

Meet Monnya Schaff, piano teacher, artist, non-fiction writer par excellence. Husband Jay Schaff is president of the eastern division of the National Power Rodding Corporation in Cannonsburg. Monnya received her Bachelor of Music degree from Northwestern University in Chicago, her home town.

Now she teaches piano at the Chatham Laboratory School of Music. She also taught at Tech (now Carnegie-Mellon) for four years. And at the Y-IKC for about the same time.

Her article "Teaching Big Fingers to Play" was accepted and published in Clavier Magazine — a professional journal for pianists and organists. And she got a nice check for it too. When you read her article and if you're an oldster, you immediately want to up and take lessons, she makes it seem so easy.

How did Monnya and Jay meet? In a very ho-hum way — introduced by a cousin. Their's wasn't even a June wedding. They married in March. But their married life has been interesting, exciting and fun.

Their daughter Pamela is 13 and goes to Ellis School. She's president of the Student Council Middle School. And currently is tutoring children in the Action Housing Program. Elizabeth is eight and attends Wightman School. And now listen to this. The Schaffs adopted Billie, a little Korean boy when he was five. He flew in from Korea through the Pearl Buck Adoption Agency known as Welcome House. And got a joyous welcome at the Schaff house. Now he's nine and a real charmer if there ever was one. He too goes to Wightman.

Last year Federal Judge Sorg made him a naturalized American citizen. He's now an honor student at the Beth Shalom Hebrew School. And one of the Pittsburgh Symphony musicians promised to play at Billie's Bar Mitzvah — for FREE.

The Schaff household is kept spic and span by their capable housekeeper Rosalie Robertson. She's a mother of two children of her own and three foster youngsters. Others in the Schaff household who act as if they own the place are two interesting cats. The big one is named Chaim Shalom and insists on having chicken soup on Friday evenings. Should you ask him how to settle the Mid Eastern problems you get no answer. He just sits and purrs. So does his small side-kick, Fuzzy.

Monnya is also an artist as said before. For her entry "Girl Reading" she received a one-year membership in the Associated Artist and $25 from Universal Art Academy as "the most creative painting." At the 7th Pennational Artists Annual she took second prize for "Worried Man." Another of her lovely work is named "Father and Child."

Our neighbor also sews, does quilting and crocheting. And is the best cook ever. Especially French and Jewish menus. Husband Jay is finding it hard to reduce.

During the school year Monnya works four afternoons at Chatham. On her day off, does she recline on a chaise reading "Lady Chatterley's Lover" with a box of bon-bons at her side? Of course not. She works as a volunteer at the Montefiore Hospital. All this and pretty too.

Monnya Schaff could also be called a Woman Who Has Everything. Everything worth-while, that is.

Honestly, ours is the luckiest neighborhood.

Gladys Schmidt
Cecil B. DeMille Got an Earful!

Now that you're rid of that sprig-has-cub cold and the Pirates have been winning like a house-on-fire, it's a good day to learn about a fabulous neighbor. She's none other than Gladys Schmidt, author of the world-famous book "David the King."

Published in 1946 it has sold over a million copies and has been translated into 10 languages including Hebrew. In private life she's the wife of Simon Goldfield, a manager at the Pittsburgh Housing Authority. Literary, himself, he's her adviser, best critic and edits all her works. The publishers marvel when she sensed in her manuscripts at how little "changing" they need do.

From the royalties of "David" — and they're still rolling in — she purchased their beautiful 10-room home at 5840 Wilkins Ave. And listen to this. Their right-hand neighbor is the Tree of Life Synagogue. Surrounded with neatly trimmed hedges, a carpet of grass, and young trees bursting with spring greenery its refreshment to the eyes.

Inside it's comfort to the spirit. Arranged with books, artistic pictures and furnished in the best of taste, you simply want to sit down and relax. And not leave.

The Goldfields shared their home with dad and mom Schmidt for many years. Also an aunt for a time. And sister Dorothy Schmidt lived with them for a while too until her recent death. Their adopted niece Betty Schmidt was a member of the family till she up and married and moved to Akron.

Their home is kept spic and span by Moena Coffy, the best housekeeper you ever met. And the best cook, too. Hand her a recipe from any cookbook or magazine and in a twinkling it's done. Occasionally you'll see the Goldfields in the supermarket pushing a cart just like ordinary folks.

Another member of the house-hold is Toffy, an unpedigreed yellow furry cat, age 5. He's never written poetry. Not even a book. But he's master of all he surveys. Currently he's going steady with a neighborhood furred beauty.

Born and bred in our city, Gladys says she comes from "plain working people." She met Si during Schenley High School days, graduating a year later than he. He had been senior editor of the Journal and she was the best-known poetess. With a name like Schmidt he pictured her as short, plump, blonde with rosy cheeks.

Instead he was pleasantly surprised to find her tall, gracefully slim, with dark hair and eyes. It was love at first sight. They started dating and graduated Pitt together.

Marriage? It was during those depression days. And even though potatoes and tomatoes were cheaper, it was out of the question.

However, in 1937, they finally made it as Mr. and Mrs. After a three-year stay in New York City, each trying to find permanent work, they got homesick for dear old Pittsburgh and came back.

Her first book, "Gates of Aulis", published in 1942 received excellent critical reception but its circulation was small. She has completed eight novels altogether. Two of them — "Confessors of the Name" and "Rembrant" — were choices of the Literary Guild. After "David" was published and acclaimed, she received a phone call from Cecil B. DeMille from Hollywood. Would she write for "Samson & Delilah" and several other movies?

Husband Si gave him an earful by replying: "She doesn't go in for that long-hair stuff."

Our famous neighbor is now full-time professor of English at Tech. And manages to do her writing catch-as-catch can. She's now working on poems and long short-stories. Already she has a publisher who will take both these works to be published in '68 and '69.

And that's not all. Because Gladys used to want to be a painter she now is interested in art. She does embroidery with crewel wool, doing her own designs. She's made 40 beautiful tablecloths, 12 artistic pillows and 20 sets of interesting place mats. She and Si enjoy the theater and symphonies. But love their home most. Constantly they have interesting dinner guests — and as constantly are invited out.

Travel? Who needs it? Si says: "Why suffer the inconveniences of travel when you have everything so pleasant at home." And you know? He could be right.

Dr. Kurt Schreiber
New Neighbor Heads School Department

The long hot summer has ended. The autumn leaves are turning a golden brown, yellow, red. And our neighborhood is filled with many interesting personalities.

How about getting to know one in particular? Meet Dr. Kurt Schreiber, a neighbor at Wightman St. Until recently the Schreibers lived in Greenfield's Loretta Street. Dr. Schreiber is head of the Chemistry Department at our famous down-town University — Duquesne.

He was born in Vienna, Austria, and even as a youngster, was fascinated by chemistry. At 16, once his family was settled in New York City, he began studying chemistry at Stuyvesant High and from there went to City College from where he was graduated with a Bachelor of Science degree in 1944.

During World Warr II, Kurt served Uncle Sam's Criminal Investigation Division in France and Germany for two years. After an honorable discharge he continued his studies in Columbia University where, in 1949 he received his Ph.D. Then on to the University of California in Los Angeles as a post doctoral fellow.

There, guess what happened? The love bug hit him. Lillian Berger had already graduated and was an elementary school teacher in L.A. And, like most schoolmarms, came back to the University for additional studies. They met at the West Los Angeles Synagogue Center. The center was starting a Youth Group in which both were interested.

As it turned out, the Group never got off the ground, but three marriages did. Kurt and Lillian among them — 15 years ago. For their honeymoon they came to Pittsburgh where the young groom got his job at Duquesne. Starting as an assistant professor of Chemistry, he's now a full professor.

The Schreibers have been blessed with three lively interesting children. Emanuel, 12, has just started at Allderdice. And has begun model railroading. So who do you think is even more interested in it? His pop! Celia Anne is 10 and is going to Wightman. And ditto for Samuel, eight. From the former owners of their Wightman Street home they inherited another household cat who acts as if she still owns the place. And what's more, in the excitement of moving they forgot to ask the cat's name. So what's in a name? The kids will soon decide.

Dr. Schreiber is a member and on the board of the Shaare Torah Synagogue. Also of the Young Peoples Synagogue. He has just been elected chairman of the Pittsburgh section of the American Chemical Society and is a member of the Scientific Advisory Board of the RIDC (Regional Industrial Development Corp.) Our neighbor has been treasurer of the Josiah Cohen B'nai B'rith Lodge for nine years. And is past chairman of that organization's Hillel Advisory Board.

Lillian Schreiber, his lovely and interesting missus, has started teaching on the Mother's Day-Out program at our neighborhood Temple Sinai and the First Unitarian Church.

Recently, as you read in the papers, there was a Symposium at the Shaare Torah synagogue on the theme "The Vanishing Jew — a Myth or a Reality?" The moderator was the synagogue's learned Rabbi A. Poupko. On the panel were Dr. Morris A. Landes, Rabbi of Adath Jeshurun Congregation; Mrs. Esther Marine, former president of Hillel Academy Parent-Teacher Association. And you guessed it — Dr. Kurt Schreiber. Is the American Jew really vanishing, or is it just a myth? The discussion was spirited, thought-provoking, and stirred the imagination. Our neighbor, being by nature an optimist, feels it's definitely a myth. While there always will be losses through assimilation, he thinks the gains will be many and will offset what is lost.

Let's wish the Schreibers the best of everything in their new home. As to their secondhand cat, may she purr happily throughout all her nine lives.

Cantor Moishe Schulhof
Young Cantor Comes Of Age

Youth — it's wonderful. Especially if the young man in question lives in our neighborhood and has a golden tenor voice. Shake hands with Rev. Moishe Schulhof, youthful cantor who came here less than a year ago — April 1st, to be exact. And lives in an Asbury Place duplex. Our neighbor became a cantor at age 19 — probably the youngest in America. Even now he's scarcely 22.

Born in New York City and when a little tike of 3 his knowledgeable grandma recognized his singing talent. And brought him to a choir-leader. There he was trained and several years later taken into the Choir. A business woman herself in grandpa's clothing store, she'd leave early each day and take the youngster for rehearsal. If not for "bobba" he says — no cantor. Grandma still lives in New York and now can proudly say to all and sundry: "See? What did I tell you!"

If you were to stop in at the Shaare Torah synagogue on a Friday evening or early Saturday morning during Sabbath services and lend an ear you'd agree that grandma knew best.

Young Schulhof attended New York's Mirer Yeshiva high school during the day and evenings went to the Brooklyn Conservatory of Music. After graduating he continued on to Brooklyn College, majoring in Biology and Liberal Arts. Later he graduated from the Beth Joseph Rabbinical Seminary. In addition he took private voice lessons and received his cantorial training from the world's leading cantor — David Kusevitsky. He got his cantor's diploma from the Jewish Minister — Cantors Ass'n in New York. Currently he's studying voice with Beatrice Krebs of Carnegie-Mellon — privately at her home.

For his first summer vacation young Schulhof took a trip to Israel. This was shortly after the Six-day War. Although the skies were cleared of all planes, who do you think zeroed in and started shooting? Cupid! With his arrows.

So what happened? The young bachelor met beautiful Ruchana Ressler, an Israeli native. And his bachelor days were numbered. Before he left they become engaged. During their separation air-mail letters came and went back and forth thick and fast. December 1967 the man-in-love returned to Israel and claimed Ruchana as his bride. The newlyweds came to New York, setting up housekeeping in the husband's former bachelors quarters — a room and kitchen privileges in a large home owned by an elderly gentleman. The youthful cantor has given a number of concerts in New York. Also while in Israel. The president of a Tel-Aviv synagogue wrote him: "Your songs and renditions thrilled your listeners. Your talent assures a great future for you. We hope to hear your voice ring again in the Land of Israel".

At the Shaare Torah, in addition to his cantorial duties Schulhof teaches in the synagogue's Hebrew School. And officiates at weddings, bar mitzvahs and — sad to say — at funerals. He's constantly studying and preparing. Currently he's working on a record with the Chassidic Choir of beautiful songs composed by Rabbi Abba Leifer, known as the "Pittsburgher Rabbi." The record will come out in April.

Our neighbor's parents and 5-year-old baby sister live in New York City. And grandma too — remember?

The learned and dedicated spirtual leader of Shaare Torah, Rev. Dr. Bernard A. Poupko has been of invaluable help to the young cantor, especially in the intricacies of dealing with the congregation. He has learned a great deal from the brilliant Rabbi, he tells you.

His young wife Ruchana teaches Art at Hillel Academy having an art teacher's degree from Israel's Teachers Seminary. As to cooking, she's the best ever, he says — especially Hungarian style. And now Guess Who's Coming to Dinner? The STORK. In March, they hope.

Let's wish our youthful neighbors good health and good luck. And to show off a little, we'll say it in Hebrew: "Mazel Tov" and "L'chaim."

Mr. & Mrs. Shlomo Segev
Social Welfare Work Objective of 'Sabra'

Anyone who says there are no more interesting personalities in our neighborhood should be asked to leave town. Actually the surface has hardly been scratched. So today, you'll learn about another outstanding fellow. And where do you think he's from? From Israel.

Say "shalom" to Mr. Shlomo Segev from Jerusalem, our neighbor at Monitor St. He's a third-generation Sabra.

Sabra? Well, say you were born in the U.S. That makes you a Yankee. In Israel you're a Sabra. And sabra in Hebrew means cactus — the popular plant that flourishes profusely in the desert areas of Israel. A cactus, as you may know, is tough on the outside yet soft inside. That describes the Israelis.

Our neighbor, 37, came here July of last year to complete social work studies in community organization. This is a vital project in Israel because of the constant inflow of immigrants from many countries. Often from ghettos, their ethnic backgraounds are varied and unique. Assimilating them into Israel's economic and cultural life requires masterful know-how and experience.

Segev had already completed studies in the social work school connected with Jerusalem's Hebrew University. On the undergraduate level, that is. They have no graduate school. Three years ago he was in Cleveland attending the international program for youth leaders and social work. Part of the program meant studying in the University of Chicago. He lived there for three weeks with various American families to better acquaint himself with our way of life.

He met a friend in high position and asked him where is the best school to study community organization. The friend suggested the University of Pittsburgh. And that's where Shlomo is now studying. He came here on a two-year fellowship from the National Council of Jewish Women. These dedicated ladies choose carefully and well. The Council pays his tuition and maintenance. Also round-trip transportation.

Our neighbor will complete his studies the end of June next year. Then he will work in Israel's Ministry of Social Welfare, teaching and preparing new recruits to work with the immigrants.

Mr. Segev is dark, strong, handsome. He soldiered in Israel's War of Independence from 1948 to 1950 — where boys were turned into men. And again in the Sinai Campaign in 1956. When the "6-days-in-June" broke out, he was all ready to fly there to serve his country. But others beat him to it. Transportation was unavailable because the priorities had been used. up.

Shlomo's lovely wife is called Yocheved. She too served in the Israeli army as a teacher. Here she will be teaching in the College of Hebrew Studies. After both were honorably discharged they became across-the street neighbors in Tiberius, Dating was uncomplicated. He simply crossed the street and there was Yocheved, waiting.

They married in 1960 and started housekeeping in Jerusalem. A few years later baby Eyal was born. Now he's 5 and has taken to English like a duck to water. The parents speak to him in Hebrew. He answers in English. Baby Amit is 2. He understands both languages but responds in a language of his own. When dad and mom attended the thrilling Israeli Philharmonic Symphony concert recently, the youngsters spent a pleasant evening at home — with a babysitter.

What about the Middle East situation? James Michener, author of "The Source" and "Hawaii" recently wrote an article titled: "Israel — Too Young to Die." The Segevs agree.

The Monitor Street house in which our neighbors live has been sold and they must move in September. But you may be sure they'll continue living in our neighborhood. They like it here. And we like them as neighbors. We wish them well.

Janet Shafer

Glamorous Spanish Dancer

The glamorous Maria-Lolita is none other than unpretentious Janet Sahfer — tall, graceful, raven-haired — living with her mother on Beechwood Blvd.

Janet was blest with not just one, but two, talents — music and the love for dancing. This created a problem: which to take up seriously as a career. Her final choice, since they are so closely related, was a natural one. She decided to study both.

Shortly before she received her Bachelor of Fine Arts degree in music from Carnegie Tech, Janet took up modern interpretive dancing. Pittsburgh's Genvieve Jones was her first teacher. She learned fast and soon was in New York continuing with Martha Graham and five other prominent teachers. Then on to classical ballet under Linda Mady and Charles Dickson of the Ballet Theatre.

By that time she knew her final goal: Spanish dancing. With her exotic looks she was a natural for it. She studied under the expert guidance of Seville and also Cansino — the latter Rita Hayworth's uncle, no less!

Now Janet gives private lessons in piano and dancing. She has performed for films and TV, doing Spanish solos on WQED a number of times. She danced and directed dancing, for a Tech play "Figaro's Marriage." In 1944 Janet danced in Charles Gaynor's Playhouse musical "After Hours." She also acted in "The Jest" all the same theatre. And she has been in a number of summer stock and Little Lake theatre plays. Summers and week-ends she entertains with Spanish solo dancing, emphasizing heel work rhythm with castanets.

Since theatrical people often have unusual experiences, here's what once happened to Janet:

She had been booked to perform at a Cleveland night club. When she arrived she learned, to her amazement, that the other four acts preceding hers were to be performed by ladies sans clothes. In other words, by strippers (you should pardon the expression). What to do! The manager, sensing problems, assured her she was to wear her Spanish outfit, and reminded her of the traditional "the show must go on."

While donning her colorful dress full of ruffles, ribbons and bows, she felt she had as much chance to make a hit as a snow-ball in you-know-where. But once on the stage, she gave her performance all she had. Her flowing dress swayed to the dizzy rhythm of her heels and clicking castanets. Much to her surprise, no one left during her act, and at the conclusion there was thunderous applause. She later overheard some gentleman remark: "You know too many naked girls become monotonous. That Lolita girl was like a breath of fresh air."

Janet left Cleveland with mixed emotions. But one thing is certain. The next time she'll know for sure, beforehand, who else will perform at the same place.

Now we are back in Pittsburgh. What about boy friends? Does she go steady? No answer. Just a mischievous smile. So it could be yes.

Maurice Shapiro
Modest Neighbor Instructor At Pitt

It's simply fantastic the interesting personalities who add luster to our neighborhood. Take for instance Maurice Shapiro of Forbes Avenue and his lively family. Mr. Shapiro teaches Environmental Health Engineering at Pitt in its Graduate School of Public Health. Ever since 1951. The School, started in 1949 is known internationally. Its students come not only from every part of our country but from around the world as well.

Let's learn a little about this tall, dark, nice-looking neighbor with a modest personality that wins you over in a minute. Maurice Shapiro was born in Denver. When he reached the ripe age of two, the family moved to Palestine (now Israel of course.) His dad was a physician member of the first Hadassah mission there. They lived alternately in Jerusalem and Haifa for 15 years. His mother Henrietta, now 80 years young, still lives in Israel. In Ashqelon, to be exact. And although crippled up with arthritis, she teaches English to a group of eager young Israelis. They come to her apartment for lessons. And what's more — paints too. Sister Ruth also remained there. She's an experienced and capable social worker.

With a background of knowledge gained in Israel, Maurice returned to the States for further education. He graduated Johns Hopkins University in Baltimore in Engineering and Biology. And received graduate education at the University of California in Berkeley. Then came World War II. Young Shapiro joined the U.S. Public Health Service and was stationed in Georgia and Florida. Later he was sent overseas to work with UNRRA in Egypt, Italy and Yugoslavia.

But long before going overseas, guess what happened? He fell in love. In the nation's Capital, of all places. With beautiful Ann Klakovich. Her parents had come from Yugoslavia but she was born in the U.S. During the same War Anne went to Yugoslavia to work as a civilian employee for UNRRA. And when soldier Shapiro arrived there, before you could say Jack Robinson he looked her up. More than likely she had made sure he had her address. They became engaged on VE Day (Victory in Europe). And were married on VJ Day (when Japan surrendered.) In the romantic Italian city of Naples. Baby Carla was born in Belgrade.

Carla, now 20 goes to Tech in the Fine Arts department. And listen to this. Now there are five more lively children in the Shapiro household. Mark is 16, Deborah 15, Joel 13, David 12, All go to Allerdice. Baby Lisa is 10 and attends Wightman School.

Mr. Shapiro has been on the board of the American Technion Society for many years. Wife Anne is a folk singer and entertains here, there everywhere. And strums her guitar as she sings.

Neighbor Shapiro has made trips to Israel since his youth. The summer of 1965 he and his entire family lived in Haifa a whole year. He was visiting professor in the Civil Engineering faculty of Technion. Their apartment on Mount Carmel overlooked the Mediterranean. At night Haifa is called "the Jewel of the Middle East" and the view from Mount Carmel is breath-taking. The children went to school there and by now are expert in the Hebrew language. Mom Shapiro substantially added to her folk-song repertoire with beautiful Israeli songs. She also did the programs at a Kibbutz near the Jordanian border.

The Shapiro home is large, with 7 bedrooms. How does Mrs. Shapiro manage the housekeeping with a maid only once a week? It's easy if you have a system and the kids get a kick out of helping. The chores are equally divided among the six of them, and rotate from week to week to prevent boredom. Each makes his own bed. Mark sets the table. David clears it. Joel washes the dishes in the machine. Lisa sweeps up the floor. Debbie has a permanent chore — ironing. Dad's job is permanent too. He washes the car — with the boys supervising.

Mothers — with no such system and cooperation, are you a little jealous mebbe?

Bob, Jim & Jules Sheer
Brothers Sing For Love Of Music

With all the moaning and groaning you hear about today's youth, it's just great to tell you about three young brothers who deserve much praise. Say hi to Bob, Jim and Jules Sheer — 23, 21 and 18, respectively. Their dad and mom are Samuel and Leah Sheer, our neighbors at Rosemoor St. Mr. Sheer is Supervisor in our downtown P.O. No other children. Just these music-loving, easy-to-look-at likeable guys. Bob is in Pitt's Graduate School of Public Health. Jim is a senior there and Jules a freshman. All sing. Bob is a tenor. The other two baritones. The youngest also plays the guitar. They had been singing around the house for years — even in the bath-tub but separately, they tell you.

Bob and Jim joined the University of Pittsburgh Men's Glee Club (45 members) in 1967. Jules followed last September. They took part in the Club's 81st Annual Winter Concert last Dec. 4 at Carnegie Music Hall. Last year Bob was its v.p. And who do you think is currently president? Jim. (Please remember which is who).

The Club travels by chartered bus to perform at Colleges in Boston, Phila., Washington, N.Y.C. Also at conventions. Most of the week they keep their noses close to their books at Pitt. Monday, Wednesday and Friday, 4 to 5:30 they have Glee rehearsals. And can hardly wait, they're so enthusiastic. From September to April they've given about 25 concerts. They sang at the Miss Pennsylvania Beauty Pageant in Hershey, which was televised all over the State. The popular TV star John Reilly, after hearing them, arranged for their coming to Altoona for a taping on his Show. Summers the boys keep fit playing football in the park. But not barefoot.

And now get a load of this. Only Jules lives at home. And can hardly wait until he's 21 so he can follow in the footsteps of his brothers. And is earning and saving his money by working Sundays and summers at Bagel-Land down Murray Ave. You see, Bob and Jim each have separate Kitchenette apts. (with separate room-mates) close to the University. Not owning even a Volkswagen they find it cheaper and timesaving than constantly paying bus fares coming and going, days and evenings for all the activities centering around Pitt. Their parents, though traditional in their basic values and beliefs, agree. They think it's good training for the boys' future years to learn getting along with others. And "make do" on their own earnings. Of course, pop pitches in when occasion warrants.

The boys fix their own breakfasts. Lunches are mostly at the Student Union Schenley Cafeteria. Dinners? They're trying, and learning. But mom's cooking is best. They come home at every opportunity, not only to eat well but to enjoy the family.

Their landlords say "No Cats". But girls? Not barred. Girls may visit and stay as late as they want and are wanted. The responsibility is their own. But with school and Glee Club work there's not much time for hanky-panky. The guys date, of course, and Jim (the middle one) goes steady. (A lovely Cleveland girl from Ohio University).

Bob also sings professionally (gets paid, that is) at two churches. One Catholic, another Presbyterian. And he a Jewish boy! Bob and Jules also sing in a Folk Group of the Glee Club. Some of their Glee Club songs are: "By the Time I Get to Phoenix"; selections from "Porgy & Bess"; "Who Will Buy?" from OLIVER. Plus numbers by Bach and other classical songs. The Club's Folk Group sang on KDKA-TV last Sunday P.M. Did you tune in? They were tops.

And now for the piece de resistance. None of the Sheers smoke. Never did, don't now and don't expect to start. And don't have the agony of trying to kick the habit. How about that?

Honestly, telling you about the Sheer boys is sheer joy.

Mrs. Samuel (Connie) Sherman
Small Town Girl Makes Good in Beauty, Music

Doctors — bless 'em — aren't supposed to get publicity. Medical ethics, you know. But it doesn't say we must ignore their wives — especially if they are beautiful and talented. So today you'll learn about Connie Sherman, wife of Dr. Samuel Sherman, chief of rehabilitation medicine at Montefiore Hospital. The Shermans have been our neighbors at Beacon St., for seven years.

The former Constance Sameth was born in Welch, W. Va. Her dad was a pioneer physician there. She's a small-town girl who made good.

Natural beauty, love of music plus an atmosphere of a music-loving family was her fortunate beginning. Her three brothers played musical instruments. At an early age Connie was performing before civic groups in her home town. She sang in high school operettas and had her own radio program while in college. Later the curvacious red-head went to New York City. There she studied voice, dramatics and the piano. Meantime doing modeling for Saks-Fifth Avenue.

And now get a load of this. New York was sponsoring a Beauty Contest for "Miss Subway of NYC." At the behest of a Powers scout Connie entered the contest. And came out the winner! The judge was the famous John Robert Powers himself. Soon her picture, taken by well-known photographer Victor Keppler appeared on all New York subways and other public transportations. Later she became a commercial photographer's model. Her picture headed ads in all leading magazines — on coffee, feminine apparel and ice-cream even.

And now lend an ear. Connie's mother became a patient in a New York hospital. Young Dr. Sherman, just out of WW 2 military service, was visiting the various hospitals. For study before returning to his practice in our city. When he chanced to see a beautiful red-head go into someone's room, he did what any smart fella would do. He paid a visit to the patient. Her mom.

An introduction followed. For a year he was kept busy in his practice here, and flying to NYC to visit you-know-who (or whom) Until the rabbi of New York's Temple Emanuel made them Dr. and Mrs. They started housekeeping near his office in Oakland. When son Jeffrey was born they moved to South Hills, and became members of the newly-built Temple.

In no time Connie Sherman became choir director and soloist there. Then for two years sang with the Downtown Chorable and later joined the Mendelsohn Choir and appeared in concerts with them. All the while studying with Ralph Lewando for 10 years.

She then sang the leading role in Pittsburgh Savoyard's production of "Pinafore". She also studied at our Playhouse for three years in its Opera Workshop directed by maestro Richard Karp. Later she became a regular performer in the Pittsburgh Opera for nine years. Thus she had the opportunity of meeting all the Met stars who came here for the various Operas and they became good friends. Like for instance Richard Tucker and Jan Peerce to name a few. However, her favorite stage-door Johnnie was none other than husband Sam.

Our neighbor was asked to entertain in Boston at the International Convention of the American Congress of Physical Medicine & Rehabilitation. She made a hit and next summer was again invited to sing for them in Philly. Last summer she once more performed for them in San Francisco.

Jeffrey is now 18 — a red-head like his mom. He graduated from Penn Hall Academy. He collects records — modern and classical. Patricia is 15 and goes to Allderdice. She plays the violin in the All-City Junior Orchestra. Also plays the piano.

Aside from Mrs. Sherman's professional performances at Sisterhood affairs, Hadassah and Bickur Cholim Donors, Sq. Hill Chapter of Eastern Star, she often performs voluntarily. She has charmed the dear hearts and gentle people of the Jewish Home for the Aged, the Anathan House and others. She appeared in the 1966 Variety Club telethon. February 19 she will be soprano soloist in the original Cantata composed and directed by Cantor Taube at Beth Shalom Synagogue. It will be shown on TV this month.

All this and more. Connie used her interior decorating skill to make her home lovely to look at and live in. And she even designs her stage clothes.

The combination of the two "M's" — Medicine and Music — has enriched the lives of the Sherman household.

Dr. Ailon Shiloh

Professor Writes Book on Mid-East

Today you'll learn about a fabulous neighbor. Dr. Ailon Shiloh of Beacon St. Dr. Shiloh is Associate Professor Anthropology in our University of Pittsburgh Graduate School of Public Health. Anthropology, in case you don't know, is the study of the physical and cultural attributes of man. It goes into the characteristics of man in relation to his origin, environment and social aspects. And because it includes peoples of the entire world the subject is deep and boundless. Dr. Shiloh is also Executive Secretary of the International Health Program. Thus, his comments on a recent TV panel discussion of "Promiscuity and the Pill" ring true and are worth noting.

But first let's learn a little about our professor's educational background and vast experience. Born in Toledo, Ohio., young Shiloh graduated high school. And during WW 2 joined the U.S. Marines in the Pacific — in Guam and Iwo Jima. Also in China. For 3½ years. After an honorable discharge he earned his B.A. degree in the University of Mexico where he worked with the Navajo Indians.

His M.A. degree he received from the University of Michigan in 1950. Then Uncle Sam sent him to Israel to do research in Anthropology. Wanting to learn Hebrew in-a-hurry he enrolled in the "Ulpan" course which takes just three months. In his class was another English-speaking student. A girl, Cynthia Amais — beautiful, idealistic, religious. And smart, too, with a B.A. degree in Psychology from London University. She was working with disturbed children in Israel's Youth Aliyah. Instead of waiting until he could do so in Hebrew, he hurried his marriage proposal in Yankee English. And Cynthia accepted in her rain-in-Spain brogue.

Then the man-in-love was discharged so he could work for the Israeli government. In Archeology, excavating the marble Roman statues in Caeseria. Ailon and Cynthia married in 1952 and lived for 15 years in a lovely old house in Jerusalem. Two years after marriage the young husband was transferred to the Hebrew University Hadassah School of Medicine. To teach Medical Anthropology (health problems) to other cultures and peoples who knew of medicine only through the Evil Eye and the Evil Spirit. After 11 years HMO sent him to Africa to help develop a Leprosy Program in Nigeria. In 1965 our Government asked him to do a study for them in a V.A. Mental Hospital in Chicago for a year. Then Pitt University called him here.

Our brilliant professor just completed a book "Peoples & Cultures of the Middle East" (Random House) out this fall. Currently he is involved in the problems of birth control and changing sex behavior presented at a conference in N.Y. Here are his findings: 1.) Today's youth is not necessarily more promiscuous than were parents, but rather more open and free in discussing it. Particularly as a result of what is seen on TV, in movies and on the bookshelves. 2) Without doubt the private and safe Pill is leading to apparently early and wide-spread sex relations. 3.) Unfortunately one by-product of this behavior is the increased incidence of V.D. (Neighbors, teach this diligently unto your children).

And speaking of children, our neighbors are the parents of three lively and interesting ones: Michael, 12½ was born in Jerusalem. He goes to Hillel Academy. Fascinated by electronics he has built a model train and a small radio. Gabriel, nine, is London-born. He also goes to Hillel. An expert in Israeli football (soccer) he has no one to play it with. Baby Dina, all of three was also born in Jerusalem. Here she attends the Y-IKC kindergarten. As to Anthropology, the Pill and other such nonsense, she couldn't care less. Captain Kangaroo, Popeye and the commericals are much more fun. Their capable and interesting Mom concentrates mostly on them and dad. Later, when the kids are on their own she, of course, will make further use of her Psychology know-how.

Steven Sieverts
Displays Capacity

When a little fella of 4 migrates with his folks to America from Germany and turns out just great, it's that country's loss and our gain. Especially when he's our neighbor. Say hi to Steven Sieverts of Northumberland St. Mr. Sieverts for the past 4 years has been Executive Director of the Hospital Planning Assn. of Allegheny County.

The Assn. is basically trying to make the health-care system more effective by improving its services, facilities and eliminating waste. Thirty hospitals are involved, each with different ideas yet compromising for over-all improvement. Steven says his work is exciting and he loves it. When you love your work you have it made. But you need a vast educational background, experience and know-how to "make it." Our neighbor has all these aplenty. So let's learn a little about him, starting 'way back.

Steve's dad, in the tea business in Frankfurt, Germany committed what was then considered a cardinal sin: He had married a Jewess! With prophetic foresight he brought his loved ones to the U.S., settling in Milwaukee. In 1938. Soon schooling became the lad's way of life. By 1956 he earned his A.B. in Political Science from Haverford and 1961 an M.S. in Hospital Administration from Columbia. His faculty appointments include George Washington U., Cornell and Pitt's Graduate School of Public Health.

Two years he was in the U.S. Army Medical Service. His professional employments comprise Phila. Presbyterian Hospital, Hunterdon Medical Center and National Blue Cross Assn. His State and National memberships read like a Who's Who. Locally he belongs to the American Civil Liberteries, on the board of Pgh. Chamber Music Society, Press Club, Zoological Assn. and World Federalists, USA. And he's only 38.

And now let's snoop a little into Steven's personal life. As you know, Haverford College is only a mile from Bryn Mawr — where the girls are. In his old jalopy the handsome students often drove there. One enchanted evening, taking out a book from the library, a Bryn-Mawrette was returning hers. With Cupid buzzing around, Steve invited her to dinner. In 1957 they became Mr. & Mrs., starting housekeeping in Minnesota. The young bride was lovely Nancy Sue Altman and like Steve's mother — Jewish. She's a member of the National Council of Jewish Women.

The Sieverts have two interesting children. Rachel, 12 goes to Ellis School. John, age 5 attends Linden. Some time ago they added a playful kitten to their household, named Peter. But guess what? Now fully mature, Peter gave birth and is a mama! To avoid future embarrassment they gave the furry baby a non-gender name — Pip. Dad has a flair for cooking. Ordinarily Nancy does it. But when company's coming pop takes over. His food? Those who try it like it.

His parents from Ithaca came for Thanksgiving and heartily agree. But Steve's greatest enjoyment is choral singing. He's a member of a fine choir and the Pgh. Oratorio Society. His lovely missus, a Bryn Mawr alumna visits high schools throughout Allegheny County in mid-term and interviews them for her alma mater. Often the girls see her after sending in their applications, hoping to make it to the College. In the past 5 years more than 50 of those interviewed were admitted.

Mrs. Sieverts helped organize the Bryn Mawr-Vassar College Book Store. Any used books in your attic, cellar, behind the piano, under the bed? Call the Book Store — 687-3433.

Our community wishes this beautiful family the best of everything now and in the years ahead.

Rabbi Phillip Sigal

Both Able And Enthusiastic

When you're enthusiastic about your challenging work, you not only do a great job, but are an inspiration to countless others. That's the type of personality you'll learn about today. He's Rabbi Phillip Sigal, our Wightman Street neighbor. Rabbi Sigal is the new director of the B'nai B'rith Hillel Foundation — a Jewish Campus Ministry for five local universities — Carnegie-Mellon, Pitt, Duquesne, Point Park and Chatham.

B'nai B'rith, among other things means Brotherhood. And Hillel is the revered name of a first century Hebrew scholar, one of the originators of the Talmud. Hillel programs serve the needs of Jewish students on campus — religious, social, cultural, counseling. It's challenging and exciting, because each campus is distinctive. Rabbi Sigal has hired two assistants who are liaisons with the students and spend much of their time on campus. And guess what? One is a gal!

Surprisingly, many students of other faiths want to become Jewish. They are welcomed but not solicited. If they show a sincere desire for the Jewish faith, they must undergo an intensive study program in Judaism.

What does it take to head a program for creative Jewish living? A highly-skilled mind; a thorough educational background; provocative, challenging ideas, and an understanding of youth. Our neighbor has all these and much more.

Born in Toronto, after public school young Sigal continued at Yeshiva University in New York. Then he was off to the University of Toronto; Columbia University where he received his M.A. in History, and the Jewish Theological Seminary, from which he earned his M.H.L. From 1954-64, he served as a spiritual leader of Congregation Beth Abraham in Bridgeton, New Jersey. There he founded the Cumberland County Guidance Center, and organized a Human Relations Committee, sponsored by the National Conference of Christians and Jews.

Since 1955 Rabbi Sigal occupied the pulpit of Temple B'nai Zion, Bloomfield, New Jersey. Then he served as a town commissioner on the Commission of Civil Rights, and as its chairman since 1969. He served on the Continuing Conference of Conservative Ideology of the Rabbinical Assembly. An active member of the Committee of Jewish Law and Standards, he was its secretary since 1968. We could go on and on but space is limited.

Getting back to Hillel campus programs, there are Sunday brunches, a dining-club of 34 members serving kosher food for those who prefer it. Wednesday luncheon sessions are called "Cafe Tel-Aviv." Coffee and cookies are available as students socialize. Monthly Saturday night socials are held for graduates and under-grads. The Director belongs to the Chaplain Ass'n at Pitt and CMU, composed of ministers, priests and one rabbi — himself. They exchanged ideas and inter-faith fellowship.

Hillel conducts Sabbath and High Holy Day Services. It invites speakers to lecture and asks faculty members to lead discussions. Rabbi Sigal also has classes in Talmud, Jewish Ethics, Hebrew and Yiddish, and Hillel sponsors a 12-unit course in Hebrew at CMU, It has a fine Judaica library, and Sigal himself has written a book., "New Dimensions in Judaism", as well as a number of Responsa in Jewish Law for the Rabbinical Assembly.

An all-out planner, he's arranging a major program for students, faculty and community leaders on the subject of family-planning and the whole spectre of population-control. He has even started a Hillel student newspaper in English.

Our neighbor's lovely wife is the former Lillian Fisher from the city where a Tree Grows — Brooklyn. She's a secondary English teacher. Their two interesting daughters, Sharon and Sabrina, 17 and 15 respectively, go to Allderdice. And you'll never guess what their dad's hobby is — coin-collecting, of all things!

Our community wishes the Sigals compliments of the season, including the best New Year's ever.

Mrs. Rita Rosini Sil Vestri
Career No Problem For Wife-Doctor

By the time brilliant lawyer Silvestri Silvestri, our neighbor at Beechwood Blvd. became judge of the Common Pleas Court, you naturally heard much about him. Today you'll learn about his interesting family — and particularly his lovely missus, the former Rita Rosini. Rita is an M.D. specializing in Pediatrics. You know, guiding mothers how best to keep their babies healthy — after they've been delivered. In her office in nearby Munhall she is best known by her maiden name — Dr. Rita Rosini. In private life she's Mrs. Silvestri Silvestri. And proud of it.

Rita and Sil were both born in Charleroi, delivered by the same doctor — just two days apart. Are you curious (yellow) to know how come Judge Silvestri's first name is exactly like his last? Let Rita tell it like she thinks it was. When the attending physician made out the boy's birth certificate he must have had a little too much bubbly. And saw double. So that's how the double name Silvestri Silvestri was registered. Believe it or not.

Throughout high school in Charleroi, although they graduated together, Rita and Silvestri never dated each other. She had her mind on Medicine and left for Pre-med at Penn State University. He thought he wanted to take up Pharmacy and went to Pitt. Then along came WW 2 and the would-be pharmacist joined Uncle Sam's air force. Rita interned in the West Penn hospital and later went for her residency in San Francisco. But she didn't leave her heart there. By the time she returned home Silvestri had been honorably discharged and changed to Law, earning his LLD at Pitt. Then opened a Downtown office in our city. Cupid must have followed both of them because when they met again in their home-town each had grown wiser with a new sense of values. So it was love at second sight. In 1947 they became Mr. and Mrs. and started housekeeping in our neighborhood, later moving right smack close to a synagogue on Beacon St. (Beth Shalom). And although they now live near a Catholic retreat, they still like bulkies and bagels and even kosher pickles. In fact, Judge Silvestri was recently made a member of the Poale Zedeck Men's Club. His acceptance speech was short and sweet. He simply rose, turned to Rita and proudly said: "Well, honey — we finally made it!"

Our neighbors are the proud parents of two interesting children. Jean Marie, 15 attends Winchester — Thurston. John Mark is 19 and goes to Indiana University, Bloomington, Ind.

Practicing medicine and being a good wife and mother was not easy when the kids were small. Getting and keeping good domestic help was difficult. That's why, she thinks, more women are not in private practice. Now, in their 4-bedroom split-level compact house things are kept in perfect order by their capable and loyal housekeeper Ardelia, affectionately called De. She's like one of the family. Others "in the family" are Rudolph and Holly who spend their days swimming around in their goldfish bowl.

Does our busy neighbor have any hobbies? Who has time? But she has taken time out to visit her folks in Florida, has held office as V.P. of the Steel Valley Business & Professional Women's Club, was a member of the Allegheny Medical Society and is currently a member of the Pediatric Society, the College Club of Pgh. and Secretary of the Homestead Hospital Medical staff. And finds time for some reading at home and to putter around straightening out closets and drawers. This way the judge can find his socks.

Of course other communities have numberless interesting neighbors. But in the parlance of teenagers, ours are the greatest.

Dr. Herbert A. Simon

Computer Aids Your Creativity

Winter is upon us but good, and brrr — it's cold outside. So it might be nice to give ourselves a warm-up into a most fascinating subject. The subject is not roses but computers. And the scientists, including a brilliant neighbor, are thoroughly engrossed and enthused. So who is our neighbor so smart with computers? Dr. Herbert A. Simon — that's who. Of Northumberland St.

Dr. Simon is a Richard King Mellon Professor of Computer Science and Psychology at CMU. His vast educational and professional background reads like a Who's Who. In which, by the way, he's listed. His honorary degrees from the University of Chicago, Yale, Case Institute of Technology and Lund University in Sweden are many. And the scientific Societies to which he belongs, the research books and papers he has authored are enough to make you dizzy. So let's snoop a little into his personal life.

Our neighbor was born in Milwaukee. And to this day, when occasion calls for a glass of beer, he chooses the brand that made his home town famous.

In 1937, then a handsome bachelor, young Simon shared an apartment with another fellow. Soon he met lovely Dorothea Pye from Chico, Calif. She was a secretary where he was studying. One enchanted evening he invited her to dinner and a play. Cost him "a young fortune" he recalls — "almost 5 dollars." But it paid off because six months later she moved into the apartment as his adoring bride. And the other fellow moved out.

Through the years many things happened, including three wonderful children. They are now grown and married. Kathy (Mrs. David Frank) lives in Cambridge, Mass. Peter resides in sunny L.A. Barbara (Mrs. Bruce Candioto) enjoys living in our city. There are 4 lively grandchildren. And a brownish cat named Cinnamon.

Before the Simon children were born their mom worked at various interesting jobs. Now she's employed in the LRDC (Learning Research & Development Center) at Pitt.

And now about Computers. Dr. Simon and his staff are interested in how people solve their problems and make decisions. They want to program a computer to do the same thing. Suppose a fellow decides which stocks to buy. In order to learn what thought processes he uses to make the decision, they programmed a computer to go through the same processes — to see if it would reach the same decision. It did! They've watched pupils studying Algebra. Then wrote a program to enable the computer to work out the problems. As another example — Contract Bridge. Suppose you give the computer the rules for bidding and playing the game. Say, the Goren system. You deal out a hand to 3 people and the 4th to Mr. Computer. By having the latter bid and play the hand, you find out the thinking process for improving your game.

But suppose you're somewhat on the stupid side and don't improve easily — and you trump his Ace? Your partner the Computer says not a word. In fact, he doesn't even raise an eyebrow.

Could a computer write plays like Shakespeare, compose like Beethoven and paint like Rembrandt? Dr. Simon believes human creativity can be analyzed and the steps involved in the creative process can be programmed onto a computer. Kind of scares you, doesn't it?

Be that as it may, we are proud of our brilliant neighbor and wish him and his co-scientists the best of luck now and in the years ahead.

Mrs. Edith W. Skinner
She's Unspoiled Despite Success

Our personality of the week is one of the country's best-known voice and speech teacher. She's none other than Edith W. Skinner, our neighbor at nearby Wightman St. In 1927 they asked her to come here as a faculty member of the then Carnegie Tech. For one year, they said. Now, 33 years later she's not only still here but was appointed Andrew Mellon Professor of Drama at Carnegie-Mellon for the current year. And last

December was honored in Drama by our Post-Gazette for sharing her time and talent for the betterment of the community.

You've heard it said that one can succeed in business without trying. But it ain't necessarily so. Not in a profession it isn't. Edith Skinner did a lot of trying, as her success certainly proves. What's more, success hasn't spoiled her. Edith is unassuming, friendly, with much charm.

First off, among Mrs. Skinner's many former students are Barbara Feldon, Shirley Jones, Theresa Wright, Soibhan McKenna, George Peppard, Judy Knaiz, Rege Cordic, and Rene Auberjonois (now in "Coco" and in the movie "M.A.S.H." playing at our downtown Fiesta). And if you're not familiar with all or some of these — shame on you!

The former Edith Warman was born in Moncton, New Brunswick, Canada. At 16 she became an American citizen and started study at the Leland Powers School in Boston. She had a sister there. Later she returned to New York and earned her BS and MA degrees from Columbia. And began teaching drama, voice and speech in the Big City. Then on to Seattle to teach at the famous Cornish School. Around that time she met Henry Boettcher, then head of Carnegie Tech Drama Dept. He was directing the Cohasset Summer Playhouse. That's how, when someone of excellence was needed at Tech, he remembered her talent and ability and sent for her post haste.

But let's not get ahead of ourselves. From 1923 to 1938 our neighbor spent summers at Provincetown, Mass., Cape Cod. There her sister owned the Wharf Theater and Edith produced O'Neill's "Ah, Wilderness!" with Sinclair Lewis, and the latter's own play "Angela is 22" starring the author. The late beloved Harold V. Cohen of the P-G Drama Desk, who spent his vacations in Provincetown where he had a summer home, was a friend and steady patron at the Wharf Theater. And wrote glowingly about her plays. Somewhere during that time, guess what? Along came a handsome and talented actor, Neil McFee Skinner, and before you knew it Edith became his lovely missus. Then another thing happened. A big avalanche of snow descended upon Provincetown and swoosh — the Wharf Theater was demolished and slid into the ocean. Edith and Neil then established a School for Acting — the first people to use the term "Learn to Act by Acting." Neil was managing director and Edith director of its Junior group. In 1927, as said above, Henry Boettcher called her to Carnegie Tech now CMU.

A member of the American Educational Theater Ass'n, our neighbor is listed in Who's Who in the American Theater, Who's Who among American Women and Who's Who in the East.

Recently Edith was invited to set up a program of speech study for the Juilliard School in its new division of Drama in Lincoln Center, N.Y. She flies there two days a week. The rest of the week she minds the store at CMU.

Mrs. Skinner never added to the population explosion. So has no snaps of kids and grand-kids to show around and brag about. But she is very proud of her more than 3,000 students and nephew Henry Hewes, Drama Critic of the Saturday Review.

She loves golf, bridge and horse-back riding. But who has time! How about that for a gal who made good and hopes to make even better?

Mrs. Rose Levin Smith

Pupil Service Aide Popular 'Neighbor'

When a certain neighbor leaves her home for some hurried errand on Murray Ave., what happens? She doesn't get back for hours. Why? Because most everybody — young and old — knows her, stops her, chats with her. And small wonder. Being friendly and interested, she chats back. So it might be a good idea to learn the why and wherefore of her popularity. Just sit back, relax and read on.

Our important and friendly neighbor is none other than Mrs. Allan I. Smith, the former Rose Levin of Morrowfield Ave. Husband Allan is a well-known attorney. He's also Section Chief at the Veterans Administration in the new Federal Bldg. Their 19-year old son Edward, a Biology major, is finishing his second year at Pitt.

And now about wife and mom Rose. She's Associate Director of Pupil Services for Vocational Placement in our public schools. That big title? What kind of a whoozit is it? Well, first let's learn about Rose's background. Her father died when she was three, leaving his widow with nine children to raise. That took great courage, of which she had aplenty. The no-nonsense discipline kids get from such an environment stands them in good stead later in life. Rose inherited her mother's great fortitude and sense of humor.

Our neighbor got her M.A. degree in secondary Education from Pitt. She has taught school at all levels — elementary, junior and senior high schools. She was guidance counsellor at Herron Hill Jr. and Fifth Ave. Sr. Highs. And an evening school Principal at Fifth Avenue High School, of which she is a graduate. And now let's digress right here. During her senior year at Fifth, Allan I. Smith was class president. But unlike present-day high-schoolers they didn't go steady. In fact they didn't even date. Each stuck to studying — with a minimum of hanky-panky.

Much, much later, when Rose was already a teacher and Allan an established lawyer, they were thrown together at a party... That evening — you should pardon the expression — Rose's slip was showing. And Allan whispered in her ear: "Your slip was always showing in High School — and still does." When Cupid is buzzing around, even an innocent whisper can lead to you-know-what. They became Mr. and Mrs.. Sept. 3, 1939 — and auspicious date not only for them but for the entire world. On that day England declared war on Germany!

In her current job Rose interviews children for N.E.E.D. (Negro Educational Emergency Drive). Last year 111 Negro graduates received over $38,500 worth of scholarship money to go on to college. And this year she has already interviewed 224 Negro students and will probably have 250 by the end of May, The other part of her duties is to find jobs for graduates, dropouts and those who are in school but have to work part-time. She has guided countless young people into meaningful careers. Every student gets her personal, sympathetic guidance — far and above the call of duty. They immediately sense she is their friend. In many cases their only friend. It often works miracles. And our community ultimately benefits.

Among their many affiliations, Rose and Allan belong to Temple Sinai. And are greatly interested in the UJF. Evenings they enjoy going to the theatre, or stay home and work on cross-word puzzles.

The Smiths built their charming 6-room Colonial home, surrounded with beautiful grounds. How does Rose manage her household tasks so well with a minimum of outside help — and do her professional job so magnificently? She concentrates on the task at hand to the exclusion of all else. And has the capacity to take everything in stride. And who do you think tends their lovely flowers and garden — digging into the good earth and pulling out the weeds? You guessed it. Husband Allan.

Mrs. Anatole (Ruth) Solow
First, Take Off All Your Clothes — Almost!

Honestly, ours is the luckiest community. We not only have oodles of remarkable neighbors who lived here for a long time. But brand new ones too.

Today you'll learn about an interesting family who came here all the way from San Salvador, Central America last September.

Meet Prof. and Mrs. Anatole Solow, our new neighbors at Darlington Rd.

Professor Solow is at Pitt's Graduate School of Public Administration and International Affairs. He's associate professor of urban and regional planning. His charming wife Ruth is starting a class in the Mensendieck System of functional exercises. More about that later.

The Solows have two interesting sons. Jonathan, 18, is a freshman at Oberlin College. Not only a tennis champion but he plays the flute and piano too. Daniel is 15 and a junior at Allderdice. He's a mathematical whiz and also plays the guitar. He was Bar Mitzvah in San Salvador. Last Mother's Day he composed a poem to his mom — in Spanish.

And there are two playful cats — Cuddles and Sniffy. Born and bred in Nicaragua, They "no spik English." Nor Spanish either. But they can meow and purr in any language.

Anatole and Ruth first met in Paris. They both belonged to the Kadimah Zionist group. He was studying architecture. They were married in 1937 in London. And listen to this. The British justice of the peace who made them man and wife was a WOMAN. After the ceremony she took Ruth's hand and said: "My dear, you are very courageous." Ruth was speechless.

In London Anatole continued with his city planning work while his young bride took up psychology at the university and a thorough course in the functional exercises mentioned above.

Two years later Anatole was called to M.I.T. to teach. Then to Yale. Eight years all told. During the war, while he served Uncle Sam, Ruth conducted a studio for her functional exercises with great success.

At war's end he was called to Washington as chief of housing and planning for Pan-American Union. After 11 years he was transferred to Nicaragua. Everything was fine there but the roads.

Danny had brought his treasured London-bought bicycle, but he couldn't use it. So he traded it for a horse.

In her interesting Darlington Road home, neighbor Ruth Solow is stwrting a class in the Mensendieck System. The "Exercise Room" has wall-to-wall mirrors. And psst! listen but don't tell the neighbors. You exercise in the nude. Or almost.

Ruth says her system teaches the importance of acquiring and maintaining precious body symetry. Each student's efforts are carefully guided to overcome posture difficulties. Scientifically designed to revitalize specific muscles and joints — help end back-ache — flatten tummy — take inches off hips and waist — tone up chest muscles — relieve fatigue and nervous tension.

You've seen supermarket shoppers in slacks who look like a sack of watermelons. And teenagers who slouch and droop as if ready to fall apart. And oldersters a bit thick here, there and you-know-where. You've watched cute little kids with knock-knees, bow-legs. They come to her from ages four to 84.

Why don't you come up and see her sometimes?

Milan Spanovich
Market Crash Baby Big In Engineering

Today's personality of the week is someone extra special. For reasons you'll agree as you read on. He's none other than our Greenfield Avenue neighbor with the interesting name of Milan Spanovich. His parents, as you may guess came from Yugoslavia but Milan is American-born. In Steubenville, Ohio, in 1929 at the height of the stock market crash. And to this day they say he was the cause of it! In spite of his vast educational background and accomplishments, Milan is so unassuming and casual, his friends and many business associates affectionately call him Mike. And you know what? He prefers it.

Mr. Spanovich came here in 1942 when Pittsburgh had earned the infamous name of "The Smoky City". Nonetheless he saw his way to school at Peabody and graduated Wilkinsburg High in 1946. Too young to serve Uncle Sam during World War II, he went to night school at our then Carnegie Tech. Two years later he continued during the day. Soon the Korean War came along, interrupting his studies. He enlisted in the Air Force, serving three years. Then back to Tech for his BS degree in Civil Engineering and his MS a year later. He then worked for eight years as consulting engineer for a local firm. In 1961 our neighbor left for the University of New Mexico to conduct research in the field of soil dynamics.

In 1963 Milan returned to our city. And wonder of wonders! All the ugly smoke had been eliminated during his absence. On that clear day he could see forever. Having lived in Denver and half dozen other cities throughout the U.S. he likes Pittsburgh best ...its general attitude, small-town warmth and big city cultural advantages.

Currently our neighbor is President and Principal of Engineering Mechanics, Inc., consulting engineers. He concentrates on applied engineering. A year ago Spanovich was named "Pittsburgh Young Civil Engineer of the Year". September 2 of last year he patented "Foundation Systems", U.S. Patent No. 3,464,215. His technical affiliations and offices held are too numerous to list in limited space. Same is true of his numberless papers written on "Soil Mechanics" and his activities associated with them.

So now a bit about Mike's personal life. A bachelor of 40 he has a one-bedroom apartment. And they say he makes the best scrambled eggs in Squirrel Hill. The best coffee, too. He attends all the ballgames. Winter vacation finds him in Aspen, Colorado, skiing. He owns a four-acre retreat in Murraysville where his young-looking Mom, Kata, lives. Mike bought her a German Shepherd dog whom she named Lady. And that's what she is — toward friends and neighbors, that is. She even tolerates the mailman. But woe be to any prowler lurking in the shadows.

Summer weekends, when there's time, guess who comes to dinner? Son Mike and his many local friends. He prepares an old-fashioned Serbian lamb roast outside over an open pit, similar to a Hawaiian Luau. With fresh vegetables from their neighbor's garden. Kata makes polachinkas (you know-like Jewish blintzes).

Our neighbor has two brothers — George in San Diego and Branko in Pasadena, California. His sister, Mrs. Mary Tiani lives in Penn Hills. Her son, Michal, just returned from Vietnam, wounded and in the Valley Forge Hospital.

Milan Spanovich is a six-footer, streamlined and handsome. And as said above, a bachelor. But girls, if you're romantically inclined and thinking of writing him a perfumed note, don't. He's already been spoken for. Lucky girl!

Mrs. Sidney Spatz

Fund Tree Drive With Enthusiasm

The long hot summer has ended, autumn leaves are gently falling. And dedicated women have been busy working and planning important affairs for the cold months ahead. Today you'll learn of one event in particular that will warm your heart.

The 14th annual Jewish National Fund Tree drive. Its capable chairman is Mrs. Phyllis Spatz, wife of Dr. Sidney Spatz, Associate professor of Oral Surgery at Pitt Dental School. And where does our chairman live? In our neighborhood, of course — on Beechwood Court. The drive opens officially Sept. 29 and culminates Oct. 19 with an all-day Dial-a-thon.

Meantime, what exactly is Jewish National Fund, and why trees? Founded in 1901 at the fifth Zionist Congress which was presided over by world-renowned Theodor Herzl, it buys land in Israel and generally prepares it for Jewish settlement. Through stone clearance, swamp drainage, uprooting of bushes and undergrowth it has created soil from fetid marshes. And transformed malaria-ridden wastes into flourishing farmland and industrial centers. And its planting of trees is known the world over. The largest affore-station project which JNF has undertaken is the planting of the Martyrs' Forest on the hills of Judea. In memory of the six million Jews who perished in Nazi Europe. The huge, swampy, rocky area has been subdivided into 18 sections — each section dedicated to the memory of one of the destroyed Jewish communities.

And you've of course heard of the John F. Kennedy Peace Forest being planted south of Jerusalem overlooking the blue Mediterranean. Because our martyred president was so young in heart, in hope and in spirit — and understood the aspirations of all peoples to build a good future for their young, the Forest will remain a living tribute to his memory. Linking America with Israel, It will cover the Judean Hills where the Jewish people fought for freedom 2,000 years ago.

And now let's snoop a little into the personal life of the JNF Tree chairman. The former Phyllis Cohen and Sidney Spatz both went to Pitt, but she was a classmate of his younger brother. The first time they met was at the Tree of Life Synagogue on Yom Kippur! On that holiest of holy days, engrossed in serious prayer — and hungry yet — who thinks of girls! So six months elapsed before he phoned for a date. But all's well that ends well.

They now are the proud parents of three beautiful daughters. Hilary Anne is at that lovely age — 16-going-on-17. Pamela Lynn 14. Both attend Allderdice. Sandra Sue, 7, goes to Linden. Another member of their household is Harvey, their pet cat. He strayed into their home five years ago, bedraggled, unwanted, hungry. After a good meal he decided to stay on. Through the years he won so much attention and love in the Spatz home he now thinks he owns the place.

Phyllis Spatz is a professional singer with a beautiful soprano voice. She has sung with the Pittsburgh Opera for seven years. And for Don Brockett's "400 Miles off Broadway" — the first of his four hit shows at Beck's Patio Theatre. And when you sing for Brockett, you have it made.

Until three years ago our neighbor was soprano of the Temple Sinai Quartet for 18 years. And has sung for weddings and Bar Mitzvahs. As to cooking — you'll never believe it. She prepares large batches of delicious foods in advance and puts it in the freezer. Even if 20 people were to stop in unexpectedly, dinner would be served — with a smile yet.

Phyllis and Sidney have done what many people haven't. They saw all of America first, before traveling through Europe. Dr. Spatz is international president of Alpha Omega Dental Fraternity. On a recent visit in Israel he met with the Chancellor of the Hebrew University and the Dean of his fraternity's Dental School. And sold them the idea of putting an addition to the school.

And now back to JNF Trees. On Sunday, Oct. 19, when your phone rings, run — don't walk — to answer. You'll be much the happier for it.

Art Spector
His Double Life Traced

This is being written on a sunny spring day when the world doesn't seem mad, mad, mad.

Our Pirates have just won three straight from the San Francisco Giants and clobbered the first place Phillies 13-4 — an ideal day to tell you about our good-humored and likeable neighbor, Art Spector.

Mr. Spector, living on Caton St., has succeeded in two different fields of endeavor. Entertainment and business. Not without trying, however. Fact is he tried like &?:! And now has made it — a comparatively young man yet.

Art and his lovely wife Dorothy have two lively children: Alan, 9 and Shelly, 7½ — both attending Minadeo Public School. Shelly takes dancing and piano at the Y-IKC. Alan goes in for sports.

Mr. Spector, reared in our city, studied voice and violin at Carnegie Tech.

At 18 his entertaining talents took him to the Catskills, right smack in the middle of the so-called Borscht Belt. He wowed them at Grossinger's and the Concord.

Often he emceed Red Buttons, Buddy Hackett and Jerry Lewis to name a few. Then came the war, World War II. Art spent four years with the Army Air Corps as an entertainment specialist, traveling far and wide.

His laugh-provoking group headed by Tony Martin was called "The Fatique Five." Once, in Calcutta, the "Five" were invited by a Jewish group to an exclusive restaurant for dinner.

The waiters, in white turbans and open sandals handed them the menu printed in Hindu. Their hosts did the ordering. The meal was fabulous, their appetites healthy.

Later, upon learning that the main course had been roasted rattlesnake they turned sick emotionally — hissing at one another all the way to their headquarters.

But soon they fared better. During Passover they were invited for Seder at a prominent Indian Jewish family. No rattlesnakes. But gold platters loaded with gefillte fish, roast chicken, matzo balls and tzimos. The stacks of matzos had been baked on their glass roof and browned on the sun, just as in Biblical times.

Again in Calcutta. The "Five's" 13-year-old house boy served them so many drinks that soon they were sprawled on the floor, fast asleep. then came the awakening. Their wallets, watches and money were missing. Also missing was the houseboy.

Later our humorist was stationed in Los Angeles, traveling to all Army Air Force bases with Danny Kaye, Roy Rogers, the Ritz Brothers, Fanny Brice, Jack Benny. He emceed them all.

Honorably discharged Art went to New York where he worked in night clubs as a singing comedian. Seven years ago he returned to our city and started the A. Spector Contracting Co. to which he gives full time. But entertainment is still in his blood. Weekends he has 'em laughing at night-clubs — on a one-night basis only.

Friday nights and on the Jewish High Holy Days he is serious. For seven years Art has headed the Tree of Life synagogue choir as tenor. All the songs are in Hebrew.

In conclusion, maybe we shouldn't have bragged so much about our Pirates clobbering the Phillies.

In baseball, as in life, fortunes often change. Besides, Dorothy (Art's missus) hails from the City of Brotherly Love!

Otto Spielbichler
'Chef of the Year' Pleases Patrons

The most popular expression these days is "Let's go to the Fair." Meaning, of course the annual Food Fair at the Civic Arena Oct. 11 and 12.

And since the best Chef in the country lives in our very neighborhood, let's get acquainted with him. He's Otto Spielbichler of McKaslin St. Our neighbor was chosen "Chef of the Year" at the American Culinary Federation convention in Chicago the past June. And small wonder.

But before we tell you more about him, be reminded that the Fair will help raise funds for the fight against polio: In spite of the Salk and Sabin vaccines, polio is not completely licked. And in addition there's the everwidening scourge of birth-defects. The Salk Institute in California is carrying on research on both of these abominable health hazards.

You'll have a chance to sample foods from around the world — not in 80 days, just two. The food will be prepared by members of the Chefs Association of Pittsburgh. Each has a specialty. They prepare it where they work and bring it to the Fair for you to enjoy. Chef Spielbichler will prepare his famous Roast Beef, and the gourmets in the know say it's simply out of this world. There also you will meet Mrs. I. Henry Katrowitz, chairman of the Fair for the past 14 years. Her first name is Pearl — and a pearl she is.

Our neighbor was born 70 years ago in a little town in the Bavarian Alps. His dad was an innkeeper. At an early age he served as apprentice in famous Bavarian hotels. Then came World 1 and Otto was called to the German Army as an infantryman. During his three-year service he was twice wounded. His hearing is permanently impaired.

Otto couldn't hear but boy could he cook! He worked at famous hotels in Munich and Cologne. And helped prepare banquets for royalty, including the King of Saxony, Crown Prince Ruprecht of Bavaria and the Queen of Rumania. The great German depression — far worse than ours — brought Herr Spielbichler to the U.S. Thousands of others clamored to get here but Otto's cooking skill got him priority.

He came on the SS Stuttgart working as its chef. In New York, without relatives, he lived with a German family two years. And joined a German Club. So he wasn't making much progress with our language.

A student, working his way through college, employed at a Cafeteria where Otto was Chef, took a liking to him and taught him English. (Today our neighbor speaks the language perfectly, with only a trace of the German accent). At the Cafeteria Cupid came a-hovering.

Otto must have found a fortune cookie which read: "Soon you will meet a beautiful woman. You will give her money. She is our cashier."

The Cashier was Susan Satiere. In no time Otto was taking Susan to dances, movies, parties. And before long they became Mr. and Mrs. The happy couple worked until 1930 when they moved to our city. The husband was hired as Assistant Chef at the University Club.

During the depression the Head Chef left and Otto was immediately asked to succeed him. He continued to please the patrons of that exclusive club for 33 years, until his retirement two years ago.

Our neighbors have a son, Otto, Jr. He just received his PhD from Ohio State University in Columbus and soon will engage in his career. His French wife is guidance counselor at the University there. They have three lovely children. Otto and his devoted Susan plan to spend Thanksgiving with them. And who do you think will cook the turkey? Chef Spielbichler.

Otto recently returned from a fishing trip to Canada. He caught lake trout, northern pike. You dip the fish in milk before rolling in flour and seasoning and it will come out brown, crisp, delicious.

See you at the Fair.

William Stark
CLO Days Mean Treat from Neighbor

Happy days are here again. The Civic Light Operas. Beginning July 8 and ending August 31 all roads will lead to our air-conditioned Civic Arena. For eight colorful and delightful hit shows that should keep the Golden Triangle swinging. Under the stars. And at the least sign of a drizzle — that retractable roof, remember?

You of course understand that such things don't just happen. Wonderfully dedicated civic leaders make them happen. And since there's always a Squirrel Hiller mixed up in everything worthwhile, you'll want to learn about him. William Stark, our neighbor at Aylesboro Avenue is secretary of the CLO board of directors. Long before he became president of the Penn Overall Co., Bill Stark was a professional musician. He plays piano and the bass violin. So naturally considers music a vital factor in our city's cultural existence.

As CLO secretary, Mr. Stark helps manage and select the artists. He is also responsible for raising — you should pardon the expression — money. And like other wonderful people, gives generously himself — although he'd be the last person to mention it. It is he who gives out a hundred courtesy tickets each week to handicapped adults and underprivileged children from hospitals and orphanages, putting a bit of sunshine into their lonely lives.

Our completely likable neighbor, in addition to his CLO responsibilities is interested in so many other important local and national organizations that limited space can't list them. Let's simply say — you name it, he's in it. Even in WHO'S WHO IN AMERICA.

So let's just snoop a little into his personal life. Our dark-eyed pipe-smoking neighbor has a personality that wins you over in a minute. At age 50 — and not coming close to looking it — he's a man in love with life.

Bill Stark graduated Allderdice. So did lovely Olga Bernstein, now his devoted Missus. In those days, always a man in a hurry, Bill never gave her a second look. And Olga couldn't care less. She went on to Northwestern University in Evanston, Ill. and Bill breezed through Pitt earning his BS degree. Thence to Harvard for a year. One enchanted evening he was invited to a friend's home in our neighborhood for a party. So was sweet girl-graduate Olga Bernstein. Another fellow, not invited, crashed the party. Dan Cupid! That's how it all started. And one fine sizzling day in July 1940, Bill said So Long to bachelorhood and I Do to Olga.

Time marched on. Today the Starks are the proud parents of two beautiful daughters. Sally is married to Fred M. Rock, a well-known local CPA. She teaches speech therapy in our County school system. Hillary Ann is a senior at Duquesne University.

The Stark' 4-bedroom Georgian style home is lovely from the outside. But even more so inside. You see, Bill's three women have elegant taste.

Now let's return once again to those ever-lovin Civic Light Operas. Their by-laws plainly state that when the time comes that their budget is balanced and out of the red, every kid in Allegheny County — even the healthy ones — will be given a chance to attend all the Operas for free. An impossible dream? Not at all, Stark says. When that happy day comes he, his dedicated co-workers and everybody else will feel real good. And as they say — what's so bad about feeling good?

Neighbor Stark says come to the Operas and have yourself a ball.

Dr. Wilbur A. Steger
California Family Makes Cold Entrance

Millions remember Pearl Harbor. Dr. Wilbur A. Steger, wife Sheila and their four youngsters remember Pittsburgh. Particularly last January 26. At seven that morning they jetted into our airport from sunny California. The thermometer read 18 below — snowing and blowing — and boy, it was cold outside! But the Stegers didn't give a shiver. Mom Sheila had prepared her brood with gobs of coats, sweaters and who knows — maybe red flannels. When Pittsburgh spread before them in all its winter beauty, they were enamored. And the kids, at their first glimpse of snow, shrieked with delight.

Now spring has come and gone, and summer is in full swing. The Stegers are settled as our welcome neighbors at Beacon Street. Edward, Francine and Harold — 11½, 9½ and 6 — all go to Colfax School. Baby Jeff, just turned 15 months, is a lively little fellow with one bad fault: he simply won't decide which school to attend.

Dr. Steger, a Harvard PhD., heads a "Brains Factory." It's called Consand Research Corp. of Pa. The word Consad is a combination of Consult and Advise. Its business is to apply the techniques of the computer to the problems of government bodies and private companies.

To date its two principal customers are the Commonwealth of Pa. and the University of Pittsburgh's Center for Regional Economic Studies. The Commonwealth is paying $50,000 for a study of the economic impact of the proposed merger between the Pennsy and New York Central railroads. Pitt is paying $75,000 for a study of how computer techniques might be applied to urban renewal problems. Consad's future possibilities range from space research to making up schedules for professional sports leagues.

Consad was first set up a year ago in Santa Monica, Calif. Its second office is right smack in Center, 3406 Fifth Ave., Oakland. Asked why the new firm decided to open another office in our city, Dr. Steger said, "It was largely because we found a tremendously encouraging atmosphere at Pitt." In addition, Dr. Steger is an Adjunct Professor at Pitt and lectures on his "Systems Analysis." Sounds exciting doesn't it?

And now let's get back to the missus. Before her marriage, Sheila Steger was a librarian — just like Marian. And until little Jeffy was born she worked half-time at her career. Here she has helped her husband set up his fabulous library — 50 boxes of books, technical and periodicals. She makes most of her children's clothes. And currently is embroidering a quilt for a soon-to-be-born niece. Or will it be a nephew?

Sheila is tall, graceful and the youngest-looking mother of four. To quote a current poet: "She's got more than a fraction of attraction, a trace of grace and a glimmer of glamour."

Our community is proud to welcome this interesting family as neighbors. May they have good health, good luck — and root for the Pirates!

Dean Erwin R. Steinberg
An Expert on English

A tall, fine-looking, unpretentious, brilliant professor lives in our neighborhood. Almost around the corner on Beacon St. He is Dr. Erwin R. Steinberg, dean of Margaret Morrison Carnegie College.

His family consists of lovely wife Beverly and two sons: Marc, 6½, is in his first grade at Davis School. Alan, 4, attends the Y-IKS nursery.

Prf. Steinberg's educational back-ground is fantastic. He is author of so many important published articles and text-books on English Literature that to enumerate them would look like a page in Britannica.

Suffice to say his writings are read, studied and used throughout the English-speaking educational world.

Dean Steinberg holds a PhD from New York University and has won a Carnegie teaching award. In 1946 he was called to Carnegie Tech as an instructor in English; became assistant professor in 1949; associate professor in 1955, and full professor in 1961.

He was appointed head of the department of general studies in Margaret Morrison College in 1956, and four years later was made dean of the college. The college, as you doubtless know, specializes in higher education for women.

This of course means that all his students are women. The dean is scarcely past his 40th birthday. Well, now — let's see. Maybe we can dig up a bit of mischief. Does the professor, by any chance, have the problem of girl-crushes about which we so often hear and read?

With a smile, he says: "No such problems. None whatever."

Incredible. How can that be?

He points out that crushes usually occur in the grades and early high school. By the time he gets them, his women are quite mature — and sensible.

Besides, Tech campus is veritably bursting with young men. Most of the women are going steady, many are engaged and some are already married. Like it or not, that's how it is.

But make no mistake about it — he does have problems with his women. Starry-eyed, they take too seriously the endings of the modern novels which invariably say "— and so they married and lived happily ever after." What they don't take to heart are current statistics which say: Among college girl graduates, 97 percent will marry, have an average of 3 children apiece, and be gainfully employed 25 years during their life-time.

Marrying at an early age they'll still be young enough after their children are full-grown, to want to work. With a college education they'll be better equipped for jobs that are more interesting and rewarding. He stresses the fact that education is as vital for women as for men.

Four years ago Prof. Steinberg and a group of other educators started an important project that has proved invaluable. It was the advanced placement program. Funds from the Ford Foundati⁰n and the A. W. Mellon Educational & Charitable Trust made it possible. The project was in the fields of English and History, with gifted students taking college courses while still in high school.

It took in several Pittsburgh high schools, including our Allderdice. The dean helped set up the program. As a result, during the last two years, the local students did better than others in the entire nation.

Originally it was a cooperative enterprise between Carnegie Tech and the Pittsburgh public schools. Later it was extended throughout all Allegheny County. Now 1,200 students in 34 schools are enrolled in the program.

The dean and wife Beverly enjoy tennis. And can ice-skate. Or think they can. Recently they took Marc and Alan to Panther Hollow to teach them. The parents hadn't been on skates for 20 years. You know what happened? The boys are the teachers now, with mom and pop the pupils.

The Steinbergs are planning to move into their own home on Sheriden Ave. the end of March. There will be more room, a large back yard and a garden. The kids will have a dog for sure, and a few kittens. And maybe a snake or two.

We'll be sorry to lose them as neighbors. And yet, we're glad for them. When they move and are settled, we want them to "live happily ever after."

Mrs. Ernest A. (Reggie) Stern
Talent Keyed For Theatres

As to this week's neighborhood personality, everything is coming up talent. Talent started out as a hobby and developed into a career without benefit of special training. Our of her own head, as the saying goes. So who is this clever woman, for goodness sakes? Mrs. Ernest A. Stern, the former Regina Abravanel — that's who. Reggie, as she is affectionately called is our neighbor at Beechwood Boulevard.

Let's see now. Regina graduated Allderdice, then went on to Northwester University — for just two years. World War II had started and her brother Ben was called to the Service. So she was wanted at home. She continued studies at Pitt and got her BS degree in elementary education. And did practice teaching for 6 months. One evening a fella took her to a performance at our Playhouse (a popular theatre even then). During intermission who do you think sauntered over — big as life — to say hello?

Ernest A. Stern, a graduate of the University of Miami. He had gone to Allderdice when Reggie did, but in those days they couldn't care less for one another. Absence, they say, makes the heart grow fonder. Or is it because each had developed into attractive personalities? At any rate, steady dating followed. And one fine day they became Mr. and Mrs. That was 24 years ago. At the time Ernest was Booking Agent for Paramount Pictures. Soon he became Manager of the South Park Drive-in — the first out-door theatre in our State. His young bride was cashier.

Together they ran the theatre for several years. When the Stork brought baby Linda, the cashier turned housewife. And continued until after Judy and later Richard came along. Linda is now 20 and a senior at Skidmore College. Judy, 19 is a Soph. at American University. Richard is 14 and is an Allderdice freshman.

Fifteen years after marriage mom Stern became interested in designing the interiors of her husband's theatres. Her first experience was the Fulton after Ernest purchased it. Its ceiling with cupids and women in flowing robes had grown almost black with age and neglect. Reggie had them restored to their original beauty by a series of rub-a-dub scrubbings. One night — in bed, mind you — she got a brilliant idea: Carpeting the theatre walls end-to-end. Putting tile in the ceiling would perfect the acoustics. She woke Ernest to tell him. Sleepily he welcomed her suggestion. After all, who has a wife with brilliant ideas? And who has a husband with nearly 50 theatres throughout the Tri-State area?

Next time you enter our neighborhood Forum or Kings Court in Oakland, take a good look around. What you see in quality, freshness, comfort and diversity originated in Reggie's head. And when you escalate down into the Fiesta — the first new down-town theatre in 30 years, you'll almost feel her presence.

At her white ultra-modern desk in the 66-year-old Fulton building Mrs. Stern develops her ideas full-time. At home, Frances, their capable housekeeper has com-plete charge. Clifford, their 7-year old dachshund — with a pedigree longer than his owners — keeps a watchful eye on everything.

Ernest and Reggie travel a lot together. They just returned from Miami for the National Association of Theatre Owners Convention. Ernest was elected a Vice Presi-dent of the Association. Three years ago they took their children to Europe for 6 weeks. Summers the family enjoy their 60-foot 3-stateroom motor yacht named Jurily IV. The yacht spends its winters in Fort Lauderdale. In the spring Capt. Jeff Mancuso brings it up across the Gulf of Mexico. up the Mississippi and Ohio to their Hideway Harbor Marina in Fox Chapel.

The Sterns are members of Rodef Shalom and Beth Shalom Congregations. Ernest is past president of the Pgh. Chapter of Variety Club, an international charity for handicapped children. Years ago a baby was found abandoned in the Sheridan Square Theatre. The Club named her Catherine Sheridan Variety, reared and educated her. Today she's married with a family of her own.

Reggie belongs to many important organizations. She's active in American Ort, the Montefiore and St. Francis Hospitals. And is Vice President of the Music Guild of Pittsburgh. You know what? Let's name our neighbor "A Gal for all Seasons."

Dr. Ernest J. Sternglass
Radiation Reduction Target of Physicist

The war news is disquieting. The stock market erratic. The cost of living is soaring above the temperature. And the Pirates are struggling. So enough's enough already. Let's concentrate, instead, on our blessings. Like for instance interesting neighbor-hood personalities. And get acquainted with Dr. Ernest J. Sternglass our neighbor at Shady Avenue.

So who is this Sternglass? A man of culture and warmth — that's who. And chock full of imaginative ideas. He is professor of radiation physics in Pitt's School of Medi-cine. And for many years prior was advisory physicist of Westinghouse Research Laboratories.

He came here 15 years ago direct from Cornell with a Ph.D. in Physics and Engineer-ing. He is now interested in developing new instruments for reducing radiation in X-ray diagnosis. At Westinghouse Dr. Sternglass and his associates were working on plans for a telescope on the moon. To be operated by astronomers on earth, using re-mote control. The telescope could provide three to 10 times finer details than any instrument on earth.

Among the chief advantages of a moon-based telescope is the view it would provide of the earth. Thus a large part of the earth's surface could be watched continuously for long periods. And could provide long-range weather forecasting. He was asked, when and if the Apollo program develops the capability to transport men and equipment to the moon, what would be the next step? Investigation of lunar structure and atmosphere.

This may provide information on the moon's origin and possibly about some form of primitive life at some time in its history. Also the study of nearby planets and explora-tion of the universe beyond the solar system.

Had enough of the technical stuff? Let's learn about our neighbor's personal life.

Dr. Sternglass is married to the former Marilyn Steiner whose mom, Mrs. Harry Steiner is our neighbor in Maxon Towers. Marilyn was working for an Advertising Agency. How did they met? You'll never believe it. They were introduced! On a blind date yet. And went to Paris on a 14-month honeymoon. For the best reason in the world. The young husband was invited to spend a year at the University of Paris — on leave from Westinghouse. They were glorious months in that romantic city. They lived on the top floor in one of those old Parisian houses with a slanting roof. Both learned French there.

Baby Daniel almost made it as a Frenchman, but not quite. His mom and dad returned home six months before the stork brought him. Two years later Susan came along. Danny, now 8, goes to Linden School. And already is interested in science like his pop. Some day they'll introduce him as My Son the Scientist. Susan is 6 and attends Linden kindergarten. She loves modern dancing and is taking lessons at the Arts & Crafts Center.

Dad Sternglass is on the board of Technion. And is past chairman of the Pittsburgh Chapter of the Federation of American Scientists. His lovely missus just got her M.A. degree in English from Tech. And hopes to teach that subject when school begins. Both recently returned from Stanford University, working on his hobby a new theory about the particles of matter.

Four years ago our neighbors moved into their modern California-style ranch house. In spite of the mixed-up world, they think it's a wonderful world and they don't want it to stop — nor to get off.

Dr. Horton Guyford Stever
Tech's President Meeting Challenge

Our personality of the week is of vast importance not only to college students but to everyone. So close your books a moment, call mom and dad — and oh, yes, Aunt Minnie too — and pull up your chairs. For today you'll learn about a most fabulous fellow. True, he isn't quite a Squirrel-Hiller, but who's going to be strict when he's so important to our entire city. Besides, he does live close by — in the Oakland Educational Center. On Devon Rd., to be exact. So let's give a most friendly welcome to Dr. Horton Guyford Stever, new president of Carnegie Tech. He took over his duties in February, 1965.

A tall, handsome fellow with an engaging smile and much charm, he wins you over in a minute. Add to this a brilliant mind, an extensive educational background plus vast experience and you have the ideal man for a herculean job.

Dr. Stever was on the faculty of world-famous M.I.T. for more than 20 years. During that time he achieved national prominence both as an educator and in service to the Federal Government. Currently he's a member of the Defense Science Board and the Advisory Panel of the U.S. House of Representatives' Committee on Science and Astronautics. We could go on and on. But you've read about him in all our newspapers. You've heard him on TV and radio. And on the lecture platform. So you know what? Let's skip the serious stuff and eaves-drop a little into his personal life.

Tech's new president was born in Corning, N.Y. When a little tike of five his dad passed away — at 34 years of age. And off Guy went to live with grandma and grandpa. The no-nosense discipline a fella often learns from grandparents stands him in good stead later in life. Among other things young Guy didn't marry during his teenage years. Instead he waited till he was able to adequately provide for the girl of his dreams; and she wouldn't need to get a job to help pay for the furniture. He was 29 before he said "so long to bachelorhood" and "I do" to lovely Louise Risely Floyd. Louise was taking a graduate course in medical social work for her MS degree at Boston's Simmons College. Guy had a fine job with well-known Bradley Dewey, head of the guided Missiles Committee of the Joint Chiefs of Staff.

How did these two meet? One enchanted evening Stever's boss asked him to his home for dinner, to be followed by a formal dance called "A Waltz Evening." Louise Floyd also was invited. But you know what? Guy didn't even ask her for a waltz! A little bashful mebbe? Later, on their first date they went on a Sunday skiing jaunt. And Louise, fortunately not so shy, invited him to a concert by the Boston Symphony. What with the charm that music hath, and Cupid lurking in the wings, steady dating soon followed. And continued for six months. On a sunny day in 1946 Guy and Louise became Mr. & Mrs. And started housekeeping in Boston's exclusive Beacon Hill. You know — the neighborhood where "the Cabots speak only to the Lowells and the Lowells only to God." Be that as it may, everyone liked speaking to the Stevers.

Time passes on. Now they have four lively, interesting children. Horton Guyford, Jr. is a Freshman at Colgate. He's 19. Sarah Newell, affectionately called "Sash" is 18 and goes to Sarah Lawrence College. Margarette Risely — "Margo" — is in the 8th grade at Winchester-Thurston. Roy Risely is in the 7th grade at Shadyside. They're proud of their dad's work and enjoy living near Tech.

Dr. Stever's lovely missus helps him in all social affairs when they entertain officially or otherwise. Like LBJ and his Lady Bird, he likes having his capable Louise around.

When Tech merges with the Mellon Institute and becomes C.M.U. next summer, its president wants to build greater strength. He hopes to make a fine University even better. He's happy and grateful for the tremendous help and friendly understanding and support he has been receiving from not only our community leaders but from everybody.

So you see — Tech's president is a far cry from the professor grandpop likes to reminisce about — the kind that was so absent-minded he put his umbrella in bed and himself in a corner. Our professor Stever is dynamic, alive — and comparatively young, too. Only fifty.

And now get a load of this. Ever since the Stevers moved to Pittsburgh they have become avid Pirate fans. So what about the Boston Red Sox? Your guess is as good as ours.

Mr. & Mrs. Stolarevsky
Double Feature Thursday Special

Actually this could almost be called A Double Feature on a Thursday Afternoon — the day your News is delivered. Because both Mr. and Mrs. Mihail Stolarevsky are gifted and interesting neighborhood personalities. But husband Mihail is one of those gracious fellows who had his druthers. He druther we concentrate on his lovely missus, the former Kathryn Fell. However, we druther tell you about both of them. So get yourself a cup of coffee, pull up your chairs, kick off your shoes, relax — and read on. The Stolarevskys live in a 7-room duplex around the corner on Darlington Road.

Kathryn Stolarevsky, affectionately called Kay, has been teaching music at Ellis School for a number of years. And weekends teaches piano at her home. During the summer she instructs at the Chatham Music Camp. The Camp was founded by her husband 14 years ago. He's still director of it.

Mihail Stolarevsky is violist for our famous Pittsburgh Symphony. He also directs the McKeesport Symphony. He's on the faculty of Chatham College and is director of the Chatham Laboratory School of Music. Born in Kiev, Russia, he came to the U.S. in 1923. He's a graduate of the Kiev Imperial Conservatory of Music and also has an electrical engineering degree from Germany.

Kay was born in New Mexico and is a graduate of the University of New Mexico in Albuquerque. She got her B.A. degree there, majoring in music. Then went on to the Cincinnati Conservatory of Music where she earned her bachelor and masters of music degrees. While in Cincinnati, who do you think was playing in their famous symphony? That musical fellow from far-off Kiev — remember? He was also a member of the Cincinnati String Quartet and on the Artist faculty. And who do you think was on the accompanying staff of the Conservatory of Music? You guessed it. That musical gal from New Mexico. And in due time became his lovely bride.

When Fritz Reiner was Director of the Cincinnati Symphony and later came here to direct our Pittsburgh Symphony — long before Steinberg — he wanted Mihail to come here also. That's how it came about that the Stolarevskys are giving of their talents in our city. And of course in our neighborhood.

Our neighbors have a cottage in Interlochen, Mich. — the National Music Camp where Milhail taught for 17 years. They go there for a few weeks after Chatham Summer School is over. As hobbies they enjoy collecting antiques. And Kay is an expert at knitting and needlepoint. Already she has ribbon knitted some of her spring outfits. And now listen to this. Kay's the best cook ever — expecially Russian cookery. Like for instance borscht, piroshki, cutleta, galupsi — to name a few. And she didn't get her know-how from Nikita Khruschev's missus. More than likely husband Mihail had a hand in it.

Mr. Stolarevsky is lucky and doubtless a most happy fella. Some married men, when they want to discuss their professional experiences with their better half, are frustrated because the little woman knows from nuthin' what he's saying. With our neighbors it's altogether different. Each understands the other. They enjoy "talking shop." And when the subject is music, it comes up roses.

So what else is news? Nothing. Oh, yes — there is! You know of course that our famous Pittsburgh Symphony is very much alive. We want to keep it that way.

Meantime let's wish our talented neighbors the best of everything.

Duella Stranahan
One of the City's Who's Who

When a lovely girl doesn't marry and must go it alone, what happens? Well first off she is constantly plagued with the well-meaning question "How come?" She can sometimes hide her personal reason with a sense of humor by saying no one wants her. Or she can pretend to have such skads of beaus that she can't decide who, which or whom. Or — we advise against it — become sour at the world for not being a wife and mother. Or, as countless single women have done, simply smile, make a huge success of her life as is, and emerge a Real Somebody — admired and often envied — by many.

In the later category belongs Duella Stranahan, a tall, graceful redhead. She lives at Wilkins Ave. with her genteel, white-haired mother, Mrs. James (also Duella) Stranahan. Duella's only brother, James is a professor at Penn State University. Frank Stranahan, the famous golfer of Toledo, is her cousin.

Duella is a dyed-in-the-wool Pittsburgher. Even her great grandmother was born here — in a house where the Nixon Theatre now stands. That was in 1830 when the roads were mud, with pigs and chickens on the streets.

After Linden Public School, Duella graduated from Peabody High School She won the Exceptionally Able Youth Award given annually by the Civic Club of Allegheny County. Soon she was attending Pitt and in due time graduated as a teacher in English, with a minor subject, Mathematics.

A stint of practice teaching proved that it wasn't for her. With her knowledge of Mathematics she leaned, rather, toward business. Pitt suggested she look into Kaufmann's Junior Executive Training Program; or see the Treasurer of the Central Division of the A&P Stores. She decided on the latter. It was a fortunate decision, because in no time she was behind a desk of her own there, as Statistician. In 1948 she was made Paymaster — the first and perhaps the only woman ever to hold that job. Is she worried about being laid off? Not at all. Without her who would see to it that all the many employes get paid?

Currently she's a membership chairman of the Pennsylvania Federation of Business & Professional Women. This is only scratching the surface. For a complete list of her volunteer activities, take a look in "Who's Who of American Women" where she's listed.

In 1961 she ran as a write-in candidate for Mayor of Pittsburgh — the first Republican woman to have that privilege. She was on radio and TV programs, and was interviewed by Carl Ide and Jane Ellen Ball. As a result of her political activities, the Post Gazette selected her as one of ten outstanding Pittsburgh women for that year.

Our red-head always gets a 4-week annual vacation. She's been to Europe; to Mexico twice; in Cuba (before Castro); in South America, and the Caribbean countries. However, many times she has snitched a week or so from her vacation-time to attend some of her many organization meetings.

People ask: Duella, a charming girl like you — so how come you're not married? She could very easily say it's none of your business and it would serve them right. But being the darling she is, she simply smiles and says: "All the nice men are taken."

Edward M. Strauss, Jr.
Busy Executive Boosts Symphony

This is about a new sound in music — the American Wind Symphony. And an important and interesting fellow who gives his spare time to it and knows all about it. Mr. Edward M. Strauss, Jr., the Symphony's President. And where do you think he lives? In our neighborhood, of course. Squirrel Hill Ave.

In private life Mr. Strauss is with Alcoa, its manager of corporate business opportunities. He looks for new products for his firm and talks with inventors, studies their new patents and works with the company's research development program.

Our neighbor was born in Omaha, Neb. — of all places. After high school he graduated Iowa State University with a B.S. degree in Industrial Engineering. He joined Aloca in 1940 at age 21 — and a bachelor. His firm sent him for additional training in NYC for 6 months. Still a bachelor. Then to Baltimore as sales representative. So what happened to Edward in Baltimore should happen to your good — looking sons. He fell victim to the sweet mystery of love.

At a party, across the crowded room was lovely Dorothy Reilly, a Goucher graduate. Even now Strauss tells you she was not only beautiful, charming, vavacious, but smart too. And still is. So his bachelor days were numbered. After a year with Uncle Sam at Fort Bragg during WW 2 in the Field Artillery, he was sent back to Baltimore by the Secretary of War. To be responsible for all aluminum needed to build fighting aircraft for the Army and Navy. Dorothy was waiting.

At the end of a year young Ed became her devoted husband. They went housekeeping in a pent-house above a garage in downtown Baltimore. Actually it was an artists studio. Then Aloca sent him to Fairfield, Conn. as sales manager. In Fairfield, guess who came to dinner? Baby Edward M. Strauss III. In 1952 Aloca needed his dad in Pittsburgh. And he's been here ever since.

Son Edward is now 18 and just graduated Shadyside Academy. He's entering Princeton University this fall. This summer he's in Norway working in a chemical plant. Then there's Cynthia, 14. She's in the 9th grade at Ellis School.

Her mom is on the Ellis School board. Also the 20th Century Club. And on the board of the Alumni of Goucher College. As well as president of St. Margarets Hospital dispensary board. She's also V.P. of the Women's Ass'n of our Pittsburgh Symphony Orchestra. The Strauss family are members of the Calvary Episcopal Church.

And now about those Wind Symphony concerts that held you spellbound 12 evenings for the past 12 summers. You know — where you and thousands others sat on chairs and benches outdoors under the stars. And music from brass, wind and percussion instruments wafted from the barge stage moored at Point Park. Along our Three Rivers. The season's concert July 4th — with fireworks yet — brought an estimated 25,000 oohh-ers and ahh-ers.

The Symphony's founder and music director Robert Austin Bourdreau visits music schools throughout the country, auditioning young musicans for his Symphony. He commissions composers too. Some are working on their advanced degrees in music. All are housed in Point Park College dormitory — walking distance to the barge for practice and concerts. They come from everywhere — Canada, Georgia, Connecticut, Texas, and of course Pittsburgh. And Pssst! listen! Several of these youngsters, away from home, with so much in common, have entered into the holy bonds of matrimony.

The Symphony gets support from the City and County. And contributions from large and small business firms. Also from Foundations. And during concert intermissions they do what is known as "passing the drum". The Symphony just finished cruising down the Monongahela, Allegheny and Ohio Rivers, on their barge pulled by a tugboat. They moored at many of the towns along the river banks, enchanting the villagers.

Neighbor Strauss and all the other wonderful people interested in the Wind Symphony wants you all at the Point next summer. See you then.

Mrs. B. (Rowena) Surloff

Hadassoh Donor Chairman

Anyone who doesn't know about Hadassah and its world-wide importance should be asked to leave town. But kidding aside, even the know-it-alls can stand a bit of reminding. Especially since in a few months this fabulous organization of 4,500 local members is holding its annual Door Luncheon. February 16th, to be exact. At Hotel Hilton.

Numberless committee members have been feverishly working on the Luncheon since early May. All are wonderful, dedicated women. But the Donor Chairman is considered the hostess with the mostest. So first off let's learn a little about her. She's none other than the popular Rowena Surloff of Avondale Place.

The former Rowena Getelman is married to well-known Bernard Surloff. He's a buyer of housewares and appliances at Binstock's in Oakland. Rowena went through the grades in East Liberty and graduated Peabody High. Later she did book-keeping and secretarial work for two different companies. Bernard Surloff used to come there on business and became Rowena's secret admirer. One enchanted evening she attended a wedding. Who was there — big as life — but bachelor Surloff. And asked to drive her home. Cupid must have hitched a ride with them because soon thereafter steady dating followed. On a beautiful June day, 27 years ago they became Mr. and Mrs. Now they are the proud parents of two interesting sons. Jerry is an electrical engineer in Tawson, Md. And don't let it get around, but his wife is "expecting". Son Paul teaches in Shaler Township and will be married December 28th to the girl-next door, lovely Francine Klein.

Mom Surloff is well known for her lectures on decorative food recipes and creative vegetable sculptures for table decorations. And lectured before the Women's Auxiliary of Westinghouse Engineers, for various women's Clubs in the Wilkinsburg area and for numerous Hadassah groups.

She is past president of Hadassah Group 6. When she was going out of office the group presented her with a chauffeur's cap. How come? Because she constantly chauffeured everybody to and from meetings. Recently Towena redecorated her entire 8-room home, with herself as the decorator. She always cooks two full-course meals every day, the second at 10 p.m. when her husband comes home from work.

The Surloff phone is constantly ringing — especially when Rowena is in the shower. But her "private secretary" — father-in-law Alex Surloff enjoys answering it and takes all messages. a widower, Alex has lived with them for 16 years. When winter really sets in, off he goes to Florida. When Rowena received that chauffeur's cap, Alex was the proudest man in Pittsburgh.

The Israeli government has asked Hadassah to raise funds to rebuild the Mt. Scopus Hospital that was vacant for 19 years. It's already in the process of becoming a new 300-bed General Hospital. Jews and Arabs alike will have access to the Hospital —the only one in that area.

Hadassah has helped rescue and redeem more than 130,000 Jewish youths snatched from every human depravity and torment of our times: Nazism. And has taken into her arms the culturally retarded, socially injured children from backward countries whom Israel must "remake" through flexible programs of work and study.

The Donor Luncheon will have a double-bill of entertainment. Johnny Ung, a Korean singer. And a humorist that will keep you in stitches. Get a new hairdo, put on your prettiest hat and join the Beautiful People at the Hilton Sunday February 16th at noon. You'll be glad you did.

Mrs. Milton K. (Minnie) Susman
Busy Neighbor Has Time For Others

Honestly, ours is the luckiest neighborhood — with so many wonderfully interesting personalities. Today, meet another and say, "We're proud of you" to Mrs. Milton K. (Minnie) Susman of nearby Ferree Street.

For 11 years, since its inception, Mrs. Susman was an instructor and now is chairman of the Department of Education of the Greater Pittsburgh Guild for the Blind — a non-sectarian Agency, on a full-time basis. She's been teaching Braille, Technique of Daily Living, Abacus, History of Blindness and Legislation.

She says her work is exciting and gratifying. Husband, Milton, is director of the Department of Continuing Education at Duquesne University, and since 1933, has been writing a weekly column, "As I See It" for the Jewish Chronicle. He travels for the United Jewish Appeal, and countless times has been guest speaker on current subjects for important non-sectarian groups. He also has headed various talk shows for radio and TV.

And now more about Milt's charming missus. The former Minnie Spero was born in Butler. After High she went on to Pitt, earning her BA, LLB and JD degrees. At Pitt, where girls often meet boys, she met handsome Law student, Susman; and fell head-over-heels. In 1936, Rabbi Freehof of Rodef Shalom pronounced them "Mr. an Mrs.".

The young bride continued law practice in Butler, staying with her devoted parents, and commuting to our neighborhood to join her husband in the home he provided for her and his parents. Winter months when driving was icy, she became a "week-end wife". She kept up her Law during WW 2, while Milt served Uncle Sam in Europe. At war's end, she gave up her practice and went housekeeping with him here in their own apartment.

As time went on, they hoped for a child; however, the doctors all said she could never have a baby. But guess what? In 1947, the stork outsmarted the MD's and delivered a bouncing boy. They were ecstatic and named him Brooks, in memory of his step-grandfather whom they loved.

Minnie's Boy turned out just great; now 25, he's a student at Hebrew Union College, Cincinnati. In two years, he'll be ordained. Meanwhile, for the past two years he's had a Congregation in Columbus, Ind. for week-ends and Jewish holidays.

Brooks is married to the former Dale Speer of our neighborhood. The past July, they were in Israel; they marvel at what that little Democracy, surrounded by enemies on all sides, has accomplished. Enroute back, they stopped in Rome and were afforded the special privilege of an audience with the Pope.

While in Butler, our neighbor was secretary of the Butler County Bar Association for nine years, and President of the Quota Club, as well as the National Council of Jewish Women, Butler Section. She organized the Civil Defense Volunteer program there. Here she was president of the Pittsburgh Section of NCJW; on the Board of the Jewish Family and Children Service; the Y-IKC; American Service Institute; Rodef Shalom Sisterhood; and United Jewish Fund.

She developed Council Lounge for Older People (now the Anathan House), and was its first chairman, with Mrs. Anathan. For 25 years, she taught pre-confirmation and confirmation classes at Rodef Shalom. In the past, she had a full-time housekeeper; currently, she has outside household help once a week. Because she loves to cook, she does it herself. We could go on and on, but limited space won't permit.

We can't end without telling you of another big "plus" for Minnie Susman — her young-at-heart mother, Mrs. Mary Spero. A more genteel, kindly golden-ager you never met...and who should know better than her across-the-hall neighbor — the writer of this article.

Mrs. Moishe (Bertha) Taube
Cantor's Spouse Willing Mate

This is being written on a clear day when you see forever. So it might be nice to look-see into the life of a most interesting personality. Mrs. Bertha Taube, our neighbor at Bartlett St. She's the lovely missus of Rev. Moishe Taube, golden-voiced Cantor of Beth Shalom Synagogue.

The former Bertha Klipper was born in far-off Czernowitz. Before the Russian occupation during WW 2 it was known as Rumania. She got a Russian education, after specializing in Pharmacy. In 1946, at age 18 Bertha embarked on a dangerous road to Palestine (now Israel). With the underground. Palestine then was under British rule and immigration was strictly forbidden. Their boat, sailing under the cover of darkness had room for 600 passengers but 2,500 homeless refugees crowded into it.

In mid-sea the ship sprung a leak. What to do! The captain flashed an S.O.S. and a miracle happened. A British plane circling the skies searching for illegal sailings sighted the ship. And made haste to capture it. And by so doing unknowingly saved the "invaders" from death at sea.

They were herded into a camp for illegal immigrants and kept there 3½ months. Among them was a young fellow with a beautiful voice. He kept up their morale by leading the captives in songs. You guessed it — Moishe Taube. He too came from Rumania but never met Bertha until that hazardous voyage. He joined the secret army known the world over as Hagana. Bertha wanted to continue Pharmacy but at the time there were no such schools. So she applied for nursing at Belinson Hospital.

It belongs to Kupat Cholim, a branch of Histradrut, the Workers' Union. Every worker automatically belongs to Histradrut and has the advantage of socialized medicine. Her knowledge of Latin, Russian, Rumanian and German was helpful. But knowing very little of Hebrew had her stumped. However they gave her five months in which to learn that difficult language. To Bertha, the sterner the challenge the firmer the resolve. She studied hard and made it.

Out of 150 applicants she was among 25 chosen for nursing. When the War of Independence broke out her soldier sweetheart was stationed in the mountains. Sometimes she didn't see him for six months. At war's end she was still a student nurse and Moishe still a soldier. In 1949 he claimed her as his bride. By the time she got her diploma son Ben-Zion was born. And dad started to study voice seriously.

They moved to Jerusalem and baby Rachel arrived. Before long the cantor's Israeli teacher admitted he could give him no further training. And suggested he go to the U.S. to complete his studies. So off they traveled to N.Y.C. where he enrolled in the Julliard School of Music. After three days he got a fine position as Cantor in a Manhattan Temple. Meantime something new was added. Baby Nina. Since the reputation of a talented Cantor travels fast, he was invited to come to Beth Shalom Synagogue at Beacon and Shady. Three years ago to be exact.

Son Ben-Zion is now 18 and just graduated Yeshiva University Talmudic Academy in New York. Rachel is 14 and attends Beacon Street Hillel Academy, 10th grade. She plans later to continue her studies in Israel. Nina, now nine also goes to Hillel, grade 4.

Our neighbors were in Israel last summer for six weeks. They visited Betha's mother, sister Aliza and the latter's two children. In Jerusalem the American Yankees and their Israeli Sabra cousins had a great reunion.

A woman of simple joys, Mrs. Taube, concentrates in being a good wife and mother. And is active in the Synagogue's many interesting programs. Her talented husband gives concerts in Cleveland, Chicago, Buffalo and other large cities. Last Spring she underwent major surgery, and came home on crutches.

When Cantor Taube needed to go to Grossinger's for a Cantors' Convention she went along. And who do you think got more attention than all the Cantors combined? Rev. Moishe Taube's lovely missus and her crutches.

The Taubes all love our city and the friendly people. And it's ditto the other way around. Our community wishes them the best of everything now and in the years ahead.

Dr. Hal C. Teal

Allderdice Principal Comes 'Equipped'

Where were you the evening of June 12? No doubt where practically everyone else in our neighborhood was. At the Civic Arena. To attend the Commencement exercises for the sweet-girl and handsome-boy graduates of our Taylor Allderdice High School. The 73rd in its history. You watched 587 high honor and graduating seniors being presented their diplomas. And if you were a mama tears mingled with your joy.

So now, in between the "school is over — hiphooray" glee it might be nice to learn a little about the dedicated and capable fellow heading Allderdice. Dr. Hal C. Teal, the Principal. With an enrollment of 3300 pupils the principal must have a solid educational background, no end of experience, patience and a sense of humor. Dr. Teal has these aplenty — and even more. Let's see now.

Teal earned his B.A. degree from Wooster College, Wooster, Ohio. And his M.A. and Ph.D. from Pitt. At Wooster he also earned something more. The heart and hand of a beautiful girl in his class. Etta Blair of McKeesport. Etta was also smart, earning her B.A. degree there. After each graduated they did what comes naturally. Got married. In 1951 Prof. Teal was called to Allderdice as one of two counselors. Now there are six.

A counselor, he says, has no teaching assignments. He interviews individual students about selecting a college or earning a scholarship. He guides them in vocational plans. When a pupil's grades are below par he tries to find the cause — from the teacher, the parents. Should a student have personal problems he wants to talk over with someone he can trust, he turns to the counselor.

Each counselor sees an assigned pupil at least once a year, inviting the parents to join in discussing problems. After five years as a successful Counselor, Dr. Teal was made Vice Principal of the Senior School. There he served diligently from 1956 to 1960. Then was transferred to Allegheny High School as Principal. Two years later he became Principal of Allderdice.

Dr. Teal has done a remarkable job in the Advanced Placement program. Superior students take college courses for a year while yet in high school. If they do well on a national Advanced Placement test they earn college credits. Later at college they thus have saved time for other courses they wouldn't otherwise have time for. Many of these start out as Sopomores instead of Freshmen.

Then there's the Pittsburgh Scholars program which is more advanced in Allderdice than average. It's for academically talented students. It gives them training in electronics, commercial art, graphic art, drafting and design. Also business courses. These courses are usually reserved for the later high school years. But the special students take them much earlier. There are also special courses for regular students interested in vocational or technical training.

Our professor's capable missus is a professionally trained librarian and works half-time in the Carnegie Library in Oakland. In the Boys and Girls Reading Room. Their lovely daughter Janis, 21, just graduated Pitt and will continue there for her M.A. degree in teaching. It includes practical teaching and class work.

The Teals were in Europe the past two summers. They flew over. But instead of rushing through the countries like average tourists, they took their time in a drive-yourself car. And saw everything. This summer, if they go anywhere it will be in the USA. Meantime dad will get in some good golfing locally.

Dr. Teal says 70 per cent of Allderdice students are Jewish. And he is proud that the school ranks very high in academic rating. In the graduating class 23 pupils were

National Merit finalists. Three received National Merit Scholarships and one of them was named one of 121 Presidential Scholars. These were specially cited by President Johnson and entertained at the White House June 10.·

Allderdice won the First City Football championship this season and came out second in baseball as well as swimming. Dr. Teal says, compared with the general pattern around the country there appears to be fewer problems of misbehavior and delinquency at our school. Honestly now — aren't you glad your kids go to Allderdice?

Wm. L. Thunhurst, Jr.

Civic Light Opera Season Looks Promising Once More

Who says there's no good news these days? Happily there is. Spring is renewing its radiance with sunshine and rain-drops for flowers to grow. And come July and Sugust, you'll be regaled with the loveliest Civic Light Operas ever. In the three years since the Civic Arena Shows, back debts have been paid off and the old Penn Theatre renovated and converted into the magnificent Heinz Hall for the Performing Arts, where the summer operas will be held.

What does it take to add such grace to our city? Talent, imagination, courage, work, fortitude — that's what. And a fellow who has all these is the new CLO Managing Director, Wm. L. Thunhurst, Jr. of nearby Edgewood. Bill is favorably known to our community. He and his talented wife, Betty Gillett, entertained our Merchants Council at the former Bubbles and Sherman's a few years ago.

Now let's learn a little more about this 6-foot-2 streamlined, likeable guy with brown eyes and smoothly-styled red hair. Born in Wilkinsburg he graduated Edgewood High. And on to Carnegie Tech (CMU). Then came WW II, interrupting his studies as he became a fighter pilot for Uncle Sam. At war's end, honorably discharged, he continued his senior year at Tech, earning a BFA degree in Drama — February 1947, to be exact.

His first job was at Mellon Bank in its training program. After a year he knew he was better suited to show-business than banking, so off to NYC where he performed in three Broadway shows. Then into musical comedies: "Arms and the Girl" and "South Pacific". When the later musical toured various cities (including ours) the Mary Martin role was taken over by talented Betty Gillett. In no time, Thunhurst fell for her charms. Soon they did what comes naturally, got married.

Together they continued to gain and broaden their experience in the theatrical, radio, TV and motion picture fields. Betty recently starred in the side-splitting production, "Never Too Late," at our popular Playhouse. Daughter, Deborah Anne, 18, is a freshman at Bennett College, Millbrook, N.Y. She has developed a fine voice and plays the guitar.

Bill is a most happy fella. Some married men, wanting to discuss professional experiences with their better half, are frustrated because the little woman knows from nuthin' what he's saying. Betty knows. They speak the same language, as the saying goes. And have fun "talking shop". And when the subject is music, it comes up roses. Both are gratified at having worked, in their apprentice years with actors who are now world-famous. The Thunhursts enjoy their charming three-bedroom ranch house which they own. It's filled with pictures of the theatre.

The summer operas? Pull up your chairs and take note: "Mame" starring Janet Blair; "Minnie's Boys" with Kay Ballard; "Camelot"; "Bye, Bye, Birdie" starring Tab Hunter and Chita Rivera; "High Button Shoes" with Jack Cassidy and our Betty Gillett of beautiful voice. Finally, "Annie Get Your Gun" starring Cloris Leechman, Oscar-winner for "The Last Picture Show". All with Saturday matinees.

Capable public-relations man Bill Mazefsky says season ticket sales have started and are going strong. He enthusiastically suggests you get busy on reservations, or you might run the chance of bumping smack up against a "Sold Out" sign.

Nice, isn't it, meeting the Thunhursts and having something delightful to look forward to this summer. There's no people like Show people.

Richard Tolusciak

Departs Old Axiom In Caretaker Role

Following in father's footsteps is old hat and not big news. But continuing the work of a father-in-law, that's something else again. Especially if it's being caretaker of a Jewish Synagogue, and both are devout Catholics. So neighbors, pull up your chairs and learn a little about this likable fellow. He's Richard Tolusicak, affectionately called Dick by one and all.

Young Dick is Jack-of-all-trades for the Beth Shalom synagogue at Beacon and Shady. He lives in a large house owned by the Shul, at Bartlet St. His wife's dad was the caretaker for 31 years until retirement. Dick has held the job for five years. He comes to work at 3:30 p.m. and is kept busy till 10:30 that evening. His duties are many and interesting, he says.

He helps put on all the synagogue's social affairs. At Bar Mitzvahs and Weddings Dick is chief bartender. He can be trusted to mix'em just right without being deadly. For Oneg Shabbats, Sisterhood and Men's Club events it's Dick who helps the women in the kitchen make tea, put cakes, cookies and fruit on trays for serving. And even cleaning up afterwards he does not consider a distasteful chore. He's also an amateur magician. Recently he put on a Show for the Sixth Grade Club — boys of the Shul. From then on he's been their idol.

Our neighbor arranges the stage for all the synagogue affairs. At the recent delightful Cantata composed by their talented Cantor Taube, the printed program listed among the other celebrities "Stage Settings by Dick." After Symphony violinist Murray Feldman completed his stirring solos, Dick came on stage to carry off the music sheets and the violin stand. And received as much applause — some say more — than the violinist. And thus became a "Celebrity" himself. So much so that Rabbi Goldblum asked him for his autograph! More applause.

We mustn't forget another very important duty for the care taker. On Friday evening, the beginning of the Jewish Sabbath, a pious Jew dare not put on the lights. And is not permitted to ask anyone else to do it for him. Dick puts on all the lights — without being told! And has earned the humorous title "Shabbas Goy."

Our neighbor is married to the former Rita Homison from Lawrenceville. When a boy of 13 Dick worked for a Jewish grocer. And delivered groceries to her home. A blonde blue-eyed beauty — smart with money. Her mother always gave her 25¢ to give to the delivery boy. Instead, she put it in her own pocket. When sailor Tolusciak returned from a four-year stint in Uncle Sam's Navy and three times around the world, he wanted a date for an upcoming dance. He knew no girl prettier than Rita. Nor richer. And since dancing often leads to marriage, that's exactly what happened.

In 1959 they became Mr. and Mrs. at St. Kierans Church in Lawrenceville. At the time the young husband was caretaker and gardener for the late Col. Rockwell's estate. And the lovely bride was selling bagels and bulkies at Silberberg's Bakery. She continued for a year, until baby Chrissy came along. Chris is now six and attends

St. Philomena School. Rickey, four, proudly marches off to Colfax Kindergarten. He has high hopes. Wants to became a janitor. Baby Judy, two, ain't talkin'. She just gives you a bewitching smile.

Since our neighbor doesn't start his synagogue duties til 3:30 p.m., so what does he do earlier? Go skiing mebbe? Nope. He attends the Universal Art Academy downtown from 8 a.m. til 3 p.m. six days a week. Learning Commercial Art for Advertising.

As a life-long Catholic, steeped in the ways of a Jewish Synagogue and its people, it might — in the proverbial 120 years from now — create a gosh-awful problem for the Man Upstairs. And Dick might find himself in the Jewish Heaven. What do you think, neighbors? Would that be bad?

Dr. Emil S. Trellis
Doctor Concerned with Human Problems

This is being written when the opening ball-game was to have begun. But the players all struck out. The seats in our beautiful Three Rivers Stadium are empty. But don't despair. Sooner or later — perhaps while you're reading this — the conflict will have been resolved and it'll be Play Ball. However, greater, deeper problems afflict our society which are not so easily done away with. But good people are trying.

So it's a privilege to tell you about a dedicated neighbor who's working seriously on some vital ones. Meet Dr. Emil S. Trellis of Beechwood Blvd. Dr. Trellis is Director of the Squirrel Hill Mental Health Center of the Western Psychiatric Institute. It's a treatment-prevention program for our community. His staff of ten includes nurses, social workers, counselors, a mental-retardation specialist, an educational consultant and a most capable secretary. Some of the Team treat youngsters and adults for various emotional ills. Several work with parents of healthy children.

There's also consultation with the Greenfield organization. His Team spent a year at Allderdice trying to deal with conflicts between students from different communities. They are working with teacher groups in two elementary schools. One of the staff developed a program where a few neighborhood residents were carefully trained to counsel selected adolescents. And our nearby Sixth Presbyterian Church donated a large adjoining home which it owned, named the Moreledge Center, as an informal meeting-place for teens. Later it saddly burned down.

What does it take to direct such vitally important work? Plenty. Let's inumerate briefly a bit of our neighbor's education, experience and know-how.

Born in our old Montefiore Hospital, Emil attended Fulton School, graduated Peabody High, then to Pitt, earning his B.S. and M.L. degrees. And his M.D. from Jefferson Medical College, Phila. In 1961 he worked in Uncle Sam's Public Health Service Hospital, Lexington, Ky. as Psychiatric Chief of the Women's Addiction Service. And Clinical Instructor at the Univ. of Kentucky School of Medicine, Dept. of Psychiatry.

Dr. Trellis belongs to many National Psychiatric Societies and has written articles titled "Narcotics Use and Abuse." Also "Drug Abuse." In 1967 he directed the Hill District Community Mental Health Team concerned with the well-being of black people. His pilot narcotic-addict-treatment project at Torrance State Hospital from 1963 to '67 put him in touch with police, courts, social agencies — you name it. What about the future of drug abuse? He's relatively pessimistic since we tend to look at the misuse of drugs as the issue rather than the complex conditions contributing to it. We could go on and on, but you, of course, want to know a bit about his personal life.

Our neighbor's lovely missus is the former Barbara Miller of New Kensington. Remember the flurry created by the recent "Kosher Calory Cook Book" printed by the

Tree of Life Sisterhood? Barbara edited it. They have three lively, interesting children. Cindy, 15, goes to Allderdice. Dan and Tom, 13 and 9 respectively, attend Colfax. The Trellis gracious home reflects mom's excellent taste. The parents most pleasant diversion is having fun with their children — doing things together. And it's mutual.

And now get a load of this. Dr. Trellis was reluctant to be written up. Fact is, he had to be literally coaxed into it. That, in our book makes him extra special. Our community is proud of him and his team. And grateful.

William Unger
A Household Name Because of Deeds

If there's anyone around who hasn't heard of William (Bill) Unger, our Ebdy St. neighbor, please stand up. No standees? Small wonder. Bill Unger has been a household name for years because of his countless deeds for the good of others. And since he's celebrating his 80th birthday Jan. 1st, you want to learn more about him. So pull up your chairs, relax and listen.

Bill's folks came from Romania when he was 9, settling in our Hill District. After public school he graduated the Hill's Central Hi and got a job as clerk with Crucible Steel. When Hitlerism reared its ugly head starting WW 1, he served Uncle Sam at Kelly Field, Tex. for 2 years. Honorably discharged he worked in the Ad Dept. of the Jewish Criterion (now the Chronicle) for 12 years. Then served as a Court Crier in Allegheny Court under Judge Benj. Lencher for over 30 years.

When a young handsome bachelor he did his socializing at the old IKC on Center Ave. There he met lovely Sara Horvitz and Nov. 1919 they married. Through the years they were blessed with 3 children, namely: Burton, now a mfgr's representative; Elaine, charming wife of Irwin Goldberg, Exec. Director of Montefiore Hospital; and Marilyn whose husband Saul Osachy is with the IRS. (If you dislike taxes don't blame him — he only works there). There are 8 grandchildren and 1 great-grandchild.

And now let's go back some. At War's end, ex-soldier Unger joined the American Legion and in 1937 organized the Sq. Hill Post. After holding many offices he was named District Commander, later becoming known as "Mr. Legionnaire". When he organized the Jewish War Veterans Post No. 49 he held every office in Allegheny County and our State. He's still active in the latter Post as well as the American Legion Post 577. As past president of the Federation of War Veteran Societies of Allegheny County, it's believed he may be the only one who received a Citation from each of the following: The American Legion, Veterans of Foreign Wars, Disabled American War Veterans, Catholic War Veterans, Polish War Veterans and, of course, the Jewish Vets.

Recently our neighbor was honored by West Va. State Veterans Dept. for cooperating in Veteran Affairs. In 1935 he established the first Good Will Dinner sponsored by the JWV Post 49 which has continued for 38 consecutive years. In addition Bill's been active in the Y-IKC, having participated in athletic events — track, basketball, baseball. He's past president of the Coffey Club, the leading non-sectarian basketball Club in the Pgh. area. Also past president of Lechem Aniyim (Bread for the Poor), ditto of the Hebrew Free Burial Ass'n and a charter member of Temple Sinai.

Oh yes, years ago at the old IKC Bill organized and took part in debates, stage productions and minstrels. His personality is best described in the book "The Hill District as I Knew it". And now sadness. Since into each life some rain must fall, Bill lost his beloved mate, Sara. Two years ago. But instead of retiring into mournful isolation, he's grateful for his beautiful family. And continues his activities in our community.

In spare time — when he finds it — he helps out in Unger's Jewelry Store, Downtown — owned by brothers Max and Ben Unger.

A philosopher at heart he knows that life can still be meaningful if you let it — and help it along. Our neighbor does just that. And more power to him.

If you don't have a hang-over from New Year's Eve and your head is clear, this will again remind you that Bill Unger will be a youthful 80 Jan. 1, 1973. Our community wishes him many returns of the day and the best New Year possible. And the same for all those dear to him. Again — Happy Birthday, Happy New Year!

Dr. W. A. Uricchio
Mercy Biology Chairman A Talented Squirrel Hiller

Mt. Mercy College, as of course you know, is in Oakland. But the Chairman of its Biology department is a Squirrel Hiller. And when you learn a little about this interesting personality you'll be glad he is.

Our neighbor is Dr. William A. Uricchio. He and wife Velma (a graduate nurse and his college sweetheart) live on Murray Ave. And there's Billy, 11; Mary Lynn, 10; Barbara, 6. Barbara attended Wightman School and now she and her elder brothers go to St. Paul's Cathedral. As to little Bobby, scarcely 3 and baby Michael, just turned 2, they haven't given school a ponder. They are too busy and curious about the many fascinating places in and around their huge 10 room house, exploring and maybe tearing apart.

Dr. Uricchio was born in Hartford, Conn., 39 years ago. But unlike Jack Benny he expects to get older — every year.

Biology — what, exactly, is it? Ask a little boy and he'll say it's about the birds and the bees. But Professor Uricchio explains it as "The science of life; the knowledge which treats of the origin, development, structure, functions, distribution of plants and animals." Which of course means us people too.

Our professor's educational background is fantastic. He received his B.A., M.S. and Ph.D. degrees from Catholic University of America, Washington, D.C. While there he was a Teaching Fellow. He also attended Massachusetts University — spending 8 full years at college. For three years he served Uncle Sam during World War II.

Mt. Mercy, from Fifth Ave. can hardly be seen because it's way up high on the hill. But inside it's a thing of beauty and joy forever. On a sunny day, between class breaks the campus simply bursts with the spirit of youth — blondes, brunettes and red-heads between 17 and 21. There are 700 of 'em from all over the U.S. and many from foreign countries. They are Catholic, Protestant, Jewish — of every race and color. Mt. Mercy's faculty consists of 70 men and women — lay and religious.

Dr. Uricchio has been a full-time professor at Mt. Mercy for 10 years. This year he was guest professor at Carnegie Tech, directing Biology programs in Advanced Placement. Our Allderdice High will benefit from this program. He is actively engaged in research and has received an NSF Grant for the past seven years for updating high school teachers. He reviews manuscripts and books on Biology before publication; reviews books on general topics for newspapers. And he wrote the recent review on "How You Were Born." Our professor belongs to many honorary scientific organizations and is editor of a Science Journal. He's on the boards of Gilmary School and McGuire Home for Mentally Retarded Infants.

His many activities in our community include around 25 lectures a year on "Role of Parents in Sex Education."

His Biology students adore him and his wife, and idolize his children. They compete for the fun of baby-sitting at his home. He can have not just one, but three-at-a-time sitters. Pretty nice.

Wife Velma takes 100 of the girls to Cook Forest in the spring for a week-end with nature. And of course husband Bill is there also, to see what's cookin'. The only man among vast pulchritude. Again — p-r-e-t-t-y nice!

Dear parents of youngsters: if you want to know how to explain the facts of life to your darlings — without stuttering — go to one of Dr. Uricchio's Sex lectures. You'll become un-confused.

Dr. Neil Wald

Nuclear Background Valuable

To date, through your NEWS you've met 218 outstanding neighbors. Anyone thinking there are no more should be asked to leave town. Because today, again, you'll meet another brilliant neighbor. He's Dr. Neil Wald of Normlee Place. Dr. Wald is Chairman of the Department of Radiation Health in Pitt's School of Public Health. And Professor of Radiology in its School of Medicine. Also Director of the Radiation Dept. in the Presbyterian University Hospital. As well as Chairman of the University's Radiation Safety Committee.

Dr. Wald's fabulous education and vast experience in nuclear radiation injury prevention and treatment; his articles written in medical and scientific journals, and his lectures everywhere would fill a book. A library even. Besides, they'd make the average layman dizzy trying to understand. The late Dr. Thomas Parran, first Dean of Pitt's School of Public Health sure understood. Our city being 'way ahead in nuclear development (Westinghouse, Duquesne Light and Nuclear Materials and Equipment Co.) has urgent need for treatment and prevention of radiation hazards to workers. Parran immediately knew Dr. Wald was the man most needed., And lost no time calling him to our University. In 1958, to be exact.

And now let's dwell on our brilliant neighbor's personal life. Born in N.Y. a mere 46 years ago, Neil received his AB from Columbia College; his MD from N.Y. University College of Medicine; an Internship and Fellowship in Immunohematology, and Residencies in Internal Medicine in N.Y.U.—affiliated hospitals. All accomplished by 1952.

Somewhere along the line the studious bachelor fell in love. With charming Lucienne Hill (part French, part American). In N.Y. studying Art and Nursing, Lucienne lived with an aunt whose next-door neighbor was Neil's close male friend. The latter had been dating her. So Neil, in good conscience could hardly ask her for a date. Later, however, when the fickle friend started dating other girls, and with Lucienne's warm encouragement, Neil quickly took over. They married in N.Y. in 1953. At the time the young husband was in the Air Force stationed at Randolf Field, Texas. They went housekeeping there in an apartment in the officers' quarters.

Years later, after Pearl Harbor, the ex-officer was sent to Japan, by the National Research Council. With his special training in blood diseases he headed a study of Leukemia and to learn the effects and treatment of A-bomb survivors in Hiroshima. Instead of the two years planned there, they stayed 3 because they loved Japan.

While there, guess what? A Japanese Stork brought them two baby boys, several years apart. David, now 17 is a drummer in a rock group "Coco-Bolo". And played at a benefit performance to raise funds for an injured Greenfield boy. Phillip, 15-½, baby-sat during the year so he could go skiing in Vermont during his Christmas vacation.

Both attend Allderdice and belong to the Young Peoples Synagogue at the Hebrew Institute. Mom goes to Pitt, majoring in Anthropology and East Asian Studies. When she's preparing for exams, pop does the dishes: She hopes to get her BA in April.

The Wald's home which they own is located on a dead-end street. With lots of outdoor ground. Their 3 cats and dog Pugsley have plenty of room to romp and play. What do they think of Radiation? They couldn't care less.

Our neighbors bought some land adjoining Moraine State Park near Lake Arthur. All are looking forward to summer to enjoy sailing and fishing.

Such interesting neighbors make our community feel good. And there's nothing bad about feeling good.

Dr. John C. Warner
...He's Nobody's Retiree

Dear friends and gentle neighbors: Today you'll meet a most fabulous fellow. It so happens, though, he isn't exactly a Squirrel-Hiller. But who's going to be strict when he's so outstanding? Besides, he does live close by — in the Oakland Civic Center. The Neville House, to be exact. So let's simply adopt him. And without further ado learn about him.

Meet Dr. John C. Warner, recently retired president of Carnegie Institute of Technology. And let's find out what he's doing in retirement.

We all know retirees — decent, average people — fumbling around trying to keep dat ole debil boredom away from their door. Their life-time work was their one and only interest. And at its end they find themselves completely lost.

How refreshing, then, is a man like Dr. Warner. Of course, his fabulous educational background and brilliance are a great asset. At 68 he's having the time of his life. His days are a satisfying blend of work he thoroughly enjoys, and some hobbies.

He's a man in perpetual motion and looks radiantly happy. He walks with a quick firm step and his warm friendly smile wins you over in a minute.

Dr. Warner's dad was a farmer in Goshen, Ind., and his mom, before marriage a country school teacher. Through the years son John graduated from Indiana University. And received so many honorary degrees that only a computer can enumerate them.

He began his career as a chemist in 1918, then a research chemist. In 1926 he returned to Tech as an instructor in chemistry. Soon he served as an assistant professor in chemistry — going higher and higher. In 1950 Dr. Warner became Tech's president.

Judging from the many news-paper articles of tribute emanating from Tech and numerous other sources; the admiration of his co-workers, and the love of his students, Dr. Warner was a president par excellence. He helped make the institute, its people and facilities far better than they might have been without him. At his retirement a year ago he was named president emeritus.

Our remarkable friend and closeby neighbor takes active interest in civic, business and professional society affairs. He's director of five outstanding corporations. Also he's chairman of the board of Nuclear Science & Engineering Corp. and holds membership in about 12 famous fraternities and clubs.

Dr. Warner has undertaken a contract with the Office of Economic Opportunity to help establish several hundred pre-college centers. These help prepare disadvantaged high school kids for college. The main office is in Washington, D.C. Locally it's at 400 S. Craig St. This project is developing with mushroom speed.

The Institute for Services to Education has organized a group of seven American universities to help build up the natural science department of the new Mindanao State University in the Philippines. And Dr. Warner has an important hand in it.

An independent Republican, his recreational interests include music, the theatre and vacations on the Maine coast. In his youth he played the fiddle — and far better than Jack Benny. Especially "Love in Bloom." And speaking of love, June 17, 1925 young Warner fell a victim to it.

On that eventful day he said "so long" to bacherlorhood and "I Do" to beautiful Louise L. Hamer of Huntington, Ind. He had been her teacher at Indiana University for several years. Took him that long to convince her that he was her man. She then taught school a year or so to help pay for furniture.

If someone had been around to get it for her wholesale, her teaching career would have been shorter.

The Warners have two successful sons: William, a professor in the University of Minnesota, teaching aeronautical and applied mathematics. Son Thomas is plant superintendent at the Screw & Bolt Corp. in nearby Mt. Pleasant. And there are three lively grandchildren: Anne, William and Katherine.

Should any of you romantic ladies become enraptured enough to write our famous nearby neighbor a fan letter — take it easy with contents. His private secretary has instruction to open and read all mail. So who is his secretary? His B.W. (beautiful wife).

Mrs. Samuel O. Wechsler

Plays 'Angel' For Hospitalized

Everyone is familiar with the world-famous moto "None May Enter Who Can Pay — None Can Pay Who Enter" of the National Jewish Hospital at Denver.

And knows that the hospital has a local committee of prominent citizens. But not everybody is aware that a favorably-known neighborhood personality has been appointed director of that committee. January of this year, to be exact.

Because the job is an important one, and she being a 'round-the-corner neighbor, you'll want to know her better. So pull up your chairs and learn about Frieda Wechsler, wife of Samuel Wechsler of Darlington Rd. You'll agree she's a "a natural" for that job if you will read on.

First, a bit of Frieda's family background. Husband Samuel represents a factory which makes maternity dresses. They met long before that apparel entered his mind. Twenty-five years ago, on a blind date. And proudly escorted her to a Marx Brothers movie at the Penn — "A Night at the Opera."

(Teenagers: Ask your mom about that one). They dated three years and in 1946 became Mr. and Mrs.

The Wechslers have been blessed with two wonderful children. Heather, 19, a graduate of Allderdice attends the American University in our nation's capital. For two summers she was counselor at Camp Deer Creek, Harmarville, Pa. Heather can cook, too. Mom saw to that.

Son Warren is 13 and the best PG delivery boy in our neighborhood. You find your morning paper smack near your door, neatly folded. Warren hops out of bed at 5:30 a.m. to complete his paper route before school.

On Tuesdays he gets to Allderdice an hour earlier to coach a friend who's slow in math. In his "spare" time he has a hobby — collecting coins and foreign stamps. He was Bar Mitzvah at Poale Zedeck Synagogue last May.

In 1889 the National Jewish Hospital at Denver first opened its doors. To the tuberculosis poor, regardless of race, religion or color. And the price was right — absolutely free for those who had no funds. Those who had, could afford treatment elsewhere.

Its first patient was a young Catholic girl from Chicago. The famous motto still holds. To date, from Pennsylvania alone, it has given 223,915 days of free care. Two Pittsburgh patients are there currently — 12-year-old Ronna Horn from Stanton Heights and Mrs. Mary Louise Lally, member of the Homewood Holy Rosary Church. And a young Negro boy, Gilbert Hollie of Homewood, just returned after 11 months of free treatment.

While there he had his schooling, played football and actually made a name for himself. In September he will start school at Westinghouse High — strong and well.

The B'nai B'rith organization was instrumental in starting the Denver hospital. And Frieda Wechsler could actually be called "Mrs. B'nai B'rith."

During her teen-age years she was president of the B'nai B'rith Girls. Soon she became regional president, during which time she helped organize seven new chapters.

Then followed the presidency of B.B. Girls District 3. She earned the distinction of being the first international president of that group.

The Denver hospital dedicated a bed in her honor, from funds raised by her girls. Thus, the local director and the hospital are compatible. Like love-and-marriage. Or a convertible with teen-agers. However, the job requires many other attributes.

What must one have to be area director of this famous medical center? She needs the ability to make friends and influence people. Be possessed of initiative, imagination, with a sense of responsibility. Frieda Wechsler has all these — and even more. She's slim, pert and attractive, too.

As a P.S., you may be interested to learn that another Squirrel-Hiller held that job for 29 years. Who, for goodness sake? The writer of this article.

Dr. Cyril H. Wecht

Coroner's Role Has Ups, Downs

Hardly a day passes that you don't read in our newspapers about a fabulous fellow who has deservedly earned national fame in his vital profession. And since he's, of course a neighbor, you want to know him a little better. He's Dr. Cyril H. Wecht of Darlington Road. Dr. Wecht, Allegheny County Coroner, was re-elected January as President of the American College of Legal Medicine at its annual meeting held in Chicago.

And as Research Professor of Law and Director of the Institute of Forensic Science at Duquesne University, he presided at the various professional meetings conducted by the College at Chicago that weekend. Senator Charles H. Percy of Illinois was the keynote speaker. The American College of Legal Medicine is an organization limited to just 200 national members holding degrees in both Law and Medicine from accredited universities in the U.S.

Wecht was chosen as one of "Outstanding Young Men of America" by the National Junior Chamber of Commerce. Through the years he has been consulted by various national groups, including those on the John F. and Robert Kennedy assassinations. Also the Mary Jo Kopechne case

Our neighbor has received scholarships and belongs to (often heads) so many Medical, Legal and Honorary Societies as well as community organizations, and has authored and co-authored such a variety of professional articles that listing them would fill a book. Maybe a library. So you know what? Let's skip the whole thing and just give you a few highlights and dwell mostly on his personal life. Which is more fun to read anyhow.

Cyril was born in McKees Rocks. At the ripe age of seven, he and his parents (Nathan and Fannie Wecht) moved Uptown near the Mercy Hospital. He was Valedictorian at Fifth Avenue High and in 1952 was a cum laude graduate of Pitt, with a BS degree. Then two years later at the University of Buffalo School of Medicine and two more at Pitt's School of Medicine, becoming an MD. He interned at St. Francis Hospital. Then two things happened. He started a residency at the Vets Hospital in Pathology and also took up Law at Pitt. Then Uncle Sam called him to the U.S. Air Force. For two years he was Captain and Pathologist at Maxwell Air Force Base.

Then something else happened. He fell in love. With the medical secretary at the Hospital. Lovely Sigrid Ronsdal from Norway. Rabbi Solomon B. Freehof of Rodef Shalom Temple pronounced them Mr. and Mrs. and they went to live with his devoted parents on Beacon Street.

The Wechts now live in a 12-room home which they own. Their four lively children are: David, Daniel, Benjamin and Ingrid...eight, seven, five and two. The boys attend St. Edmund's Academy and go to Rodef Shalom Religious School. They take swimming, judo and skiing lessons. And since Pop plays the violin they also take music lessons and hope to play ensemble music. Their pet Irish Wolfhound Moisha takes no lessons. Mostly he watches the household and their four goldfish. And sits near baby Ingrid as she revels in Bugs Bunny, Pop-Eye, Porky Pig and such. When he gets bored he curls up and takes a snooze. Mom Wecht is interested in various civic organizations.

The family enjoys doing things together. Last spring they were in Israel and Greece. In 1967 they took the boys through the Scandinavian countries.

Being Coroner of our County is more than a full-time job. He averages between 75-80 hours a week. He's on call every hour of the day — on murders, accidents, suicides, suspicious or unexplained deaths. Even on holidays his office never closes. He has a small Pathology Laboratory in the Iroquois Building. He's consultant for attorneys throughout the nation on medical-legal problems involved in their cases, to help determine cause of death.

Our neighbor organized and is chairman of a committee which looks into the medical and legal aspects of heart transplants, and gives lectures on their problems.

A handsome fellow, in perpetual motion, loves his work, looks radiantly happy and is only 39. Not the Jack Benny 39 but for real. How's that for a fabulous neighbor?

Nathan Weiner

School of Hard Knocks No Problem for Him

As you know by now, our neighborhood is filled with wonderfully interesting personalities. They live blocks away, down the street, around the corner, next door. They all have a story. Some are gay, some gayer. Others not so gay. But each is a slice of life. Today you'll learn about a fellow next door whose leisure time is filled with worthy doings. He's the well-known and likable Nathan Weiner of Forbes Ave.

But don't look for college degrees. He has none such. He didn't even graduate high school. In fact, he never went to school at all. Except the school of hard knocks.

Born in Minsk, Russia, Nathan was 17 when an uncle in New York arranged for his passage to the Land of Liberty. It wasn't the Mayflower. Nor the Queen Mary. Not even the Shalom.

A steerage no doubt — the kind of ship our grandparents migrated on. At about the same time young and lovely Rose Einbund, also from Minsk, (or was it Pinsk?) was brought over by a cousin in our city. Nathan had another uncle here. And guess what? The uncle, a natural "Fiddler-on-the-roof" matchmaker, invited the new American to Pittsburgh for a visit. You guessed it. By the time he was 20, Minsk, Pinsk — Nathan Weiner was a settled married man, with Rose Einbund his adoring wife.

Potatoes and tomatoes being cheaper then, the young husband, a paper-hanger by trade, was able to pay for groceries. Later he went to work in a cleaning plant. And for five years was a Union organizer. In 1940 Weiner went into business for himself, manufacturing wire hangers. Nineteen years later he sold out. Now he's retired.

Never having had an education himself, our neighbor saw to it that his four children did. Son Abe Weiner, a graduate of Tech's Art department, is assistant director of the Ivy School of Professional Art, Downtown. Considered one of the most promising painters in the U.S. he has exhibited in Chicago, New York and other large cities. He's a member of the Associated Artists. His wife Anne is a piano teacher.

Bernard also is a Tech graduate. He works in the Engineering Dept. of the U.S. Government as an architect. His wife Selma is a kindergarten teacher.

The daughters are Beatrice Schechter, whose husband Milt owns the Liberty Incandescent Lighting. And Barbara is married to Jerry Dinovitz, a manufacturer's representative with a show-room in the Penn-Sheraton. There are 10 grandchildren. All are Squirrel Hillers.

Since retirement, dad Weiner has been on the board of the Senior Citizens Club of the Y-IKC And is house chairman of that group. He arranges the card games and other recreation activities. He even perks the coffee. And now listen to this. He visits sick people through the social service department of the Montefiore Hospital — after they get home. Mostly those without family. These include two friendless men at the Jewish Home for the Aged. And 76-year old Wm. Hamlet of Robinson Court — a blind negro without kith or kin. Hamlet was a handyman at the Rodef Shalom Temple for 20 years. Weiner visits him every week. And once a month takes him to the hospital for a check-up. Often he brings him goodies. Even bagels — you know, pretzels with a superiority complex at their best in Squirrel Hill bake shops.

Never having had a honeymoon, Nate took his Rose to Miami Beach last November — their first trip South — for a three-month stay. To celebrate their 50th wedding anniversary. The only thing that marred the trip was having to leave his blind friend all alone. He didn't even have the heart to tell him he's leaving. Upon his return in March, Mr. Hamlet was in tears from joy. So was Weiner.

The Weiner children welcomed their sun-tanned mom and dad's home-coming with a fabulous Anniversary Dinner at Canter's restaurant March 18th. Wedding cake and all. Near and far relatives, including all their kissin' cousins, were there.

Our neighbor has Merit Awards for devoted and unselfish service from the Montefiore Hospital, the Jewish Home & Hospital for the Aged, the United Fund of Allegheny County, to name a few. As they say — if everyone would light but one little candle what a bright world this would be. May the Weiner's world be bright now and in the years ahead.

Dr. Irving Wender
Area Chemist Notes Future of Cooking

Dear neighbors — especially women and bachelors who do the cooking at your house. We have news for you. Fascinating news. In the not-far-distant future you'll be making dinner out of petroleum and coal. And in about 10 years no one in the entire over-populated world need go hungry. But the nice part about it is that a brilliant Chemist in our neighborhood has the inside know-how on the project. So say hello to Dr. Irving Wender of Denniston Ave. He's Chief of the Chemistry Section of Pittsburgh Coal Research Center. And has worked at our Bureau of Mines since 1946. He also has a class at Pitt in Organic Chemistry.

Dr. Wender says you grow yeast or bacteria on certain parts of petroleum or coal. It develops fast and comes our a thick mass. Then it's made into a white tasteless powder. But it has all the food elements, particularly meat proteins. You simple flavor it to your taste and shwoosh — dinner is ready! Already animals in France, Czechoslovachia and Russia are lapping it up. Of course it's not as simple as it sounds. But give 'em time. Our neighbor is also working on cheaper synthetic gasoline from coal, and ways to combat dat ole debbil, Air Pollution He says the Bureau of Mines is a great place to work in. His group of 18 (7 with Ph.D.'s) are given an opportunity to let their imagination, skill and diligence hold full sway.

Born in New York City, Wener earned his BS degree from City College, his MS from Columbia. And had the good sense to come to Pitt for his Ph.D. Now his reputation is world-wide. He has lectured in Belgium, England, Germany, France, Italy — you name it. Recently he received the highest honor of the U.S. Department of the Interior — a gold medal for Distinguished Service, for his contribution to fundamental research at the Bureau of Mines.

And now let's snoop a little into his personal life. As a know-it-all bachelor from the Bronx, he often chided his brother for dating a girl in Brooklyn. Get a girl closer to home, he kept saying. But guess what happened to Irving? He fell for lovely Reah Margolin, a yo-all shugah from Chattanooga, Tenn. Served him right! On his first visit to her home he had to drive all the way to Miami (3 days), and catch a Chattanooga Choo-choo to her home. Another 28 hours. But he was well rewarded with the best meals he ever ate. Reah didn't entice him with miniskirts. Instead, she cooked dinner. By the end of the week Irving returned to the Bronx an engaged man. Reah, a graduate of the University of Chattanooga, with a scholarship to Columbia University, soon followed. But instead of college she took a job to help pay for the furniture. They didn't get it wholesale.

Our neighbor now enthuses when he talks of his family. Their twin sons, 16-going-on-17, are juniors at Allderdice. Both are Eagle Scouts. Edward, and "A" student in Math and Sciences, plays the clarinet in the all-City Orchestra. Donald has a leaning toward Science and plays the tuba. Richard is 13 and goes to Linden. He plays the violin and sings in a wild combo, "The High Tide." He will be an Eagle Scout come spring.

Then there's their basset-hound, Mona Lisa. Her former owner is now in Italy and sent her a card saying "Having a good time — wish you were along." Not long ago they had two guinea pigs — Adam and Eve. But pop Wender became allergic to them. What to do? They couldn't just turn the little critters out on the street. So they gave them to the Nature Museum in Frick Park. And the kids visit them.

Mom Wender was president of the Linden PTA. Now she holds that job with Allderdice. She's active in NCJW and works in the WICS. Two days a week she's secretary at Pitt. Dad is on the board of Rodef Shalom Temple Brotherhood and assistant Scout Master of Troop 14. He has met the most interesting people through his Scouting — a complete cross-section of all occupations and interests. He's active in the American Chemical Society. And loves sports. He predicts, with Clemente and now Maury Wills, our Pirates will murder 'em. Allevei! The Wenders are celebrating their 25th Wedding Anniversary this March. Many happy returns.

Mrs. Gerome S. (Lu) Wenneker

Adventuresome Wennekers Recall Fond Memories of Stay in Italy

Been to Europe and beyond lately? And came home with empty pockets? Well — if you were as knowledgeable, imaginative and adventuresome as the Wennekers, your pockets might still be jingling. So who are the Wennekers, for goodness sakes? They're our interesting neighbors at Wightman Street — that's who. And you'll learn the why, when, where and how-come if you will read on.

Mrs. Gerome S. Wenneker, the former Lu Beery of Monesson (kissin' cousin of the late famous Wallace Beery) teaches Drama at our well-known Ellis School for Girls. She's a graduate of Chatham College, having majored in Drama and Art. And guess who was — and still is — Drama teacher?

Tall, easy-to-look-at Gerome Wenneker. And because, as he proudly says, Lu was the most talented and prettiest girl in his class, he did what came naturally. Married her. In 1950, to be exact. After a honeymoon in N.Y.C., Gerome resumed teaching Drama at Chatham. And his lovely, talented bride took a job at Gimbel's Art Display department. She arranged their inside displays. And enjoyed getting discounts on all purchases toward furnishing their home.

Their marriage has been blessed with three lively children. Gordon, now 13 goes to Shadyside Academy, Laura, 12 and Lucy 8, both attend Ellis School. And are proud of the art teacher — their mom.

Their household cellar is enlivened by two guinea pigs named Piglet and Apricot, who became the proud parents of a blessed event right before Christmas. Which became an ideal gift for an eager friend. Their rabbit, Harvey, scarcely two months young, is in the process of being house-broken. Then there's the neighbor's dog Benji, a shaggy toy Schnauzer who thinks the Wenneker home is his. Every evening he slips in, curls up at their cozy fireplace and takes a blissful snooze.

And now for the piece de resistance. When Gerome's remarkable missus received a Fullbright Fellowship a year ago, he himself was granted a Sabbatical leave from Chatham. They gathered up the kids and off they went to Florence, Italy, for 10 months — an ideal place to learn art history. And for visiting other fascinating places. The Fullbright furnished Lu's round-trip to Florence, her living allowance, and for books. They did not — like you-all — travel on a luxury liner but took instead passage on a student-boat to LeHave, France. Before leaving home, dad ordered a microbus Volkswagon in Germany and later picked it up in Hanover. Thus saving approximately $1,500 because of his know-how and foresight.

From Hanover they toured in their huge bus down along the Rhine all the way to Florence, Italy. There they rented an apartment close to the Art Library where Lu began her work. The children went to an English-speaking school and in no time learned Italian. The parents also studied the language. Daughter Laura, interested in ballet, went with her mom to the Royal Ballet. Gordon became fascinated in Archeology and may some day go to Israel to make further use of it. From Florence they traveled in their bus through Yugoslavia, then on to Athens and surrounding places. They attended many theatre festivals in Epidaurus and Sparta. These, and the monasteries and paintings were unforgettable.

Throughout their sight-seeing travels they spent nights, not at the Hiltons, but in highly organized camp sites along the Mediterranian. The parents slept in tents. The kids bedded down in the huge back area of their bus. Occasionally they even cooked supper in it.

Our neighbors came back last August — autobus and all — to their charming, comfortable 3-bedroom home. With the best beds ever. The memories of the experiences will remain with them always. More so since they shared as a family group — together. And Benji once again snoozes at their fire-place.

Morris Wise
...'No Wonder His Name Is Wise'

Constantly these days you hear about people living longer and because of automation, retiring younger.

So what should senior citizens do to keep dat ole debbil boredom away from their door? Suggestions and plans are afoot everywhere. But a well-known fellow in our neighborhood didn't wait for suggestions. He made plans himself. And they have proved worthwhile and meaningful.

Our neighbor in question is none other than the popular Morris Wise, of Douglas St. He has developed an absorbing hobby which not only gives him happiness but affords pleasure to others.

Mr. Wise always loved music. But the responsibilities of making a living for his sizeable family left him no time for lessons. However, he never missed a concert, symphony or opera throughout his entire life. Thus his musical yearnings were kept alive.

At 65 Morris Wise retired from his men's furnishings store on the North Side.

A year later he started taking piano lessons, through Mrs. Anne Perlow, music director of our community's popular Y-IKC. His good friend Nathan E. Snader, who recognized the latent musical talent of neighbor Wise, encouraged him to join the center's Senior Citizen's Social Club of which Mr. Snader is president.

The club believes in combining social fun with study — that it's never too late to learn.

Morris joined and by age 70 has made such remarkable progress that his friends call him "The Miracle of the Century."

But that's not all. One day, while Mrs. Perlow was in another room, pianist Wise began singing "My Hero' in a rich baritone voice. You guessed it. She and friend Snader urged him to study voice too.

Now his musical talent is so rounded out that he is sought constantly for entertaining. He performs at any and all charitable groups that cannot afford to pay. For free, of course.

He has entertained at the Negley House, at PTA meetings, at the Anathan House and the Senior Citizens' birthday parties. When he sings "Rose Marie," "There is No Tomorrow" or "Bless This House" the applause is deafening. Instead of Barry, it's 'We Want Morris! We Want Morris!''

And who do you think often plays the piano while he sings? Gwyn Hamovitz, his young granddaughter. She started piano lessons at age nine — on the exact day grandpop at age 66 began studying voice. When entertaining together, Morris Wise is "the happiest man alive."

Mr. Wise, who has lived in Squirrel Hill for 35 years, has three married daughters: Norma Zilker, Bernice Weltman and Edith Hamovitz, all living in Pittsburgh. There are nine grandchildren, including a set of eight-year old twins.

And now listen to this. In between practicing, he spends much time visiting the sick. Are there shut-ins in hospitals or at home without a family, who are lonely or discouraged? He brings them cheer and hope. He stays as long as they want. Even shops or does errands for them.

Our neighbor says he has no ambition for riches, but only to serve. He asks not what others can do for him, but what he can do for others. No wonder his name is Wise.

William Wolfson
'Willie The Fireman'

"Fireman, save my child!" How often do they hear that anguished cry? Too often — what with careless smokers, deserted houses filled with rubbish, arsonists, bombings and just plain mischiefmakers for a thrill. So today you'll meet a local fireman who retired after 35 years of courageous service. Say "hello dere" to William Wolfson of Negley Ave., fireman par excellence. His countless friends call him Willie. At retirement in 1965 he was honored with a banquet at a night club and given a watch and badge, both solid gold. His eldest brother, Dave, was a local policeman for 30 years. The latter's two sons are now on our police force. Why did Willie become a fireman? Fate mebbe. Let's see now.

Mr. Wolfson was born in NYC. His father, a house-painter, fell off a scaffold which proved fatal. Willie was just a little tyke of 3. Two years later mother Lena and her boys moved to our city. She opened a kosher boarding-house on Clark St. and Carpenter Alley where they lived. Willie went to Franklin School Logan and Epiphany Sts. At age 13 after the 6th grade he had to drop school and start working. One of the boarders Louis Kaufman took a liking to the boy and gave him a job huckstering fruits and vegetables on a horse-drawn wagon, starting in the produce yards at 5 a.m. Salary: 50 cents a day.

Willie also sold newspapers, buying them wholesale — two for 1 cent and selling each for a penny. A tidy profit! When mom married Mr. Kaufman, Willie was actually working for his stepfather. Later mother had saved enough to buy the son a horse and wagon of his very own. So young Wolfson became his own boss. Thus, as he grew older, he found time for a bit of socializing and meeting girls. Soon he did what comes naturally — fell in love and got married. To lovely Ethel Turner (now of blessed memory).

They were blest with one child — a son who later worked his own way through college and turned out just great. He's none other than Marty Wolfson, well-known artist and head of the Marty Wolfson Associates, Gateway Center. He has three interesting children. Todd and Marla go to Mt. Lebanon Hi and Paula attends Penn State. A far cry from grandad's humble 6th-grade schooling.

Now back to the horse and wagon days. After marriage huckstering became boring. So the young husband tried for a fireman's job. Now, due to the constantly increasing fires, it's a simple procedure. You apply and if accepted you immediately pitch in full-time. Years ago, you had to sub sometimes 5 years prior to a permanent position. You worked 12 hours a day, 7 days a week, day or night shifts. No day off, not even Sundays. Between fires you wash the hose, clean the apparatus. Saturdays were spent scrubbing floors. Through the years, seeing buddies perish fighting fires and not being able to save trapped victims in burning buildings brought deep heartaches. Willie served his 35 years with only a permanent scar on his hand from flying glass. He says the young firemen want to be heroes and take dangerous chances. Several hundred have lost their lives.

When ex-fireman Wolfson became a widower he was lonely. In due time his uncle told him of a nice widow "rooming" nearby. A meeting was arranged and several months of "going together" Fannie Levine became the second Mrs. Wolfson. They are very companionable together. An excellent cook, and Willie being on a restricted diet, she prepares exactly what he needs. Fannie doesn't gad about to women's clubs and won't go anywhere without Willie. After teaching him Canasta they play the game at the Y-IKC and the Anathan House in our neighborhood.

There's much more to tell but space is limited. The Firefighters Union Local No. 1 is working on a book giving the complete life histories of all retired fireman. Watch for its publication.

Meantime, when you hear the sirens screaming and the red engines and ladders racing through the streets, pray that no one will be hurt. And thank your lucky stars for our brave firemen, guys like Willie Wolfson. Lord bless them all.

Sterling Yates

What Ain't He Got?

It's simply fantastic the interesting personalities we have in our neighborhood. Consider the well-known and popular Sterling Yates of radio and television fame, our neighbor on Kinsman Road.

Tall, sun-tanned, with a million-dollar smile and voice — honestly, it's enough to make one forget Cary Grant. And the Beatles even.

You too will be won over if you listen on KDKA Sunday mornings 8 to noon. Sterling Yates regales you with jazz, news, the weather.

And even his commercials are easy to take. And if you turn the knob on Channel 2 Saturday mornings 9 to 10 you'll chuckle with the kids on "Wing-ding" — a program he co-hosts with Josie Cary and Johnny Costa. You may even win one of the giveaways.

The Yates comedy talent took another form recently. In "Take Her, She's Mine" which packed the Pittsburgh Playhouse, Ster played the dad and he himself really had a ball. So did the audience.

Now there are more plans afoot. When the Playhouse opens next season at the end of September, our neighbor will have the leading role in "A Thousand Clowns."

And Mr. Yates is the world's best salesman. At the Variety Club Charity Telethon recently, he sold more hot-dogs then you can shake a stick at.

His versatality as an actor before broadcasting dates back to when he was a tike of five. Since then he has been charming audiences big and small. A native of Chicago, Sterling graduated from Chicago Tech in 1951 with a degree in music. Before broadcasting days he was with seven orchestras — the Pittsburgh Symphony and the Pittsburgh Opera to name a few.

Sterling is married to the former Jeanne Negley of the pioneer Negley family. They met in high school. Allderdice no less. And there's Sterling Jr. (nickname Skipper), age 11. He goes to St. Edmund's Academy. So does his cousin Douglas Malone, 9, who makes his home with them.

Daughter Lindsay is at the most interesting age of 16 and attends Winchester.

Then there's Heidi, an over-sized German dachshund. And a fluffy French poodle who answers to the name Poolie. Until recently there was another member of that fascinating household — a pet monkey.

However, after just six months he couldn't take the goings on any more — and departed for the Great Beyond.

Mr. Yates is on the board of the Alpine Cabana Club, a new swim club. He also plays ice hockey with Dick Groat on a McDonald Farm owned by former football star Joe Zombeck.

And in his own back yard he reigns supreme at the charcoals. His grilled steaks are the talk of the town.

Many would consider Sterling Yates as A Man Who's Got Everything. So he has. But no — wait! What ain't he got? He ain't got bangs!

James D. Yeiser
Loss of Playhouse Is Loss Of Talent

In tennis, the buffs tell you, there's "No Love After 40." But there's plenty of it when James D. Yeiser is concerned and this in spite of the fact that Yeiser's role as general manager at the popular Pittsburgh Playhouse has been terminated.

Everyone was particularly chagrined when the announcement came that the Pittsburgh Playhouse, for lack of financial support, wouldn't be opening for its 40th season.

Yeiser, of nearby Wilkinsburg, was called here in June of last year by S. Joseph Nassif, the executive director for the Playhouse.

Scarcely 29, this imaginative fellow has a vast educational background, experience and know-how ideally suited to his vitally important duties. Kentucky-born, Yeiser was age 2 when the family moved to Chicago. Hence no hill-billy accent. In High School Jim was always in plays and on debating teams. After a year at Kentucky-Wesleyan he continued at Hanover College. Then to the University of Evansville, graduating with a BA degree. After a hitch at Fort Knox for Uncle Sam he got a job with Texas Gas Transmission Corp. His business experience acquired there and other sources has proved invaluable. When Nassif guest-directed a summer show he hired two of Jim's best friends for a year in our city. Coming to see the shows and visit the friends, Yeiser got hooked on Pittsburgh — its hills, its panorama, its character. And the friendly people. Joe made him an offer as Production Manager which he accepted. And worked during all of last year's productions. A play he himself wrote ("The Deaf") which the Playhouse produced mid-November was a sure-fire hit. He even created boots and shoes for the actors. Jim also plays the piano and loves reading.

Somewhere along the line, guess what? He met beautiful Bonnie Davies, a student in the Playhouse Professional Training School. Cupid stepped in and March of last year this near-6-footer and itty-bitty Bonnie (5 foot - 2) became Mr. and Mrs. Next May, guess who's coming to dinner? The Stork! Meantime he and Bonnie share their affection with Arlow and Taffy, two pet kittens. Are the pets interested in their master's responsibilities at the Playhouse — like for instance hiring personnel, public relations, business activities, box-office, bookkeeping, etcetra etcetra? They couldn't care less. But Jim's Bonnie does. Some men can't discuss business with their better-half because the little woman knows from nothing what he's talking about. But his little woman knows theatre. They speak the same language, as the saying goes. And enjoy talking shop. And what's more, Bonnie knows how to cook. When husband Jim comes home after a hard day, dinner is ready.

So the talents of this fine young man will go elsewhere we're sure. Meanwhile Pittsburgh theatre-goers are saddened because of the demise of the Pittsburgh Playhouse. Six outstanding plays had been arranged for the 1974 season.

The city's loss, therefore, is not only the loss of the theater, but also the loss of the talents of a young man destined for success in the world of show business.

Mrs. Joseph (Vera) Zahm
Creator of Dolls

Often, these days, when a woman is asked for her profession and she happens to be married, she meekly answers "Oh, I'm just a housewife," as if to aplogize that she isn't one of those glamorous career women. She's doubtless unaware that many married women, burdened with the added responsibilities of running a business, would be thrilled and grateful to be "just a housewife." And career be danged!

Mrs. Joseph (Vera) Zahm, of Phillips Ave., doesn't need to wish she were one or the other. She has been — and still is — both. When she married Joseph Zahm 34 years ago, at a time when a career for women was almost unheard of, she at once became a devoted wife, full-time.

But later (8 years ago to be exact) when their two daughters were grown and married, Vera found herself with spare time. Soon her naturally talented fingers began itching to create and "make things." From remnants of silks, chenille and cottons purchased at year-end sales, she has made thousands of dolls, colorful little aprons, flower pots, corsages, Christmas trees, Chanucka candles — and all sorts of intriguing novelties.

In fact, you name it and Vera can make it. At present her basement game-room is a veritable "little girl's paradise."

Vera's fabulous hobby has turned into "big business," except that the money she raises from it goes for charitable organizations exclusively. And what makes her extra special is that although Vera is of Jewish faith, her charities extend to all, regardless of race, creed or color.

"When I was a little girl in Russia," Vera reminisces, "I never knew what it was to have a doll. There were times we didn't have enough food or clothes. I always wanted to help people in need."

And she sure does. Through the years Mrs. Zahm has furnished dolls and all sorts of lovely handmade novelties for children. She reached them through the Salvation Army; Pittsburgh Assn. for the Improvement of the Poor; The Home for Crippled Children.

She has made cookies and corsages at Christmas time for the lonely elderly ladies at the Old Fullerton Home in Wilkinsburg. She has made and trimmed Christmas trees and Chanucka candles for Colfax School. Vera has taught doll-making to members of Haddassah and B'nai B'rith women's groups, as well as a Girl Scout Troop. And she has raised funds for the Save-A-Life Seniors. Her dolls and little sweaters even reached children at the National Jewish Hospital at Denver and the Leo N. Levi Memorial Hospital at Hot Springs, Ark. And she even knitted a black wool sweater for a nun in Philadelphia. Vera has and treasures a large box of thank-you letters from appreciative people all over the country.

Vera's husband is now part owner of a brake-shoe firm. Does he have a hobby? Yes, two to be exact. The first is their lovely garden where he and his wife (believe it or not) raise all sorts of vegetables and flowers. But his labor-of-love hobby is to fill his car evenings with Vera's dolls and other lovely novelties and help her deliver them to the various institutions for the children.

What about diversions such as night clubs? Do they ever step out? Yes, Aug. 26 on their 34th wedding anniversary Joe took Vera to a night club. Did they do the Twist? "We never had time to learn" she answered with a smile. "But it was great fun watching."

Mrs. Ben (Celia) Zeligson

Plenty of Kids... and Love, Too!

The personality of the week is our close by neighbor who has had a total of 43 children. No, she's not the Old Woman Who Lives in a Shoe. Neither has she drastically added to the population explosion. Only three are her own.

The others — 40 of them infants — were foster children, youngsters born to others, whom she has mothered like her very own.

Meet Mrs. Ben Zeligson, foster mother par excellence.

The former Celia Rosen arrived in the U.S. from Austria when she herself was an infant. She matured into a supercharged bundle of sentiment, caring for the welfare of others. And what she accomplished through the many years is a tribute to her blend of goodness, sense of humor and down-to-earth wisdom. So let's look further.

When teenagers, Celia Rosen and Ben Zeligson first met at a summer camp. He and his five adoring sisters were guests there. Cele waited on tables and washed dishes. Dish-pan hands or no, all became friends.

Many years later back home, she had an extra ticket for the symphony concerts. Phoning the Zeligson home to invite sister Anne to share the symphonies, who do you think answered the phone? Brother Ben.

He slyly hinted that he too liked music. You guessed it. Anne stayed home. He and Cele enjoyed the concerts. And since music hath charms, that did it.

They married on a shoe-string and lived on love. To help her husband finish Pitt's School of Social Work, she did typing at home. Sometimes got only two or three hours sleep. After graduation and several years in St. Paul, Minn., they returned here. Mr. Zeligson became business manager of the Centre Avenue Irene Kaufmann Settlement. Now he's director of the Senior Citizens at our neighborhood Y-IKC.

About 10 years ago a newspaper ad captured their imagination. It read: "WANTED — Foster Parents." Celia tested the idea in her brain. The more she thought about it the more urgent it seemed. Then it became a "cause." And Ben agreed.

The Zeligson seven-bedroom home on Wightman St. belongs to the writers of that ad — the Jewish Family & Children's Service. That agency places into their temporary care infants of unwed mothers. Or orphans of legitimate parents who are ill or unemployed. Also refugee children from foreign countries — like Hungary during the revolution. And recently three stranded children from Castro's Cuba.

Celia gives the children TLC (tender loving care) until their real parents or suitable adoptive couples are found.

Mrs. Zeligson takes in a maid five days a week. She herself does the washing, shopping and cooking. Ben helps too but balks at getting up during the night when a baby cries for attention.

The Zeligsons have three children of their own. DeDe is "16-going-on-17."

Marcia is 15 and son Wayne will soon be 13. All attend Allderdice. They treat the new - comers as their own brothers and sisters. And they idolize the babies and enjoy helping care for them.

The foster children are brought for approximately three months' care but sometimes remain for as long as five years. Parting is sweet sorrow and often brings tears. But the new parents become permanent friends.

Celia is song specialist for Girl and Boy Scouts. And conducts song workshops. She started a Folk Song group at her home 10 years ago. It meets monthly and has performed at folk festivals.

For diversion, do the Zeligsons ever do anything gay and mad and daring? Sure. They go to dinner at Weinstein's. And once a month socialize with relative at their Cousins Club parties.

Sara Writes About Herself

By now, via this writer's feature articles in your News you've gotten to better know 250 wonderfully interesting neighbors, many known nationally. And now listen to this. Readers have written the editor: "Sara has told us about so many personalities, we'd like to know about HER." And often during interviews prior to writing, they've said: "Someone should write YOU up." So who? Well, at this stage of the game, guess what? I'll up and write about Sara myself.

Born in Kovarsk, a Russian Village, during the Czarist regime, we migrated to the United States on a luxury liner—steerage class; and were met at Ellis Island by the Statue of Liberty. We settled in Connellsville where father opened a small tailor shop. I was age six then. To this day I remember the utter confusion of my first day at school. English was Greek to me. But kids learn fast and in due time I was a sophomore in high school. Then dropped out. Father made a bare living and I had to earn. After a short secretarial course I got a job with the H. C. Frick Coke Co. in nearby Scottdale.

By then I was at the most interesting age. And had opportunities galore for dating the nicest boys. But a handicap stared me in the face. There were scarcely any Jewish fellows. And father, strictly Orthodox, forbade inter-faith dating. Now when I pass the Y-IKC and see the lively socializing among the Jewish youth, I'm glad for them but saddened at what I missed. We didn't even have a synagogue.

When my parents died, I came to Pittsburgh, rented a room with a private family and tried various jobs. They were hard to come by during those depression years. I sold books for Houghton Mifflin Co. Two summers, with a friend, hired a cottage in Atlantic City, rented out rooms and prepared dinner for our guests. Two following summers I was a counsellor at a children's camp in the Catskills.

Without any camp training, my natural love for writing was needed for their weekly paper. Another summer I did likewise at a Western Ranch in the Rockies. Visiting the famous National Jewish Hospital in nearby Denver, I was offered a job to represent it locally—raise funds and arrange for TB patients needing its free non-sectarian care. Accepting, I was later named Director of its Western Pennsylvania Committee, continuing for 29 years. At retirement Judge Samuel A. Weiss and other prominent members of our Committee honored me with a luncheon at the William Penn Hotel. Here's what the Hospital wired me that day: "May the love and devotion you've given NJH the past 29 years be returned to you in countless blessings. Accept our deep appreciation for many difficult tasks brilliantly mastered." My wonderful sister (Naomi R. Blum of Great Neck, N.Y.) treated me to a three-month trip to Europe and Israel. Unforgettable!

A life-member of Hadassah, I was Donor Chairman twice of my group (now Hadar). Ditto of membership and HMO. And served in various capacities including other worthy causes.

And now I'll answer the $64 question constantly confronting me: "How come a lovely girl like you never married?" (With a compliment yet). My pat answer was: "No one wanted me." And more recently: "Didn't want to add to the population explosion." Today you'll get the truth and nothing but.

Here I had many, many dates but fell head-over-heels for one and one only. And believed it mutual. Steady dating went on and on and on. Marriage was always postponed. He needed to provide for his parents; felt he should wait till his older sister married. I offered to continue working. But in those days "it didn't look good" for a wife to work. At long last—too long—I saw the handwriting on the wall. And started breaking off. It took several unhappy years to completely forget. If someone were to offer me a million dollars to relive those years I'd say "keep the change."

After retirement I started writing about interesting neighbors for our News. They came to my home for the interviews. Meeting them (mostly for the first time), questioning and relating their deeds and skills into simple language has been like a college education for me. But the greatest fringe benefit was getting to know them, resulting into warm friendships. There's much, much more to write but space is limited. I'll end with: Neighbors, you're beautiful!

Pace Setter Sara Rosenblum

by Barnetta Davis Lange

"Because of my high regard for her personally and her magnificent accomplishments for the National Jewish Hospital at Denver, I have planned a luncheon in her honor at Hotel William Penn Sept. 14. I would be very happy if you can attend". We have quoted Judge Samuel A. Weiss. And his "high regard" echoes eloquently the community's high regard for Sara Rosenblum, recently retired director of the Western Penna. Committee of that hospital.

Sara devoted 29 years of service to this institution—29 years of service that was born in the depression, attained adolescence during the days of the "Gathering Storm", and reached maturity during war and post-war days. While everything around her spelled death and disaster, she doggedly continued to devote her life to the improvement of the human condition.

How does one become a director of such a famous Hospital? A royal whim can change the fate of nations; a chance meeting can initiate a career. In Sara's case a job held some thirty years ago as a counselor at a Children's Ranch resulted in a long and felicitous affiliation with the Denver institution.

Sara had been employed in a secretarial capacity with the H.C. Frick Coke Co. in Scottdale. During the summers her office closed, but financial pressure necessitated Sara's year-round employment. Two summers found her counseling at eastern camps. Eventually she obeyed that oft-repeated dictum to "go west", and became a counselor at a Western Ranch in the Rockies, some forty miles from Denver. Inevitably Sara's "day off" found her in Denver, where she promptly visited the National Jewish Hospital. The authorities there, discerning in their visitor an instant rapport for their humanitarian work, as well as a tremendous potential ability that her ultimate position would demand, asked Sara if she would espouse their cause.

Her beginnings were fraught with difficulties. Collecting at best is a laborious and thankless task. During the height of the depression, the obstacles were herculean. Nonetheless Sara began her campaign in our city and surrounding small towns, all by means of employing all of her sincerity, her total capacities—mental and physical—and a disproportionate amount of shoe leather, she gradually built up friends locally for the Denver Hospital. Sara approached anybody and everybody, from humble workers to presidents in swank executive offices—approached them all with equal ease. The years have tallied up a tremendously favorable percentage of success, both in obtaining contributions and in acquiring life-long sponsors.

When Sara became the local director for the Hospital, Richard S. Rauh was chairman; Judge Weiss succeeded him. The list of sponsors joyously bears the names of the area's most prominent citizens. Members of the committee who have received Judge Weiss' invitation to the luncheon include such luminaries as David Lawrence, Anne X. Alpern, H. J. Heinz II, Gwilym A. Price, James G. Fulton and many others, as well as prominent members of our own Jewish community.

We join these local committee members in congratulating Sara on her "magnificent accomplishments". We also wish her the fun and relaxation that her retirement should bring, and which she so fully merits. Her plans for the future are indefinite, but somewhere along the line she'll turn to creative writing, a hobby which has won her several prizes, including $100 received for a one-page story. She'll doubtless also devote additional time to Hadassah and enlarge her work in American-Israeli affairs. Or conceivably will visit her sister, Mrs. Naomi R. Blum of Great Neck, Long Island, N.Y., her only surviving close relative. But wherever she turns, this able woman will probably in some measure continue to benefit society.

It Happened in Eilat – 1962

By Sara Rosenblum

An all-day trip to Eilat is an exciting adventure to say the least. But when, in addition, on the same journey, one meets an outstanding personality from Pittsburgh whom one knows and always admired, it becomes something extra special.

Eilat is in the extreme south of Israel, in the hottest part of the desert. It became world-famous because the King Solomon Mines were unearthed there. You get to Eilat from Tel-Aviv in two ways: by bus which takes 8 hours and means staying overnight; or by plane which gets you there in an hour, giving you the entire day for sight-seeing and a chance to return that evening. The bus trip, they told me, although scenically magnificent, is "killing" because of the intense heat. So I chose a plane — the 19-passenger air-conditioned "Arkia" run by the Israel Inland Airlines.

On the small plane were tourists from everywhere: from the U.S. of course; from Africa, South America, Canada, Switzerland, Mexico. All friendly, all eager to become acquainted. An interesting engineer from Mexico City sat near me. He couldn't speak a word of English. I know nothing of Spanish. Yet we conversed easily and fluently in what until recently was the universal language of Jews: Yiddish. (Now of course, there's a leaning toward Hebrew). We were bemoaning the fact that even though each of us had traveled for over two months through Europe and now Israel, neither of us had the pleasant surprise of running into a "landsman" from our respective home towns. Actually we were a bit homesick.

Just then I saw a distinguished-looking white-haired gentleman slowly ascending the plane's runway. My heart stood still; Judge Michael A. Musmanno, of all people!

Famous Tourist

When the other passengers learned (from me) who the latest tourist was, they buzzed around him — the men shaking hands, the women smiling admiringly. The name Musmanno was known to all. They knew he is a brilliant jurist from Pittsburgh; had been a prosecuting attorney at the Nuremberg trials in Germany; was summoned to Jerusalem by Ben Gurion to testify at the Eichmann trial. His testimony was often quoted in the JERUSALEM POST; the social columns frequently mentioned that he was a guest for tea at Ben Gurion's home; or had lunched with President Ben Zvi.

By the time the pretty Turkish hostess was serving us ice-cold fruit drinks and handing out colorful souvenir ash-trays, the plane was zooming over the mountains and desert. Saudi Arabia, Jordan and Egypt were plainly visible.

At the Eilat airport we were met by a huge bus, headed by a sun-tanned driver and a bronzed guide. The latter admitted he was 28 years old and that he already was considered "an old man". That's how rugged their life is! The pioneers who live and work there, are just beginning to have families. Until recently they refused to bring children into that neglected, forsaken country. There were no doctors. The nearest hospital was an hour's plane flight.

New Hospital

Now, thanks to Hadassah, they have a beautiful air-conditioned hospital, with adequate doctors for all. There are miles and miles of air-conditioned housing units. Flowers are blooming, trees are in abundance. And the fields are lush with planting and harvesting. When a new baby is born there is general celebration; and recently when two sets of twins arrived, the whole town celebrated far into the night. The guide told us that in spite of wondrous improvements, people don't rush to settle there. He said they have 600 unmarried men and only 25 single girls. Their jail is air-conditioned and equipped to serve kosher meals, but there are no prisoners. The only tenants (nights only) are the 25 single girls — just to play it safe!

It was lunch-time. Prior to going into the beautiful dining-room in the Eilat hotel, I wrote cards to Judge Samuel A. Weiss and Eugene B. Strassburger whom I proudly call my friends. The Judge added the notation: "Regards from Mike."

The meal was roast beef with all the trimmings. The Judge wondered if, with his dessert, he might have tea and milk. The waiter looked shocked. "This is a strictly kosher hotel," he said, "we do not serve milk with meat." I explained that the Judge is not of our faith and may drink milk any time in good conscience. The waiter stalked out. Soon he returned with a suggestion. "If the honorable Judge is not well and his doctor prescribes milk, he might go to the terrace and order whatever dairy food he desires". "But even then," he added, "he must wait two whole hours after his "fleishig' meal."

A Healthy Jurist

We wondered if a good "cough" would serve the purpose. But the Judge looked too healthy. So he went back to work on his notes and other data which bulged from his brief-case. And I went for a swim in the Gulf of Akaba opposite the hotel. The water was cool, clean, refreshing — and welcomed me like a caress. Nature evidently tried to compensate for the burning heat by furnishing cool, cool water.

On my way back from the swim to dress, I caught a glimpse of the Judge at a small table on the terrace. He was drinking tea with milk. He looked very contented. And I never had it so good, because where in Pittsburgh is there such delicious swimming?

We learned that David Niven and other movie stars from Italy and France were in Eilat working on their new movie, "Best of Enemies". I was hoping to catch a glimpse of the handsome Niven and perhaps get his autograph. But was told it was still siesta time and he was in his suite relaxing — or whatever else one does during siestas.

Mines of Solomon

The King Solomon Mines were a sight to behold. Enormous rock formations too high for the eyes to reach, with narrow paths winding through them. It reminded me of Wall Street — copper color. The mining operations and machinery were too complicated for description. But I'll always remember and marvel. The judge had a camera and asked some gentleman to snap our picture — right in front of the Mines.

From there our group took a glass-bottom boat and traveled for miles on the Gulf of Akaba with our hands swishing through the cool water. Below were beautiful coral formations, built like miniture castles.

The plane ride back to Tel-Aviv was restful and welcome. All were tired. But not too tired to marvel at the wonders below — wonders that were hidden from human eyes for thousands and thousands of years. And we had the privilege to look and see and admire and remember. Judge Musmanno went on to Jerusalem.

That night, thinking of the unbalanced men-women ratio in Pittsburgh I began wondering how it would feel to be one of the 25 single women in Eilat with 600 handsome unmarried men to choose from.

I Meet Yehuda Lev – 1962

By Sara Rosenblum

Yehuda Lev, as you doubtless know, is the Criterion's special correspondent from the Middle East. Barnetta Lange calls him "the Huntley-Brinkley of Israel." I call him a darling! I fell in love with him, from afar, through reading his fascinating article, "Letter From Israel" the past two years. His articles carried serious news from Israel — often very serious. Yet they were always interspersed with bits of humor about his wife, Idell, little Dani and baby Daphna, and their dog, Whiskey.

Last month I had the pleasure of meeting two members of that interesting family: Yehuda himself and Whiskey. I didn't actually meet Whiskey. I just "talked" with him over the phone. Here's how it happened.

Before leaving on my three-month trip through the Continent, Greece, Turkey, and Israel, I called my dear friend, Sadie Alter, Criterion publisher, to say good-bye. She told me to call Yehuda Lev when I reached Jerusalem.

Jerusalem was the last city I visited during my four-week stay in Israel. I was there for six days. The morning I was scheduled to attend the Eichmann trial, I was told that Mr. Lev would doubtless be there as one of the many reporters. I called his home first and his wife, Idell, answered the phone. She was pleased I was from Pittsburgh and a friend of the Alters. She said Yehuda would be delighted to meet me; that at the moment he was at the Kol Yisrael Broadcasting Station preparing his daily program. "Jerusalem Calling." But before she had a chance to give me his office phone number, she hurriedly said, "Hold on a minute. Someone's at the door." Then I heard a dog barking. Of course it was Whiskey. Who else?

Later, when I called Yehuda at his office, I sensed his personal charm. He invited me to his office at the radio station. I had expected to find his office in a tall office building. Instead it was in a sprawling one-story gray stone building surrounded by a beautiful garden radiant with flowers. Centuries ago it had been an Arabian palace.

Several minutes before 4 o'clock I was sitting opposite him while he was about to start his broadcast. His program from 4 to 5 is the only English-language broadcast in the Middle East. I knew about it because many times during sight-seeing trips on buses, after the radio program had rambled on in Hebrew for hours, an impatient American tourist would call out, "Put on Yehuda Lev!" And there I was, scarcely a yard away, watching and listening to him say, "This is Yehuda Lev starting off another edition of 'Jerusalem Calling.'" He then gave some important news bulletins, introduced a Frank Sinatra record, and followed with more news. Then with a mischievous twinkle in his eye, he announced, "We have in our studio just now a charming friend from Pittsburgh, Pennsylvania, U.S.A. — Miss Sara Rosenblum. She has been touring Israel for four weeks. She loves Israel and we love having her."

After my initial surprise subsided, I felt thrilled and quite important. In addition to the tourists, the inhabitants of Israel, Syria, Lebanon, Jordan, and Egypt all have access to that program. And all who listened were informed that Sara Rosenblum of Pittsburgh was in Israel! Maybe Nasser heard it too.

As I was leaving, Yehuda said, "Be sure to kiss Gerry Buerger for me." I did just that.

It Happened in Istanbul – 1962

By Sara Rosenblum

"Are you related to Charles Rosenbloom?"

That question, through the years, has confronted me many times in and around Pittsburgh. But when I heard it in far-off Istanbul, Turkey, the inquiry made me gasp in surprise.

The questioner was the night-maid at the Istanbul-Hilton hotel. She had served the Rosenblooms during their various visits in that city and when she saw my name and address on the register, she came to an obvious conclusion. I expressed regret that I was not related to such a great philanthropist.

Her name was Rosa. In her early forties, she was born and raised in Istanbul. She was unmarried, without any living relatives. And she was Jewish. She spoke Turkish, French and Hebrew fluently, and English unusually well. Yet the only job available to her was that of a hotel maid. Not because of her religion. There is no evidence of anti-semitism in Turkey, she said. But jobs in Istanbul were very scarce.

Rosa asked me where I had traveled. When I told her I had been in Israel for four weeks and had just come from a six-day stay in Jerusalem, she, put her arms around me and said: "I want to touch and kiss someone who has been in Eretz Yisroel." And with pride in her large grey eyes, added, "I am preparing to move to Israel when my papers are ready. It will be soon."

My new friend helped me plan my sight-seeing in her city. Because of her, I saw more and enjoyed more than most tourists traveling alone.

Downstairs at the Hilton, the night-club featured a French band and twin exotic belly-dancers from Casablanca. The show was available to guests who ordered mid-night supper. Since I don't eat late suppers, particularly when alone, I had no thought of seeing the show. But Rosa felt differently. If I told the concierge at the desk, she suggested, that I was a tourist, and alone, he might possibly permit me to see the show without ordering supper. The concierge proved to be most obliging.

Promptly at 11:45 p.m., I was led to a table in the huge ballroom, so close to the entertainers I could almost touch them. The tables were mostly small, suitable for two. Most of the couples were older men with young, beautifully dressed women.

The orchestra played tunes but the words were either Turkish or French. So were the jokes which of course I couldn't understand. But it was fun to hear the laughter and wild applause. The exotic dancers were identical 16-year-old twins, dancing in perfect unison. They were graceful, artistic and beautiful. My bill was a fourth of what it should have been — all because of Rosa.

The City tour the next day, was fascinating. Istanbul was built 2,000 years ago. It is smoky, hazy and mysterious — with a promise of something unusual at every turn. Of the 500 mosques, the 16th-centruy Blue Mosque stood out in all its splendor. The several Moslems in our group removed their shoes and washed their feet at the hundreds of water spigots surrounding the huge circular entrance. We infidels just took off our shoes, sliding our feet into a pair of flat straw slippers that lined that hall. From a high minaret, through loud speakers, the faithfuls were called to prayer. This happens five times a day.

In the Seraglio Palace, we viewed fabulous jewels, art objects and beautiful clothes worn centuries ago by the women in the harems. We went through an underground cistern built by the Romans 2,000 years ago. It was very cool there — nature having air-conditioned it from the start.

The Turkish Bazzar was the answer to a shoppers dream — 4,000 shops all under one mile-long roof. But in spite of the lowered prices and a bit of "haggling", limited luggage space prohibited much buying.

We took a complete tour of the University of Istanbul. Its buildings were beautiful, the grounds spacious. The men-students often walked in pairs, or sat on benches, engrossed in conversation.

On Friday evening I wanted to go to the synagogue, to see and meet Turkist people of our faith. Rosa told me which one to attend. Evidently, not many guests at the Hilton went to the synagogue because the taxi-driver had no knowledge of the address given him. He stopped several times to inquire. After riding up and down through many narrow streets and one long steep alley, the cab suddenly stopped at the schul. From the outside it looked pretty much like the old Shaare Torah Synagogue when it was located on Washington Street. The Shamos greeted me with "shalom" while his little 7-year old son eyed me with curiosity. Other than the greeting, we could not exchange a word. My fluent Yiddish and my broken German did me no good. They speak only Turkish, French and Hebrew and I am ignorant of all three. The boy, at a signal from his father, guided me up-stairs where the women sat. I was an hour early so the balcony was deserted, except for one aged woman praying. When she learned that I was a "tourista," she motioned for me to sit near her. Soon other women appeared and soon I was surrounded by a large group, shaking hands, smiling, some putting their arms around me. We spoke not a word but I felt I was among friends who were happy I came. The men down-stairs concentrated on their prayers, hardly aware of the stranger in the balcony. At the conclusion of the services, many of the men came over to shake hands. It was a heart-warming experience. The Shamos didn't want to accept my contribution and it took a bit of coaxing. Two women, with their arms around me, walked with me to a taxi. They stood smiling and waving until out of sight.

Rosa was waiting when I returned, and was eager to know how I enjoyed the services. Since it was my last night in Istanbul, she brought me a beautifully tinted china ash-tray carrying the message "Greetings from Istanbul." A going-away gift, she said. When I offered her some money as my going-away gift, she refused. Only after much persuasion was I able to press the gift in her hand. She asked me to write her and I promised to do so. After a warm embrace we parted.

Early the next morning, before leaving my room I took one long look through the huge picture-window. I again saw the lovely blue Phosphorus sea, with Asia at the other end, visible even through the morning mist.

I had come near skipping Istanbul on my itinerary. I'm happy I didn't. I'll always remember that fascinating city so very far away. And most of all — Rosa.

Sara in Manhattan — 1963

By Ida Rubenstein

One of the most amazing people we know is our friend Sara Rosenblum, feature writer for the Squirrel Hill News. She has a rare talent for squeezing two weeks worth of activity and pleasure into five or six days of vacation. Last week she did it again.

Lucky Sara spent Monday to Friday in New York and once again she was invited by an executive friend — one still appreciative of her devoted years of service to the National Jewish Hospital in Denver — to be his guest at four Broadway shows. Not just one ticket but two orchestra seats for any hard-to-get shows of her choice!

Accompanied by her friend Mildred (Mrs. Jack) Rubenstein for the evening performances and a matinee with her sister Naomi Blum of Great Neck, L.I., she saw four hits: "Promises, Promises," "Forty Carats" with Julie Harris, Woody Allen in "Play It Again, Sam," and the rock musical, "Hair." There's nothing prudish about our pal; to prove it, she took in a certain infamous movie that will not hit Pittsburgh for awhile. And nothing happened! She got in without throwing one photographer — Jackie Onassis style.

A highlight of Sara's trip was a luncheon date she had with a former Pittsburgher, Gene Forrell, now a known name in New York music circles. She saw him last when, as 16 year-old Eugene Finkelhor, he was present at a dinner she had with his parents. His older brother, Herbert Finkelhor, and sister-in-law Dorothy are founders of Point Park College. Mr. Forrell is now conductor, "Master Virtuoso of New York," who frequently performs in Philharmonic Hall, Lincoln Center. He received an Academy Award for his scoring of the film, "To Be Alive," the Johnson Wax exhibit at the New York World's Fair.

With still a few spare hours to fill in between appointments and show time, Sara gadded around Manhattan, wandering as far downtown as Greenwich Village which she found interesting. Much larger than Shadyside and dirtier!

So there is the Saga of Sara, the lady who knows how to enjoy each hour of life!

Lucky Sara

By Ida Rubenstein

Any theatre-goer headed for New York knows there is little chance he'll pick up tickets for the shows, "Funny Girl", "Fiddler on the Roof" or "Golden Boy". All three in one trip? Impossible! But these were precisely the golden ducats that were set aside for her at three Broadway ticket offices — two for each production — for herself and sister Naomi R. Blum of Great Neck, Long Island. And best of all they were presented as a gift from one of Sara's former associates. This, for our lucky colleague was just the start of a glorious vacation trip. From New York she embarked on a 24-day Grace Line casual cruise southward to the Caribbean and through the Panama Canal to the west coast of South America. "Wish you could share the lovely trip", is the message on the post card we received this week. So do we, Sara....so do we!

South Seas: Yellow, Pink, Blue and Charming — 1963 By Sara Rosenblum

Today, instead of writing about an important neighborhood personality, I'll take the privilege of writing about myself — for no earthly reason except that I just returned from a 24-day boat trip all the way down into Venezuela.

And because you may want to learn "what happened" during that interesting cruise, come along. I won't describe the port towns and cities much. The travel folders do that. I'll just try sharing with you the various interesting experiences I had. Mostly unplanned. Which made them more fascinating.

But before taking you on the boat, let me tell you about my three days in New York City. And you'll forgive me if I brag a little. A wonderful local executive friend treated me to a pair of tickets for each of three Broadway hit plays, for which you almost have to sell your grandmother to secure.

I'll mention one in particular: "Fiddler on the Roof." Even if you must WALK to N.Y. see that play. If you can get a ticket, that is. You'll be under its spell for weeks. As I was — and as was my sister Naomi Blum of Great Neck, Long Island, who joined me.

Friday, May 14 my boat set sail. A Casual Cruise it's called. Not too much dressing up. Just what you'd wear for dinner at Weinstein's or Bubbles'. An out-door swimming pool at which bikinis and mesh suits were permissible — as long as they weren't topless. Nor bottomless!

The boat had rooms for 52 passengers. But evidently because of the Dominican danger many chickened out and canceled. Of course we by-passed Santo Domingo like a hot potato. Who wants to get shot — especially since we had nothing to shoot back with. We were a mere handful. The captain, purser, doctor, chef, steward, engineer, waiters and the crew went all out in friendliness to compensate for the smallness of our group.

Our first stop May 16 was Savannah, Ga., called the City of Southern Charm.

During our two-hour sight-seeing trip we saw and learned much from our cabbie whose southern drawl you could cut with a knife. Tuition for their state college for colored people is only $84. There's no prejudice nor restrictions, he assured. And there's very little unemployment. He then took us to a place he said "people are simply dying to go to". Their cemetery! Full of marble statues of all kinds.

He ended the trip with these words of wisdom: "Savannah is owned by Jews, run by Catholics, paid for by the Crackers, and enjoyed by the Niggers." No prejudice??

And now the foreign ports. Laguaira May 21. The Atlantic is on one side. The peaked Andes Mountains on the other. The little houses, peeping through thick foliage, are painted yellow, blue, pink, aqua. From a distance they look like radiant flowers among the miles and miles of mountain greenery. And did you ever watch a cargo ship unload its contents? Hundreds of eager native workers, suntanned, shirtless, working in perfect precision with modern machinery.

Wish you could have seen them lift dozens of Chevrolet station wagons from the boat's bottom; thousands of burlap sacks of beans and the like. They get good pay, we were told. They sure earn it.

Instead of making a trip into Caracas — the nearest city on that hot Saturday, we decided to go swimming. At their famous Macuto - Sheraton Hotel beach. Like Miami Beach but with charming Spanish atmosphere. We shared a cab. Cost, including dressing room at the hotel, totaled $8 apiece.

Next day I ventured there alone, via a public "libre" (jitney) to see if, without speaking Spanish, I could make it for less money, more adventure — and to have something to brag about on the ship later.

A little shoe-shine boy helped me catch the libre. He motioned for the driver to wait, held up his both hands to stop all oncoming traffic, took my hand, led me across the street, put me into the car and told the driver where to let me off. Fare — 1 boliva (22 cents).

The return trip was a cinch. As I was walking up the gang-plank to the boat I heard someone calling loudly. "Sara, Sar-rra!" On top of the nearby terminal my little shoe-shine friend was waving and smiling in recognition. Before our ship left he came to say good-bye. Hardly 11, already he was working to help support his widowed mother. We filled a box with sandwiches, apples, wash clothes, soap and all the nickels and quarters available.

Now we're at Maracaibo — May 24. The others took a taxi for sight-seeing. I had better luck. Raquel and Ilsa, wonderful mother and daughter who sat at my table, got off there. It's their home town. The husband met them at the boat.

They invited me to join them in their large Buick and they showed me around. They left me off at the colorful Market Place a few blocks from the ship. The hundreds of outdoor shops carried things we get at Woolworth's. But the variety of shoppers made a fascinating sight.

A man, carrying a live chicken under his arm, asked if I would buy it. He showed me how plump it was. I pointed to the ship. Seeing it was a lost cause he shrugged and sauntered away. But he was a good loser because he turned, waved and smiled.

The chef later said he would have helped me cook it.

Aruba — May 25. We planned to just browse and shop for souvenirs in this little Dutch town. It was noon, the beginning of their two-hour siesta time. The shops were closed tight. After window-shopping in the noon-day sun we sat down on the curb, waiting for the shops to open.

Meantime we admired the lovely little divi divi trees all bent in the same direction by the trade winds. The men purchased mostly perfume for their women back home. We — all sorts of interesting novelties.

Puerto Cabello — May 26. The stay here was the trip's hightlight. Three of us unattached women were invited by the handsome captain, purser and chief steward for an all-day sight-seeing trip and beach party. They brought along delicious box lunches.

We taxied to the beach one way and returned via another. Most of the day was spent swimming, eating, joking, laughing. A romance mebbe?? Well — it's like this. Our escorts had looks. personality, charm. Everything. They also had wives.

Guanta — May 28. First thing heard were children's voices yelling "Hey, amigo (friend) — monney!" Little boats filled with naked brown-skinned youngsters, eager to dive in for whatever was thrown down. Like fish, only swifter. They clamored also for apples, soap, clothes — anything. Kids who have nothing.

Caracas — May 31. We got there by public bus. Then hired a taxi for two hours of sight-seeing. Called "The Paris of the Andes," it's like a huge bowl surrounded by jagged mountains. As always, there's the contrast between magnificent sections occupied by American business tycoons, native millionaires — and the little shacks in the slum areas.

The Nelson Rockefeller Super Market is something to behold. All our neighborhood markets could be put in one small corner of it — and be lost. "My Fair Lady" was advertised everywhere — with Spanish subtitles. We saw many signs like "Death to the Yankee Invaders." Also Nazi swastikas and slogans scrawled on walls. One in Spanish read "In one year we'll steal the country."

We went up to their famous cable car which gives you a view of the entire city. It has room for 24 passengers, is a 12-minute ride and costs $1. Then wouldn't you know it — we needed to "wash our hands." The door marked "Senora" was locked. The caretaker motioned us to use the adjoining room marked "Cabellero." He stood guard so that no man could enter. And had the will-power not to crack a smile at this hilarious situation.

On the crowded bus returning, I sat down near a little boy. He was engrossed in some comic books. In Spanish. Soon he handed one to me, to share his enjoyment. I said "No Spanish." He gave me an understanding smile. As did his parents sitting behind us.

Port de France, Martinique — June 2. In the French West Indies. Being completely free, the handsome Creoles looked relaxed, without tension. The statue of Empress Josephine, Napoleon's wife who was born there, graces the public park. We saw the spot where Columbus landed when he discovered the island. The coastline is a succession of picturesque fishing villages in romantic settings.

That evening, a few hours before sailing I went down to the dock to buy one of their charming little Creole dolls. A little youngster came over, took my hand and led me walking along the ocean. Soon more urchins joined, babbling in French and battling to be the one closest to me. The passengers aboard ship looked down with great amusement.

A few more days of sailing. Then Baltimore. Then New York — June 7. I visited my sister Naomi for several delightful days. Her home in Great Neck is a short drive to the Fair. You guessed it. We spent an entire day there.

It Happened in Maui – 1945

By Sara Rosenblum

To visit the Hawaiian Islands is a rare treat to say the least; but when one has a most unusual, unexpected experience there, it is that much more velvet.

I learned that a Hula Dancer is "A woman telling a story with her hands and trying to wiggle her way out of it." I also learned, if you get stranded, try to find a Jew. If you are Jewish yourself, that is.

After much island-hopping and fascinating sight-seeing, my next stop was in the Island of Maui. There I was scheduled to spend a whole week-end at the Puulani Ranch. This ranch is world-famous. The owner died years ago, leaving a fabulously wealthy — and lonely — widow. To off-set her isolation she decided to permit twelve tourists to visit her magnificent ranch every week-end — for a price, of course. I couldn't wait for that week-end.

Upon landing at the Maui airport, the travel agent who met me said apologetically: "Miss Rosenblum, I'm so sorry to disappoint you. One of the employees at the Puulani died this morning and all reservations have been cancelled. I have made a reservation for you at a commercial hotel on the main highway — the only one available."

That was a let-down. I was alone, far from home, frustrated and generally unhappy. After unpacking I decided to look around the town. Maui, it seemed, was the least attractive of the Hawaiian Islands. It chiefly featured the beautiful and rare Silver-sword plant — and the Puulani Ranch. I sauntered down the street, browsing in the little shops. All were Japanese and the merchandise cheap and uninteresting. I wondered if there might be a Jewish family in this predominantly Japanese town. Jews, they say, are found scattered everywhere...in the remotest parts of the world. I walked and walked for blocks and blocks. No signs that looked remotely Jewish. Just as I was about to start walking back to my hotel, I saw from far off a sign which read: "HYMIE MEYERS." It was a large automobile accessory store. I almost ran towards it. But it was closed. I remembered it was Saturday morning. It seemed unbelievable that Jews in Hawaii would be more "fruom" than our Squirrel Hill people. However, there was nothing to lose — and much to gain — if I went around to the back entrance. Maybe they were closed for appearance sake. The back door was open! Inside, at a desk sat a very dark young man, evidently engrossed in bookkeeping. He looked up, questiongly. I told him my story — that I was a tourist from the States, stranded and alone — and Jewish. And that I thought it would be nice to meet someone of my faith. He smiled and said: "I am Hawaiian. My father, Hymie Meyers, is part Jewish. His farther was all Jewish." He closed his books and resumed: "My parents are quite a drive from here, watching their new home being built. They will be delighted to know you; and I'll be happy to drive you there." In his car sat a lovely blond young woman. While we were driving she told me she was the young man's wife, and that she came from Sweden. She also said the Meyers were the only family in the Island remotely Jewish, and that they are loved and respected by all.

We found Hymie Meyers and wife sitting under a huge banyan tree, on rocking chairs. They were very dark with pure white hair — about the same age around 70. She had on a colorful mumu (Hawaiian house-dress) and he wore cotton dungarees. Both were barefooted. They looked cool, relaxed and comfortable. The foundation of their new home which they had been watching over-looked the most beautiful valley I ever gazed upon. The son hurried back to his bookkeeping, leaving me to repeat my story to his parents.

They greeted me with open arms. Mrs. Meyers said she was very sorry their new home wasn't completed. They took me to their old Hawaiian style home, which I loved. While she went upstairs to dress, Mr. Meyers told me his father had come from Russia to the United States but wasn't permitted to settle there. So he migrated from one country to another and finally settled in Hawaii — the only place he was welcome at the time. He found a job in an Hawaiian pineapple plantation. There were no Jews in Maui; and of course no synagogue. Later he did what many others would have done — what came naturally: he married the boss' daughter — a pure Hawaiian. Hymie was their first and only son. He in turn married a Hawaiian, the present Mrs. Meyers. He said he remembered his father telling him about Jewish holidays and of praying in Hebrew many times. His father, he said, later took a trip to California, became ill there and died. He is buried in a Jewish cemetery in San Diego.

Soon Mrs. Meyers came downstairs, dressed in perfect American style. First they showered me with all kinds of beautiful tropical flowers grown in their own conservatory nearby, and with tangerines, oranges, apricots and bananas grown in their back yard. Then they drove me to each of their married children's homes. There were three sons and two daughters living in the same town. Each had charming Hawaiian-style homes, including beautiful children — some dark, some blond. One little fellow was so dark and looked so Jewish that I told him, between hugs and kisses, that if he lived in Pittsburgh I'd take him to the synagogue! He evidently wasn't sure what I meant, but it seemed to please him anyway because he was all smiles.

Mrs. Meyers then explained that they had to go to the cemetery. It was the anniversary of their son who died during Pearl Harbor. They wanted to visit his grave. I asked if I might have the privilege of going too. This pleased them greatly. When they stood bowed in prayer, I prayed too, and in my heart I asked God to bless them. I put my flowers on the grave.

When we returned to their home, their married sons and daughters were dressed up and waiting. They had already arranged for baby-sitters for their youngsters. They seemed eager to join their parents for a family dinner at a beautiful Japanese restaurant, in honor of their unexpected Jewish visitor from Pittsburgh, U.S.A.

It was a charming restaurant, with doll-like Japanese waitresses dressed in colorful kimonos. The main course was a huge Roast Pork! What to do. Mr. Meyers immediately sensed what was wrong and he ordered all kinds of delicious vegetables, salads and desserts which he hoped I could eat in good conscience. A husband of one of the daughters told me he was an American soldier from Montana, during Pearl Harbor. He married Mr. Meyer's youngest daughter and settled in Maui. He seemed eager to learn if I had ever been in Montana and asked me many questions about the States. He never missed a chance to sit near me and ask me questions of news about the States. I felt that he was homesick.

It was near midnight. Everybody kissed me good-night and the Meyers' drove me to my hotel. Strange how pleasant the hotel looked now, when early that same morning it had appeared so dull and uninteresting. I was refreshed, happy, grateful to a wonderful family — part Jewish, Part Hawaiian...all delightful.

The next morning Mr. Meyers and daughter drove me to the airport headed for Honolulu. The wife sent her regrets because she was attending an early Mass.

That was nine years ago but I remembered it all with much tenderness. No one was happier than I when Hawaii became our 50th state.

Sara Looks Up Old Friends

A former Connellsville woman—who had not been back to the old home town in a great many years—had "the time of my life" Saturday as she spent several hours strolling through familiar looking streets looking for faces she could recognize.

The visitor was Miss Sara Rosenblum, once a resident of East Crawford Avenue. Today she is Director of the Western Pennsylvania Committee for the National Jewish Hospital at Denver, with headquarters in Pittsburgh, were she also resides.

"I've never lost interest in Connellsville nor all my friends back here," said the visitor as she stopped briefly at The Courier office. "And I'm having the time of my life today as I greet some of those old friends."

"I came up on Baltimore & Ohio train this morning, got off and walked up town," she related. "I stopped in to see Julius Harris and Leon Kingley, then I saw Patsy Gigliotti. After that I went across the street to Sammy Oppenheim's store. I walked up to him and said 'I want to buy a pair of trousers for my husband'. He never recognized me and said 'about what size would he wear?' I replied that I don't know because I don't have a husband yet. Then he knew I had been kidding him. He took a good look and remembered me."

At The Courier office Miss Rosenblum found an old friend in Louis H. Simons, a member of the reportorial staff. As Editor James Driscoll walked by, Simons mentioned that "you ought to know this man." Miss Rosenblum said:

"I'll bet he's a Driscoll—and I well remember his father." Then a quick second glance and she added: "There are too many to remember you by name but I do recall you as a young man." She followed that remark with: "But I'll bet you don't remember me?" A smile lighted up her countenance as the editor came back with: "I don't exactly recall your first name but I do know you lived in a big white house on East Crawford Avenue."

"You do remember!" ejaculated Miss Rosenblum. "You know this has been a truly wonderful day for me. I often see Clyde Whipkey and Ray Wetherell (both former Connellsvillians) in Pittsburgh and when I do we always talk for a while about this good old town."

It was shortly after noon when Miss Rosenblum left the newspaper office.

"I'm going to go up in our old neighborhood and see if any of the people who lived there when we did are still around," said Miss Sara. "It will be nice to talk to them again."

Asked about her sister, Naomi, Miss Rosenblum said:

"Naomi is fine. She lives in New York, her hair is white and she is still quite beautiful."

The Rosenblums were quite well known in Connellsville and have many friends here despite the fact they have been gone for several decades.

Thank You Notes

My sincere thanks and heartfelt appreciation for the magnificent article you wrote about Hadassah and me. Your deep feelings and love for Hadassah showed in this beautiful article and I know how helpful this will be in getting women to give, and participate with an open heart and hand in our Donor campaign.

—Mrs. Martin D. (Ann) Adler, Hadassah Chapter Donor Chairman, Jan. 7, 1972—

Your article was just delightful. I wish I could have had a tape-recorder with me so that I would have been able to give you an oral report on all the comments that people made. My family was delighted at their inclusion and it gave all of us a nice, warm glow.

—Mrs. Elliot (Freda) Alber, Hadassah Chapter Donor Chairman, Feb. 18, 1968—

On the occasion of our 50th Anniversary we wish to thank you for your friendship and thoughtfulness and your beautiful article about Charles and me. The many calls, telegrams and people from everywhere and the Maxon Towers (my residence) have praised YOU. And your article gave us much joy.

—Mrs. Charles (Rose) Bronk, Aug. 10, 1968—

I want to thank you very much for writing such a lovely article about me. It's been a wonderful experience. People called to tell me they read it and how nice it is. And last night we were at the Home for the Aged Dinner Dance and many people came over to tell me about the write-up. It is very thrilling and exciting and everyone is so happy about it.

—Mrs. Steven (Marian) Beck—

Dear Sara:
Thanks a million for the beautiful article you wrote about me. Only Sara Rosenblum can write like that. And I also enjoy all your articles about other personalities. Shalom!

—Jacob Becker—

Mrs. Bergman and I thank you most sincerely for your kind interest in us, and for the very nice little biographical sketch you developed about our joint lives. You have a fine gift for the orderly arrangement of your material derived from our pleasant but brief chat over the teacups; and importantly a felicitous way of expressing your very generous thoughts. I have procured half-dozen copies of today's issue of the NEWS so that we can share them with our son and other members of our family who, I am sure, will enjoy them with us.

—Sidney M. Bergman, March 17, 1972—

I am writing this on my lunch-period at the Hadassah office. I have a new name now: ''Mrs. Celebrity''—thanks to you. I have received so many phone calls—one from my sister-in-law in Uniontown. She said she showed the article to ''All Uniontown''. I am stopped on the street. They liked my son's way of calling me ''Sadie'' and they all thought your quote on Jack Benny was wonderful. Everyone is so pleased with your talent and your wit.

—Mrs. Jack M. (Sarah) Davis, June 28, 1971—

Sharon and I want to thank you for the beautiful article you wrote about us. It was well-written and expressed, and was a reflection of your warm and friendly personality. Thank you for the time and effort you devoted to us.

—Marilyn and Sharon Davison, March 11, 1972—

Many people have already told me how much they enjoyed reading the wonderful write-up in the NEWS. Margie Weiner and other Chapter executives agree with me that it is a beautifully written article which will help our Campaign tremendously. Thank you very much for taking the time and effort to write such a beautiful article. And my children even liked it!

—Mrs. Jonathan (Bobbie) Duker, Hadassah Chapter Donor Chairman, Jan. 21, 1974—

Your article about me was written with so much gentleness and understanding that I am genuinely delighted. You wrote about me—but the great big HEART of Sara Rosenblum comes through like a shining light! It isn't just the fact that you write so well—that has made you so well-liked. It's that innate KINDNESS and sincerity that one recognizes about you immediately.

—Aaron Gross, Oct. 30, 1964—

Some time ago you sent me your special article on Gladys Schmidt. I think it is beautifully written and you deserve the highest commendation and warmest congratulations.

—Herman Hailperin, Rabbi Tree of Life Synagogue, June 30, 1966—

I have the article you did about me, and I must tell you it is one of the important tear sheets in my collection.
It was a joy meeting you.

—Peter Hamilton, July 3, 1974—

The article you wrote for the News was satisfactory in all respects and my wife and I got a thrill out of it. I believe you handled the subject matter with care and precision and produced an article which was readable and, I might say, somewhat flattering to me. I am most appreciative for the effort expended and for the time you gave me.

—Milton E. Harris, July 7, 1969—

This is to thank you for your beautiful article about me. I must say that you have to be a genius to get as many facts about my complicated life in the allotted space allowed you by the paper. It was an excellent article and written in good taste.

—Ross Harris, Dec. 30, 1970—

It is a most difficult task for me to pen the fitting words to tell you how highly honored I feel for your precious article. You have so wonderfully given my long-life history, from teenage to golden age. The many letters and phone calls since Thursday make me very proud and therefore want to keep up my interest in humanity as long as the good Lord will let me.

—Mrs. Sophie Hoechstetter, Oct. 17, 1963—

Many thanks for your article about Mrs. Posvar. It certainly was beautifully written and provides a very good picture of her. She is an especially fine person and I am sure that she will continue to contribute to the musical world and to Pittsburgh.

—Dr. Walter Jacob (Rabbi, Rodef Shalom Temple), April 6, 1970—

I want to take this occasion to thank you for the wonderful article you wrote recently, which I thought was grand. I received many phone calls and personal comments which were most flattering.

—H.I. Katz, Executive V.P., Papercraft Corporation—

THE WHITE HOUSE
Washington

Thank you very much for your letter to the President. It was thoughtful of you to send him your article about Dr. Hays, and he has asked me to express his appreciation.

The enclosed autographed White House card comes to you with the President's best wishes.

—Evelyn Lincoln, Personal Secretary to President John F. Kennedy, Feb. 4, 1963—

The Tuesday Musical Club's Benefit was a real success, and consequently I want to thank you for the part you played in making it that. The figures aren't in yet, but I'm told that several tickets were purchased from the Squirrel Hill area, and that can only be from your article. A number of our members complimented me on the article, and I pass the credit right on where it belongs. I was glad to tell them how cooperative you were, not just in writing about Miss Krebs, but in doing it in time to appear before the Benefit. Miss Krebs was thrilled with it and judging by the number of clippings I've received, so were all who read it.

—Mrs. Stefan (Cecilia) Kruger, April 2, 1971——

This is to thank you for the exceptionally fine column with which you honored me. I have had about a dozen phone calls and additional verbal comments from many people who saw your column. Thank you again for the pleasure you gave my family and me.

Alvin L. Kushner, Director, Community Relations
—Committee of the United Jewish Federation, July 6, 1970—

Been traveling around so much I haven't had a moment to say a proper "thank you" for the loverly article you wrote about me in the NEWS. I had many people comment on it and thought it very warm and well written.

—Esther Lapiddus, March 15, 1968

I want to thank you so much for the beautiful article you wrote about me. I have received many compliments on it. I'm very happy the article gave us a chance to meet. I admire your enthusiasm toward everything you do.

—Joyce Levenson—

Your article about me was charming. My family and I thoroughly enjoyed reading it. Why don't you write an article about Sara Rosenblum? I'm sure there is lots to tell about this self-made, capable woman. I wish I were a writer, I would love to.

—Mrs. Samuel (Rose) Levinson, March 9, 1966—

It's a very nice interview indeed, and I must thank you for the care and thoughtfulness and generosity which went into it. I picked up several copies and sent one to my mother in Alabama who will enjoy it particularly.

—Sara Henderson Hay (Mrs. Nikolai Lopatnikoff, Dec. 14, 1963—

My wife and I appreciate very much the warm and entertaining article you wrote to introduce me to the Squirrel Hill community. Thanks so much for the time and concern for accurate detail you put into the article. It was a pleasure getting to know you, and I trust we will have an opportunity to become better acquainted in the future.

—Rev. John S. McCall, Pastor Sixth Presbyterian Church—

Peggy, the kids and I enjoyed your delightful article. My mother was pleased too. It was a pleasure meeting you.

Mead J. Mulvihill, Jr., Attorney-at-Law
—Member, Pgh., School Board of Public Education, June 30, 1972—

The article you have written about me has given us genuine joy. I will long remember your kind gesture with pleasant memories of congratulations by notes, phone calls, hearing from old friends, relatives and tenants' praises. P.S.—Chapter liked the Hadassah publicity presented in such an "off the beaten path" style, and it did a lot of good at the Convention.

Mrs. Leo (Rose) Noon, President
—Business & Professional Women of Hadassah (now Hadar), Aug. 28, 1962—

I have had so many favorable comments concerning the wonderful article you wrote about me. I was especially pleased with the heading; you managed to come up with something different.

—Mrs. Wesley (Mildred Miller) Posvar, April 7, 1970—

Hi, how are you? I'm writing to thank you for the wonderful article you wrote. I think you made me seem a lot better than I am—but thank you. The most important task that we as American Jews have is to remember our brethren behind the Iron Curtain. You have done a "mitzvah" by informing your readers of the plight of Soviet Jewry. For this there is no possible way of thanking you enough.

—Jay Rice, Nov. 5, 1969—

Thank you so much for your beautiful article in the NEWS about me. Particularly for all the time and attention you gave to the myraid facts, and yet turned out such a human story.

—Noel Riggs, Sept. 19, 1969—

Thank you for the beautifully written article. Everywhere I go people stop and tell me how much they enjoyed it. You have made me a local celebrity and I will never forget you for it.

—Norman Roth, Dec. 1, 1970—

Your very interesting and informative article concerning "The Sacks" was one of the most descriptive we've read in a long time. Your poignant style and easy reading was a joy. My family and I thank you.

—Nathan Sack, O.D.—

Thank you so much for your lovely article. I have sent copies of it to my family and friends and they are all thrilled.

— Ronald Satlof, Artistic Director, Pittsburgh Playhouse, April 15, 1968—

Just a short note to thank you for your wonderful article which appeared in the NEWS. We have received many compliments on it and my parents are already sending copies to all of our out-of-town relatives.

—Jules Sheer—

Thank you for giving your special touch to the JNF TREE Drive. I appreciate it more than words can fully express. The humorous and light development you have applied—while hitting squarely on the serious side—will gain many new friends for JNF.

—Mrs. Phyllis Spatz, Chairman, Jewish National Fund Drive—

Since my family is still in New York and will be there until Friday, I read the article to them and my in-laws over the phone. Everyone thought it was a lot of fun and nicely captured the spirit of our being in Pittsburgh. Thank you for your interest and fine effort

—Wilbur A. Steger, President, Consad Research Corporation, July 9, 1963—

Thank you for the article you wrote about me. You are most kind. I can't help thinking of the farmer whose old, broken-down cow was being lauded by the auctioneer. The farmer stopped him and said: "Hold on. If she's that good a cow I'll keep her myself". Thank you very much for your gracious remarks.

Dr. H. Guyford Stever, President
—Carnegie Institute of Technology, April 3, 1967—

I very much appreciate the way in which you wrote the article in the Sq. Hill News. In spite of my reluctance to participate, I am pleased that I did. As I mentioned to you, you are a highly skilled interviewer.

Emil S. Trellis, M.D.—Director Squirrel Hill Mental Health Center
—Western Psychiatric Institute & Clinic, University of Pittsburgh School of Medicine—

I should like to thank you very much for your gracious article that appeared in the NEWS. You certainly have an ability to condense much factual material into a relatively limited amount of space, while at the same time sprinkling your remarks generously and warmly with personal observations.

—Cyril H. Wecht, M.D., J.D., County of Allegheny, Aug. 18, 1970—

INDEX